CONSTRUCTING
THE PATRIARCHAL CITY

Constructing the Patriarchal City

Gender and the Built Environments of London, Dublin,
Toronto, and Chicago, 1870s into the 1940s

MAUREEN A. FLANAGAN

TEMPLE UNIVERSITY PRESS
Philadelphia • Rome • Tokyo

TEMPLE UNIVERSITY PRESS
Philadelphia, Pennsylvania 19122
www.temple.edu/tempress

Portions of this book were previously published as Maureen Flanagan,
"Private Needs, Public Space: Public Toilets Provision in the Anglo-
Atlantic Patriarchal City; London, Dublin, Toronto, and Chicago," *Urban
History* 41, no. 2 (2014): 265–290. Reprinted with permission from *Urban
History*, Cambridge University Press. Copyright Cambridge University
Press.

Library of Congress Cataloging-in-Publication Data

Names: Flanagan, Maureen A., 1948– author.
Title: Constructing the patriarchal city : gender and the built environ-
    ments of London, Dublin, Toronto, and Chicago, 1870s into the 1940s /
    Maureen A. Flanagan.
Description: Philadelphia : Temple University Press, 2018. | Series: Urban
    life, landscape and policy | Includes index.
Identifiers: LCCN 2018008481 (print) | LCCN 2017050963 (ebook) |
    ISBN 9781439915691 (hardback) | ISBN 9781439915707 (paper) |
    ISBN 9781439915714 (E-book)
Subjects: LCSH: City planning—Illinois—Chicago—History. | City
    planning—Ireland—Dublin—History. | City planning—Great
    Britain—London—History. | City planning—Canada—Toronto—
    History. | Patriarchy—Illinois—Chicago—History. | Patriarchy—
    Ireland—Dublin—History. | Patriarchy—Great Britain—London—
    History. | Patriarchy—Canada—Toronto—History. | BISAC: HISTORY /
    General. | SOCIAL SCIENCE / Sociology / Urban. | SOCIAL SCIENCE /
    Gender Studies.
Classification: LCC HT168.C5 F53 2018 (ebook) | LCC HT168.C5 (print) |
    DDC 307.1/2160977311—dc23 LC record available at https://lccn.loc
    .gov/2018008481

For Gaia Sophia and Madeline June
Forza e coraggio

Contents

Acronyms

AO   Archives of Ontario
BMR   Bureau of Municipal Research (Toronto)
CCC   Commission of Conservation of Canada
CHM   Chicago History Museum
CMIL   Chicago Municipal Improvement League
CPC   Chicago Plan Commission (early)
CPC2   Chicago Plan Commission (later)
CWA   Chicago Woman's Aid
CWC   Chicago Woman's Club
DADC   Dublin Artisans' Dwellings Company
GCAJ   Gerritsen Collection of Aletta Jacobs
HTPAI   Housing and Town Planning Association Ireland
LCC   London County Council
LGB   Local Government Board
LMA   London Metropolitan Archives
LSE   London School of Economics
MDC   Model Dwellings Company (London)
MOL   Municipal Order League (Chicago)
NAWLH   National Association for Women's Lodging-Homes (England)
NH&TPC   National Housing and Town Planning Council (England)
NLI   National Library of Ireland
OAA   Ontario Association of Architects
RIBA   Royal Institute of British Architects
TCA   Toronto City Archives
TCC   Toronto City Council

TLCW   Toronto Local Council of Women
TPI   Town Planning Institute
WCC   Woman's City Club of Chicago
WLL   Women's Labour League (England)
WMP   Women's Municipal Party (England)
WNHA   Women's National Health Association (Ireland)

CONSTRUCTING
THE PATRIARCHAL CITY

Introduction

"Our Cities Are Patriarchy Written in Stone, Brick, Glass, and Concrete"

It was not the custom to build on demolished areas. The modern
idea was to get people out into the country.
> —Andrew Beattie, Dublin Citizens Association (1910)

The city is becoming conscious of itself as a city of homes . . . as a
place in which to rear children.
> —Anna Nicholes, Chicago settlement house resident (1913)

There is a revolt of the Working Woman against home life and home
cares. . . . Love of a home, however meagre, is no longer the aim and
ambition of a working woman.
> —Tissie Sparrow, "In a Woman's Doss-House" (1894)

In the incipient domestic order—electric, hygienic, eugenic—the
drudging charwoman, the futile fine lady alike disappear, and
woman at once elemental and evolved, vigorous yet refined, will
reappear within her home, and be at once effective in the kitchen
and inspiring in the hall.
> —Patrick Geddes, *Cities in Evolution* (1915)

By the mid-twentieth century, the built environments of cities of the transatlantic Anglophone world shared a number of distinctive characteristics. Residential, commercial, and industrial areas were separated from one another. New housing construction favored the single-family, preferably suburban, home. Slum clearance policies had removed many poor, working-class, and minority residents from the center of the city. Decisions about urban development were focused on protecting property values and fostering economic growth. Slum clearance allowed the construction of new types of buildings and monumental public spaces to promote the city's economic and cultural prowess.

These shared features did not arise by chance. They resulted from a discussion within the English-speaking, Anglo-Atlantic world that began in the late nineteenth century and soon engaged participants on both sides of the ocean on how to reconstruct cities in the wake of the disruptions caused by industrialization. This was a discussion dominated by a comparatively small group of men who wrote extensively, traveled in both the United Kingdom and North America, and organized conferences in both places where they could set forth their ideas about how cities should be built or rebuilt. Eventually their efforts would lead to the creation of paid advisory positions with city governments and to academic positions within universities, both of which they and their followers naturally came to fill themselves. Whether acting as private citizens or professionals, though, these "experts" promoted a vision of the city that imposed a conceptual and geographical division between public spaces, intended mainly for men and their economic activities, and domestic residential areas reserved for family, home, and women.[1]

Though this patriarchal vision of the city was eventually successful in shaping the development of twentieth-century Anglophone cities, it met challenges almost immediately from the women of these cities, who had very different ideas of how a city should work and how it should be built. Just as the men found international audiences for their ideas, so too women in North America and the United Kingdom knew of one another's activities and attempted to implement them at home, often despite the delays and opposition of their male countrymen. Contesting the male vision of cities as places where men made money, these women maintained that the city should function for the good of all its residents.

This book compares the ideas and activities of these activist men and women in London, Dublin, Toronto, and Chicago from the 1870s into the 1940s, the crucial decades for shaping these Anglo-Atlantic cities into their present configurations. The four cities were chosen as representative examples of how, despite different specific historical contexts, shared ideological, professional, and cultural history underlay construction of the patriarchal city.[2] They also demonstrate the role that the municipal governing structure derived from English law, with its tradition of the city as the property of its male economic leaders, played in enabling this patriarchal construction while minimizing the influence of women.

Scholars have recognized that patriarchy—"the promotion of male privilege," as Allan Johnson defines it—has different manifestations in different contexts.[3] Lynn Appleton has argued that "all cities are patriarchal, but neither all cities, nor all patriarchies are the same." Yet "each city has a gender regime that it shares with equally constituted cities."[4] I use the term here to refer to the determination of men in cities to use power to structure the urban built environment to create and maintain both public and private patriarchy.[5]

I am not, however, concerned only with how male leaders of these cities used the power vested in them by urban institutions. I am also interested in women's resistance to men's projects and the underlying ideas of women acting individually and, especially, in groups. Specific processes of urban infrastructure development—transportation, sanitation, water, and power networks, for example—have been examined for these cities.[6] Scholarship on the impact of the built environment on class, ethnic, labor, and racial groups reveals how different groups of urban residents experience the city as they work, live in, and navigate it.[7] But urban scholarship has largely ignored how ideas about women and proper gender roles shaped the built environment.

Feminist social scientists have analyzed the city as a network of social relations and gender segregation, resulting from a "distinctive relationship between its political, economic, and familial systems," all determined by men. The city becomes "a version of patriarchy" in which the values and behaviors of men are presumed normative and thus embedded in urban institutions and structures to privilege male control.[8] The final result is a city, according to Jane Darke, in which "assumptions about roles and the proper place for different categories of people are literally built into towns and cities. . . . Our cities are patriarchy written in stone, brick, glass, and concrete."[9]

Yet as Helen Jarvis observes, except for observations such as Darke's, feminist analysis "rarely engages systematically with the built environment."[10] Urban historians, for example, generally ignore the impact of gender on decisions about the built environment. Before going further, I need to define how I use gender in this book. First, gender is not monolithic or essentialist. Not all men and all women think and act alike. So, what interests me is how specific activist groups of men and women viewed the city differently and proposed different solutions to its problems. Gender above all is a social construction through which values, behaviors, and norms are determined. History, experience, and centuries of male privilege produced the gendered visions of the city. Women were historically told that the private home was their sphere, and even the lives of women working outside the home revolved around taking care of home, children, and family. As women extended their activities out into the city, they conceptualized the city as a home for all its residents and applied their experiences and that knowledge to the city. Men were historically accustomed to believing it was their role to produce in the public sphere of the city. They conceptualized the city as the masculine space of work and production separate from the home as the feminine space of reproduction. Any threat to this division for men challenged public patriarchy, their power and authority to structure the city as they wished.

Public patriarchy is a historical construction. As bourgeois women moved into the urban market economy of the late medieval period, western men passed new laws that reconfigured "the market as male space." They began inserting walls, hedges, and gates between the house and the street to spatially divide the productive from the reproductive, while simultaneously delineating the private domestic spaces as "those associated with womanhood containing things made intimate by their relegation to private, hidden, spaces."[11] In the mid-fifteenth century, Leon Battista Alberti contended that the best city would be one planned rationally and scientifically within a structure that placed women in private under control of their husbands.[12]

Choice of subject matter, modes of analysis, and professional practice and training have focused urban studies on explanatory elements other than gender. Overall, urban studies practices what geographer Helen Jarvis terms the "'macro' grandstand views of the city."[13] The macro analysis privileges the work and ideas of men. In the Marxist (or neo-Marxist) interpretation, the city is primarily the site of class conflict and struggles over ownership of means of production and property.[14] Doreen Massey contends that this analysis assumes "that the only axis of power which matters . . . is that which stems fairly directly from relations of production. No other relations of power and dominance are seriously addressed. The fact that patriarchy, for instance, is not reducible to the terms of a debate on modes of production, is not considered."[15] According to Andrew Merriman, even neo-Marxists who advocate a less structural analysis of the city mainly mix gender and race into their existing interpretations.[16] As Liz Bondi and Linda Peake argue, even Manuel Castells's analysis that recognizes the diversity of urban oppositions to capitalism reduces the urban "to reproduction of labour," a spatial unit for reproducing labor power. For Bondi and Peake, this split between production and the reproduction is fostered by looking primarily at "those aspects of the reproduction of labour power that are provided, at least in part by the state." Ignoring how "the processes that ensure the reproduction of labour occur in the home or in the community rather than at the workplace" has embedded a gendered conceptualization of the city in the literature.[17]

Finally, the practices and tools of the building professions designed by men more than a century ago continue to determine the shape of the built environment. Engineers, architects, and urban planners assumed they knew how to construct the city using the tools of their trades. A common result, as architectural historian Lynne Walker contends for that profession, is that "architectural practice is a case study in patriarchal control and economic hegemony."[18]

The quotations beginning this introduction reveal the contrasting gender visions of the problems facing industrializing cities. Those visions of men that would reconstruct the built environment emanated from three ideas about the city. First, many men saw the city as a disorderly space that needed to be controlled and made modern, a situation that could be achieved only if living and working spaces were separated. The city's productive and reproductive spaces had to be physically inscribed by reconstructing a new built environment.[19]

Second, men believed that women were a significant cause of urban disorder. Women were less free to travel, barred from much university education or training in new professions such as architecture, and held very few university positions, but they too were communicating ideas across the Anglo-Atlantic world. They were leaving the home, asserting their rights to appear in public, demanding that the built environment be reorganized to accommodate their needs, and rejecting the idea that a woman's only proper place was inside the home. For men, fashioning a new domesticity was necessary for controlling both the public and private disorder of women.

Third, men sought to apply impersonal professional and structural solutions to urban problems. For men, the city was an organism that needed to be cleansed of its diseased parts. It could be reconstructed only using technological innovations wielded by professional men. Women, instead, advocated people-centered solutions focused on how people lived in and experienced the city.

The refusal of men to build public toilets for women, an issue that I develop later for each city, is one example of public patriarchy. Women wanted cities to build public toilets for women, a seemingly benign request, since cities were building these facilities for men. But public toilets would allow women equal freedom to travel through the city and tacitly acknowledge that women had the right to be in the city's public spaces and to expect the city to meet their needs. Men in all four cities strenuously resisted furnishing such facilities for women.

The ideas and activities of London housing reformer Octavia Hill provide another brief example here of urban patriarchy. According to planning historian Helen Meller, Hill "took the urban fabric as she found it." For her, "urban renewal was first and foremost an activity involving people and improvement in the built environment followed from this. . . . Citizenship was a matter of personal caring and urban renewal took place around a healthy community."[20] Hill focused on bettering the conditions in which people lived and not restructuring the city to control them. She believed that personal human interaction across social classes was necessary for a better city.[21] One of Hill's contemporaries, Lord Shaftesbury, who was president of the Society for Improving the Conditions of the Labouring Classes, promoted instead a new domesticity to reorder the city. He claimed that people "were beginning to realize that a nation's happiness was in the domestic system of living and it was impossible to calculate the great good that would result if every man could have a place of dwelling to himself—a home in which he could have the comforts and decencies accruing from such a state of affairs."[22]

From the mid-nineteenth century onward, men feared the city was a disorderly, chaotic place needing massive change.[23] John Ruskin called London "that great foul city . . . a ghastly heap of fermenting brickwork, pouring out poison at every pore."[24] The frontispiece of Patrick Abercrombie's plan for Dublin, "Last Hope of the Night," depicted Dublin with the monster of death sweeping overhead. For the later modernist theorist Le Corbusier, the city should contain nothing contradictory: everything arranged hierarchically and in its proper place. According to historian Elizabeth Wilson, these were specifically gendered fears of the modern city that were not necessarily shared by women: "Perhaps the 'disorder' of urban life does not so much disturb women. . . . [I]t may be because they have not internalised as rigidly as men a need for over-rationalistic control and authoritarian order." Unlike for many male writers and professionals, for women the modern city brought new possibilities and freedoms for which "modernist women writers" often "responded with joy and affirmation."[25]

Although men and women alike believed that the built environment of the industrial city needed change, they sought different ends and asked different questions about what was needed to reform the city.[26] Helen Meller suggests that women asked "people-centered questions"; they focused on asking what was needed for everyone to live decently in the city: "how to live in a 'modern' city."[27] Women began to ask these questions as they publicly encountered the city's defects and observed its social injustices. Their response was to apply their private domestic experiences to the public city, envisioning it as a reproductive and cooperative living space, the larger home of all who lived there. To make the city a home necessitated the "opening of the domestic to the space of the city" rather than enclosing the domestic inside the home.[28] Lest women have their way, men had to reassert their public patriarchy through new ways to restructure the built environment.

THE DISORDERLY BODY OF WOMEN

Because the concept of the disorder of women revolved greatly around ideas about women's bodies, this book discusses how the ideas of appropriate norms of masculinity and femininity influenced reconstruction of the built environment.[29] Ideas about these norms produced dualistic visions of the late-nineteenth-century city. The masculine was dynamic, changeable, movable; it embodied gravitas and time. The feminine was the absence of the dynamic; it always lacked something; it was emotional and restricted in space.[30] As the city offered women more freedom, their presence became "a growing threat and paranoia to men." Men were coming to fear the city as a "realm of uncontrolled and chaotic sexual licence, and the rigid control of women in cities has been felt necessary to avert this danger." In her analysis, Elizabeth Wilson argues that for men, women represented the crowd, liable to rush to extremes of emotion; they "represented feeling, sexuality, and even chaos; man was rationality and control."[31]

> The city is "masculine" in its triumphal scale, its towers and vistas, and arid industrial regions; it is "feminine" in its enclosing embrace,

in its indeterminancy and labyrinthine uncentredness. We may even go so far as to claim that urban life is actually based on this perpetual struggle between rigid, routinised order and pleasurable anarchy, the male-female dichotomy.[32]

Richard Dennis interprets it as "the dilemma of reconciling licence and order, liberty and responsibility that lay at the heart of the planning and regulation of modern cities ... producing top-down representations of space that translated into responsible spatial practices."[33]

When industrialization "loosened the patriarchal, familial control of women, and provided the preconditions for their greater independence," it undermined the city as a duality of the masculine public, productive space and the feminine private, reproductive space.[34] It gave women more access to public spaces. It brought young female migrants into the cities, many unaccompanied by family. It compelled even married women to join the paid labor force or to bring strangers into board in the private household. Other women turned to street-selling and prostitution. Middle-class women shopped and strolled. Women increasingly represented disorder and a threat to male control of both public and private patriarchy. Women became the sphinx who threatened to devour the city, according to Elizabeth Wilson's analysis of male fears of women in the city.[35] The feminine, for the influential Le Corbusier, had the power to "engulf," "swallow up," and bring "death."[36]

A number of recent works in gender studies recognize the patriarchal nature of the city.[37] In this book I push beyond that recognition to analyze how the intersection of ideas about gender and patriarchy reconstructed the built environment of the city. Women's new public freedom not only intensified "public patriarchal struggles to control women's use of the city as a whole";[38] it produced renewed efforts to reassert private patriarchy through a domestic ideology that "intensified [the] ideal of the wife and mother in the home" in the face of its erosion by enormous economic changes.[39]

Doreen Massey chastises scholars for not realizing that "the public city which is celebrated in the enthusiastic descriptions of the dawn of modernism was a city for men."[40] The deeply rooted ideas of public patriarchy have meant, as Clara Greed concludes, that despite women's attempts to call attention to their ideas and needs in the city, "again and again, mainstream planners seem unable to take in what is said, and continue to make quite basic mistakes because they are just not thinking about women's needs."[41]

Organization of the Book

These four cities provide for excellent comparison because they were sufficiently equally constituted as corporate entities for men leading these cities to assert their claims to power to reconstruct them as patriarchal regimes. Part I focuses on the unplanned city to provide the historical context of urban development in the Anglo-Atlantic world. Chapter 1 discusses the development of these cities as corporate, chartered entities, with clear divisions between the private and the public embedded in their political and economic structures. Chapters 2 and 3 focus on housing to see the early manifestations of the gendered ideas that underlay differing male and female approaches to the city. Chapter 4 examines ideas of modernity: what it meant to be a modern city and how these ideas occupied male discourse and decision making on reconstructing the built environment and how men used their ideas to marginalize women from the discussion of reconstructing the built environment. By the turn of the century, men were undertaking "purposeful intervention" in the built environment, focusing on infrastructures such "drains and sewers," for example. Such structures, as Helen Meller points out, were "not seen as the province of women," so men purposely shut women out from decisions on such undertakings. By accepting what Michael Batty identifies as "the single-minded force that cities, their developers, the capitalists required to finance them, even the workers and residents that occupy them demand to make their mark: to exhibit their difference from the past," by the early twentieth century, professionally trained men argued that only a comprehensive plan would produce a modern city distinguishable from the past.[42]

The chapters in Part I also introduce women's alternative conceptions to reconstruct cities that would produce a more equitable social infrastructure and guarantee the welfare of all urban residents. Comparing the ideas and actions of women rather than focusing solely on the male arguments for modernity, or on professional men's organizations and plans, or even on women's activities, produces a broader picture of the city, what it would become, and why certain paths were chosen by men to construct the city. It also demonstrates how as men saw themselves as the gender capable of understanding the city's problems, they assumed theirs was the appropriate vision of the city.

Finally, Part I considers the central role played by housing in the struggle over reconstructing the patriarchal city. Housing had deep implications for the public-private divide. Examining how early housing decisions were made, by whom, and the rationales for these decisions provides a crucial entree into the comparative study of urban built environments and the influence of gender.

Part II devotes a separate chapter to each city to examine how the men dominating business, professional, and political institutions directed the reconstruction of its built environment. An introduction to this part identifies the ideas of modernity, the city as a diseased organism, and the concept of creative destruction on which men rationalized their decisions. Each chapter then discusses how male-dominated professions cast men as the capable professionals who understood the city and its needs. Each chapter also discusses how women attempted to influence the city's reconstruction as men rejected their ideas, marginalized them in public discussion, and exercised their power to construct the city as a public patriarchy. By planning all its concrete manifestations, determining who would have access to municipal services, building new housing forms, and redesigning the interiors of housing to redomesticate women, men consolidated the patriarchal city for the future.

This was not a conspiracy; it was an exercise in power to rebuild the city along the lines desired by men. Each chapter ends with a discussion of the ongoing implications of professional planning and earlier decisions for the city's development through the 1940s. As a recent book of essays on European cities, women, gender, and planning demonstrates, women are still struggling not just to obtain equality in cities but also to have their ideas implemented as municipal policy.[43] The patriarchal city of the Anglo-Atlantic world has remained firmly in place, with decisions about its built environment still shaped by gendered ideas. Men did not get everything they wanted, and women constantly challenged them. But new professional disciplines and practices in architecture, engineering, and city planning and developing academic disciplines in the social sciences allowed men to apply their ideas to reconstruct the patriarchal city.

PART I

THE UNPLANNED CITY

1

LIBERTY, PROPERTY, AND GENDER
IN THE CORPORATE CITY

There is an enormous and increasing number of single women in the
nation, a number quite disproportionate and quite abnormal, a
number which, positively and relatively, is indicative of an
unwholesome social state, and is both productive and prognostic of
much wretchedness and wrong.
　　—W. R. GREG, *Why Are Women Redundant?* (1869)

THE CHARTERED CORPORATE CITY
OF THE ANGLO-ATLANTIC WORLD

The historical development of Anglo-Atlantic cities determined the
patterns of later nineteenth-century city growth. From the later medieval era, English towns had become largely self-governing. Royal
charters set a town's physical boundaries, granted immunities from outside
interference, and acknowledged the rights of the town's burgers to control
political, economic, and legal affairs within the town, including the control
of public space and property. The concept of town liberty derived from ancient Roman law that assumed an "urban conception of civic freedom" with
"corporate rights that accrue to the citizens of a self-governing republic."[1] By
at least the thirteenth century, London and other English towns were considered "autonomous public spaces" of a "civic community." As civic community, the town was defined as "a legal, structural, and elective entity
containing a range and concentration of public offices."[2] But power within
this civic community was largely confined to the town's economic elites,
merchants, property owners, and master craftsmen in the organized guilds,
the freemen of the city. As Richard Holt and Gervase Rosser argue in their
introduction to *The English Medieval Town*, "Political power was largely an
expression of economic influence." Freemen possessed "contingent privileges, liberties, and freedoms—and indeed responsibilities, reciprocities, and
obligations," as Phil Withington points out, but in essence they were able to
consider the town their property because they produced its wealth. The town
was a private corporation that they controlled politically and economically.[3]

In this context of the town as a private corporation, public and private
interests were combined and freemen carefully controlled their prerogatives.

Very few men were admitted annually to freeman status; "the theoretical concept of free status" was based "on the comparatively firm ground of economic function" that provided "a critical link between city and crafts," and "nearly everywhere the practice of regularized urban enfranchisement had been originally developed to augment the wealth and power of the town patriciates."[4] Few women, of course, were ever admitted to freeman status, and those who were admitted were primarily widows of freemen who were allowed to retain their late husband's status as long as they did not remarry.[5] It was thus men, and only a small portion of the town's male residents, who shaped the town's built environment: erecting new types of public civic buildings, restricting the use of public spaces for official parades and rituals, and sanctioning and controlling all marketplaces.[6] The city developed simultaneously as a limited and patriarchal corporation.

The model of the town as a chartered corporation spread through England. It was extended to Ireland following the Anglo-Norman ascendancy with Dublin receiving its first royal charter from King Henry II in 1171.[7] Ultimately, cities of British North America were organized under the same model with colonial assemblies and governors granting rights and privileges to the city. After the revolution against Britain, corporate charters were renegotiated in the United States as groups of men challenged the idea of the city as a private corporation as undemocratic. Individual states began to charter cities that loosened the control of small groups of men over all political and economic decisions and broadened the powers of a city government.[8] Chicago received its first town charter in 1833 from the state of Illinois. Toronto was incorporated as a city in 1834 with its name changed from the earlier York. Britain began to reorganize its towns with the Municipal Corporations Act of 1835 that created a system of town boroughs with town or city councils elected by ratepayers to replace the closed corporation. Boroughs thereafter were able to petition Parliament for incorporation.[9] Parliament officially established the municipal Dublin Corporation by separate act in 1840.

THE CORPORATE CITY: PRIVATE PROPERTY OR PUBLIC GOOD

These changes technically lessened control of the city by groups of private individuals or organizations, but in practice propertied men continued to dominate local government. In the United States, for example, the new Boston charter of 1822 replaced the town meeting dominated by a "merchant oligarchy" with an elected mayor and city council, but between 1822 to 1851, almost all mayors and council members were either businessmen, merchants, or lawyers. Boston men accepted the new charter only when they were assured that incorporation would not "deprive them of their accustomed rights and liberties," some of the men perhaps concerned because the state had just previously eliminated property qualifications for male voters. Bristol, England, replaced the older corporation with an elected council, although still restricting voting to male ratepayers, and most of the elected council members were either manufacturers or merchants.[10] Despite businessmen and manufacturers replacing the older merchant oligarchy, and abolition of the title "freeman," economic status still conferred municipal political power and kept the municipal government's focus on economic growth through private enterprise.[11]

Municipal incorporation also gave the city more control over its public spaces, resources, and services. Councils in incorporated cities were able to initiate and consolidate infrastructure developments. Water supply, garbage removal and sewer systems, new roads and bridges, and professional police and fire forces, for example, had previously been wielded by different entities. With more centralized authority, men were able to begin reshaping the built environment. Theoretically the municipal corporation was responsible to the community of the city. Yet there was no new definition of what comprised that community, so new charters created a quasi-public city. Prominent men continued to assume that the taxpaying (ratepaying) property owners had the right to decide how and for what purposes these tax revenues were spent. Various acts extended the franchise with property restrictions in British cities. The new Dublin Corporation extended the civic franchise to ratepayers who owned a minimum of £10 of taxable property and expanded to all ratepayers in 1899. After 1841 Chicago had no property qualifications for men, but Chicago's leaders "made policy decisions that recognized both their personal dependence on Chicago's growth and the ways in which government could be used to encourage that growth."[12] Urban women remained largely disfranchised. The 1869 Municipal Franchise Act gave English unmarried female ratepayers the franchise. Unmarried women who owned property worth $400 could vote in Toronto from 1885. Chicago women could not vote in municipal elections until 1913.

As industrialization magnified the city's physical, economic, and social problems, both residents and businessmen demanded more and better services from government. The corporate town tradition, however, could not be easily dislodged. In each city, leading men continued to identify the public interest with the private interests of property and wealth. But by the mid-nineteenth century, urban problems multiplied to challenge the hold that these men had on preserving the patriarchal city. A brief synopsis of the situation in each city illuminates the growing challenges.

That Great Foul City of London

London was the entrepôt of the far-flung British Empire and the central node of commercial and industrial development within the United Kingdom. Its expansive docks along the Thames River received, shipped, and stored goods from all over the world. All railroads led to the city so that rail lines criss-crossed the city and several great railway stations accommodated the rail traffic. Tunnels were bored beneath the city for the new Tube lines, the first of which, the Metropolitan line, was opened in 1863. Production required capital, and capital required financial institutions. Before the end of the century, the City—that small geographic center of London that had received the city's first charter—would become the financial capital of the world, its residents displaced by new office, banking, and other financial buildings. Factories and warehouses, roads, rail lines, and bridges across the Thames were needed to produce, store, and transport goods. England's abundant reserves of dirty-burning coal fed the boilers of railroad steam engines and factories while producing London's notorious air-polluting coal fog.

As industrialization transformed the economy, London's population grew from 1.8 million in 1831 to 2.6 million by 1851 and to 3.8 million by 1871. Vast numbers of largely unskilled rural migrants created a pool of excess labor that drove down wages and made job insecurity a way of life for hundreds of thousands of London's poor. The newcomers had to find living space in an unregulated private marketplace, often competing with older residents whose dwellings were being demolished to make room for new commercial buildings, tracks, train stations, roundhouses, loading docks, and factories. More and more of London's people crammed into older and deteriorating dwellings to produce massive pockets of poverty and disease. Charles Booth's 1880s survey of life and labor in London estimated that more than 30 percent of the city's residents lived below the poverty level of 21s (shillings) per week. In the growing chaos, businessmen and property owners increasingly turned to government to solve their infrastructure needs while city residents demanded that the government attack the city's poverty, disease, and filth.

London's governing structure was ill-equipped to meet these demands. The London Corporation was an anomaly in England in that since its 1215 charter, its merchants and guilds had resisted any expansion of its geographic territory or diminution of its powers, with the result that population growth occurred outside its boundaries. Services and government were left to seventy-eight civil parishes until mid-century. With property owners in the parishes resisting centralization of power, legislation to replace this fractured system advanced slowly. The Metropolitan Police Act (1829) replaced the parish constables; the Metropolitan Commission of Sewers (1847) was limited to overseeing sewers; the Metropolitan Local Management Act (1855) created a Metropolitan Board of Works with responsibility for health and safety over the entire London area, except the City; and the Metropolitan Poor Act (1867) abolished the administration of poor relief by parish vestries. Finally, the Cross Act (Artisans' and Labourers' Dwellings Improvement Act, 1875) gave local authorities power to build municipal dwellings on newly cleared sites. Slow progress toward government responsibility for confronting the city's condition did little to satisfy demands for more reform.

Parliament began centralizing urban governments with the Local Government (England and Wales) Act (1888) that established the single London County Council (LCC). The city corporation retained its separate powers and wealth. The LCC also had no control over police (the "Met" is still directed by the Home Office), schools, or poor laws.[13] Nevertheless, progress was slow, and many of its residents probably agreed with John Ruskin's assessment of London as a "great foul city—rattling, growling, smoking, stinking—a ghastly heap of fermenting brickwork, pouring out poison at every pore."[14]

Dear, Dirty Dublin

At the beginning of the nineteenth century Dublin's population of 180,000 made it the second largest city in the British Empire. Its economy was based largely on artisanal trades of cotton and silk weaving, watchmaking, and the book trade enterprises that the Irish Parliament had helped finance. Following the unsuccessful 1798 uprising against British rule, however, the 1801 Act of Union dissolved the Irish Parliament and subjected Dublin to England's free trade laws. Unable to protect its artisanal production against cheap English goods, Dublin entered a downward economic spiral. Whole areas of production collapsed, and the city's environment steadily degraded. Many of the city's wealthier inhabitants abandoned the city for legally separate, sparsely populated suburban townships, depriving the city of tax revenues to halt the degradation or tackle existing environmental problems.[15] At the beginning of the century, for example, there were almost 100 privately owned slaughterhouses in the city. In 1805, surveying city conditions, James Whitelaw witnessed the appalling conditions surrounding the slaughterhouses. In one tenement, he was interrupted "by an inundation of putrid blood, alive with maggots, which had, from an adjacent slaughter yard, burst the back-door, and filled the hall to the depth of several inches." The building's residents were so accustomed to such incidents, he reported, that they just calmly walked through the blood.[16]

Beginning with the famine years of the 1840s, rural migrants flocked into the city, which could offer them little in the way of housing or employment. Newcomers crammed into the city's deteriorating core housing vacated by the fleeing middle class, now subdivided into the multifamily rooms that characterized Dublin's notorious tenements. Living conditions were so dire that by mid-century 62 percent of children born in one poor city ward died within ten years of birth.[17] The best jobs for men were in the Guinness brewery and on the docks on the Liffey River, but growing numbers of poor

Dubliners subsisted on day-to-day casual labor and street selling. Lack of manufacturing meant that there were few jobs for women outside domestic service and street selling.

By 1891, the city's population had increased to about 245,000, but Dublin was unable to expand its territory. Its boundaries had been set in the 1780s and 1790s by a circumventing canal system. Suburban residents outside these boundaries resisted incorporation into the city. Thus, all Dublin's old and new residents shared a restricted geographic area.

Unlike London, Dublin did have a more unified municipal corporation with passage of the Municipal Corporation Reform Act (Ireland) in 1840. The following year, Daniel O'Connell became the city's first democratically elected Lord Mayor. The 1849 Dublin Improvement Act expanded the corporation's power over the previous decentralized powers of the Wide Streets (1757) and Paving (1807) Commissioners, and subsequent English legislation gave the corporation more authority over poverty and sanitary measures. But low taxable property values; stubborn property owners, especially the remaining small tradesmen who fought to keep their taxes as low as possible; and England's refusal to provide funding to implement infrastructure and sanitation reforms left the Dublin Corporation drastically deprived of revenue. Moreover, the Corporation Council was largely composed of tenement owners and building tradesmen with little interest in enacting or paying for reforms. Dublin may have been dear to James Joyce's Leopold Bloom, but for certain it was a poor and dirty city.

Toronto the Good

Toronto was an infant city compared with London and Dublin. In the 1830s it was a small, rudimentary settlement huddled along the banks of Lake Ontario with a few thousand inhabitants. Toronto's location on flat lands connected to other rivers and lakes made it a natural shipping center, especially as British Canada expanded westward. By the 1850s, the city was Canada's main railroad hub connecting east and west. Its population reached 56,000 by 1871 and rose to 181,000 twenty years later. Timing was crucial for the city's rapid development. Toronto grew simultaneously with the age of railroads; it had space for railroad lines, terminals, and the factories and industrial plants that were beginning to drive the economy of the British Empire. Growth required attracting new settlers, so city leaders welcomed in migration. Middle-class white men from eastern Canada saw Toronto as the site of new economic opportunity, especially for land speculation, and they streamed into the city.

The English model of the corporate city promoted Toronto's growth and ensured that its built environment would resemble that of the cities across the Atlantic. Well into the nineteenth century, mayors and city councilmen

were wealthy and propertied men. They and their non-office-holding counterparts viewed the role of city government as promoting economic development. An election circular of 1834 exhorted Toronto voters to elect only
those men who would endeavor "to improve your City and manage with
judgment your finances . . . those who possess a commercial, trading, and
scientific knowledge."[18] The men leading the city wanted limited interference
in private enterprise. They focused instead on land use regulation to profit
the city, brought in fire codes, and attempted to enact nuisance ordinances
to regulate nuisance-producing businesses such as slaughterhouses and
butcher shops. Even these rulings were often objected to as violating property rights and were subject to petitions against economic restriction. The
council was susceptible to such petitions as that of a group of butchers asking it to rescind certain restrictions as injurious to their trade. The council
granted the petition.[19]

As a transportation and shipping hub, Toronto also attracted some dirty
industries, and poor migrants to work in them, that taxed the government's
ability or willingness to confront the ensuing problems. Between 1870 and
1890 Toronto's industrial establishments had increased from just under 500
to 2,100. Among these establishments were slaughterhouses located along its
lakefront. Slaughterhouses, along with other factories, polluted the harbor
with their waste products while raw sewage from the city poured into the
lake and rivers for lack of a general sewage system. Rolling mills and distilleries contributed to the pollution problem.[20]

The administration of Mayor William Howland, 1886–1888, began confronting the city's sanitary problems and municipal corruption. But Howland, a convert to evangelical Protestantism, was most interested in moral
reform. He instituted a department of morality inside his administration
and closed saloons, gambling dens, and brothels. Howland's attacks on immorality and municipal corruption earned the city the nickname "Toronto
the Good." While Howland's term did make the city's residents more at-
tuned to the city's social problems, the majority still did not accept that the
purpose of municipal government was to pay for or to resolve them. They
worried about the immorality of the migrants who resided in the overcrowded and deteriorating housing in the city's center and whose presence
was threatening to impede economic growth. Ratepaying property owners
generally opposed government responsibility for financing public works and
were even more adamant that government not assume responsibility for social welfare.

Chicago: The Second City

Chicago resembled Toronto in location, timing of settlement, and its corporate model of government beginning with its first town charter in 1833. By

the 1850s, Chicago was the rail hub that linked the Midwest with the East. As with Toronto, middle-class white men flocked to Chicago for economic opportunity. Chicago's growth also benefited from the country's unrestricted immigration policies. While British control restricted immigration into Canada to British—including Irish—migrants, Chicago became a favored destination for foreign migrants from across Europe. As a result, Chicago grew faster than Toronto; in 1871 its population was almost 300,000 and ballooned to over one million by 1890.

After 1841, all white Chicago men could vote in municipal elections, but prominent men sought to control the city. In the 1840 municipal elections, voters were told that "we want the affairs, character, and dignity of our city protected and represented by men of responsibility and character—who have some stake in the institutions and interest in the laws which they are called upon to maintain and create."[21] Behind such rhetoric was the desire to keep general funding of public services to a minimum so as not to raise property taxes. Chicago's early municipal policies were largely devoted to developing a physical infrastructure to benefit economic development through private enterprise. The city's early bridges over the Chicago River that connected the north and south sides of the city center, for example, were built by private subscription of businessmen. Decisions on where to build them provoked struggles among competing economic interests. Other public works were carried out through a system of special assessments levied on property owners who stood to benefit from the work.[22] Garbage collection was awarded through a franchise to the highest private bidder.

As a railroad hub, Chicago also attracted some of the "dirtiest" industries: slaughterhouses and iron and steel rolling mills proliferated. Slaughterhouses were noisy, bloody, noxious places that produced irreducible waste, and the city's Union Stockyards were the largest in the country by the late 1860s. The situation in Chicago was perhaps not as bad as that of Dublin, with its slaughterhouses side-by-side with housing, because Chicago's slaughterhouses were located on the near south side of the city, close to rail lines, in an area not heavily populated until later in the century. Slaughterhouses produced so many jobs, however, that ultimately the immigrants working in the stockyards crowded into insalubrious housing in the surrounding neighborhood, which in turn was overhung with a pall of black smoke. Its nearby waterways were polluted with waste products and "blood pouring undiluted" from the slaughterhouses.[23] Until the late 1850s, Chicago had no reliable drinking water or sewer system, a particular problem because the city was built on a swampy area that permitted little natural drainage.[24]

Chicago reveled in its stockyards and industrial establishments that earned it status as the country's second city. This status as an economic engine of the nation enabled businessmen and political leaders to secure millions of dollars in outside funding to rebuild the city following the catastrophic fire of October 1871. The fire had left 100,000 residents homeless, destroyed 15,000 buildings, and razed the commercial and government center of the city. New York businessmen and bankers heeded the pleas of Chicago businessmen that the fire presented a splendid opportunity for starting new businesses in Chicago so that the economy of the country would not be damaged by the failure to rebuild its second city immediately. They quickly invested millions of dollars in this effort.[25]

In the aftermath of the fire, prominent men seized the opportunity to exercise more control over the city. The mayor gave the Chicago Relief and Aid Society, a private organization run by the city's wealthiest businessmen, all power to decide how to dispense the relief funds that were pouring into the city. The group's first priority was to protect and rebuild private property, including guarding and maintaining their own positions within the city by using donated funds to rebuild their own businesses. The directors of the relief society even sold materials needed to rebuild the city to the Relief and Aid Society, handsomely reimbursing their own losses. At the same time, these men adopted strict definitions of eligibility for persons applying for relief, often based on property ownership. No person or family left homeless was eligible to receive shelter relief funds, for example, unless they had owned the home that had burned.[26] When the Common Council tried to collect rent monies from businessmen whom the council had allowed to set up their businesses on public land, men refused to pay, responding, "Who made Chicago? Was it the Common Council? Or was it the individual enterprise of her citizens?"[27]

WOMEN'S BODIES AND THE BODY POLITIC

With the corporate city functioning as a self-governing public civic community run by men, in all four cities men not only resisted incorporating women into that community; they began to identify women, especially single women, as a danger to the community. By the late nineteenth century, women were moving into the city's public spaces, breaching the barrier between the city's public spaces and the private home. To restore patriarchal order, many men fell back on another centuries-old western trope of equating women and their bodies with the unhealthy and disorderly spatial organization of the city. A London mayoral proclamation of 1590 had singled out women selling outside the regulated marketplaces, one of their few means of employment at the time, and blamed them for increasing prices. The proclamation characterized these women as "sinks of lewdness": "women not onely of lewde and wicked life and behavior themselves but procurers and drawers of others also servauntes and such like to sundry wicked accions, the number of which people are of late yeres soe wonderfully encreased."[28] Men equated the feminine with disruption of the orderly city as they attempted to keep control over all aspects of the city. This disruption, according to historian Elizabeth Wilson, extended to "the many layers of physical, social, historical, geographic, cultural, symbolic, and embodied/lived associations and relations" in the city.[29] Moreover, masculinity became associated with citizenship. In New York City, for example, men accused the old charter of being "sickly and effeminate" for limiting male suffrage. Men claimed that "any man born within the city of New York is 'by birthright a freeman.'"[30]

Fears of women taking advantage of new urban opportunities produced texts specifically referencing women's bodily or supposedly naturally ordained functions as reasons for concern. The quotation from manufacturer W. R. Greg that introduces this chapter was only one piece of his diatribe against women. He inveighed against the proliferation of unmarried women in England. These were single women, according to Greg, "who, not having their natural duties and labours as wives and mothers . . . [and who] in place of completing, sweetening, and embellishing the existence of others are compelled to lead an independent and incomplete existence of their own." Greg worried that if the single state of women rose to about 6 percent of the marriage-age female population, the laws of nature would be violated. But, he assured his readers, this was a "curable evil," solved by removing five hundred thousand single women "to the colonies."[31]

Greg and other writers feared that their "natural" world of private and public separation was threatened by women's unnatural act of being single and thereby increasing the disorder of the urban world.[32] Greg's idea to transport single women may have been tongue-in-cheek, but the more women moved into public view, the more men were determined to reassert control. Planning historian Barbara Hooper, examining the writings about mid-nineteenth-century Paris, sees the direct connections they made between women's bodies and the disorderly city:

> In the texts of planners, public hygienists, sanitation engineers, city fathers, and heads of family and church and state, the female body becomes synonymous with that which disorders, threatens, undoes the work of Man, the idea of the plan. Female factory workers and department store clerks, housewives and matrons, female utopianists, socialists, and revolutionaries, bourgeois women whose first "respectable" unescorted excursions into public space were into department stores—all these women, in addition to prostitutes, had their movements throughout the city restricted, controlled, and monitored by what masculinist power produced.[33]

She concludes that "the ordering of body space is absolutely central to the organization of city space, to all social order and control. . . . [B]ody and city, body and body politic, are implicitly and explicitly linked."[34]

Overlapping linguistic and literary traditions reflected this fear of women, the need to cure their disorder, and the desire of men to keep them invisible in public. Modern English (as opposed to Old or Middle English) is a gender-neutral language. Nonetheless the city has been conceptualized as feminine and referred to this way when writing of its dangers and failures. In *English Hours*, Henry James calls London an "ogress who devours human flesh" and then notes that "the ogress herself is human."[35] In *Le Città Invisibili*, Italo Calvino gives each of his imagined cities a female name ("le ho chiamate ognuna con un nome di donna"). He does not explain why, but one story, "Cities and Desire" ("Le Città e il desiderio"), recounts recurring waves of men coming to Zobeide dreaming of and seeking a woman, but they could not find her. They "changed position of arcades and stairways to resemble more closely the path of the pursued woman and so, at the spot where she had vanished, there would remain no avenue of escape."[36]

Historian Leonore Davidoff notes that even when women were in public or successful in business or commerce, they remained largely ignored or unseen, except to be monitored and controlled. Even as the public sphere grew to cover "an immense variety of forms, levels, and functions, they were with a few notable exceptions, founded and run by men." Moreover, the assumptions of this expanding public sphere—Davidoff cites railroads and police as examples, but we could easily add firefighting companies, financial institutions, and law courts—were "that they would be entirely staffed by men."[37]

Given such preoccupation with women as a disorderly, potentially diseased, private body threatening to corrupt the body public, it is not surprising to recognize that, as Elizabeth Wilson remarks, this "particular division [public-private] became inscribed on urban life and determined the development and planning of cities to a surprising degree." What is surprising, she goes on to say, is that it remains so "in an extraordinarily unremarked way."[38] Women were becoming a threat, an intrusion, a natural redundancy because they refused to follow the natural gender order that men designated for them. Because this was happening at the same time that cities were assuming more power and authority over their public spaces and economic affairs, many urban men found it imperative to restore the so-called natural gendered order of things, to control the intrusion of women into the economic, political, and social spaces of the city, and especially to cure the evil of the single woman. One magazine article warned that London was becoming the place of "glorified spinsters," who "remapped the city as 'like meteors [they] wander free in interfamiliar space obeying laws and conventions of their own.'"[39]

With such fear of women's disorder, reconstructing the public patriarchal city required refashioning the modern city into a place where, once again, men could be sure of their control. Yet if the modern city was again to be the property of men, they needed to identify the first crucial change to restore control. New housing arrangements became a focus for restoring the proper balance between the private and the public, between production and reproduction, and return the city to public patriarchy while simultaneously strengthening private patriarchy.

2

Housing, Boundaries, and Gender in the Quasi-public City

> In every country, old and new, the people were being rapidly
> urbanized, and if the urbanization of the poor were not controlled,
> devitalization of the people must occur.
> —John Burns, Labour leader, LCC member (1907)

The leading men of each city had four goals for housing reform. They wanted to protect private property and private enterprise; keep municipal expenses restricted; focus on the city as an economic site; and reinstitute the boundaries between the public and the private. As men sought to implement their goals, by the late nineteenth century women in these cities began to contest male solutions to housing, offering a different perspective on human needs and working against boundaries between public and private.

Philanthropic Housing and the 5 Percent Solution

London

The initial forays made by London men into housing reform focused on private enterprise whereby wealthy individuals endowed new housing projects. In 1862, George Peabody, a wealthy American banker transplanted to London, organized a group of friends into a board of trustees. He gave them £150,000, with the promise of more funds to come over time, to build and manage new housing schemes, and he instructed them to keep building so that "there may not be a poor working man of blameless character in London who could not obtain comfortable and healthful lodgings for himself and his family at a cost within his means."[1] The trust began erecting four-story model tenements. Within two decades it owned 3,500 dwellings, housing almost 15,000 people. Beginning in 1890, Lord Edward of the Guinness family joined this effort and established the Guinness Trust, to which he donated £200,000. For London officials, the work of the Peabody and Guinness Trusts relieved them of responsibility to erect housing, so they helped facilitate the purchase of land for these buildings. The Board of Works sold land to the trusts at one half the asking price, and the Bank of England and the Commissioners of Public Works lent them large sums of money at reasonable rates with which to finance land purchases.[2]

Such charitable philanthropy, however, failed to attract many other similarly inclined individuals and other means had to be found to confront a growing housing crisis in the city. The Torrens Act (1868) and the Cross Act (1875) gave British cities powers to clear slum areas and build on these sites. The individual vestries assumed such power in London. But they were restricted to clearing sites and building housing for the working classes only on the cleared land. Vestry ratepayers tended to resist paying for such new building schemes, and the vestries possessed little means to raise enough money to build on cleared sites even with favorable public loans. There was, however, no thought that the vestries should build and operate housing on their own. R. A. Cross, for example, saw his legislation as a means to facilitate investment:

> There is . . . good reason for believing that with increased facilities for obtaining possession of dilapidated and notoriously unwholesome property, as well as of property in which conflicting interests are concerned, there would soon arise a class of investors actuated as much by sound commercial principle as by benevolent considerations who would be willing to engage in judicious building schemes for the better housing of the poor.[3]

Thus, once they had cleared their land, vestries sold it at a favorable price to private model dwellings companies (MDCs). MDCs were for-profit companies whose investors bought shares in the company for a promised 5 percent return. This so-called 5 percent "philanthropic capitalism" kept housing a private, profit-making enterprise.[4] According to the deputy chairman of the Metropolitan Association for Improving the Dwellings of the Industrious Classes (MAIDIC), its purpose was to demonstrate that "decent buildings could be constructed for the dwellings of the industrious classes, and still return a fair interest for the outlay."[5]

Relying on the MDCs to provide housing promoted the idea of the quasipublic city. It was governed by public officials but confined itself to facilitating private enterprise. London MDCs were able to borrow funds from the government at 4 percent interest, to be repaid over forty years, making them private investment bodies partially funded by government. Government would invest in housing without being obliged to finance it directly. This was a market solution for social problems.[6] One early-twentieth-century investigation of government lending found that up to 1905, 40 percent of £3.4 million went to "private undertakings."[7]

The MDCs aimed to "reconcile private and public interests" in order "to demonstrate that there was no necessary contradiction between private profit and social welfare objectives."[8] But such market solutions produced a pattern of housing that the poorest and most needy urban residents could not afford. To turn a profit and pay dividends, room rentals in MDC buildings were well beyond the means of the city's poorest residents. The secretary of the Improved Industrial Dwellings Company remarked that "the company could hardly be expected to house the 'degraded classes,' for that would be an impossible speculation."[9] The poor displaced by land clearance projects were almost never housed in the new dwellings because they could not afford the rents. Only Londoners with regular employment at decent wages could afford the buildings of the Peabody Trust, the MAIDIC, and the other thirty or so MDCs.[10] The Cross Act mandated building only new working-class housing on cleared lands and that the number of residents be the same as the original displaced persons. But the act did not demand housing the same people. MDCs carefully chose their sites and who would be housed, either through an interview process or by rents too high for the poorest Londoners to afford.

Only one model housing project deviated from that pattern of a market solution. The Columbia Square Building, erected by Baroness Angela Burdett-Coutts, accommodated the lower classes. She limited dividends to 2½ percent and made rooms more affordable for some of the lowest-paid and least welcome Londoners, among them the common laborers and costermongers. She even built shelters nearby for the donkeys of costermongers.

In the 1880s, the liberal London Municipal Reform League and the social democratic Fabian Society, led by Sidney and Beatrice Webb, sought more municipal government responsibility for housing. The new centralized London County Council had administrative power to formulate comprehensive plans to secure a public good, which opponents to private provision believed included housing. But shifting to public provision of housing was not easy. Prominent men in the City opposed extending government action or viewing London as a unified metropolis lest it mitigate their power. Ratepayers controlled vestry expenses, and they too were reluctant to surrender that power to the LCC to pay for public works outside their own boundaries.[11] Even the LCC, elected by the ratepayers of the new metropolitan area, remained reluctant to undertake any expansive new municipal housing or sanitary schemes that it would have to subsidize.[12] Moreover, housing reformers themselves rarely agreed about the best methods for financing new housing, where to locate it, or what better housing would accomplish for the city.

Dublin

In Dublin, the poor and working classes squeezed into multistory tenements converted from the city's old abandoned Georgian mansions. By the middle of the nineteenth century, those houses formerly occupied by the city's tradesmen were more than two hundred years old. As historian Mary E. Daly notes in her examination of Dublin housing, working-class housing was neglected until it collapsed.[13] Yet Dublin faced several impediments to bettering the overall state of housing even with the limited powers given by the Cross Act. Good buildings often intermingled with decaying buildings, making complete clearance of such areas difficult, and the city hesitated to destroy some of its Georgian buildings because of their architectural value. As applied to Dublin, the Cross Act mandated that the city pay compensation for property owners of any buildings destroyed for new housing. It was too expensive for the Dublin Corporation to acquire many properties, and ratepayers objected to financing large clearance projects.[14] While the corporation had authority to improve housing based on the city's sanitary conditions, it was limited by needing to appeal to the British-controlled Local Government Board and then to receive parliamentary permission to undertake any improvement schemes.

In 1877, the corporation borrowed almost £20,000 from the Commissioners of Public Works to demolish and rebuild in the poverty-stricken Coombe neighborhood and spent an additional £37,000 for another scheme at Plunkett Street. But the corporation could barely pay for the cost of purchasing and clearing the property when it was obliged to compensate Coombe property owners for over £14,000 and to pay similar fees in Plunkett Street.[15] The corporation had to lease both sites at extremely favorable rates to the Dublin Artisans' Dwellings Company (DADC), an MDC founded in 1876 as a business venture paying 4 to 5 percent on investment. The DADC secured low-cost public loans and when built, its properties housed predominantly "the more respectable tenants." The *Freeman's Journal and Daily Commercial Advertiser* publicly congratulated the company in 1884 for its "noble work," for being "well managed by competent businessmen," and for being a model showing how housing could be accomplished within a "commercial point of view."[16] Yet the DADC built most of its housing on empty land on the city's outskirts and charged rents that only the more well-off working class could afford. The DADC was such a profitable business enterprise, paying a high of a 5 percent dividend by 1899, that the following year the *Freeman's Journal* wondered whether there was "such a thing . . . in such a company as being too successful."[17]

Philanthropy and MDCs made such minimal progress toward solving the urban housing crisis that by the 1880s Parliament was alarmed that private enterprise could never do so. Still, men in both London and Dublin continued to promote building by private enterprise. When Parliament constituted a royal commission to investigate the housing of the working classes in 1884 (more details about this commission later in the chapter), Dublin men defended private enterprise. The attitude of one Dublin alderman, who was also the solicitor for a company that had been formed to clear one area of the city, build a new market, and widen its streets, reflected the lack of concern for the fates of those displaced through private rebuilding. Although the parliamentary act authorizing clearance schemes specifically mandated that the company "rehouse" those evicted, the alderman felt little concern for the fates of the 714 families (3,570 people) cleared out. The evicted families were compensated according to rates previously paid, he noted: "They signed agreements, we paid the money, and they went away."[18]

Nevertheless, by the late 1880s the Dublin Corporation began to undertake limited building schemes, although with rentals sufficient to operate without a loss. Dublin's Lord Mayor praised one of the first of these new building schemes "as an additional incentive to private enterprise to follow in the footsteps of the Corporation."[19] The directors of the DADC, however, were not pleased. They "regretted that the Corporation have determined on the further erection of classes of dwellings which cannot fail to compete unfairly with those erected by the company as they are to be let at rents involving an annual loss to the ratepayers. The effect must be to discourage private enterprise."[20] Another Dublin man, who was both an MP and an associate of the building firm Lombard and M'Mahon, insisted that only by lowering property rates would the city find "the only real solution to the question of the housing of the poor."[21]

PROPERTY RULES: THE NORTH AMERICAN CITIES

By the time dramatic housing problems developed in Chicago and Toronto, private enterprise was virtually enshrined in each city's way of life.

Chicago

In Chicago, almost every aspect of the city's growth was undertaken either by private enterprise or by property owners paying for infrastructure amenities. Chicago used general operating revenues to fund sewers to the "most valuable property" areas but balked at paying to extend sewage provision into a citywide system. As historian Robin Einhorn concludes, in Chicago, property ruled.[22] The men of Chicago did not envision much responsibility at all for housing, or the built environment overall. In the process of rebuilding after the 1871 fire, Chicago men claimed the city as the realm of propertied men. Without national housing laws or state laws to challenge their authority, Chicago men were able to rebuild the city largely as they deemed fit. Their only significant challenge came when they sought to pass a comprehensive citywide fire ordinance to limit the erection of wood buildings in order to protect the rebuilt city center. Here too competing interests revolved around property ownership. Working-class men argued that such a restriction would impinge on their ability to acquire property at reasonable prices. A compromise ordinance limited its geographic application so that the working classes could build and own cheap housing.[23]

Failure to enact the comprehensive ordinance did not stop prominent Chicago men from considering the city their realm. In the 1880s, the male-only Citizens' Association, formed in 1874, argued that only private enterprise should erect housing. As Chicago's population surged over one-half million, the association suggested that "the most influential capitalists, manufacturers and merchants" form a joint stock company so that housing could be built at "a very fair rate of interest obtained on the investment." The men claimed that "our system of business needs no governmental aid or advice" on the issue of housing. Few influential Chicago men at the time, however, were interested in investing in housing, but as the Citizens' Association noted, they also did not want any government interference.[24]

Still, the housing situation in Chicago was becoming dire. When the residents of the near west side Hull House settlement systematically surveyed their neighborhood in 1894, they counted nearly twenty thousand people living within one third of a square mile. Much of this housing was small, poorly built, wood-frame structures, often placed back-to-back, or backing onto insalubrious alleys. By the end of the century the generous estimate was that 40 percent of Chicago's 1.7 million residents continued to live in substandard housing.[25]

Toronto

Toronto residents similarly paid little attention to housing for its poorer residents, and hastily erected "shacktowns" sprang up to house them. Toronto entrepreneurs were as uninterested as Chicago's in investing in housing. When a few philanthropically minded men led by Goldwin Smith proposed to form a joint stock company—the Artisans' Dwelling Company of Toronto, Ltd.—they sought to capitalize it at $100,000 by issuing $10 shares modeled on the English 5 percent philanthropy. Smith even purchased land on East Gerrard Street that he intended to donate to the company for the housing. But his plan generated little interest among other Toronto men, and the scheme was abandoned in 1907.[26]

Toronto men, however, were prepared to spend money on a new city hall to symbolize the wealth and modernity of the city. It was constructed at a cost of $2.5 million, and its opening in 1889 inspired Mayor John Shaw to celebrate this triumph:

> Why people will spend large sums of money on great buildings opens up a wide field of thought. It may, however, be roughly answered that great buildings symbolize a people's deeds and aspirations. It has

been said that, wherever a nation had a conscience and a mind, it recorded the evidence of its being in the highest products of this greatest of all arts. Where no such monuments are to be found, the mental and moral natures of the people have not been above the faculties of the beasts.[27]

Toronto men, as was the case with many men in Anglo-Atlantic cities, saw monuments and great buildings as the physical representation of the good city. They also sought to promote the city by focusing on its economic prowess. So, even as Toronto ignored its housing situation, the city council formed a special committee to decide how to portray the city at the 1893 Columbian Exposition in Chicago. The council allocated $10,000 to publicize the city as "a manufacturing, commercial and educational centre."[28]

GENDER AND HOUSING IN THE QUASI-PUBLIC CITY

The year after the Toronto Council made this $10,000 allocation, it refused the request of women's groups for funds to help maintain a night shelter for homeless women.[29] This refusal, the extremely favorable loans given to the MDCs in London and Dublin, and Chicago men's assumption that property ruled reflect a patriarchal vision of the city under male control. The first sustained challenge to this control came from women who were formulating different solutions to the housing situation. Octavia Hill's housing activities in London have been well documented but not in the context of investigating the city's built environment as a patriarchy. Nor has the general scholarly analysis of housing reform taken her work seriously as a challenge to this patriarchy or been concerned to understand why it differed from male housing reformers.

In literature Hill has been viewed as a middle-class woman attempting to instill middle-class values in her tenants. She has been labeled "the self-appointed school mistress of the lower classes"[30] or placed in similar context to the "bible-tract women" who "invaded working-class homes," satirized by Charles Dickens in *Bleak House*.[31] Although such patronizing characteristics were assigned to Hill, she was also acknowledged for bringing a "much needed humane touch to housing reform."[32]

So much analysis of Hill's work has been on the social history of housing that its context within prevailing ideas about nature of the city and about how its poor residents were connected to the city has gone widely unnoted. Anthony Wohl concludes that "she never acknowledged the desperate extent of the housing crisis," but Elizabeth Darling and Anne Anderson suggest that Hill did not think of it so much as a crisis or a problem but as a condition of urban life that needed to be better managed.[33] Moreover, a comparative study of housing reformers has noted that unlike the MDCs or housing philanthropists, Hill did not have specific plans for the reorganization of society. Instead of building new housing structures that would reflect specific beliefs about proper housing for families, Hill was managing old buildings.[34] Many male housing reformers, such as Lord Shaftesbury, wanted new housing that they hoped would provide a new domestic arrangement to guarantee the future of England. Shaftesbury did not neglect the profit motive, contending that "benevolent persons" could make a 4 percent profit on investing in housing.[35]

Hill's approach to housing was defined by three ideas. First, she did not believe in building new housing that would move residents out of their neighborhood or make a profit from housing. She worked instead to renovate existing properties and to train women to function as property managers and rent collectors so that London's poor could have improved living conditions where they currently resided. Hill began her work managing several small buildings owned by John Ruskin. Prominent women gave her additional properties to manage. In 1869, Julie, Countess of Ducie, bought six ten-room houses in Marylebone and turned them over to Hill to manage.[36] Maud, Lady Selborne (daughter of Lord Salisbury), built twenty-four three-room tenements in Southwark for Hill to manage. Lady Jane Dundas gave her a gift of £1,200 to underwrite the later construction of the Red Cross Cottages. Hill's recordkeeping reveals that the overwhelming majority of outright donations given to her to help her maintain her properties came from women. Hill was not dispensing charity. Managing buildings meant collecting rents, fixing up dilapidated properties, and keeping accounts of expenses and income. Many of the landholders expected earnings from the rents she collected.[37]

Second, Hill's efforts were designed to reach some of London's poorest inhabitants. The residents of her houses in Marylebone, she wrote, "were mainly costermongers and small hawkers and were almost the poorest class of those amongst our population who have any settled home."[38] Most of the buildings she managed were already occupied, and she did not intend to evict people. She believed that proper management could rehabilitate buildings and allow rooms to be "re-let at the same prices at which they had been let before."[39]

Third, Hill did not recoil from older forms of housing. She recognized that buildings clustered together on very narrow streets with their doorways opening directly onto the street fostered a sense of community among London's poorer residents. Often the buildings on those streets were arranged around courts enclosed on three sides. Courts troubled other housing reformers because they hid residents from public observation and allowed women to congregate in those doorways and courts without being observed. Hill believed that if tenants felt a sense of community with those living around them they would better their own living conditions. Hill had arranged common meeting rooms in her buildings and involved tenants in the work of keeping up the property, paying them for their labor, to encourage that sense of community. Hill believed that there was a profound connection between housing, communal space, and living space. According to Darling and Anderson, Hill rejected the "spatial transformation approach" of the trusts and MDCs. She was interested in transforming "patterns of inhabitation . . . rarely manifested in (new) bricks and mortar." She wanted to produce "model dwelling practices, rather than model dwellings." She believed that how a building was used was as important as how it was designed.[40] After four years of managing the Marylebone houses, Hill believed "that a consciousness of corporate life is developed in them is shown by the not infrequent use of the expression 'One of us.'"[41]

Hill's focus on how a building was used by its residents and how people lived in the city, rather than how a building was designed, clashed with the ideas of men building the model tenements. The men directing the trusts and MDCs intended to transform society through new types of buildings and new housing arrangements that would dictate not only where but how the working classes and poor would live. It was easy for these men to ridicule Hill, her small cadre of housing managers, and her "small knots of tenants"—when they even paid her any attention at all.[42]

Hill's ideas of improving existing housing clashed also with the emerging ideal that, as expressed by architect Thomas Blashill, cities needed "to get rid of the slums, leave the owners the true value of their interest, and actually rehouse the whole of the people displaced, without throwing an unreasonable burden upon the rates."[43] As Richard Dennis notes, categorizing areas as slums allowed cities to believe that the "housing problem was simply a collection of problem areas, not a fault of the structure of housing provision as a whole, let alone an inevitable consequence of the economic system."[44] Hill may have looked to her tenants as people in need of middle-class values, but she did not see them as pawns of capitalism to be moved around to suit the needs of the men controlling the city.

The trusts and the 5-percenters were engaged in a specific type of social engineering. Where they chose to build and the types of edifices they built would change class relations as well as reconfigure the built environment. New building on sites scattered throughout the city would ensure that working-class areas would not proliferate. The Peabody trustees had accepted that certain aspects of communal living were necessary—flats shared common washing facilities, lavatories, sculleries, and baths. According to John Tarn, "communal lavatories were sensible because they were capable of easy supervision."[45] But the buildings of the Improved Industrial Dwellings Company in London, organized by housing reformer Sydney Waterlow in 1864, enclosed the family inside its dwelling space by giving each flat its own water closet and bath so that families would be able "to live segregated from one another in individual units."[46] Such provision was not merely a nicety for residents. As an 1874 report of a cooperative building company in Boston, which had modeled its housing schemes on the London ones, put it:

> We have learned by experience that such tenements with common corridors, water rooms, and "above all common privies, are a disgrace to modern civilization, and public nuisances, inasmuch as they incroach upon the family relations, tend to make them impure, and thereby sap the very foundations of the State."[47]

As Anthony Wohl notes, the model dwellings were "the architecture of stern paternalism and social control. The railings around the Peabody estates, and the entry ways off a central, closed courtyard represented both the Victorian concern for privacy and for the social immunization of the 'deserving poor' from the contaminating influences of the slum."[48] You can still see this arrangement in London's extant Peabody and Guinness buildings. The buildings physically remove the residents from the streets; they usually face away from the street with doorways leading into staircases—not directly into flats—that are accessible only from internal courtyards; access to the courtyards is limited by surrounding fences, gates, or narrow passageways. The message is that outsiders are not welcome. (See Figure 2.1.) As historian Martin Daunton summarizes it, housing reform in late-nineteenth-century

Figure 2.1 Peabody Clerkenwell Building, Islington, London, February 2012. (Photo by author.)

Britain intended to rearrange public and private spaces by opening up the older model of crowded inward-facing courts that had shared public and private space in order to clarify, regulate, and control the boundary between public and private spaces.[49] Private patriarchy and public patriarchy came together in the drive to change urban housing conditions.

As part of this effort to control the residential spaces, all model buildings had strict rules for accepting residents. Peabody tenants had to be vaccinated; no one was allowed to be late on the rent; no dogs were allowed; and no shops were allowed in the buildings. There were "strict regulations about washing and cleaning steps and staircases [and] tenants have to distemper and whitewash their rooms once a year." No home working was allowed, thereby eliminating one means that women had to help support their families, or guaranteeing that poor women would not reside in the trust buildings.[50] Similar restrictions pertained in the Guinness buildings on Columbia Road in 1892: they forbade animals, noise from children, ball games, and hanging washing to dry inside the flats, and there was a list of cleaning that tenants were obliged to do. Children were forbidden to play, loiter, or make noise in the stairwells, landings, and passages. These latter restrictions often meant that mothers had to stay inside with their children, keeping them quiet.[51]

Despite Peabody's claim that his trust should ensure that poor, blameless working men should have a comfortable home that they could afford, his buildings charged rents that the poor working man could not afford. Trustees were forbidden to use funds for any purpose other than housing. Peabody directed trustees to remove from his second deed the provisions that would have given them leeway to fund any hospitals or dispensaries in the buildings or their neighborhoods. Peabody also demanded that the trust deed specifically describe and limit the types of housing projects.[52] The bricks-and-mortar approach also allowed Peabody and Guinness to have their names clearly associated with housing as a personal legacy and to let anyone know what class of people lived in the buildings. Hill refused to have her name put on any buildings.[53]

Octavia Hill and Housing Management

Hill and her coworkers were not interested in such large-scale social engineering. She pointed out the reality that decentralizing housing to outer areas of the London would negatively affect the poor: "But the widowed charwoman, obliged to run home and get the children's dinner, the dock-labourer, the costermonger how shall their needs be met," she asked. "For these and many others, cheap dwelling would have to be provided in the neighbourhood of their present homes."[54] When Hill assumed the management of properties in Southwark that were owned by the Church of England,

she expressed to the Ecclesiastical Commissioners her concern that some of
the property was to be cleared and let to private developers:

> I was most anxious to have leased to me the portion of the ground
> allotted to the permanent housing of the poor, which was then unlet
> to builders. It would have rendered the personal work that we are
> doing among the tenants tenfold more useful, because we could have
> continued our work among them, and kept them together, with some
> sense of a corporate body, when the time came for the destruction of
> the present houses, instead of their being either scattered or handed
> over to the government of an ordinary builder.[55]

She rejoiced when the commissioners decided to turn another property over
to her rather than to building companies. The commissioners realized, she
wrote to her fellow workers,

> that in the years to come . . . they will have managers to supervise in
> detail the comfort and health of their tenants, so far as these depend
> on proper conditions in the houses in which they live; managers who
> will be interested in the people, will have time to see thoroughly to
> the numerous details involved in management of such areas.[56]

Hill rejected the Victorian notion that the people who lived in deteriorating
housing were innately depraved or inferior. She believed that the conditions
in which people were forced to live and taken advantage of by landlords and
rent collectors were responsible for what might be termed unsocial behaviors. Good and just management of existing housing, she believed, could
induce people to take responsibility for at least some of their own conditions.
Hill never gave up that idea.

Hill recognized that women would work outside the home and needed to
live near their work. In one of the few housing schemes she built, the Red
Cross Cottages and Hall in Southwark—on Redcross Way, which runs directly into the Peabody Marshalsea/Mint Street buildings—she laid out a
garden (Figure 2.2). These gardens, she said, would serve as "an open-air
summer sitting room . . . where we hoped working women will sit and rest
and do needlework, and tired men sit and smoke."[57] In the Red Cross Cottages, Hill was able to demonstrate her idea that readily accessible outdoor
spaces were important to people in developing a sense of community. At the
Red Cross Cottages she employed Emmeline Sieveking and her sister Mi-
randa in the Kyrle Society to do the original landscaping. The Kyrle Society
was dedicated to beautifying the surroundings of poor neighborhoods, including creating small gardens for public use.[58] The gardens, a children's playground, and the multiuse Red Cross Hall would be open to everyone who
lived in the neighborhood to enjoy. Hill rejoiced that not only were the Red

Figure 2.2 Red Cross Cottages and Hall, Southwark, London, May 2009. (Photo by author.)

Cross gardens a "great success" for the residents, but even the "rough characters" and "boisterous boys" of the neighborhood were behaving well there.[59]

Hill also called on wealthy landowners to create public spaces available to the poor. London's magnificent public parks were generally impossible for the poorer residents of the city to reach. She wanted these landowners to open their lands to the public and advocated the creation of small spaces, places that "may be enjoyed without effort or expense. . . . [P]laces to sit in, they should be very near the homes of the poor, and might be really very small, so that they were pretty and bright, but they ought to be well distributed and abundant."[60]

Hill's work at Redcross Way was supported by women. Hill's accounting of the donations made to the building of the adjacent Red Cross Hall in 1887 demonstrate this fact. Most donations came from women, many of whom gave small sums. Of sixty-five donors whose gender could be ascertained (some were identified only with initials), fifty of those donors were women and two were couples. Their donations ranged from 5s to £100 along with Lady Jane Dundas's £1,200.[61]

Housing Management and the Alexandra Guild

Beginning in 1898, the alumnae of Dublin's Alexandra College adopted Hill's housing management idea. The women organized the Alexandra College Guild Tenement Company and raised money to purchase several tenement buildings on two of the poorest streets on the north side of the river: Summer Hill and Grenville Street.[62] The company sold shares at £5 each with the possibility to return a 2 percent profit. The women hoped that by operating the company on a sound financial basis, they would inspire others to invest in similar efforts to rehabilitate, not destroy, the city's housing stock. The guild's mission was "to provide decent and comfortable housing at rents within the reach of the poor and without proving a financial loss to the owner." Their tenants were "of an extremely poor class, hawkers and such like, and many were almost destitute," so it was not always possible to pay a dividend. In 1903, for example, they used their funds to repair buildings damaged after a particularly bad storm rather than pay a dividend. The following year, when its finances had recovered, the guild paid a 2½ percent dividend.[63]

The three guild houses on Grenville Street each contained ten rooms with one family occupying each room for a total of 150 occupants. The women cleaned, painted, and whitewashed the buildings, fixed roofs, installed drains, and cleaned yards and ashpits. At the end of their first year, the women reported that "those of the original tenants who stayed with us were quite pleased with the improved conditions of affairs."[64] The few extant photos of the guild's buildings (which have been destroyed) were identified only by a small *A.G.* on the doors as part of the address. Like Hill, who refused to have her name on any buildings, the guild women were not interested in claiming personal identification for their work.[65]

To enhance a sense of community among the buildings' residents, the guild women purchased a small cottage in Grenville Street and converted the ground floor into a children's playroom. They organized playroom areas in the Summer Hill tenements in 1910 and 1911. They led outings outside the immediate neighborhood, organized sewing and cooking classes inside the buildings, began a coal fund to sell coal to their tenants more cheaply than they could buy individually, and organized used clothing sales.[66] The guild kept an emergency fund for the rent collectors to provide bread and milk, coal, or medicine to tenants in times of need and to aid sick children. They sought to beautify these tenements by organizing current students at the Alexandra College to bring flowers to the tenements. The guild's activities were significant in a city that was starved for public recreational spaces. Dublin had only two public parks because most open space in Dublin was enclosed by wealthy property owners. Mountjoy Square in the immediate neighborhood of Summer Hill and Grenville Street, for example, was private and would remain so until purchased by the Dublin government in 1938.[67] When another women's organization, the Women's National Health Association of Ireland, appealed to the corporation to provide small recreational spaces for children and the general public, they were unsuccessful.[68]

Dublin men were loath to support women's housing activities and in fact were downright hostile. Standard studies of Dublin housing detail how lax the corporation was in investigating housing conditions. Several members of the corporation owned tenement buildings. A building owned by alderman Gerald O'Reilly collapsed in 1902, killing one person; he was elected Lord Mayor of the city six years later.[69] Such indifference, however, did not extend to the properties of the guild. As the women sarcastically reported in 1903:

> We certainly have no reason to complain of any lack of Corporation Inspection. . . . Their inspectors are with us morning, noon and night; they jostle our rent collectors on the stairs; and if their methods sometimes strike us as curious, surely the number of their visits makes up for that. No rates could pay for the inspection we get, and the Guild should accept these constant attentions with becoming gratitude.[70]

Five years later nothing had changed, as the women recorded:

> The vigour of the Corporation is amazing. Their inspectors are ever with us, and we get full value for the taxes we pay in the matter of inspection. We wonder if other people are as highly honored. The only way I can account for their unremitting attention is by the hypothesis that all the inspectors gather together on Monday morning to decide where they will inspect. They have perhaps an alphabetical list of names and Alexandra Guild Tenements Co. stands first on the list. They all decide they must visit our premises, and do so. The same thing possibly happens on Tuesday and the following days. Do they ever reach XYZ?[71]

The *Freeman's Journal* chastised Dubliners who constantly expressed concern for poor children but did little to ameliorate their conditions. "We should very much like to know," wrote the editor, "what support has been given to the [Alexandra Guild] project and what practical steps have been taken to carry out the object of the company." Although the guild's activities were not copied by other Dubliners, they had raised £1,000 in £5 shares. There is no accounting as to who bought these shares.[72] The rents in guild buildings were comparable to those in the rest of the neighborhood, and no other housing schemes charged rents as low as did the Alexandra Guild: 1s to 3s/6d (pence) per week. Still, the guild was paying a 2½ percent dividend by 1908.[73]

THE ROYAL COMMISSION ON HOUSING OF THE WORKING CLASSES

The royal commission on housing—a group that the *Times* labeled as of "representative and influential character"—excluded women; led to the adoption of the 1890 Housing of the Working Classes Act, applying to all British cities;

and confirmed the direction in which men in London and Dublin wanted to pursue housing reform.[74] The commission refused to appoint Hill under the pretext that no woman had ever been appointed to serve on a royal commission. She was allowed to testify before the commission in London, where she pointed out that the private housing companies were not adhering to the mandate to rehouse the people displaced by new housing. They were getting around the mandate, she contended, "by getting rid of the people, by paying landlords to evict tenants before the company took over the site.[75] The commission also heard testimony that the Peabody Trust's demolitions had displaced thousands of people while rehousing only a small percentage of them and that their buildings were producing increased rents in surrounding areas.[76]

The commission's refusal to appoint Hill and its hearings and subsequent report demonstrate that men assumed it was their role to reconstruct the built environment and, in the process, to mute women's voices. First, the commission had relied on testimony from the men it considered housing experts; engineers, sanitary and medical officers, philanthropic housing builders, officials of MDCs, clergymen, and local officeholders were called on to testify.[77] In Dublin, where women living in abysmal conditions far outnumbered men, no women would testify before the commission. As Jacinta Prunty put it, "women were in general still excluded from the closed circle of engineers, medical officers and local government officials which 'controlled' discussion and hence the 'resolution.'"[78] The actual experiences of Hill and her housing managers could not stand against male professional determination to control the housing situation.

Second, testimony before the commissioners exposed the fact that men were concerned with reorganizing family life as a moral question in reconstructing the built environment. Testimony of London's medical officer of health that the presence of overcrowding "was corrupting the morals of the nation"[79] led the commission to conclude:

In considering what are the effects moral and material of the present conditions of the housing of the working classes, especially in the Metropolis, it will be convenient still to deal with over-crowding as a centre evil around which most of the others group themselves. The facts and figures which have been quoted in known instances where persons of all ages occupy the same room at all hours would be sufficient to establish the moral evil of the single room system, even if specific corroborative evidence were not forthcoming both as to the prevalence of this evil and also as to the widespread existence of the system which is the cause of it.[80]

Lord Shaftesbury testified that "the effect of the one room system is physically and morally beyond all description. . . . [Y]ou will generally find one bed occupied by the whole family, in many of these cases consisting of father, mother, and son; or of father and daughters; or brothers and sisters. It is impossible to say how fatal the result of that is."[81]

Contemporary publications shared this opinion. The London *Pall Mall Gazette* published a three-part exposé, "The Housing of London Workingmen— Not in the Slums," that had helped spur the organization of the commission. The paper was indignant that "mere overcrowding" could not "compare in indecency . . . with a case like that of a man living in one room with his grown-up daughter . . . or of a mother in one room with two grown-up sons and a grown-up daughter."[82] The *Times* noted in its commentary on the commission's report that "striking, and sometimes painful evidence, the report shows, had been given as to immorality."[83] The Reverend Andrew Mearns, author of the sensationalist twenty-page penny pamphlet *The Bitter Cry of Outcast London*, in which he had declared that immorality was the natural outcome of living in squalid conditions, was consulted for his "expertise."[84]

In Dublin, Dr. Thomas Grimshaw declared that housing must be built so that males and females were "compelled to occupy separate rooms." The Gentlemen's Society of St. Vincent de Paul asked the commission whether they were able to guarantee that sexes are "separated in night" in any new housing schemes.[85] The Housing of the Very Poor in Dublin, subsequently established in 1898, would construct its model dwellings with this idea in mind. It published a pamphlet stating that some of its buildings provided "a small but thoroughly ventilated separate sleeping compartment . . . thus affording a means for the separation of the sexes, if necessary."[86]

Third, the commission concluded that correct regulations and oversight and exercise of sound fiscal controls would result in better housing. For London, the commissioners recommended changing the configurations of future buildings, such as making the height of the first floor higher above the street, mandating better enforcement of existing laws, and consolidating overlapping municipal authorities. They spent much time evaluating the best ways to finance housing improvements, always taking into account what would be asked of ratepayers. They identified the most fiscally efficient means for securing housing for the poor and working classes as clearing the slums by extending the city boundaries to where cheap land could be purchased and the people rehoused outside the center.[87] In Ireland, the commissioners contended that the "chief remedy for the deplorable conditions of the dwellings of the working classes lies not so much in the amendment of existing statutes as in the carrying of them out more strictly."[88]

WOMEN AND THE QUALITY OF LIFE

In the face of such male power, and without recognized "expertise" on housing, women found it virtually impossible to have their voices heard. This

circumstance is especially pertinent because sources on women's organizations in all four cities contain evidence that women were not concerned with
reorganizing family life inside housing.[89] Rather they were seeking to ameliorate the conditions in which the poor lived, not cast them out and isolate
them. Moreover, women's organizations worked together, going directly into
the cities' poorest areas. At their Grenville Street buildings, the Alexandra
Guild opened a branch of the Women's National Health Association and
supported the WNHA's campaign for open playgrounds in Dublin's poor
neighborhoods. The WNHA, for its part, opened Babies' Clubs, with a female doctor in attendance in poor neighborhoods where mothers could
bring their children for health checkups. They operated a restaurant in another neighborhood serving food to women and children at a "nominal rate,"
supplied free milk and eggs for infants and young children, and opened a
pasteurized milk depot. Babies' Clubs, milk stations, and playgrounds
brought women, children, and the poor out into the streets rather than isolating them from the rest of the city.[90]

Neither Chicago nor Toronto had women's groups similar to Hill and the
Alexandra Guild, but activist women in both cities worked within similar
ideas about community and social responsibility for all residents. In Chicago, the women of the Hull House settlement used new techniques of mapping and surveying to map their immediate neighborhood economically,
socially, and ethnically. Publishing the results in the *Hull-House Maps and
Papers* in 1895, they asserted that "the aim of both maps and accompanying
notes is to present conditions rather than to advance theories—to bring
within reach of the public exact information concerning this quarter of Chicago."[91] Rather than classifying people and neighborhoods as impersonal,
bounded areas, the Hull House survey sought to demonstrate the neighborhood as a home to people who lived and worked in difficult circumstances.
The women acknowledged "the painful nature of minute investigation and
that the personal impertinence of the questions asked would be unendurable
and unpardonable were it not for the conviction that the public conscience
when aroused must demand better surroundings for the most inert and
long-suffering citizens of the commonwealth." This was the first survey that
"graphically details the plight of immigrants and documents their work
ethic, blaming the economic system rather than the individual for social
conditions in the slums."[92]

When Toronto women organized their Local Council of Women
(TLCW) in 1893, its first president declared that women's concern for the
individual home, children, and family should be extended outside their own
domestic sphere to embrace the community.[93] Early in the twentieth century,
the women became especially incensed about the deteriorating conditions of
the city's rental housing occupied by poor immigrants. They organized a
public meeting to arouse awareness on "how some people in the city live."

They discussed the possibility of raising money to erect a cooperative home for thirty families in cooperation with the Evangelia social settlement.[94] Women never eschewed attention to laws, enforcement, and finances, but they saw them as components of housing reform, not as the motivating factors.

Chicago and Toronto had no official housing inquiries in the late nineteenth century, although by the early twentieth century men in both cities had begun to see poor housing as a threat to the cities' prosperity. And, like the men testifying before the royal commission, Chicago and Toronto men were preoccupied with the morality of bad housing. The Chicago Association of Commerce declared that "bad housing means death and disease . . . means inefficient workers . . . makes bad citizens . . . gives the city a bad appearance and a bad reputation."[95] The Toronto department of public health described the poorer areas of the city as "hot beds for germination of disease, vice and crime. . . . We can scarcely hope for people to rise much above their environments."[96]

Men in Dublin and London had also voiced their concern for the health and efficiency of the working man. A participant at an 1889 meeting in Dublin of the National Labourers' Dwellings and Sanitary Association declared that "the strength, and energy, and physical vitality of workingmen depended on the homes they occupied. . . . The idea of 'the home beautiful' was surrounded by the happiest thoughts and holiest associations; every effort should be made to realise it in the case of the labourers."[97] In London, C. M. Knowles wrote that "the efficiency of the worker must also be reckoned with as a factor in the cost of production, and the healthier homelife obtainable outside London must undoubtedly conduce to greater energy and alertness in industrial pursuits."[98]

Nevertheless, women continued to pursue their visions of the quality of life owed to urban residents. These concerns ranged from attention to women's desires for organizing space within the home to benefit women (which was generally ignored by male professionals who told women what they needed), to providing adequate and affordable housing for single women, to such basic questions as how to find appropriate accommodations and how to engage with the labor market. All such concerns, as Helen Meller proposes, were "people-centered" and emphasized the "experiential aspect of urban life."[99] As the founding members of the Toronto Local Council of Women expressed it: women should "be concerned with their communities, especially with those social issues which directly affect children and the home such as education, housing, pure food, and so on. Women's special material concern for the home and family should be extended outside their own domestic sphere to embrace the community."[100]

The literature's tendency to conceptualize women's ideas through a male lens has often produced a mistaken analysis of women's perspective. One recent work discussing Toronto women's public activities describes them as wishing to create the "city-as-parlour."[101] Since many of these women and those in other cities were working to break down the boundaries between the city and the home, not just to make the city a more comfortable sitting area, such an analysis risks dismissing women as serious urban actors. By breaking the public-private divide, women were not seeking to create a public matriarchy. Sandra Haar, a scholar of the architecture of the Hull House complex in Chicago, provides a more apt analysis. She argues that in its internal arrangements, Hull House "challenged the way in which the house—the domestic sphere—was sited within the city." Both the "architecture and urbanity of Hull House shaped, or more specifically reconfigured the relationship between the public and private spheres, allowing these spheres to co-exist, yet protecting their distinctions." Hull House residents "went out into the city and the city and its people came into Hull House." Addams and the other Hull House residents understood that the boundaries between the private home and the public city were being transformed, and they wanted women to take part in transforming that public city. According to Haar, they "did not desire to recreate nor reconfigure the domestic. . . . [T]hey were responding to changes in domestic life already occurring."[102] Octavia Hill had promoted this same idea when she built the Red Cross Cottages with their open garden and community hall. WNHA founder Lady Ishbel Aberdeen's presidential address to the International Council of Women encapsulated these sentiments:

> But when it is spoken of as if [women's] home duties clashed with the public duties, surely it is a wrong conception of what home means. . . . [L]et us recognize that it is good for us now and again to come together to realize that there is a common aim uniting us all in a great international sisterhood the world over—a sisterhood of work for the benefit of humanity.[103]

Women's emphasis on the quality of life for urban residents, on breaking down the boundaries between the home and the city for a common welfare, and of learning how to live in the city ran counter to the male emphasis on controlling the city to implement their own political and economic agendas. With women presenting a challenge to male control of housing, men began to prioritize finding ways to reinstate the boundaries between the public and the private. So, as women were pushing out of the home and connecting the health of the home with the health and welfare of the broader community, men simultaneously sought ways to push women back into the home and maintain public patriarchy. Reconstructing the private patriarchal home became inextricably entwined with reconstructing the public patriarchal city. In tandem with the male focus on economic development and protecting the property culture of all four cities, this ideal would largely determine how and why the built environment would follow certain forms in the coming years.

TRANSIT TO THE RESCUE

It may seem strange to finish a chapter on housing by bringing in the issue of transit. But to maintain patriarchy, new transit systems became inextricably bound to decisions about housing, domesticity, and breaking and resetting boundaries in the built environment. The chapters in Part II of the book explore the major role that transit and traffic would play in reconstructing each city, but introducing the issue here is helpful to understanding how gendered this issue was.

When Octavia Hill testified before an 1882 parliamentary committee, she had pointed out that casual laborers could not afford to travel any distance to work. She had especially emphasized the difficulties commuting to work imposed on families. When only one member of a family worked, she noted, the commute was not difficult. But when several members of a family, including children, worked, then workmen's trains disrupted the family circumstances as they might work at different times and in different places, and the amount of money spent on train fares mounts up.[104]

New transit systems, however, would make it possible to decentralize the city's population into the city's outer areas. By building on the periphery, or even constructing new suburbs connected by transit lines, men would be able to erect new types of housing that would not just move the working class out of the city but would embound women into a new domesticity in isolated homes and surroundings. Rather than follow Hill's line of reasoning and keep housing near to work, men in London as well as in other cities would make decentralization through new transit systems a priority.

As early as the 1860s London men had been working to facilitate decentralization by mandating cheap-fare workmen's trains. In 1864, trains offering cheap fares to artisans and labourers were instituted. Cheap-fare trains, however, left for the city by 6:30 A.M. to accommodate male workers in trades. Women workers' employment in the city usually began at 8:00 or 9:00 A.M, so if they wanted to use the cheap fares, they had to arrive in town well before their employment opened.

Simon Abernethy's recent study of transit decisions in London argues that working men's trains were more "accessible to a much broader spectrum of the working class before 1914 than has previously been supposed."[105] He fails to appreciate, however, that the early timetable of running the cheap-fare trains primarily to accommodate working *men* constrained working women's choices. He concludes that the inconvenience for wives and children of having a long wait in the city before their work began if they took the early trains was "apparently acceptable" because they took the trains.

"Loitering, while problematic," he argues, "was not so inconvenient that women and children gave up commuting."[106] Yet his own evidence suggests that the proportion of women taking the trains rose with the later, more costly trains, which he attributes to them perhaps not wishing to loiter in the city.[107] Moreover, his assertion that by the 1890s "households which required children or wives to earn subsidiary wages" were taking the working men's trains downplays the fact that if their wages were so necessary, they would have been reluctant to take the costlier trains no matter the inconvenience.[108]

Dismissing the travel issues of households as inconveniences does not take into account how gendered was the discussion about decentralization and working men's trains. And although it was not the point of this article, it also does not address the needs of single women working in the city. Rather, the article refers only to working men's households, with women restricted to the marginal role of wives and subsidiary workers.

3

THE DISORDER OF UNEMBOUNDED BODIES

I asked [my aunt] why she left her Wisconsin farm for the city of Milwaukee. What was there to do, she asked in return. Meet a boy down at the bridge? What did she do in the city, I asked. She said she had first worked in a candy factory and roomed with the family of a young friend. The year was 1916. What did you do after work, I persisted. We went dancing, she replied, every night except Monday. Why never on Monday, I asked. Because, she responded with a smile, the dance hall was closed on Monday.[1]

Here was the new urban single woman: working in a factory by day, spending her money by night, unescorted and dancing with unfamiliar men. She was far away from her family and lodging with strangers. She might be unemployed, working as a prostitute to earn enough money for food and a night's shelter. She might be a destitute woman sleeping on the floor of a police station or an abandoned woman with children and no means of support. She might even be a single, self-supporting woman living and working in decent circumstances. Whatever her situation, the single woman, working or not, was a public figure. She violated the gendered ideal of women inside the family home under the watchful eyes of a male authority figure.

But there were also tens of thousands of single, often unemployed, men circulating through the Anglo-Atlantic cities. Without a fixed abode, they too threatened the ideal of family life and social order. They might frequent saloons, use brothels and prostitutes, and loiter on the streets. They could not be counted on to fulfill the gendered trope of masculinity: the hardworking male who supported his family and obeyed the law.[2] Such men might feel no allegiance to the city and maintaining its order. While both single women and men were then subject to new types of urban control, single or homeless women posed a potentially more disruptive threat. Not only did they challenge the four male goals for housing reform set out in the previous chapter; they were out of place as public women. The debate in all four cities about providing lodging houses for the homeless or marginally employed men and women reflected the gendered nature of ideas about the proper place of male and female bodies in the city.

LONDON

By 1851, the bulk of the London's population of almost 2.5 million was crowded into the city's inner boroughs. Here, the only accommodations affordable to the poor and marginal were often the insalubrious common lodging houses that charged by the night. One group investigating the condition of these lodging houses claimed that every night "tens of thousands" of Londoners "take up their quarters at some of the lodging-houses that are scattered about the poorer parts of London" and wherein the respectable poor mingle with the "very worst of mankind" and where "promiscuous accommodation of the sexes" is allowed.[3] Publications of this sort, along with more salacious tales published in the series *Mysteries of London*, persuaded Parliament, led by Lord Shaftesbury, to pass the Common Lodging Houses Act and the Labouring Classes Lodging Houses Act in 1851. The former act gave local governments the power to register, regulate, and inspect the lodging houses based on new sanitary laws. The latter act authorized local parishes over a certain size to appoint commissions to consider providing lodging houses.[4] An estimated eleven thousand lodging houses existed in London at the time the acts were passed. Ten years later Henry Mayhew worried that there were at least two hundred "low lodging houses" in which "no fewer than 10,000 persons domiciled, more or less permanently."[5]

When the LCC assumed regulatory control of lodging houses in 1894, jointly administered by the council's Public Health and Housing of the Working-Classes Committees, concern about common lodging houses extended beyond issues of sanitation and morality. London men feared that the number of homeless single men congregating in these dwellings threatened the family life and the social order they were promoting. Carefully distinguishing between the impoverished and the "respectable workingman," they feared that the lodging houses were debasing the latter. Lord Rowton, a wealthy philanthropist who had worked with the Guinness Trust, built the first of his working men's hostels, called Rowton Houses, in Vauxhall to provide a better type of lodging house for that respectable working man. Rowton put up £30,000 for the original endeavor and in 1894 he formed the Rowton Houses Company, which attracted sufficient investments to erect several more Rowton Houses by the early 1900s. Rowton Houses were intended to be profitable ventures and the original charge at a Rowton House was 6d per night. The *Times* reported that by 1896 the company was paying a dividend of "no less than 4%," and the paper predicted "that the time would come when artisans' dwellings stock would be a security equal to first-class railway debentures."[6]

Rowton House accommodations were far superior to the common lodging houses. They ranged in size from that for several hundred men to just over a thousand. Each man had a separate sleeping cubicle, and each house was furnished with common lavatories, smoking and reading rooms, and dining rooms. The houses also provided "respectable" intellectual entertainment and leisure activities for the residents: libraries, reading and smoking rooms with newspapers, chess sets and dominoes. The *Times* assured readers that such establishments were not charity. Rather, they needed to be self-supporting, "free from the charge of pauperizing and to encourage manly independence of spirit."[7]

At the same time, the LCC decided to furnish municipal lodging houses for men. Between 1893 and 1895 the council built the Parker House (Drury Lane); the Bruce House (Kemble Street), which ultimately accommodated up to 1,000 men; and the Carrington House (Mill Lane, Deptford). When a dispute arose between the LCC and the Rowton Houses as to whether the Rowtons were common lodging houses that should be registered and inspected, they were ruled legally exempt from the common lodging house acts.[8] By the beginning of the twentieth century, the common lodging houses, the five London Rowton Houses, the three municipal lodging houses, and other smaller philanthropic lodging houses provided thousands of lodgings for men.

There was not universal support for providing any type of lodging house. C. S. Loch, head of the Charity Organization Society, claimed that providing shelter increased "homelessness and celibate unsettlement. . . . [P]auperism is fostered and congested." On the other hand, W. Bramwell Booth of the Salvation Army regretted "this new danger to the world that we all understand by the word 'home,'" but he believed that the present economic system would not allow everyone to attain this desirable situation and men in such reduced circumstances should not be denied shelter.[9] Even the progressive LCC councillor John Burns, a strong supporter of the LCC lodging houses, worried about building too many such establishments. In a 1907 speech opening the International Housing Conference, he declared that "for single men who ought to be married . . . London was more than sufficiently supplied with housing for this class of person." He claimed that the "housing problem . . . [was] the problem of the home . . . the nursery for the young, a seminary for the youthful, a refuge for old age, the root-tree of character." Burns made no mention of women's housing needs except to list "female labour" as a London problem.[10]

Single women in London generally avoided the common lodging houses, which were considered one step above the workhouse. They offered few amenities and little privacy. Not all common lodging houses would even accept women, and lodging houses that did accept women often charged women more than they charged men. The LCC's joint public health/housing of the working classes committee reported that of seventy-three lodging houses it investigated in 1898, only eighteen admitted single women, providing a total of 801 beds for women. The report did not comment on

the number of single women in the city, but four years later another report by the committee estimated that there were around seventy-five thousand working women in London's central districts.[11] Both reports recommended that the LCC investigate building a model lodging house for women.
This recommendation would seem reasonable, since the LCC was building lodging houses for men. But the LCC never built any lodging houses
for women. No wealthy men championed lodging houses for women. Wom-
en's housing needs continued to be ignored even after a health committee
survey of licensed common lodging houses in the inner boroughs found
that there were 5,625 beds, but only 40 of these beds were licensed for single
women.[12]

The male philanthropic and investment-seeking housers and the LCC
failed single women for two main reasons. First, the low wages paid to
women meant that many of them could not afford even the 6d charge that
made the Rowton and LCC houses profitable. Sydney Waterlow, chair of the
housing of the working classes committee, urged the LCC to consider building a women's model lodging house but admitted that they "had not yet been
able to bring it within the financial requirements of the Council."[13] Several
times in 1902 the LCC postponed even accepting its joint committee's report. The LCC finance committee desired "to point out that the [commit-
tee's] hope to bring up a scheme for a women's lodging house in connection
with working-class dwellings which, as a whole, shall be self-supporting,
[does] not expect to avoid a deficiency on the lodging house."[14] The LCC
subsequently failed to follow through on an architect's proposal to build a
small lodging house for fifty-seven women in Southwark for a sum of £7,500.
By early 1909, the LCC's housing of the working classes committee dropped
the idea altogether, conceding that "exhaustive inquiries had been made with
the view of ascertaining whether the Council could make such provisions
without a charge upon the county rate, but up to the present it had not been
found possible to provide a house of the necessary size and description on a
self-supporting basis."[15]

Providing housing for single, homeless women threatened the male ideal
of urban order through family domesticity. Some women were already proclaiming that the wave of the future was women escaping the patriarchal
home. In a 1894 essay in the *New Review*, journalist Anna Mary (Tissie)
Sparrow declared that there was a "revolt of the Working Woman against
home life and home cares. . . . Love of a home, however meagre, is no longer
the aim and ambition of a working woman."[16] Sparrow advised society to
accept this fact and provide well-regulated lodging houses for women. In
1900, the Women's Industrial Council (WIC, organized in 1894) declared
that "there is an ever-increasing number of women demanding comfortable
but inexpensive lodging" and that women wanted such lodgings to "enable
them to devote themselves to their various callings undeterred by domestic

worries or privations." The WIC circulated a leaflet asking working women to fill out a form about their housing needs.[17]

Despite the obvious need for women's lodging houses, by 1904 there was only a small lodging house for women opened by the religiously oriented Shaftesbury Institute Mission. The mission solicited funds for a larger establishment, saying that "nowhere else can a poor, hard-working, respectable Christian woman obtain a fitting lodging for a night for a trifling payment." The mission succeeded in funding a larger establishment, the Portman House on Harrow Street, Marylebone Road, that accommodated 104 women at 5d per night.[18]

As women were struggling to find decent housing in London, Shirley F. Murphy, London's chief medical officer of health, assured the LCC that it need not concern itself about providing municipal lodgings for women. Such "unfortunate" women, he declared, could find room in the common lodging houses that accommodated the "class of person" who would go there. A model lodging house, he told the LCC, was unnecessary because respectable women would not wish to associate with unrespectable women even in model lodgings. Murphy asserted that women preferred a home to a lodging house and thus would not stay in the latter. Besides, he warned the LCC, "a lodging house for factory women and girls would [not] be successful from a financial point of view."[19]

Women did not agree. That same year as Murphy's report, Mrs. Marianne Dale, treasurer of the National Association for Women's Lodging-Homes (NAWLH), published a pamphlet describing the need for women's model lodging houses. She asked the LCC to rescind its standing order that such establishments be self-supporting, pointing out the particular plight of middle-aged and older women who could no longer work and could not afford decent lodgings. "It is only common sense on the part of the community," she wrote, "to try and remove women from casual wards, workhouses, common lodging houses, and houses of ill-fame, and give them a chance of clean, modest, decent living in Municipal lodging houses—like the men."[20] In the same month that Murphy rejected the need for women's model lodging houses, Dale led a women's delegation to the housing of the working classes committee to urge the LCC to build model lodging houses for women. She again emphasized the conditions of older women: "I plead specially for the middle-aged women. Work for them is scarce and difficult, they can only pay night by night." But she qualified her statement: "not that I underrate the importance of the young girl." She also asserted that fourteen of the London boroughs did not even have common lodging houses for women.[21]

In May 1911, the NAWLH held a conference in London to publicize women's housing needs and reject the men's ideas. "Women are citizens of this country," declared Lady M'Laren. "Their health, happiness, and convenience should be as important as any other section of society. . . . Everywhere we see public money poured out like water for objects in which men are interested, while reforms of first necessity for the well-being of women are denied. Women earn less than men, their need is the greater."[22] The Duchess of Marlborough rejected the notion that model lodging houses "will destroy home life." The widowed mother, the factory girl, unemployed women searching for work, single women—all were in need of decent lodging.[23] It is significant, as the organization's title notes, that these women saw lodging houses as homes, unlike Burns, who conceptualized homes as the family home. Titled women such as the duchess opened the conference, but they were not alone in speaking out for lodgings for single women. Mary Higgs, who had been investigating the lodging conditions of working and poor women for several years and who had founded the NAWLH in 1909, pointed out that in London only the common lodging houses charged a rate that working women could afford. She had investigated all the privately owned, philanthropic, or common lodging houses in the city in which women could stay and found that only fifteen of them had any places for women, and in several there was only one such lodging for a small number of women. She concluded that it was a "civic duty" of the city to provide "a place where a poor woman can, at her own cost, sleep safely and keep herself clean."[24]

Dr. J.F.J. Sykes, the medical officer of health for St. Pancras borough, dismissed Higgs. Providing housing, he contended, "requires a sense of proportion and perspective. . . . You must say what proportion of each particular class of persons requires lodging. When it is known what class of houses or homes exists you might prepare schemes and get out plans to stimulate enterprise under proper supervision. . . . My last words are: privacy and modesty in not-over-regulated houses under homely supervision."[25] The women rejected Sykes's patronizing statements, first, because they knew that it was impossible to know how many women needed shelter on any given night or whether they would be accepted into any shelter. The Providence Row Night Shelter, for example, required women to supply references before they could be admitted. As Dale asserted, the solution was not more study of classes of women but immediate action and recognition of the gender bias.

> The Council has built houses for men, with splendid accommodations. There are also the Rowton Houses, to which men go. At none of these are references to character required. However vicious or unsatisfactory men may be they have the run of these working-men's hotels. For poor women there is nothing but the common lodging-house. In the opinion of the deputation [that had met with the LCC], the right solution lies in the providing of medium-sized houses with accommodations for about 100 women each in some half-dozen selected areas.[26]

When the Duchess of Marlborough and other women organized the Women's Municipal Party (WMP) in 1913, one of its principal demands was that the LCC build lodging houses for women. The duchess continued to accuse the LCC of gender bias: "The London County Council in the past has spent thousands of pounds in providing municipal lodging houses for men, but has so far refused to spend money in constructing them for women. . . . [T]he need for such lodging is even more urgent in London than in other cities." She also argued that it was "absolutely necessary to have women's inspectors of common lodging houses for women" rather than have only male inspectors.[27]

Without support from the LCC, women had to use their own resources. Unlike the monetary investments for the Rowton Houses, however, women had only a few wealthy investors. The Ada Lewis House was a conspicuous exception. In her will Lewis had bequeathed £50,000 to endow Ada Lewis lodging houses "run on lines of Rowton Houses."[28] It took the appointed trustees of her will seven years to open one such house, on New Kent Road in Southwark, and they never opened any others. The trustees also decided to name it the Ada Lewis House because they believed it a more respectable title than *lodging house*. The house affiliated with the NAWLH in 1914.[29]

The women did not intend that women's housing should be a money-making endeavor. Lodging houses for women were opened and furnished by soliciting donations, often at the request of prominent London women. The Duchess of Marlborough helped open the Mary Curzon Hostel in late 1913 on Kings-cross Road. The hostel accommodated fifty-five single women and had six additional accommodations for women with children. The charge was 6d per night.[30] Mary Higgs reported in 1915 that the Curzon Hostel was "constantly filled by poor women needing such shelter" and that the Ada Lewis House was averaging 142 lodgers per night.[31] The purpose of the NAWLH, according to Higgs, was to link all organizations and individuals who were interested in opening and maintaining lodgings for women.[32] The Ada Lewis House, the Curzon Hostel, and a few other private or philanthropic lodging houses for women could hardly begin to meet the need, and women continued to agitate for the LCC to provide more lodging houses for women. But the LCC refused to do so. In the mid-1920s women organized the Women's Public Lodging House Fund to solicit donations for a new series of lodgings called Cecil Houses. The driving force behind this initiative was Ada Elizabeth Chesterton (widow of Cecil Chesterton), who was an investigative journalist and the organizing secretary of the fund. A letter to the *Times* announcing the fund's initiative made the same case for this need as before, pointing out the real gender disparity of the situation:

We find that homeless men are admirably cared for. There are municipal lodging houses in plenty, and every district owns its Rowton

House. . . . But neither philanthropic trusts nor municipal bodies will provide public lodging houses for women. Of the total sleeping accommodations in London thus licensed by the L.C.C. only 9.42% is available for women. . . . Hundreds of women are without shelter, night after night because there is no place where for a small sum they can find a roof.[33]

Lady Violet Bonham-Carter chastised people for assuming that homeless women "must of necessity be a shady character" while thinking that homeless men were "merely unfortunate." She pointed out that while accommodations were being provided for men, for women there was one casual ward in Southwark and a few free shelters.[34] Despite women's claims, the chief medical officer of health flatly denied that "hundreds of women tramp the streets of London nightly." By his account there were beds available for them in free shelters and casual wards.[35] Ada Chesterton countered that casual "wards" were unacceptable and that besides 90 percent of lodging house accommodations were for men.[36] George Bernard Shaw supported her assertion, saying that the problem was "that people still did not feel like providing for women what was looked upon as right for men."[37]

The first Cecil House was opened in January 1927 on Devonshire-street, and by the mid-1930s, there were four additional houses: Wharfedale-road (Kings Cross), Kensal-road in North Kensington, Harrow-road, and Waterloo-road. They were all founded on the principle that they were to be solely a social service where "in no circumstances will any profit be made" with funds to sustain the houses secured through public appeal, not by private investment. The houses were also to be strictly nonsectarian. They were to supply at cost beds, bathing, and washing accommodations for "homeless or vagrant women."[38] The annual reports indicate that the fund achieved its aims but also that the demand still far exceeded the need, so contributions were constantly being solicited. By January 1928, during its first year of operation, the Devonshire house had supplied more than eleven thousand beds. By October the number had risen to more than eighteen thousand. The houses accommodated casual workers; flower, paper, and match sellers; itinerant charwomen; waitresses; unemployed domestics; and "a percentage of women of middle-class education," including women with children, as the Cecil House furnished children's cots. A late October 1928 public meeting to support the Women's Public Lodging House Fund noted that the houses needed to increase the number of cots. By 1932, the Cecil Houses had furnished 311,468 beds and 27,924 children's cots. By 1937, those numbers were 626,640 beds and 38,315 cots.[39] The cost of a bed was 1s per night, which included a hot bath, washing facilities, and tea and biscuits. A child's cot could be had for 3d per night. Yet no one was ever turned away as long as there was an available bed, whether she could pay or not, and there were no questions asked. Despite these successes, the Cecil Houses fifth annual report in 1932 asserted that lodging house accommodations in London for women had increased to only 11 percent of the total available lodgings.[40]

DUBLIN

Dublin faced an influx of rural migrants with its economy in decline and ruled by a distant and largely indifferent Parliament that expected the city to finance any municipal undertaking out of the rates. Under these circumstances, Dublin government paid little attention to the housing of single men and almost none to the needs of single women. Between 1883 and 1888, the Dublin Corporation did erect some buildings on Barrack-street (soon renamed Benburb-street) for "artisans and laborers," mainly to accommodate families, but the complex did include one lodging house for men with one hundred beds at 4d per night. The rents in the tenement buildings ranged from 5s for three rooms to 1s/6d for one room.[41] By all accounts over the next twelve years, the lodging house weekly accommodated a small number of women. The Artisans' Dwelling Committee of the Dublin Council reported that during the first week of October 1889, 532 men and 58 women had used the lodging house.[42] The gender imbalance remained. In 1898, the committee reported that since its opening, the lodging house had accommodated 28,772 men and 1,392 women.[43]

Dublin's one equivalent to the Rowton Houses was a men's hostel with just over five hundred beds at 7d per night for men, furnished with bathrooms with hot water, erected by Lord Iveagh as part of his trust buildings. Iveagh and Rowton happened to be good friends. In 1912, the Catholic Church established a free night shelter, the St. Vincent DePaul Home in Great Strand Street for homeless Catholic men, that offered fifty beds.[44] Many Dublin men made connections to home and laborers, as had London men. The Reverend D. Mahoney told a meeting of the National Labourers' Dwellings and Sanitary Association, "The strength, and energy, and physical vitality of workingmen depended on the home they occupy. The idea of the 'home beautiful' was surrounded by the happiest thoughts and holiest associations; and every effort should be made to realise it in the case of the labourers."[45] In such a context, men could hardly have been eager to provide shelter for homeless or poor women whose choices were the workhouse, a rough night asylum designated for the homeless poor, or a religious charity.

The tight connections between religion and ideas about the home affected Dublin's attitude toward women. Unlike London, where women acted on their own to compensate for the institutional indifference to single women, in Dublin the Catholic Church opposed such efforts. Women, in effect, were forced to channel any efforts to help other women through sectarian night asylums run by members of either the Roman Catholic Church or the Protestant Church of Ireland. The purpose of such asylums was to protect the virtue of young homeless girls and women.[46] For Catholics, this typically meant that asylums were run by congregations of nuns, who themselves were controlled by the church's male hierarchy. Since records from these women's congregations are scarce, it is difficult to discern how much work these congregations did for other women in the nineteenth century. Catholic clerics denounced any other women's public activities. One pastoral letter declared that lay women would be under pain of ostracism if they formed their own organizations:

> "The daughters of our Catholic people, be they matrons or virgins, are called forth under the flimsy pretext of charity to take their stand in the noisy streets of life. The pretext of charity is merely assumed; for already we have associations of holy men and women, who with the full blessings of religion, do the works of mercy, corporal and spiritual for the poor and afflicted." . . . [W]omen are being asked to "forget the modesty of their sex and the high dignity of their womanhood." . . . [C]lerics [should] deny these women access to "sodalities" because they are unworthy of a "child of Mary."[47]

The Protestant women of the Alexandra Guild were not controlled by the Church of Ireland. The guild was able to extend its concern for housing to the plight of single women. It invited London activist Marianne Dale to be a featured speaker at its annual conference in 1911. In a speech titled "Where Shall She Live?" she urged the women to concern themselves with the plight of homeless women and advised them that it was "an absolute necessity for women's lodging houses to be provided by the municipal polities."[48] But aside from the small number of accommodations at Benburb-street, the Dublin Corporation did not fund such lodgings. As in London, therefore, it was left to women to help other women. The Alexandra Guild solicited donations to buy and furnish accommodations for single women. In December 1912 it opened the Alexandra Working Girls Hostel on Castlewood Avenue in Rathmines (a suburban township). The charge for full room and board was 5s/6d per week, about 1s less than the average working girl's wage. The hostel could accommodate twenty-five to thirty girls. The hostel was strictly nondenominational, making it the only accommodation for women in the city that was not religiously affiliated.[49] In 1915, the guild reported that it had housed ninety-six working girls during the year, with it always being full and at times needing to turn girls away for lack of room.[50] The hostel remained open until 1920.[51]

TORONTO

Toronto's population and economy expanded during the 1890s as immigrants, mainly British, arrived seeking the opportunity promised by a new industrial city. Immigration produced a new gender problem for the city. The number of single women in Toronto was outpacing that of single men. In 1881 the ratio of single women per single men was 105.4 to 100; twenty years later it was 120.9 single women to 100 single men.[52] Even in the face of this imbalance, Toronto men clung to the ideal of Toronto as the place of the single-family home, believing this image would best continue to produce economic growth.

This emphasis on the single-family home worked to the detriment of single women or poor women immigrants. Toronto single women had to depend on other women to provide them with shelter. One shelter for home-less Toronto women was the night shelter mentioned in Chapter 2, superin-tended by Agnes B. McIntyre, that the city council had refused to support. McIntyre was also matron of the Women's Christian Temperance Union shelter for girls. By 1905, the TLCW had organized a Women's Welcome Hostel located at 52 St. Alban's Street for women and children. They secured a grant of $1,000 from the Ontario provincial government—not the city—to set up this hostel as temporary lodging for newly arriving immigrant women while they looked for work. The grant allowed them to lodge these women from twenty-four to thirty-six hours at no charge. The TLCW reported in 1907 that they had sheltered 550 women and children since opening and that they had secured another $1,000 from the provincial government to con-tinue the work. Although it was a temporary shelter, the hostel was more than either the city or any private entity had provided for the now-daily in-flux of women migrating into the city in search of work.[53]

The TLCW's housing committee recognized that the Women's Welcome Hostel was a dire necessity: "it is impossible to give an idea of the value of the Hostel to the women arriving at the Union Station often with only enough money to carry them to their destination and who, without the Hos-tel, would have been left without shelter for the night."[54] But it was not suf-ficient to solve the problem of housing for single women. The TLCW unsuccessfully sought to have both the city and private enterprise provide regular housing for single women. In 1909, they called for a public meeting to address the issue, but in lieu of any further progress in housing women, they began to investigate what it might cost to build cooperative housing complete with a central nursery and laundry. The TLCW proposed building a working mothers' home of four stories of ten tenements, to include a cen-tral nursery, laundry, kitchen, and dining room, with rents no higher than $1.75 per week. Such a building and at those rates meant that it could never make money but would need an endowment and a steady influx of gifts to keep it going.[55] As in London, few women could afford to put up that kind of money, so the cooperative never materialized.

In 1912, the women asked the city council to establish its own housing committee that would consider building municipal lodging houses, both temporary and permanent, for single working men and women.[56] The council did not consider this request, although chief medical officer Charles Hastings was concerned, mainly from a public health perspective, about overcrowding in private lodging houses and proposed that there might be a civic lodging house at St. Paul's Hall on Yonge Street. Residents of the area immediately objected that such an institution "would bring a very undesirable class of people into what promises to be the best retail district in the town."[57] In August 1913, he informed the council that there were 2,240 lodgers "in the various lodgings houses in the city" that violated the Public Health Act. He again suggested that the city arrange some type of lodging house for men, located perhaps in the General Hospital Building on Gerrard Street. Hastings was motivated by concern over the growing population of unmarried, non-British, immigrant men who could best be assimilated into Canadian culture in "lodging houses under proper supervision."[58] Hastings also assured the council that he was investigating how such an endeavor could be profitable for the city. He contended that many of the men who were currently overcrowding the city's lodgings "are receiving sufficient wages to pay for better accommodations that the city would provide, and our lodging house would not be a burden on the citizens."[59] Hastings also wanted new licensing regulations for private lodging houses[60] and declared that they "would close up about 25 percent of the lodging houses of the city"[61] and that this "would be a splendid move in the interests of the city."[62]

Hastings continued to raise the issue of housing in the council, but always in the context of public health concerns, the evils of overcrowding, and the need for laboring men to afford a house. Promoting a municipal lodging house was always secondary to home ownership.[63]

A Social Survey Commission, appointed in 1913 to survey the state of the city's social morality, calculated that there were even more men in unsuitable lodgings than Hastings had claimed. According to the survey, at least five thousand unmarried men in the city had no lodging other than a bedroom, a condition that the survey obviously deemed a potential harm to the city's moral life. The survey recommended that men's hotels be built, on a business basis, "where men could have home comforts, club rooms, reading rooms, ample baths, and lavatory accommodations." The survey also wanted to eliminate overcrowded conditions that they believed resulted in young women sharing space with fathers, brothers, or male boarders. Such conditions, its report stressed, "must necessarily tend toward immorality" as "they deprive young people of that sense of modesty which is one of the most valuable barriers girls possess in safeguarding them against the temptations they are exposed to." The report used the phrase *young people*, but it was really concerned with girls being tempted into sexual impropriety. On the other hand, the survey made no recommendations about better housing for women beyond recommending that all boardinghouses be inspected by the public health department to ensure that they had parlor and lavatory accommodations. Many of these accommodations, apparently, did not have such facilities, a situation that the survey believed was "a genuine menace to the health and morals of the young women who live in them."[64]

Neither Hastings nor the Social Survey Commission was inclined to recommend municipal lodging for women. Yet the need was clearly there. In 1913, the TLCW reported that across the previous year 1,395 women had been sheltered in the Women's Welcome Hostel, almost triple the number of women who were sheltered when the hostel first opened. The hostel survived only because it continued to receive grants from the provincial government.[65] With no help coming from the city, by 1915 the TLCW was left with few options for securing housing for single women. At that point, they would turn to the private Toronto Housing Company (THC) and ask it to build "adequate housing for self-supporting women." But the THC was a profit-making venture and focused on erecting housing for working men's families, not for working women. Only when it could not find sufficient buyers for the buildings did the THC agree to rent some buildings to the TLCW.[66]

The best accommodations that Toronto working women could experience were privately endowed houses for "business" women and girls.[67] In 1909, Georgina Broughall, the wife of an Anglican minister, opened the Georgina House at 106 Beverley Street. The Georgina House provided housing mainly for women who were finding work in new occupations, such as stenographers, telephone operators, and bookkeepers. In 1912, the house built an addition that increased its accommodations from thirty-three to eighty-five, and it added another wing in 1914. The Georgina House was "under the auspices of the Anglican church," but there was no religious requirement for the residents.[68] Although the *Toronto Star* assured its readers that this was not a "transient boarding house," by 1922 the women running the house admitted that it had become necessary to make "an emergency cot" into a permanent fixture and to add more temporary cots "to take in an occasional transient." The house was also being obliged to turn away women for lack of space.[69]

The Georgina House Association recognized that single unemployed women had an ongoing desperate need for shelter that the house could not hope to meet. To expand lodging "for unemployed women and girls, as well as those on reduced or half-time wages," the association in 1914 opened Spadina Lodge at 184 Spadina Avenue. Room and board was "arranged to meet the circumstances of the applicant." Unemployed women and girls were able to have two weeks' free board and lodging, including free meals in the lodge's lunchroom, which helped pay for the lodge, as the lunch room was open to "all business girls."[70] The lodge's only other sources of support were monetary gifts—such as they occasionally received directly from the association— and donations of provisions.[71] The lodge remained open until 1925.

Businessman H. H. Fudger, president of the Robert Simpson Company, endowed a house for working women, the Sherbourne House Club, which opened in early 1917. The residence was described as a club for women who live out of the city (presumably meaning young women migrated into the city for work) and especially for the women employees of the Simpson Company. The endowment envisioned that ultimately it would accommodate three hundred residents. The club opened to great fanfare, with the *Toronto Star* extolling the furnishings of the bedrooms, the beautiful dining room, and the "splendid club rooms." The charge was $4.50 per week—a sum far greater than that of the Curzon or Cecil homes in London. The newspaper assured its readers that "no fond mother could wish for her dearest daughter, a fairer home than this."[72] At the same time, the newspaper worried about the precedent set by this club. It wondered whether providing such amenities to young women carried a threat to the City of Homes. The club's superintendent, Mary L. Bollert, was asked, "Will there not be a likelihood of their [the women] becoming so attached to Sherbourne House that other homes will appear small and mean, and of large numbers of girls resolving not to exchange quarters so elegant for the humbler abodes of wedded life?" Bollert assured the paper that this would not happen, but clearly the prospect of single women avoiding the married life troubled men. And providing a few hundred businesswomen with shelter did not come close to meeting the housing needs of Toronto's single women.[73]

CHICAGO

As migrants flooded into Chicago to take advantage of its economic opportunity, the number of single and homeless men and women multiplied. This situation challenged men's prevailing ideals of masculinity, family, and property. Chicago's businessmen, for example, believed that men should work to support themselves, and their first efforts—modeled on the English Rowton Houses—were directed toward those unfortunate men who were doing so but could not find, or afford, decent accommodations. Two Chicago businessmen opened the Friendship Hotel on Clinton Street in 1891 with 540 rooms designated for "the best classes of laboring men and single men with trades."[74] The nightly rents ranged from 15 to 25 cents, and weekly from $1.00 to $1.50. There was a reading room, a lunchroom, a bathroom, and a hospital ward. The hotel's proprietors described it as a model lodging house, a business venture, and practical philanthropy that would solve social and labor problems and afford "every workingman the means of living respectably if he so desired,"[75] allowing him to "retain his self-respect and manhood and continue to be an industrious and useful member of society."[76] Although there were proposals to build more such lodgings, few Chicago men were interested in doing so.

While male city leaders saw homelessness as a threat to moral standards and masculinity, women viewed the situation as a social crisis. By the time

the Friendship Hotel opened, Chicago women had been agitating for housing for single women for several years. Ethnic and religious groups would
organize boardinghouses for women of their ethnicity and faith, but other
women saw housing for single women as a citywide issue.[77]

In spring 1887, a group of socially active Chicago women invited sev-
enty-seven of the city's clergy to attend a large organizing meeting to push
for housing for self-supporting women. Only three clergymen attended, but
led by Caroline Brown, the former president of the Chicago Woman's Club
(CWC), women moved ahead on their own. They secured a house at 221
Illinois Street for a rental of $80 per month to furnish "comfortable and de-
cent places for women having small means and earning low wages." According to Lucy Flower, vice president of the home's board of managers, the
lodgers "could come and go as they please."[78] The facility opened on May 1,
charging 15 cents per night or 90 cents per week for a bed or 25 cents per
night for a single room. Department stores in the city paid around $3.00 per
week, making the home affordable to shopgirls. Women's organizations
raised money and furnished the home to make it self-sustaining with no
intention of making a profit. By 1890, they purchased a new building at 275
Indiana Street to accommodate an average of sixty "young women who
[otherwise] are unable to live comfortably on their wages," and where they
could live in a cooperative, "self-supporting, and self-respecting" fashion.[79]
By 1892, the number of lodgers at the home had increased to seventy, but by
1894 the charge for room and board had increased to $2.50 a week, making
it difficult for all but the best-paid working women to stay there.[80]

Given this difficulty, and in the wake of the 1893 economic depression,
the CWC turned greater attention to unemployed women and founded a
Women's Model Lodging House and Workshop at 186 Polk Street to be
a "permanent protection to the unemployed woman." They proclaimed it a
benevolent association "without capital stock."[81] One of the city's wealthiest
women, Bertha Palmer, gave $1,000 to help start the model lodging house.[82]
The lodging house provided temporary shelter for unemployed women, deserted wives including those with children, and destitute women with no
other place to stay. The managers of the lodging house noted, with sad
understanding, that they were living in an economic system that valued
youth and masculinity. Many of the women applying for shelter were over
fifty, "thrown out of work" with little hope of gaining another position, the
situation that Marianne Dale had recognized for London women. In just
one month in 1898, 511 women resided at the lodging house. Women were
paid for working in the sewing room, which by 1913 would be self-supporting. Between 1895 and 1916, the CWC contributed almost $1,200 to sup-
port the lodging house. Almost twenty women's clubs worked to maintain
the lodging house, including Catholic, Jewish, and neighborhood women's
clubs.[83]

The first municipal effort to aid homeless men, generally designated as tramps, began in 1900. Early that year Franklin MacVeagh, president of the Bureau of Charities, suggested that the city solve the tramp problem by establishing a lodging house with municipal powers to house "the man without a home who is willing to work for what help he gets." All men so housed who refused to work for their lodging were to be "arrested as vagrants and sent out of the city." MacVeagh wanted a municipal lodging house to replace those provided by the Salvation Army, which he believed lacked the power "to make a man do any work."[84] MacVeagh's proposal set the tone for subsequent ideas about lodging houses for homeless men. The city would provide some type of emergency lodging, especially in winter, but with minimal comfort and with all "able-bodied lodgers offering no pay . . . required to work for their keep, and this labor [being] a means of testing their actual situation." In early winter 1901, the *Tribune* accused able-bodied unemployed men of keeping warm inside two private so-called lodging houses when they should have been put to work shoveling show.[85]

The first nonprofit men's lodging house, operated under the auspices of the private City Homes Association, opened on December 21, 1901, at 12 S. Jefferson Street. It was controlled by the police department; lodgers were restricted to staying only four days per month and required to work. The *Chicago Tribune* hoped that having to pay for lodging or work for it would "diminish its popularity."[86] When a new municipal lodging house for men opened the next year in a three-story building at 12 (now 160) North Union Street on the city's near west side, the *Tribune* emphasized the duty of the men to work. The lodging house was "intended to be a place for transients," not for residents; it was a "sociological laboratory" in which

> if instead of receiving alms [the men] are sent to the lodging-house they are there given an opportunity to support themselves by their own exertions. . . . If they refuse to work they become proper subjects for police supervision. It is not tolerable that in a city like Chicago any man should be a "floater." . . . [The lodging-house] can be used as a sieve through which the deserving will pass into honest labor.[87]

By 1914, Chicago was operating three municipal lodging houses for men that could accommodate close to four thousand men, always on the basis that their stay was temporary. The number of lodgers always swelled during the brutal winter months, when men crowded into a reception hall for admission. Despite early photos of nice clean beds, the number of homeless men so overwhelmed facilities that most of them slept on the floor, with a blanket if they were lucky, or just on the bare floor if unlucky. Police and private guards were posted inside to keep the men orderly. The economic downturn of 1907 created such a desperate need for shelter that the *Chicago*

Tribune, no friend of the homeless, opened its own emergency lodging house during the recession of the winter of 1907–1908 at 59–61 Canal Street. The lodgers were required to perform work for the city. When the house closed in March 1908, the newspaper reported that 36,792 lodgings had been furnished and the men had put in 5,186 days of work for the city.[88]

While the city was prepared, at least reluctantly, to deal with male homelessness as a problem of social order, it was not prepared to deal with female homelessness. The Women's Lodging House was overwhelmed by the demand. In the winter of 1902, the house reported turning away almost a dozen women a night for lack of space when it was still "practically the only place in Chicago where a lonely penniless woman may go at any hour of the day or night and be sure of finding protection and shelter—always supposing too many other lonely, penniless women have not applied for these benefits before her."[89] By 1906, the house reported that it had sheltered over 19,000 women, of whom over 3,600 were "absolutely destitute."[90] Responding to the need for women's lodgings, women raised money for a larger building to continue to support the older Home for Self-Supporting Women, to be renamed the Indiana House. The new building accommodated 103 lodgers rather than the 60 in the older building.[91] Neither this home nor the Women's Lodging House could provide sufficient lodging, so women again turned to the city, demanding that it establish municipal lodging houses for women as it had begun doing for men. They informed the city council that in 1909, 1,000 "respectable women" had been forced to shelter in police stations while the city had spent $7,500 to shelter men in the same period.[92]

When the city's health commissioner responded that "so many more men were in need of accommodations that they should be cared for first,"[93] *Tribune* reporter Harriet Ferrill pointed out the gender discrimination in a statement that closely resembled the statement that London's NAWLH would make a few years later:

> The Henry George sign, "I am for men," should be placed above the door of the municipal lodging house of Chicago. . . . The city says to the woman, "Pass on to the hard bunk behind the iron bars in the police station"; but to the man, "Come in and be my guest for three days and longer if you are earnestly seeking work." . . . For women, who for various reasons suffer more from poverty than men . . . the city does little or nothing.[94]

After women appeared before the city council asking the city to fund the women's municipal lodging house, which by then had moved to South Calumet Avenue, the city agreed in early 1910 to budget $1,000, from which it would pay 25 cents to the lodging house for every woman sent there by the police. But such largess was deemed "entirely inadequate in every way for the purpose," and would require that a woman go first to a police station to ask for help.[95]

The housing situation was worse for African American women, as the few lodging houses generally would not accept them. In 1908, the Phyllis Wheatley Club opened the Phyllis Wheatley Home for young working women and girls. Between then and 1915, the Phyllis Wheatley Home sheltered more than three hundred young women, at 25 cents per night or $1.25 per week, while it also operated as an employment agency. When it received $5,000 from the Elite Social Charity Club, the home was able to purchase a larger place, but even so, its capacity was always limited. Other women opened homes for African American women. The Melissa Ann Elam Home opened in 1923.[96] YWCA branches were racially segregated by national Y policy, so the existing branches in Chicago were for white women only. In 1915, a group of African American women founded a branch for black single women on South Indiana Avenue. African American men had already raised funds to build a YMCA. White philanthropist Julius Rosenwald pledged $25,000, and business leader Cyrus McCormick also contributed to the fund. The institution opened in 1912. But it was left to African American club women to finance building a YWCA a few years later.

The 1910s saw a continuation of the same gendered pattern. Since proper masculinity demanded that men work and pay their own way, and support women and children, Chicago's leaders never accepted municipal lodging houses as a permanent arrangement. Some men in Chicago were even convinced that other cities sent their homeless and jobless to Chicago and that many men using the municipal lodging houses actually had money.[97] During a winter storm of early 1918, the *Chicago Tribune* informed its readers that "dwellers at the municipal and other lodging houses learned trench warfare yesterday when shovels were placed in their hands as implements of honor and a means of earning a honest night's rest together with hot coffee and warm bread." The municipal lodging house reported "every able bodied man working."[98] Despite such ideas, in 1915 voters approved a $100,000 bond issue for municipal lodging, and a site for the men's house was purchased. But it was never built: local businessmen's organizations mounted a strong protest against it, evidently fearing that the presence of so many homeless men would scare off potential customers.[99]

Chicago never floated any bonds for a women's lodging house and never assisted in sheltering working women, and Chicago women were never able to convince the city to provide such lodgings. Even after women received the municipal franchise in 1913, men still had the power and the votes to stymie women's efforts. One member of the Stevenson Lodging House board complained, "We have asked for appropriations before, but the city council has always said that inasmuch as only men are municipal voters they alone are entitled to protection from the city." She had hoped that with the franchise, women could now demand equal protection.[100] The Women's Model Lodging House, renamed in 1911 for one of its founders, Sarah Hackett Stevenson, remained one of the few shelters for unemployed or marginally employed women in the city. Unlike the men's lodging houses, the women running the Stevenson House considered their building a temporary residence, not merely an expedient shelter. There was a six-week limit to a stay, which gave women time to find a job and other housing, but such a time limit was believed necessary in order to make room for other women in need. Rather than thinking about their lodgers as profligate tramps or floaters, the women supporting the Stevenson House believed that there were thousands of women who needed temporary shelter but could neither find nor afford decent housing. The house rule was that if a woman could not afford her night's stay, she was able to put in an hour's work around the house so that she was contributing to the upkeep of her place and thereby assisting other women.[101] By 1917, the Stevenson House had relocated into a larger building at 2412 Prairie Avenue that accommodated sixty women and twenty-five children. It then purchased three adjacent buildings to again expand the number of women and children it could house. It was the only shelter in the city that kept women and their children together. If a woman found work while living there, her children were cared for in the house's day nursery.[102]

Single working women in Chicago did have a few additional limited housing resources at their disposal, equivalent to the businesswomen's housing in Toronto. The Eleanor Clubs were first opened in 1898 by Ina Robertson, the managing trustee of a wealthy estate left to her guidance by a member of the United Presbyterian Church. By 1920, there were six Eleanor Clubs accommodating six hundred women. Although that number of accommodations may seem like a lot, by 1920 Chicago's population exceeded two million. And, as was the case with the Toronto Clubs, the charges were too high for marginally employed women. The Eleanor Clubs shared another cultural characteristic with the Sherbourne House Club in Toronto. Their architecture was intended to represent a safe haven for businesswomen where, as Ina Robertson expressed it, women could find "companionship [and] . . . homelike surroundings" that would not violate cultural expectations about women's proper behavior and needs.[103] Hull House organized the Jane Club, a self-supporting, self-governing, cooperative boardinghouse for working-class women that, as one scholar noted, was an aspect of the settlement's offer of "an alternative lifestyle for all working women."[104] The charge for room and board was $3.00 per week in 1893, by which time it could accommodate around thirty women.

One wealthy Chicago man, banker Charles Dawes, was moved to open a Rowton-type hotel for men in memory of his son. The Rufus F. Dawes Hotel on South Peoria Street opened in January 1914, where a bed for the night cost five or ten cents. The *Chicago Tribune* reported that it was immediately besieged by homeless men seeking shelter from the winter cold, and although the hotel could accommodate three hundred men, many had to be turned away once those rooms were taken. By the end of the year the hotel was able to accommodate five hundred lodgers—carefully called *guests* by the management to make it clear that the Dawes Hotel was not a lodging house.[105]

Once the Rufus F. Dawes Hotel was established, Charles Dawes built the 275-room Mary Dawes Hotel for self-respecting working women. Named in honor of his mother, it opened in early 1917 on South Throop Street. The *Chicago Tribune* called it "an interesting experiment": "the first hotel of its kind to be built for women." Mary Dawes described it as a place "with a large attractive living room with a piano where the girls may entertain their gentlemen friends. Say what you will young people just will have company even if they are forced to seek it on the streets, and it's much better to have them entertain their men friends in a pleasant, well-lighted place with others about and under the care of a responsible person."[106] The Mary Dawes Hotel, like the Eleanor Clubs, did not accommodate women with children. Rather the Dawes hotel resembled Toronto's Sherbourne House, where young, single women could be supervised.

London's Rowton Houses, Dublin's Iveagh Trust hostel, and Chicago's Friendship House and Rufus F. Dawes Hotel were private establishments where respectable men could reside. Charles Dawes claimed that guests at the Rufus Dawes Hotel "are not to be considered as a class or a species or anything but American citizens."[107] On the other hand, when men's municipal lodging houses were established, they were to be temporary shelters where single men could be kept off the streets and under surveillance, combining surveillance with compulsory work. In 1918, the city council attempted to centralize under its control supervision of any such facilities. It created a new Bureau of Employment, Woodyards, Lodging Houses and Gardens, whose superintendent would direct the operation of all facilities for homeless men, and whose charge would be to establish working conditions, wages, and hours of labor. Mayor William ("Big Bill") Thompson rejected the bureau on a technicality, believing that such an ordinance violated state statute.[108] But the idea of keeping watch over homeless, unemployed men continued to interest Chicago men. In late 1921, Alderman Robert Mulcahy raised the question of having the city furnish a municipal lodging house for men during the economic squeeze following the end of World War I, urging the city to allocate money toward this project for "examining, classifying, and disposing of the men who would frequent it." If such men were "gathered in one or more central places each night, where they would be under the eye of the police it is probable that their opportunity for crime, if not their inclination would be lessened."[109] The city then began plans to reopen the previous site on North Union Street. But within a month, the council was debating whether to use an allocated $18,000 to send building trades workers back to the cities they came from, a measure supported by the city's unions.[110] The men of the City Club had supported the possibility of reopening the municipal lodging house, but they also advocated providing temporary shelters such as in the city's armories, where homeless men could spend the night under surveillance.[111] Every proposal for lodging homeless men was bound up with concern for their status as "unworthy" men who both failed to conform to the expected standards of masculinity and were a potential threat to the city's resources and well-being.

Chicago's businessmen and politicians had an additional political reason for not providing municipal lodging houses for men. In the United States there were no property requirements for voting. In Chicago, a man merely had to have an address to vote, and a lodging house was a residence with an address. Thus, it was believed crucial to limit the numbers and political influence of transient men. A man without property did not have a stake in the city and could not be trusted with its future; a man without work, family, or property was a triple threat to the city.

As disorderly, unembounded bodies, single women were perceived as a different type of threat. Employed or unemployed, they were a threat to patriarchal order, but they were not judged as worthy or unworthy or likely to commit crimes. They were just not going to be taken care of with municipal lodgings. In May 1922, the Women's Protective Association reminded the city council that a $100,000 bond issue passed in 1915 had intended to use $50,000 for a woman's municipal lodging house. The association claimed that in the current circumstances, no more than 25 percent of women needing shelter could be accommodated in existing facilities, but their plea went unanswered by the city council.[112]

As much as men might have wished to ignore the housing needs of women, these needs were only one of the threats that women posed to the patriarchal city. Women in all four cities were occupying public space, demanding new types of housing, and demanding rights of urban citizenship, not just to vote but to make other decisions about the directions and obligations of the city toward all its people. Women could no longer be counted on to stay in their private sphere or to "domesticate" the marginal men whom the cities were trying to control. Moreover, the late-nineteenth-century city presented new challenges as the relationship between the urban environment and society was changing. The city was now far more open, public, diverse, and flamboyant than previously. Restaurants, cafés, theaters, department stores, popular exhibitions, other sites of shopping, entertainment, and production drew crowds of men and women into the city streets day and night. Prostitutes, pickpockets, street urchins, flower sellers, and common laborers going to and from work added to the mix, moving along the same streets as their "betters." The city was becoming a spectacle both celebrated for its new possibilities of public freedom and feared for its disorder, especially that of women. A disorderly and chaotic city was as much a deterrent to continued economic prosperity as was a dirty and unhealthy city. So, reforming housing would no longer be sufficient for reordering the city in such a rapidly changing world. New modes of thinking about the built environment were needed to make sense of the modern city.

4

The Urban Modern

> When a girl leaves her home at eighteen, she does one of two things.
> Either she falls into saving hands and becomes better, or she rapidly
> assumes the cosmopolitan standard of virtue and becomes worse.
> —Theodore Dreiser, *Sister Carrie* (1900)

We cannot speak of the modern city without considering what this meant to urban residents in the late nineteenth century. Generically, *modern* can be applied by any group of people seeking to distinguish its society and environment from a past that it conceptualizes as traditional or perhaps backward. In the context of the four cities of this book, even when urban residents did not use the word *modern*, both men and women were grappling with the desire to separate the city from its past. Industrialization, urbanization, and technological innovation had disrupted the social order of the city, altered its daily experiences, increased the urban poor, and degraded the city's livability. But there was a distinct gendered approach to creating the modern city.

For many urban men, chaos, disorder, lack of control, and failure to plan characterized their cities. A modern city meant overcoming these conditions through a well-managed, scientifically rational regime. To advance their ideas, men formulated new terminology to describe the problems. Areas of deteriorating housing were no longer pockets of poverty, they were slums. Places were labeled overcrowded according to new statistical analyses of the correct ratio of people to place. The movement of people, goods, and transit on the city streets was termed congestion. People and places also had to be classified and sorted. There were no longer simply poor people, there was poverty with gradations: the worthy poor and the unworthy poor; those who had been reduced by economic circumstances and those who were responsible for their own failings. There was a respectable working class that needed to be separated from the lower classes of wanton immorality and criminality. Richard Dennis calls this a "language of modernity," a new "conceptual modernisation—new representations of space and society, focused on collectives of structures, classes and areas, rather than the particularities of individuals."[1]

This new language of modernity also spoke of cities in dichotomies. The past was uncontrolled chaos and disorder; it had to be completely rebuilt to eliminate or to control its disorderly elements. The modern city could be either a masculine space or a feminine space; it could not be both. Romantic notions of place had to be countered by matter-of-fact scientific rationalism applied to rearranging the city. The femininized domestic private places of home, family, and women had to be separated from the public spaces of masculine work, enterprise, profit. The old city had to be destroyed in order to build the new city.

In their dichotomous view of the city, men identified themselves with the city.[2] They were the modern, the orderly, the rational, the new. Women were the disorderly "other," a threat to the male ideal of the modern city. The prostitute was the most evident threat to control and order, flaunting her sexuality and tempting men. For the German social critic Hans Ostwald, behind urban corruption "lurked the female prostitute, a recurring figure in [these] texts, who threatened physical and spiritual contagion with her ability to transgress 'all of the boundaries that were set up to contain her.'"[3] But, as David Harvey contends, the sexuality of all women threatened urban modernity and the male desire for control. In Paris, there was a "pervasive fear [of] the unsubmissive, independent woman."[4] The new space of the department stores presented such a threat. On the one hand, they were celebrated for their potential to increase the city's wealth. On the other hand, they spawned fears of women's licentiousness and vice as even respectable middle-class female customers were seen as tempted by, and unable to resist, shoplifting. The ostentatious display of goods in the department store was seen as "arousing women's sensual and impulsive nature" and fostering a new type of urban crime.[5] As retailers extended their husbands' credit to women, they collapsed the private and public separation and placed husbands in an inferior economic situation to their wives. "The female shopper," according to Erika Rappaport, "inherently disrupted the supposedly separate spheres and the traditional balance of power between spouses and thus was often accused of a moral crime akin to adultery."[6] If such uncontrolled sexuality were allowed to exist, if sentiment and feeling were to control the city rather than rationality and control, public and private chaos would result.

Moreover, as historian Elizabeth Wilson points out, in this modern city men were separating themselves from traditional restrictions of social orthodoxy and seeking to restructure their own lives. Women were perceived as a threat to this new male freedom. "Women represented feeling, sexuality, and even chaos, man was rationality and control. . . . There is fear of the city as the realm of uncontrolled and chaotic sexual license and the rigid control of women in the cities" was necessary to "avert this danger." Woman was the sphinx in the city—"female sexuality, womanhood out of control, lost nature, loss of identity"—threatening to devour men.[7] By identifying women as the enemy of modernity, men not only were able to rebuff women's attempts to bring a different perspective to reconstructing the built environment but rejected women's ideas as a direct threat to male control.

Most of the literature analyzing the modern Western city has simply accepted the male perspective without questioning its gendered underpinning. If the male perspective was rational, then alternatives proposed by women could be dismissed as not understanding the realities of the modern city. When the League of American Municipalities began publishing its magazine, the *Modern City*, it spoke only to and about men as creating the modern city. It also extolled new definitions of modern masculinity. Its inaugural edition described its annual conferences as the place where men could engage in "heart-to-heart talk . . . in the spirit of brotherhood, where questions can be discussed in man-to-man fashion open and above board." The magazine claimed that it would "present the view of the idealist, the dreamer, the man who plans and thinks and ferrets out, the man who catches the vision of those things, puts them in position to be of service to mankind." It would present "sketches of the men who are doing things, contributing to progress and development."[8] As Richard Dennis contends, it is difficult to separate the idea of what constituted the modern from the concept of progress.[9] The language used by the *Modern City* clearly equated the idea of the modern with both progress and masculinity.

Urban scholarship has accepted what men said about women and their motives, rather than investigating what women actually said and did. Filtering everything about women through a male perspective fails to understand the inherent contradictions of the male view of women. On the one hand, men feared women for their sexuality, disorder, and intrusion into public spaces. At the same time, men generally celebrated women as the civilizing gender. Here was another dichotomy. The problem for men was that the modern woman had forgotten her civilizing role by intruding into public. Women needed to be reordered and placed back into the home so that their disruptive nature—sexuality—could be controlled. Reformers such as Patrick Geddes and Ebenezer Howard held both perspectives. Both men envisioned women as perfecting the city with their feminine qualities, but only if embounded in cities reordered along masculine ideals. Seeing women as opposites of disorder and civilization are two sides of a patriarchal vision controlling the modern city. Rather than contradictory, these ideas are mutually reinforcing.[10] Theodore Dreiser's Carrie, who used her sexuality to pursue her cosmopolitan desires, ends up "sitting alone . . . an illustration of the devious ways by which one who feels, rather than reasons, may be led in the pursuit of beauty."[11] She had learned her lesson of stepping outside the boundaries that were designated for women, at least in the eyes of a male writer. But, as Elizabeth Wilson notes, modernist women writers such as Virginia Wolfe "responded with joy and affirmation" to the city,[12] and one Berlin woman published *What a Woman Must Know about Berlin* as a guidebook for women to use and negotiate the city unafraid to challenge male-defined boundaries and become "an energetic and outgoing woman who embraced the metropolis as her own."[13]

GENDER AND THE SETTLEMENT HOUSE

The settlement house movement is an iconic symbol of the late-nineteenth- and early-twentieth-century city, but it was highly gendered in its perspective on the modern city and the roles of men and women in confronting its problems. Historian Seth Koven contends that the purpose of English settlements was to establish a new "brotherhood of men," to create "'The New Man' in the Slums" in the face of women's demands to control their own lives and have equal citizenship.

> If brotherhood seemed to promise the way to escape the horrors of urban class warfare, it was also linked to the sex wars and gender anxieties of the *fin-de-siècle*. The language of fraternity was unabashedly male and framed the major problems and solutions confronting modern Britain—poverty, class conflict, and debates about citizenship—in wholly masculine terms.[14]

A glance through Toynbee Hall's *Annual Reports* confirms this reality. Only men were residents or associates there, and only a handful of women were among the hundreds of associated members and subscribers.[15] A 1914 description of Toynbee Hall's Boys' Clubs acknowledged, "We cannot here begin to speak of Girls' Clubs; they have never existed in connection with Toynbee Hall. A kind of Club formed by Mrs. Barnett for Factory Girls is the only exception." There they could cook their lunch and have "a little dance."[16]

Founded in 1884, Toynbee Hall has been described, apparently without irony, as the "Mother of Settlements." Its purpose was to reorient public and private life by educating its residents to become a generation of public decision makers. As one contemporary source explained it, "the importance of the Settlement lies in the educational influences it exercises on Residents and which in many cases has given the direction to their whole life."[17] Since numerous residents of Toynbee Hall pursued successful public careers in positions from which they could influence and direct the private and public reconstruction of the city, this claim was justified.[18] In an edition of papers given by settlement residents, Canon Samuel Barnett declared that his establishment would mitigate class suspicion and foster better local government.

> A settlement, by bringing into the neighborhood people whose training makes them sensible to abuses and whose humanity makes them conscious of other needs does what [political] machinery as machin-

ery cannot do. It fits supply and demand; it adapts itself to changing circumstances; it yields and goes forward; it follows or guides according to the moment's need; it turns an organisation which might be a mere machine into a living human force. Above all, it brings men into touch with men, and, by making them fuller characters enriches their work.[19]

The settlement houses founded by women in London differed from Toynbee Hall in organization, purpose, and their focus on people. The Women's University Settlement in Southwark, organized in 1887 with the assistance of Octavia Hill, declared that its aim was to "promote the welfare of the poorer people of the districts of London, and especially of the women and children by devising and promoting schemes which tend to elevate them physically, intellectually, or morally and by giving them additional opportunities for education and recreation."[20] The settlement sponsored boys' and girls' clubs and labor exchanges for both boys and girls. Margaret Sewell and Eleanor Powell, representing the Women's University Settlement, characterized women's settlements throughout England as aimed to "give local help, which was so scanty before, to existing organisations, whether the parish or the special society."[21] The settlement's activities supported medical missions and hospitals, managed dispensaries and sick benefit funds, and organized workrooms for unemployed, especially elderly, women. "To put it simply," the women wrote,

> the Settlement is an effort to reproduce, in large towns and cities, where the population tends to sort itself according to its means, the more natural conditions in which all classes live more or less together, and can, if they choose, and without any trouble, know a great deal about one another. . . . To know our neighbours, to be touched by local grievances, interested, not by sympathy, but by right, in local schemes, should be the aim of any Settlement worthy of its name.[22]

American settlement worker Sara Libby Carson established the first settlement in Toronto, Evangelia House, in 1902. The house was originally a center for female factory workers, informally called the Young Women's Settlement, but it quickly expanded to include children's activities and toward meeting the needs of the neighborhood's women and children (Figure 4.1). University women and graduates joined its staff. Female student organizations formed settlement chapters to help support the settlement's work. The TLCW and YWCA supported its work.[23]

Protestantism was an important motivator for establishing some Toronto settlement houses, but Central Neighbourhood House, headed by

Figure 4.1 Evangelia
Settlement Baby
Clinic, Toronto,
1914. (Courtesy of
the Toronto City
Archives, Fonds 200,
Item 335.)

Elizabeth Neufeld, who was Jewish, refused to have any religious affilia-tion.[24] The women of Central Neighbourhood House, like those of the Evan-gelia settlement, were occupied with fostering the lives of the women and children of their neighborhood located in the heart of the ward. They made small, but ultimately futile, attempts to provide housing for women and chil-dren. Neufeld returned to Toronto after a tour of housing movements in the United States to suggest that the settlement build "two-storey houses on the plan adopted by Philadelphia,"[25] by which I assume she was referring to the Octavia Hill Association in that city. The settlement also proposed to establish a women's residence, and the TLCW solicited donations toward such a building. At the same time, the TLCW and Evangelia House explored the possibility of setting up a cooperative home for thirty families that would take care of daily needs by including a laundry and central nursery. The TLCW had established a provisional committee to investigate raising the money for such a venture.[26] Neither of these ventures, however, was ever realized.

Toronto men organized University Settlement in 1910 along the lines of Toynbee Hall, including not allowing women as members, although women were subsequently allowed to join. The impetus for this settlement came from, among others, S. A. Cudmore, a lecturer in political economy at the university. Cudmore called on "the Empire's 'best men'" to engage in this work to "provide university men with first-hand experience of urban slum conditions." Sara Z. Burke observes that after organization of the University Settlement, social services in Toronto had a distinctly gendered approach. Men were to draw on their professional expertise, applying their profes-sional, scientifically based training in economics, political science, and soci-ology to solving social problems. Women's work became downplayed as soft female "social" work.[27]

This division in gendered labor was also happening elsewhere as academic men sought to professionalize their disciplines as scientific. In Chicago, after the largely female-directed social service Chicago School of Civics and Philanthropy affiliated with the University of Chicago, the women were relegated to a gendered place within the university. The idea of social service became the purview of the School of Social Science Administration, where the women were to train social workers. The separate department of sociology, from which women were excluded, focused on scientific investigation of social problems.[28]

Jane Addams might have taken Toynbee Hall as her inspiration for founding Chicago's Hull House in 1889, but her objectives were quite different. In her 1892 lecture "The Objective Value of a Social Settlement," she enumerated the civic activities of the settlement. It had persuaded the board of education to purchase land for a neighborhood school; had sent 1,037 complaints about health conditions in her ward to the female Municipal Order League, which then submitted them to the Department of Health; worked vigorously to assist women by providing space for female trade unionists to meet, arbitrating a strike at a knitting factory; and secured financial support for widows and deserted women. For Addams, these activities were just the beginning of the settlement's civic work.[29]

In "The Subjective Necessity for Social Settlements," Addams asserted that Hull House "endeavors to make social intercourse express the growing sense of the economic unity of society. It is an effort to add the social function to democracy."[30] A decade later she warned that "'reform movements,' started by business men and the better element are almost wholly occupied in the correction of political machinery and securing better methods of administration rather than the ultimate purpose of securing the welfare of the people." Reformers, she went on, "give themselves largely to criticisms of the present state of affairs, to writing and talking of what the future must be and of certain results to be obtained."[31] Her objections to these preoccupations can be compared with the celebratory statement of Charles Mostyn (C. M.) Lloyd, a Toynbee Hall resident, self-identified Fabian socialist, and future head of the social science department at the London School of Economics. Mostyn declared that "Toynbee Hall is a vantage ground for the study of the conditions of poverty. . . . [I]nside Toynbee Hall he will be able to modify and correct and amplify his ideas by discussion with other men who are engaged in various sorts of work in East London."[32] Addams wanted more social activism: more work in the neighborhood rather than studies about the neighborhood.

The women's club at the University of Chicago settlement headed by Mary McDowell negotiated with the city to build a free public bath for the neighborhood and secured manual training and kindergartens for several public schools. To keep abreast of social and political problems, the club held a weekly speakers program. In 1900–1901, the women heard talks about the democratic, republican, and socialist labor platforms; the growth of the factory system; and the work of the women's Chicago Political Equality League. In January 1901, a leading member of Chicago's African American community, Fannie Barrier Williams, gave a talk titled "What the Colored Women Are Doing for Humanity." The outward focus of the settlement and its lack of need to control was apparent from its organization of a day nursery and a dispensary, which, once established, moved out of the settlement house and operated independently, cooperating with the settlement but not directed by it.[33]

Graham Taylor's Chicago Commons settlement, on the other hand, was internally focused. Its women's club was dedicated to women sharing stories about themselves and their cultural backgrounds rather than discussing social and political conditions. The Chicago Commons settlement brought people inside to educate them, not to have settlement residents go out into the neighborhood. Its articles of incorporation stated, "The object for which it is formed is to provide a center of a higher civic and social life, to initiate and maintain religious, educational and philanthropic enterprises, and to investigate and improve conditions in the industrial districts of Chicago."[34]

For McDowell and Addams, investigation did not preclude social activism; being a social center likewise did not obviate the need for direct action in the neighborhood. The investigation undertaken by the residents of Hull House of living conditions in their neighborhood combined all these objectives to produce the previously mentioned *Hull-House Maps and Papers*. Rather than stigmatize the neighborhood as Charles Booth's work had done for London neighborhoods, Addams wrote, "We offer these maps and papers to the public, not as exhaustive treatises, but as recorded observations which may possibly be of value. . . . [They] have been chiefly directed, not towards sociological investigation, but to constructive work."[35] Color-coded maps that designated areas as slums would not lead to "learning about the needs and circumstances of actual people" in their environments.[36]

PATRIARCHAL CAPITALISM AND THE MODERN CITY

In the mid-twentieth century, economist Joseph Schumpeter analyzed capitalist economic development as predicated on the continuous need for "creative destruction—the constant destroying and inventing of new means of production." Creative destruction, according to Schumpeter, "is the essential fact of capitalism."[37] Urban historian Max Page and geographer Richard Dennis adapted the concept to explain that the urge to tear down the old and replace it was an essential feature of the modern city. For Page, "the process of creative destruction [was] at the heart of the story of urban development."[38] Dennis contends that by seeing the city as a morphology—a structure or a form—men were able to rationalize creative destruction.[39] For

London, thus, deteriorating housing now constituted slum areas, and "slums were no longer individual properties in need of improvement or demolition [but] an *area* for clearance, large enough to allow redevelopment, but small enough to suggest that the housing problem was simply a collection of problem *areas*, not a fault of the structure of housing provision as a whole, let alone an inevitable consequence of the economic system."[40]

Page describes the urge for creative destruction as the tension between "stability and change; between the notion of 'place' versus undifferentiated, developable 'space.'"[41] Space signified that the city was provisional; place signified permanence. According to Ruth Livesey, Octavia Hill "resisted the production of the putatively abstract, quantifiable, disciplinary, urban spaces." Men could thus dismiss her as romantic and unrealistic, out of step with male modernism.[42] Moreover, Hill's system of female housing managers brought more women into the streets of some of London's worst neighborhoods, where they functioned outside male control. Their experiences on those streets gave them a social understanding of the city and the needs of its residents in their place. Even if to contemporary standards their attitudes may seem patronizing, Hill and her coworkers knew the city differently from the men who endowed money or who theorized about proper housing without experiencing the streets and their residents.

As Page also notes, "The literature on cities has either listed toward a nostalgia for a better, lost time or veered sharply toward an embrace of 'improvement' or 'modernization.'"[43] But whichever perspective taken by scholars, their analysis either celebrates or decries capitalism as an economic system. The patriarchal foundations of capitalism go largely unremarked in the literature of urban history because scholars overwhelmingly consult sources left by men, look at laws written by men, read the records of men's voluntary, civic, business and labor organizations, city council minutes and reports.[44] Even when women were involved in urban legal and political issues, mainly the records of women's clubs document their activities, and most urban scholarship neglects these sources. The literature on the urban built environment thus implicitly denies that gendered ideas played any role in reconstructing the built environment.[45]

Accepting that men's ideas of the modern city were rational accepts patriarchy. Economic historian Martin Daunton's analysis that a market-driven, property culture shaped the modern urban form may be correct, yet it does not consider how this stemmed from particular ideas about controlling the city for the benefit of men.[46] When men in these four cities decided there was indeed an urban housing crisis, they wanted market forces and private enterprise to determine new housing. London architect Thomas Blashill warned against allowing the LCC to build housing because the private speculator could make "economies which do not decrease the stability of his buildings . . . [and] the speculator would get the whole of his work done either as piecework or by the employment of inferior hands or learners at lower prices."[47] The Peabody trustees rejected fireproof floors in their building because they would increase expenses. Blashill also calculated that if private enterprise erected buildings that "in the long run . . . might suffer" because of cheaper standards, ultimately it did not matter because they could be kept "to the very low standard which such tenants we are speaking of demand."[48]

Because the built environment was ultimately shaped by such ideas, much urban scholarship views cities as the triumph of engineers and architects who applied new learning and technology to clean up, reorder, and beautify industrial cities. These men have been congratulated for clearing out slums and cleansing the urban landscape. They have been faulted for creating urban sprawl, or for negatively affecting the poor or minority groups.[49] Whether the analysis in such work is heroic, laudatory, cautionary, or even accusatory, the gendered origins of their ideas and work remain unquestioned. The result is a distorted view that these ideas were the norm and that the main arguments were among different groups of men about such things as how involved government should be or which men should have the strongest voice in determining the built environment. Beyond this distortion, relying on the male narrative makes it possible to denigrate the work of middle-class or elite women who pursued housing policies other than those of clearing areas, moving people out, and rebuilding through private enterprise. Hill's efforts have been described as "bordered on the romantic," or as opposed to the practical reality of the 5 percent philanthropists who "grasped the essence of the housing question to be one of supply and demand."[50] Hill has even been dismissed as anti-urban, as if the city's lack of "natural beauty, cleanliness, fresh air, and recreational spaces" signified hatred of the city, rather than a desire to change the urban environment to make it more livable for everyone.[51]

Such negative analyses also ignore how urban men routinely dismissed women as uninformed about problems or patronized them. The mayor of Toronto in 1908 invited women to attend city council meetings because "their presence at all times lends a charm and casts a refining influence over an assemblage which nothing else can replace."[52] But groups of Toronto women were trying to force the city council to build a water filtration plant. The mayor and city council had been resisting this effort, contending that its potential benefits were insufficiently investigated. When Florence Huestis of the TLCW accosted the Board of Control on this attitude she surely was not gracing its proceedings. She castigated the men for accusing women of "jumping at conclusions" while they were "told that men reason." "If they reason to come to a conclusion," she went on, "when may we reasonably expect them to arrive at a decision regarding the water supply?" As Huestis sarcastically continued, "Civic rulers have taken thirty-three years to think over this problem" while the people of Toronto remained without pure water.[53] Huestis was quoted in a newspaper, but there is little other indication that Toronto men gave attention to the women's ideas. There is no mention of the TLCW's meeting with the Board of Control in its reports to the city council or in the council's *Minutes* or its appendices.

The fact that when men and women used similar language they meant different things has not been acknowledged. Men and women in Toronto and Chicago both used the phrase *City of Homes* to refer to the city, but men meant single-family home ownership, and women meant that the city was a home for all its residents. In 1888, Chicago men heard a Chicago real estate board member ask, "Is it not better for a city that its citizens should be made up of those that own their own homes? Let a man once own his own home, he becomes an advocate of law and order." For the reform-oriented Citizens' Association, Chicago should be a "city of homes—as few tenants as was possible and as many owners as possible." The *Daily Inter-Ocean* praised the city's building and loan societies for providing money "for the most part going into homes for the laboring and salaried classes . . . making them home owners."[54] "To convert a city of tenants into a city of home-owners is to work a marvelous transformation."[55] Chicago workers valued home ownership, according to historian Margaret Garb, because it was a hedge against low wages and job insecurity, it generated extra household income from taking in boarders, and homes could be used as collateral for loans.[56] To promote home ownership, one Chicago newspaper even castigated women for wanting to live in apartments rather than buying homes. "Social-climbing wives who were too anxious to move to the latest fashionable neighborhood" were preventing Chicago from becoming a city of homes.[57]

Toronto businessmen promoted a city of homes to lure new investors, developers, and other businessmen to the city.[58] The city's medical officer of health, Charles Hastings, declared that "if we are to develop along judicial lines we must make Toronto a city of individual homes."[59] The city's reform-oriented Civic Guild urged employers to encourage the construction of "attractive, healthy and comfortable homes . . . to ensure their work-people being contented and efficient." As Richard Dennis points out, Canadian cities "prided themselves on being 'cities of homes': cities of single-family, owner-occupied dwellings."[60]

Neither London nor Dublin men used precisely the same rhetoric, but they also emphasized the need for single-family home ownership as they turned against block buildings for their lack of domestic privacy. English planning advocate Henry R. Aldridge declared that block dwellings were expensive to manage and unhealthy, but one of his more critical objections was that they do "not give the maximum amount of encouragement to a healthy family life."[61] Dublin chief engineer P. C. Cowan remarked, "give a man comfort in even the humblest cottage and the glow of patriotism may, and probably will, give an added warmth to that which shines on him from his fireside."[62] Ebenezer Howard worried that "the present physical condition of the people in our great towns is a serious danger, not only to our national life, but to our capacity to compete successfully with other countries." "Healthy homes in healthy areas," Howard argued, "must be provided if we are to maintain our position among the nations."[63]

When many urban women envisioned their city as a city of homes, they saw the city as a collectivity in which all people were responsible for the common, daily welfare. For Anna Nicholes, a resident of Chicago's Neighborhood House settlement, the city should be "a place in which to rear children. . . . a spiritual city, where the watchword is 'personal welfare.' . . . This new city would care because babies die from preventable diseases . . . [and] will open to all greater industrial and social opportunities." Nicholes and other women who dominated social settlements in Chicago saw the distinction between the private home and the public city as an artificial boundary. Rather than recapture domesticity inside the home, they sought "the opening of the domestic to the space of the city, the extension of domestic services (bathhouses, coffeehouses, meeting spaces) to their neighbors."[64] In Toronto, the TLCW declared that women's concern "for the home and family should be extended outside their own domestic sphere to embrace the community."[65] In Dublin, the city's chapter of the Women's National Health Association made the security of private lives into a public endeavor when they raised money to fund district nurses, to open and maintain a Babies' Club with a female doctor and a boys' camp to feed and shelter homeless boys, to support a restaurant to feed women and children, and to provide milk and food to infants and young children.[66]

Through their rhetoric and actions, women-directed social settlements and women's organizations threatened disorder and a public-private collapse. They took women out of the home and into public, insisting not only that women belonged in public but that they must be there. Sandra Haar suggests that women saw that the modern city was creating "a fluid condition between private and public spheres" and that what was occurring was "the making of a new domestic and urban environment."[67] The work of Octavia Hill and her landladies, the women of the Alexandra Guild, and the Hull House women who went door to door investigating neighborhood conditions all threatened disorder because their work brought women's concerns into the city's public spaces and thereby pierced the patriarchally imagined boundaries between the public and the private.

Feminist geographers argue that constructions of space and place are symbiotic with gender relations.[68] As such, the contest over housing was not just a modernist contest between the romantic and the realistic; it was a gendered contest over the nature of the city as both place and space, and where women would fit. Men spoke of the public city as the economic spaces of production where men worked and from which they needed to return to the orderly private home after their hard day's toil. Many women saw the entire city as a reproductive, cooperative, living space. For them, public and private places and spaces had to be ordered so that all their residents prospered. Underlying an anonymous writer's flippant dismissal of women as the "Glorified Spinsters" who moved through the spaces of the city and who "remapped the city as 'like meteors [they] wander free in interfamiliar space, obeying laws and conventions of their own'" was fear of women's transgression of the public-private divide.[69]

The housing plans advanced by urban men through the first decade of the twentieth century in all four cities sought to satisfy creative destruction, maintain class order, facilitate private enterprise, and reorder the public-private divide to solidify appropriate gender relations. Slum clearance and new, decentralized single-family dwellings could achieve such ends. All rhetoric supporting these objectives emphasized that all housing reform had to divide the feminized, domestic space of the home from the masculine, public space of the city. New types of housing and neighborhoods were now needed to secure this public-private divide, and men were ready to propose how to do this with the help of government.

MODERNITY: EMBOUNDING NEIGHBORHOODS AND HOMES

The findings of the 1885 Royal Commission on Housing raised alarm that private enterprise and philanthropic trusts alone could not confront the housing situation. Prominent male housing reformers then convinced Parliament to give British and Irish cities authority to build housing. The 1890 and 1891 parliamentary Housing of the Working Classes Act and the Public Health (London) Act gave London's now centralized municipal government the power to control housing development. The Dublin Corporation possessed the authority to rehabilitate, manage, and control existing slum properties courtesy of the Cross Act of 1875.[70]

The first new housing schemes promoted by men in these two cities had several distinct elements. They prioritized embounding neighborhoods by creating inward-looking estates. When possible, they also wanted small single-family cottages rather than multistory buildings. They also preferred new housing decentralized away from the center of the city. Chicago and Toronto would follow the lead of their cross-Atlantic counterparts and adopt similar new housing plans. The result for the built environment of all four cities would be the resegregation of the productive and reproductive spaces of the city to re-embed male privilege back into the modernizing city and secure it for masculine production.

Elizabeth Wilson argues that new housing schemes "represented one answer to this threat of female independence. . . . They constituted an attempt to gain control over women, although this was rarely if ever explicitly stated as a goal." Professor of urban planning Clara Greed expresses it more bluntly: "The creation of separate, residential neighbourhoods, was one means of enforcing divisions spatially between male and female, and of preventing women combining work inside and outside the home in their daily lives."[71] One example each from London and Dublin serves to illustrate the truth of her statement as men promoted new types of housing for the city.

London's Boundary Street Estate

The Boundary Street Estate in Bethnal Green, east London, was one of the first examples of London men and the municipal government working together to clear slums and build residential neighborhoods that would separate the public and the private. The area, known as the Nichol, was among the most overcrowded, poverty-stricken, and crime-ridden of London's neighborhoods; 5,719 people lived on fifteen acres with a death rate more than twice that of London overall. Its buildings had been shoddily constructed, and covered virtually every piece of land. Houses in its narrow streets and alleys intermingled with stables, cowsheds, and workshops.[72]

There was little doubt that this neighborhood needed redevelopment: the issue was how to accomplish this. The LCC acquired the land, demolished the buildings, and completely replanned the area to construct the city's first municipal housing scheme. The council hired Owen Fleming, who would subsequently become the chief architect of the LCC, as architect-in-charge. Fleming and his team created a master plan for the area that "envisaged a picturesque urban village."[73] While the resulting Boundary Street Estate with its four- and five-story buildings replacing the older two-story ones was far from a village setting, several of its elements presaged the redomesticating patterns that would soon emerge and dominate twentieth-century urban planning. Building the Boundary Street Estate as a cooperative working arrangement between an architect and the LCC also signaled the waning of private philanthropy in housing and the turn to a partnership between professional men and municipal government to rebuild the urban environment.[74]

The Nichol had always mixed residential and work spaces. The tiny ground-floor shops used the street frontage to display their goods. Street sellers and costermongers passed along shop fronts and doorways hawking their goods to both shops and residents. The intersecting gridlike street system made it easy for sellers and residents to move around and through the neighborhood. Old pictures and accounts of the Nichol demonstrate that many women were involved in these shops and in street selling and that they socialized with one another standing in the doorways of their shops and homes (Figure 4.2).

Figure 4.2 The Nichol before destruction with women in doorways, London, 1894. (Courtesy of the London Metropolitan Archives, Image 249433, available at https:// collage.cityoflondon.gov.uk/quick-search?q=249433.)

The new building scheme of the Boundary Street Estate followed the examples of the Peabody and Guinness estates in clearly separating production and reproduction. Ground-floor shops and small workshops were eliminated, and remaining workshops and a factory were relocated away from the residential buildings to the outlying margins of the area. The design and layout of the buildings and streets embounded women's movements through the neighborhood. The new four- and five-story buildings made street selling and socializing in streets and doorways impossible (Figure 4.3). The design of the estate isolated women inside their buildings and made shopping more difficult and time-consuming by eliminating shops on the ground floor of the buildings. Shops, including a central bakery, were arrayed mainly along Calvert Street at one corner of the estate. The more time it takes to get to stores, the less often one is inclined to make the trip; the fewer trips women made to the shops, the less time they were likely to spend in public without men to accompany them.

Figure 4.3 Clifton and Molesey Buildings, Boundary Estate, London, 1906. (Courtesy of the London Metropolitan Archives, Image 253562, available at https://collage .cityoflondon.gov.uk/quick-search?q=253562.)

Small side streets and interior courts were demolished, and seven new diagonal streets replaced the old warren of intersecting narrow streets and alleys. Each of the new streets led into a central ornamental garden, with an ornamental bandstand, inside a circular drive called Arnold Circus. Now residents would rarely be able to socialize in the streets or visit one another simply by going around the corner in any direction. The new street design also turned the estate inward by eliminating several of the previous street entrances to the neighborhood and directing all the interior streets toward Arnold Circus. As the Guinness Trust building on Columbia Road (near the Nichol neighborhood) had forbidden children to make noise or play ball,[75] so did the Boundary Street Estate restrict children's activities by locating their play area atop the circle. Fleming's rather pastoral vision of his setting was one in which there would be "happy couples promenading in the ornamental gardens after a hard day's artisanal toil by the head of the family, as music from a central bandstand played."[76] Waiting for the male worker to return from his toils outside the neighborhood to take them outside would have women promenade under male control.

Area clearance projects such as the Boundary Street Estate became emblematic of the housing projects that removed the poor from older areas and replaced them with lower-middle-class residents. When the estate was finished, only 11 of the 5,719 evicted Nichol residents moved back in. The others could not afford the higher rents, especially since the buildings contained few one-room flats, and they had not been able to retain their small shops. In the process of renting the new flats, female heads of households apparently disappeared from this area. In the enumeration of occupations of heads of households, the occupations that poor women might have had—food hawkers, general-goods dealers, and the like—had reduced from 280 to 23 between 1891 and 1903, although household heads listed as washerwomen and chars had increased from 44 to 46.[77]

The LCC was pleased with the new development, although financial considerations had reduced many of the original plans. The LCC then moved quickly to continue the process of clearing and replanning poor neighborhoods and then turning a large part of the work over to private enterprise. By 1899, the LCC calculated that the total number of people displaced by clearance in London was 18,029; the number rehoused was only 6,812, despite legislation requiring that people displaced by new housing schemes be rehoused.[78] Between 1902 and 1904, a report to the LCC estimated that private enterprise had destroyed another 4,186 rooms that were not replaced by rooms for housing with another 6,279 people displaced in those years. The report also noted that displacements would be increasing in "central crowded districts, which are becoming more and more valuable for business purposes."[79] By 1905, the population of the Boundary Street Estate had been reduced to 4,184.[80]

Dublin: The Iveagh Trust

The Dublin Corporation had begun some housing schemes by the 1880s with the twin objectives of clearing areas and fostering private enterprise for the actual rebuilding. When the corporation did undertake a few building schemes on its own, the Dublin Artisans' Dwelling Company (DADC) protested on behalf of the semiphilanthropic housing organizations that the corporation was misusing rate revenue to compete unfairly with their efforts.[81] But the corporation was not getting into the business of owning housing, and instead it demolished tenements on land that it owned, erected new dwellings, and then turned them over to the DADC for a nominal yearly rental. The corporation continued to acquire land and demolish unsanitary tenements under provisions of the 1890 Housing of the Working Classes Act when it was extended to Ireland, but it never had sufficient funds to erect a large number of suitable buildings. Building owners impeded the process by insisting on high compensation for loss of their property, and the corporation generally complied with such demands. Complicating the acquisition of property at a reasonable rate was the fact that some corporation and city council members owned buildings in condemned tenement areas. Mary

Daly notes that there was much speculation that slum properties were being acquired in advance of corporation schemes for the purpose of acquiring compensatory profits.[82] Despite receiving two ratepayers "memorials" protesting the award of £4,200 in compensation to public house (tavern) owner Michael O'Reilly—who, as a member of the council, had voted on this payment—as too much, the Artisans' Dwelling Committee defended the award. On the other hand, an elderly woman who was going to lose the clothing shop that she had leased for twenty-five years and was "her sole means of support" received just £15.[83] As Jacinta Prunty remarks in her study of property acquisitions by the corporation, "The sacredness of private property, even if tumbledown and seriously endangering the health of occupants and neighbours, had to be respected."[84]

As the corporation debated how to clear a designated area along Bride's Alley just south of the Liffey River, in 1898 Lord Iveagh proposed to acquire a patch of land between Bride's Alley and Bull's Alley to build "artisan and other dwellings, a Lodging house for men, Shops, etc., and also a Concert Hall, combining therewith a Reading Room, Gymnasium, Lecture Room, etc." as the perfect solution.[85] Two years later he proposed extending this development by building an indoor old-clothes market to replace the street selling on Patrick Street and to include a wash house.[86] Since his scheme would involve evicting more tenants in order to destroy old buildings, and compensation would need to be paid to property owners, the council was more than willing to accede to Iveagh's plans.[87] The Iveagh Trust's Bull's Alley scheme comprised eight E-shaped, five-story blocks "separated by communal paved playgrounds" bounded by Bull's Alley, the new Bride Road, Bride Street, and Patrick Street. Fences and entry gates closed off the area. A hostel for single homeless men was included.[88] In 1906, the trust added a public bath and swimming house with eighteen private baths for men and nine for women, the covered market, and then a new play center in 1911. Certainly, these building vastly improved living conditions in this area, as the Boundary Street scheme had done in London. But the configuration of the buildings and new street schemes changed the patterns of daily life. And as with the new Boundary Street Estate, the people who moved into the new Iveagh flats were the better-off members of the working and lower middle classes, not the poor who had lived there before.[89]

The Iveagh Trust complex was the first embounded housing scheme in Dublin. Old photographs of the former streets and buildings reveal neighborhood women congregating in the streets, in their doorways, in front of the street-level shops, or outside the buildings that surrounded the area's typical semienclosed courts. Women had been highly visible and unsupervised in these public spaces, communicating daily with their neighbors, passers-by, or the ubiquitous street sellers. The higher residential buildings of the Iveagh Trust with their limited number of entrance doorways impeded easy pursuit of such former daily practices. The building scheme also removed many street-level shops. Ground-floor shops were allowed on only two streets, so women who had owned or rented such shops were removed from the streets. Patrick Street had been the site of an open-air used-clothes market. The gathering and selling of used clothing was almost exclusively a female occupation. Women collected, cleaned, mended, sold, and bought these items on their own (Figure 4.4).[90] The new covered market on Francis Street to replace the street market was several blocks away. In his study of the Iveagh Trust, F.H.A. Aalen described the complex:

> The search for order is evident, not only in the new regular street lines and straight building facades but in the provision of new activities in clearly defined precincts and the segregation of formerly intermixed activities. . . . [A] separate covered market [is] provided for trade previously on the streets; dwelling blocks [are] for residential purposes only, shops being confined to specific sites on their edges.[91]

Myriad regulations structured the lives of residents. Cats and dogs were not allowed, no one could take in lodgers, taking in washing or mangling was forbidden, and no nails or screws could be put into the woodwork.[92]

Figure 4.4 Patrick Street Used Clothing Market, Dublin, 1903. (Courtesy of the Dublin City Library and Archive.)

Eliminating separate doorways, interior courtyards, and street-level shops; installing perimeter fences and gates; and removing the street market all removed women's socializing and economic activities from the streets and into fewer and more easily regulated and supervised settings. Such new development was shifting the nature and locations of public and private spaces in the city where women could function. Eliminating direct entrance from the street and eliminating the older type of courts both embounded the private home and made public surveillance easier. Street markets were moved indoors where both buyers and sellers could be more easily controlled and regulated.[93]

The council agreed to Iveagh's request to enforce the removal of the used-clothing market from the streets and also to decide whether items other than clothes should be sold in a new covered market so as "take steps to obtain the removal from the neighbouring streets and concentrate the sale of these articles in the Market." Iveagh promised to assign the deed to the land in this area to the corporation as long as it did not alter its use and purposes.[94] Removing the clothes market from Patrick Street to a building on Francis Street to the west of the trust buildings required women to travel farther from their homes to sell or to buy—that is, if they continued to live in the neighborhood. Having to rent stalls inside the market undoubtedly reduced the possibility of women having their own stalls.[95]

A new block of Artisans' Dwelling Company buildings just to the north of the Iveagh buildings also did not contain any shops, further funneling women's public presence into prescribed market places.[96] The Boundary Street Estate and the Iveagh trust buildings restructured the boundaries between the home and the city, between the private and the public, in their bricks-and-mortar building schemes (Figure 4.5).

Housing developments in Chicago and Toronto proceeded differently from the already crowded cities of Dublin and London. Chicago's population was heavily foreign, religiously mixed, and expanding rapidly. Toronto's population was also growing, but it remained much smaller and was largely English Protestant. Municipal government authority also differed. The United States had no national housing laws, agencies, or funding, and no sense that housing was the responsibility of government. Canadian provincial governments had the power to legislate on specific urban issues and gradually extended money and power to municipalities. Neither Chicago nor Toronto had to confront already extensively built-up areas, but they also did not have wealthy, titled residents to endow housing monies or philanthropic housing entities. In both cities, businessmen and male civic organizations were free to control housing reform and to ensure that private enterprise determined all housing. As each city expanded, housing development prioritized real estate speculation, preserving the property culture, and reconstructing the private-public boundaries in the city.

Figure 4.5 Gated entrance to an Iveagh Trust building, Dublin, October 2009. (Photo by author.)

Chicago

In Chicago, the elite Citizens' Association never convinced influential capitalists, manufacturers, and merchants to build housing.[97] But private entrepreneurs took advantage of the city's exploding population and its surrounding empty land to push housing toward the city outskirts. The most successful example was Samuel E. Gross, who built as cheaply as possible by using standardized house plans and mass-produced materials. Beginning in the late 1880s, Gross built about ten thousand single-family homes in new areas of the city and into yet unincorporated townships beyond its boundaries. His flyers and advertising exhorted both male workers and the middle class to stop paying rent, stop paying city taxes (in yet unincorporated areas), and become home owners. Home ownership was the reward for masculine labor (Figure 4.6).

Gross's advertising and the Citizens' Association report on tenement housing also reflected a perceived uneasiness about gender in a changing industrial society. The tenement report had advocated that all boys age fifteen and older living in tenements be consigned to live in dormitories on the top floor so that they would not be able "to eye their young sisters." Photos and sketches from Gross's flyers depicted men doing a man's work—clearing land and building new homes. Once built, these homes would become the cozy domestic place: husband, wife, and children were pictured sitting and

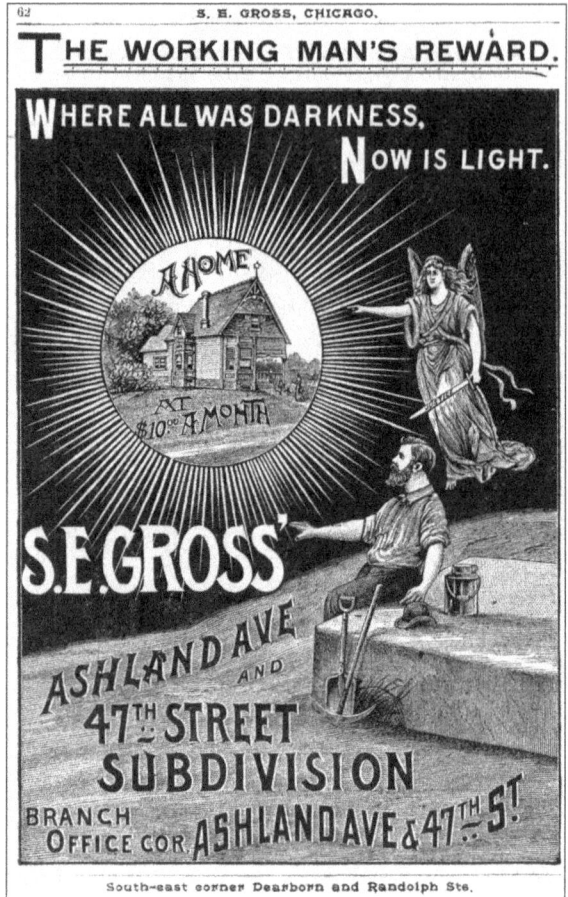

Figure 4.6 Samuel
Gross flyer from Samuel
E. Gross, *Tenth Annual
Illustrated Catalogue of
S. E. Gross' Famous City
Subdivisions and
Suburban Towns*
(Chicago: S. E. Gross,
1891), 62.

playing in the parlor. Redomestication was consciously linked to property
ownership and the single-family home. His advertising, according to historian Margaret Garb, suggested that home ownership carried an even more
significant function: "reinforcing a husband's authority within his household. . . . [P]roperty rights in housing marked an assertion of manhood and
a move to reclaim male authority within the home . . . [and] explicitly acknowledged that industrialization wrought profound, and what he [the hus-
band] perceived as disturbing, changes in the late nineteenth-century gender
relations."[98]

With ownership of the single-family home touted as the means both to
prosperity and restored patriarchy, Chicago's leaders paid little attention to
the housing conditions of masses of the people, even after William T. Stead,
the former editor of the London *Pall Mall Gazette*, excoriated them during
visits to the city in 1893 and 1894. The old central area of the city was a mix

of factories, railroad lines and terminals, and old mainly frame houses, many of which had not even weathered half a century before falling into disrepair. Stead's message drew directly from Toynbee Hall's Protestant male evangelism. He wanted to transform the moral values of the city's male leadership so that they would take a more active part in making the city the kingdom of Christ on Earth. The frontispiece of his publication, *If Christ Came to Chicago*, depicted Christ casting sinners out of the temple from the gospel of Matthew. Like the Hull House maps and papers, Stead provided a map of buildings. Unlike the Hull House maps, Stead's maps were not concerned with the conditions of the people living there. Instead, they located the places of vice: pawnshops, brothels, saloons, and lodging houses.[99]

In the middle of Stead's visits to Chicago, the city experienced the disastrous economic depression then sweeping the country. The first concern of Chicago's leading men of the city's Central Relief Agency was to find "sleeping places for the three to four thousand [unemployed] men who slept in police stations, City Hall, and the Pacific Mission Garden."[100] Such unemployed and homeless men were not fulfilling their masculine duty to work and own property. The agency's handbill admonished Chicago residents that

all who give money to men on the streets or at the door are doing harm. They are increasing pauperism, and doing wrong to the individual and to the State. Do not give tickets that will entitle the recipient to food or lodging without investigation, or without an equivalent in work. It is just as harmful to give food, shelter, or clothing to the unworthy as it is to give them money, since the one as well as the other gives support to lazy and dishonest people.[101]

This handbill did not mention the plight of destitute and homeless women.

After Hull House published its neighborhood housing survey in 1895 and a 1900 investigation by the private City Homes Association revealed that 40 percent of the population lived in substandard housing, more concern developed for the city's overall housing situation. On the one hand, the City Homes report acknowledged that Octavia Hill's management techniques had demonstrated that much unsanitary tenement housing resulted from landlords' poor management and not tenants' immoral behavior. Rather than advocate Hill's methods, however, the report had two main conclusions. It urged the city to better regulate buildings and sanitary conditions, a process that would challenge the prevailing emphasis on property rights. In fact, when the city did enact new building regulations in 1902, they applied only to new construction, and even these were scarcely enforced as property owners resisted complying with them.[102] The report's second conclusion echoed the stance of London men that the primary solution to the city's housing situation lay in controlling and dispersing the population by providing "workingmen's trains."[103]

Toronto

By the early twentieth century, Toronto's central area was a mix of old wooden housing and factories. By 1907, the city's inner St. John's Ward housed ten thousand residents in what Lawrence Solomon describes as "more a shanty town than a tenement slum."[104] Despite this situation, in 1905 Mayor Thomas Urquhart had announced that he was "pleased to see that private enterprise is endeavoring to alleviate in some measure the present necessity [for housing]." He was willing to concede that "if private enterprise does not supply this need in the very near future, it may become necessary for the City to consider the question of house accommodation." Toronto's leading men, however, were more focused on creating a "Greater Toronto" by incorporating outlying townships than on the plight of the ward's residents. They sought this expansion to control the financing and development of the city's infrastructure of water supply, sewers, roads, and transit to enable economic growth and safeguard its property culture.[105] More concern for the location and configuration of new housing development in Toronto would not begin until the next decade. Then, as Toronto housing scholar Sean Purdy observes, increased concern about housing arose from "a stress on the family home, with its segregated gender roles aimed to offset the instability in gender relations provoked by declining marriage and fertility rates, the significant increase of women in the wage labour force, and the development of socialist and feminist organizations that fought for women's rights."[106]

Such relative uniformity in thinking despite national differences led men in all four cities to embark on new housing schemes to secure the private single-family home that would foster a new domesticity, preserve the property culture, and restore order to the city. By the end of the nineteenth century, men began to propose building garden cities and garden suburbs in which embounded clusters of homes could create an embounded city.

MODERNITY: EMBOUNDING CITIES

The English parliamentary stenographer Ebenezer Howard proposed a singular blueprint for the embounded city. In 1872, the year following Chicago's tragic fire, Howard had moved to Chicago, where he stayed for five years and worked as a legal stenographer for the firm of Ely, Burnham, and Bartlett. Daniel Burnham would design much of the 1893 Columbian Exposition in Chicago and become the favorite planner of the city's businessmen. Howard claimed he began to develop his idea for a new type of city while in Chicago.

By 1892 he had drafted a "master key" to embody his vision that he would then successfully promote in his book, *Garden Cities of To-Morrow*.[107] Howard declared the existing city a failure. He cited as authority numerous anti-urban sentiments from men in the Anglo-Atlantic world. He cited Lord Rosebery's declaration that London was "a tumour, an elephantiasis sucking into its gorged system half the life and the blood and the bone of the rural districts," as an example.[108] Howard proposed to excise the tumor by building garden cities with limited populations. People would be drawn from major cities such as London to build and reside in these smaller cities that would harmonize town and country, capital and labor into a new way of living and working. Individual garden cities would be self-contained, but linked by railroad networks. No city would be allowed to grow beyond a limited size, and agricultural lands were to surround each city, never to be built on.[109] Howard believed that rural life lent dignity and health to life that could not be found in large cities.

Beyond a shared nostalgia for rural life, Howard's book appealed to men who saw the city as the site of growing class conflict. On the left of the political spectrum were calls for more municipal responsibility—or even municipal socialism. The defenders of private property and limited government interference were resisting any attacks by government or organized labor against their propertied privileges. Howard and his followers saw his garden city ideal as a middle ground that would prevent government interference and that would break the economic power of property and satisfy the demands of restless labor. His garden city would defuse labor tensions without enacting municipal socialism, while the most predatory aspects of capitalism and private property would be abandoned because there would no longer be vast fortunes to be made from controlling urban property. Howard's middle ground was a different way of managing and governing the property culture. Its focus was primarily on rents, rates, consumption, and leisure. Buying the land and building the city were to be acts of philanthropic land speculation, not much different from the earlier 5 percent philanthropy.[110]

Howard's proposed new living and working scheme, moreover, was aimed at restoring a lost masculinity. He labeled the "over-crowded cities" of his time as "effete." Although he never explicitly explained what he meant, his rhetoric implied that "vested interests" of economics and politics had impeded proper (manly?) enterprise of labor and life. They had entrapped men in a vicious circle of paying rents and rates to large landowners.

> Such a task as the construction of a cluster of cities like that represented in our diagram may well inspire all workers with that enthusiasm which unites men, for it will call for the very highest talents of engineers of all kinds, of architects, artists, medical men, experts in sanitation, landscape gardeners, agricultural experts, surveyors,

manufacturers, merchants and financiers, organisers of trades unions, friendly and co-operative societies, as well as the very simplest forms of unskilled labor, together with those forms of lesser skill and talent which lie between.[111]

Howard drew inspiration from past ideas about urban reform that had been articulated previously by men such as John Ruskin, whom Simon Parker identifies as among a group of anti-metropolitans.[112] Ruskin had called for "the cutting down of vested interests that stand in the way," after which new planning could build new small communities, with "clean and busy street within and open country without, with a belt of beautiful garden and orchard round the walls."[113] As Ruskin had advocated that London's size should be significantly reduced, Howard now advocated reducing the city's residents to no more than one fifth of its present population. Once the city had been so emptied, new systems of railways, sewers and drains, lighting, and parks could be constructed on the site of demolished slums for use of the remaining residents.[114]

Parker calls Ruskin and Howard prophetic "civic revivalists" seeking to create utopian forms of living. Such utopian dreams shared some of Toynbee Hall's religious orientation. Future city planner Patrick Geddes credited Ruskin's influence for his own developing ideals. Geddes praised Ruskin for believing that urban reform must be wedded to the age-old goal of achieving the "kingdom of God upon earth."[115]

Despite the declarations of men engaged in the garden city movement that women were eager proponents of this ideal, many women shunned these ideas. The relationship between Ruskin and Octavia Hill suggests some reasons for women's disinterest. Ruskin had given Hill her start in housing management, yet he broke rather bitterly with her. The precise cause of their break remains unclear, but Hill wanted to provide better housing for people in the city rather than moving them out of it, and she wanted gardens and parks for people to use in the city: "places to sit in, places to play in, places to stroll in."[116] Hill was also not imbued with the religious fervor that characterized Toynbee Hall or with the ideas of Howard's master key that linked science and religion as the key components to reform.

Moreover, Hill spurned Howard's gender-based ideas on which he based the organization of his garden city. For Howard, a self-contained garden city would need self-management, and it would be women's role to bring this about by civilizing its society through their domesticating practices inside the private home. Hill's methods would bring random, uncontrollable, public women into his city. Howard held that dual vision of women—a threat in public, but necessary for civilizing society—that feminist scholars have argued characterizes the largely unacknowledged male view of women. In 1903, the Garden City movement organized a women's league to persuade women of the benefits of living in a garden city. From this context, housing scholars see Howard as either gender neutral or according women equal status in his proposed cities. But in the same way that he thought of town and country as complementary, Howard believed that each sex had a complementary—not equal—role to play in the city. For Howard, as it had been for Ruskin, women's role was profoundly domesticating, and civilizing society took place inside the home. According to Meryl Aldridge, Howard's garden city "would celebrate difference and the complementary nature of this difference, rather than questioning the social construction of gender."[117] The women's league was never self-sustaining. It had to be reconstituted in 1907 and again in 1920. It is striking that a glance through the official publication of the Garden City Association, *Garden Cities and Town Planning*, from 1908 through 1923, shows almost no mention of women or of the women's section.

For Howard, building the garden city was the male task, and managing the domestic realm was the work of women. Howard's garden city was a carefully segmented one where each neighborhood was its own world with its basic unit being "the family living in its own home surrounded by a garden."[118] Male and female realms of life were to be carefully segregated from each other, with individual homes carefully isolated from one another and the living and working sections of the city also carefully separated.

In its interior layout, the garden city was to be bounded within a circular system similar to the Boundary Street Estate. Movement within the city would be directed inward toward a center circle called the Central Park. Encircling the park would be a Crystal Palace where recreation, learning, and shopping would take place.[119] In Howard's garden city scheme, there would be no idle circulation on the streets, no standing in doorways talking, no ground-floor shops tended by women. Howard intended his Central Park to be "an impressive and meaningful setting for the 'large public buildings'" such as a "town hall, library, museum, concert and lecture halls, and the hospital." This area would be the "second cohesive force" for holding together the community: a civic spirit, embodied in these buildings and their central location, bringing together "the highest values of the community . . . culture, philanthropy, health and mutual cooperation."[120]

Howard's vision of a civic spirit inspired by grand buildings clashed distinctly with the vision of civic spirit being proposed by women. Chicago settlement house resident Anna Nicholes appealed for women to engage in municipal reform by developing a "city sense." "A general demand for better community life, a vision of a purified city," she claimed, "is not enough." The city must be made to "work for human betterment."[121] Howard was proposing the "purified city" of Ruskin's imagination. Nicholes was following the more personalized vision of Hill. For both these women and many others, the city had to function within a cooperative sense of caring for the environment in which all residents lived. For Hill and settlement workers, cooperation on the neighborhood level would lead inexorably to cooperation on the city level; people needed to be brought together, not separated from each other.

Although Hill's work and philosophy had spread to the United States by the end of the nineteenth century, it was not even necessary for Nicholes to have heard of Hill to envision the city as she did. Since the 1890s, groups of Chicago women had been thinking along similar lines in their settlement houses and women's voluntary organizations. Nicholes's city sense, which she articulated fully in volume 9 of the *Woman Citizens Library*, came from women's personal experiences investigating the social conditions of the city. In Chicago, these women had been developing an alternate sense of citizenship that resembled Hill's belief that "citizenship was a matter of personal caring and urban renewal took place around a healthy community."[122] As the University of Chicago–trained political economist Sophonisba Breckinridge expressed it: there ought to be public standards of housing "below which no living in the community will be allowed to continue."[123] The women of the Chicago Woman's Club used the word *civic* when calling for the municipal government to ensure good housing for everyone in the city. "What civic ideal," the club asked, "could be more inspiring than that of comfortable, healthful homes for all citizens and their children[?]" For these Chicago women, the fate of every individual had to be considered before the city could be renewed.[124]

Recent feminist scholarship on notions of urban space and place point us to new possibilities for understanding the gendered ideals that underlay the reconstruction of the urban built environment.[125] While few garden cities were ever built, Howard's vision of the decentralized and embounded population living in separate houses (or cottages), with its notions of a patriarchal nuclear family composed of the working man and the dependent wife and children, took hold and shaped the path of overall town planning ideas in the coming decades. As David Pinder notes, Howard's ideal orderly city necessitated eliminating anything disorderly and whose interests "were supposed to be restored in their reassertion of 'natural' order, balance, and harmony." Such natural order, balance, and harmony did not specifically require garden cities, but for many men, in some fashion or the other, an orderly city required that women's disorderly bodies had to be restored to their proper place in the private home.[126]

The Cottage Home

By the beginning of twentieth century it was becoming an article of faith for many male urban reformers that housing had to be moved out of the central city. Howard's utopian vision provided a blueprint, but only in a few exceptional instances were such garden cities built before World War I. Instead, an emerging cadre of professional men, university-educated in social and practical sciences, seized control of directing the built environment by destabilizing the city as a residential site so that it could be reconstructed as a patriarchal economic and monumental entity. In doing so, they premised their urban vision on the ideal of a new domesticity that would push women to the periphery of the city, embound them in their homes or immediate neighborhood, and build the city to ensure the stability of its economy and property culture.

Men who turned their attention to housing London's population obsessed about the type and location of housing that was needed to ensure a viral, healthy English population and England's place in the world. The London Reform Union declared in 1899 that "the efficiency of the worker must also be reckoned as a factor in the cost of production, and the healthier homelife obtainable outside London must undoubtedly conduce to greater energy and alertness in industrial pursuits."[127] Howard asserted that "the present physical conditions of the people in our great towns is a serious danger, not only to our national life, but to our capacity to compete successfully with other countries."[128] Housing philanthropist Sydney Waterlow, who chaired the LCC Committee on Housing of the Working Classes, told the LCC and metropolitan borough councils that housing reform was needed "for the sake of the children. . . . [F]or the health of our people, I appeal to you for the virility of our race; I appeal to you for the greatness and glory of our empire."[129]

By 1908, such obsessions had even turned to comparing England to Germany and the need for England to provide good exercise for young men as an element of all housing schemes. T. C. Horsfall feared that "unless we at once begin to protect the health of our people by making the towns in which most of them now live, more wholesome for body and mind, we may as well hand over our trade, our colonies, our whole influence in the world to Germany." The lack of organized athletic games, he contended, was linked to excessive use of alcohol and "sexual licentiousness." His focus of exercise and physical conditioning, of wholesome bodies and minds, was about men; young girls barely earned a mention in his talk.[130]

In Dublin, concern about the physical and moral health of the population began to play a greater role in discussions over the shape of housing. P. C. Cowan, the chief engineering inspector of Dublin's local government board, warned against municipal building schemes because "when the State is making many general provisions to improve the lot of the people [then] the moral fibre of the individual may be slackened and enfeebled." To avoid such enfeebling, new housing estates had to be built so that all residents shared common areas such as bowling greens, clubrooms, and tennis courts; common spaces would simultaneously provide residents with athletic stimulation and focus their attention inward rather than out to the city's streets.

According to Cowan, such a scheme was so "economically sound, practically independent of State or municipal aid, that it fosters and develops many qualities of good citizenship."[131]

In 1903, at the request of the Dublin Trades Council, a conference presided over by the Lord Mayor and attended by members of Parliament for Dublin and the Dublin Trades Council—no women were invited—proposed to shift housing development to the "suburban solution." The Trades Council proposed building cottages or self-contained buildings on the outskirts of the city, linked by "cheap means of transit to and from the city for workers." According to the investigations of this Mansion House Conference, only 5,394 families had to that date been rehoused (out of 59,263 total families in the city). At this rate, the report concluded, "it would be a fatal mistake to continue to put a premium on bad sanitation and improper housing by purchasing up, at a ruinous rate, insanitary areas and rebuilding them."[132] Unlike London, the Dublin Corporation did not have an equivalent to the LCC's Housing of the Working Classes Committee. In Dublin the Public Health Committee, the Artisans' Dwellings Committee, the Estates and Finance Committee, and the Improvements Committee shared overlapping responsibility for investigating the city's housing. These committees tended to view the housing situation as primarily a matter of health and were most concerned to facilitate the work of the DADC and reluctant to experiment with any municipal housing schemes analogous to the Boundary Street Estate. Only in 1910 did the Dublin City Council form a standing Housing Committee.[133]

Once the Housing Committee was formed, it was directed to undertake "concentrated and sustained effort to deal with 'abolition of the slums' and substitute them with 'decent dwellings at moderate rents.'"[134] The Dublin Corporation thenceforth made housing decentralization its preferred course in dealing with housing. Dublin men were as concerned as those in London to ensure that most housing remained a private enterprise and that new housing would provide for home-ownership as a domesticating goal that would simultaneously increase rateable property and preserve the virility of the Irish race.

The role that women and family life were to play was clear in the proposals and ultimately the decisions that followed from them by men in all four cities. Women were to provide the domestic stability and tranquility of Henry Aldridge's happy little home. They were to be removed from the streets, removed from work in shops, and kept in the home, where, as Cowan reported, in his inspections he had "been delighted by the comfort and comparative beauty imparted by a good housekeeper."[135] Healthy working men and a viral race for the nation would be secured in this manner. It was not merely the residuum that reformers wanted to remove from sight, it was also women; whether middle-class, working-class, or poor, women were all to be bounded into the home. New transit systems that catered to the working man would help ensure that this happened. William Thompson, councillor in the London outlying area of Richmond, claimed that "the great majority of workers in London do not, and need not, live near their work. . . . [C]heap and rapid transit [would make] suburban districts" accessible.[136] Women would be staying in the home with the children, cloistered out in the suburban colony. Architect and planner Raymond Unwin proposed that the interior of the cottages built in these districts be specifically designed to foster a new domesticity. Cottages were to contain a large living room/kitchen where "the bulk of the domestic work will be done, meals will be prepared and eaten, and children will play, while the whole family will often spend long evenings there together."[137]

Planning historian Helen Meller concludes that "of all the pressures which dictated the form of nineteenth century cities, there was not one related to finding new ways for women to live in modern cities outside a rigid interpretation of the Two Spheres."[138] Her analysis extends to the important role that men believed new housing schemes could play in redomesticating urban life. While men in control of the cities could not imagine breaking the private-public dichotomy of the two spheres, women were challenging that divide by entering public spaces. Moreover, the working man was threatening the stability of the economic life of the city. The solution to both problems was clear: put women back into the home and persuade the working man that his best interests lay in a cozy domestic setting upon his return from work.[139] As Martin Daunton claims, working-class men were complicit. According to Daunton, "the respectable working man would argue that the streets were for those who did not have a decent home."[140]

The separate dwelling would thus bring happiness to the nation, but the physical structure itself was not sufficient. The structure had to be accompanied by a "domestic system of living." The Scots sociobiologist Patrick Geddes posited the rationale for this system. According to Geddes, the city was a living organism whose built environment was of cultural importance for the national identity. Cultural ideals had to be transmitted from one generation to the next. For Geddes, women would fulfill this role because their "biological roles as wives and mothers kept them untainted by the artificial machinations of the world." The public world of the city, wherein men moved and were prone to be so "tainted," could be preserved and bettered only by a matriarchal domestic (private) world as its counterpoint. Social science rationale meshed here with utopian ideals, for Geddes was a follower of Ruskin.[141]

Along with other male-dominated professions, the emergent social sciences played a crucial role in determining the reconstruction of the city. These new disciplines allowed men to present their ideas as the rational, scientific ones and to connect them with Ruskin's idealistic civic revival while bypassing the religious orientation of Toynbee Hall or Howard. Departments of political science, such as that at the University of Toronto, preached a political economy that only "scientific" knowledge acquired through statistics and facts should be applied to solving social problems. Acquisition of this knowledge was the province of university-trained men who would then move into positions of municipal policy making. Men such as James Mavor and S. A. Cudmore at the University of Toronto became important figures in promoting new scientific approaches to reconstructing the city. The Anglo-Atlantic relationships of professional men extended beyond planners. Mavor was a close friend of Geddes, and he had trained Cudmore in political science. Before moving to Toronto, Mavor had been a professor at the University of Glasgow and was acquainted with the London men's settlements. Once his focus turned to social science, he eschewed what he considered the sentimental outlook of social settlements and instead worked to train members of the Toronto University Settlement to ground their work firmly in the social scientific methods of political economy.[142]

Using social science methods, men depicted their visions in graphic representations intended to impress the viewer with their authenticity and rationality. Patrick Geddes's publications were replete with diagrams. One diagram titled "Action and Reaction" between "Organism and Environment" demonstrated how the relationship between a biological organism and its environment could be applied to the city as a living organism that responded similarly to its surrounding environment. Other diagrams ranged from simple to extraordinarily complicated representations of the application of the sociological interrelationship of acts, deeds, facts, and thoughts that led him to contend that civics was applied sociology. The city could be surveyed, observed, and interpreted "on lines essentially similar to those of the natural sciences."[143]

Howard also used sketches to present his garden city plans. His "master key" was drawn as an actual key. Written inside the head of the key, labeled the lever, were the necessary ingredients for a good urban existence: health, education, recreation, and a series of municipal reforms. Science and religion were the shaft of the key (or barrel)—the ideological components. The teeth of the key, called the wards (the places where people were to live), described the principles of a new city among which were to be a new city on new land, unity of town and country, and free association. Below the diagrammed key was another diagram showing teeth (parts) cut away. Overcentralization, attacks on liberty, and parliamentary interference would be eliminated in his vision. Color was significant. The new key was in blue; the cut-away parts were in red. Below them Howard provided a quote from the American poet James Russell Lowell's poem "The Present Crisis" (1844) that ended with the words, "nor attempt the future's portal with the past's blood-rusted key."

Howard's graphic of "three magnets" was a fully visualized representation of his garden city (Figure 4.7). It promoted the symbiotic town-country relationship through "three magnets" that would draw people and places into each other. On both the Town and the Country magnets he elaborated all the drawbacks of living in one or the other. Then his third magnet, Town-Country, listed all the good things that would result from his garden city. "As man and woman by their varied gifts and faculties supplement each other," he wrote, "so should town and country."[144] Howard also provided an elaborate drawing of a site plan and an even more detailed section of that plan, showing where everything in the city would be located.[145]

When women had the opportunity and the resources to publish their ideas, their representations contained sketches or photos of people and the neighborhoods, most especially of women and children. Unlike Charles Booth's London maps that focused on categorizing areas with an eye to demonstrating what needed to be eradicated, the *Hull-House Maps and Papers* attempted to draw a picture of the neighborhood and accompanied the maps with essays to describe the lives and circumstances of the people living there. In London, the women of the Kyrle Society's decorative branch decorated the interiors and exteriors of private spaces, semipublic spaces, and public spaces. They intended to "work within the existing fabric of the city . . . to

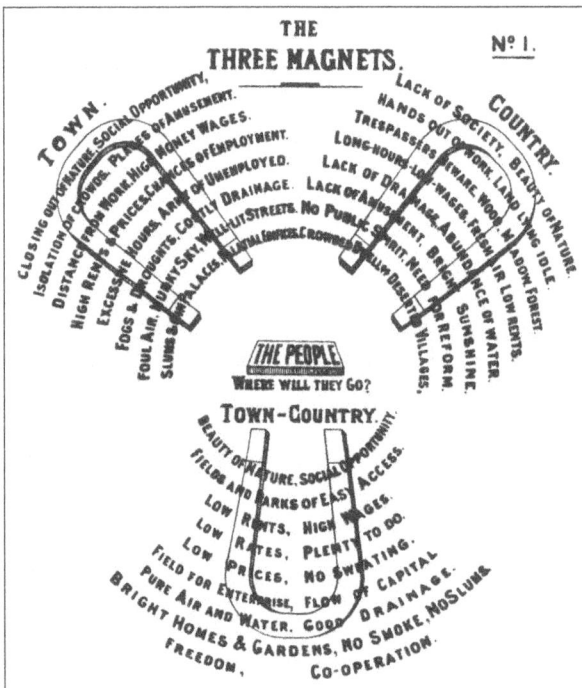

Figure 4.7 Three magnets diagram from Ebenezer Howard, *Garden Cities of To-Morrow* (London: Sonnenschein, 1902), 16.

enhance, not demolish and begin again."[146] In Dublin, the women of the Alexandra Guild took pictures of the neighborhood children in front of their buildings. Women's concerns for housing consistently focused on human conditions, while men's concerns focused increasingly on structures. As women were trying to breach the barriers between the private world of the home and the public city so that all city residents could be made to feel responsible for each other, men were seeking to reprivatize the home by removing women from public spaces and formulating new structural plans to embound women into the home.[147]

The Garden Suburb

Neither governments nor private entrepreneurs were much interested in Howard's completely new cities. But early town planning advocates promoted another scheme: the totally planned garden suburb. These men argued that building new areas on vacant land would decentralize the city and clear out city centers of unwanted population, buildings, and even factories. In London, the Hampstead Garden Suburb Trust answered the cry that "the main objective of all housing reformers should be to get the people out into the suburbs."[148] The trust purchased acreage in the far northwestern section of London from private owners, including Eton College, expressly to develop a suburb on Hampstead Heath. A driving force behind this activity was Henrietta Barnett, wife of the founder of Toynbee Hall. Her activity in developing this site is one of the examples that scholars often use to demonstrate the absence of gendered ideas in reconstructing the built environment. In reality her ideas were more complicated. On the one hand, Barnett's explanation of the plan resembled the ideas of other women. The Garden Suburb, according to Barnett, was to be built to "preserve the rightly valued beauty and amenities of the neighbourhood of Hampstead Heath, and will provide houses with gardens for persons of all classes, so that the rich and poor may live within one another's knowledge, as members of the same community."[149] Barnett also saw Hampstead as an opportunity to build housing specifically for working women, and she persuaded Sydney Waterlow and his Improved Industrial Dwellings Company to build Waterlow Court at Hampstead for that purpose.[150]

On the other hand, Barnett's ideas reflected those of many male housing reformers that there was something wrong with a built environment of "long monotonous streets, with their rows of cheap houses, all alike gardenless and treeless, always noisy because they are the only playground for the children." Such conditions "do not refresh the tired worker by stirring his interest in nature or awakening purer sympathies."[151] Barnett accepted the domesticating ideal. In her publication *The Making of the Home: A Reading-Book of Domestic Economy for Home and School Use*, she took her cues about women's duties from male praise of women as homemakers. She quotes Arnold Toynbee that "the greatness of no nation can be secure that is not based upon a pure homelife" and another "great [male] author" that "a true wife in her husband's house is a servant, in his heart she is queen."[152] Given her association with Toynbee Hall, her acceptance of male ideas about domesticity is not very surprising. It is important to acknowledge this attachment. She is more exception than rule.

When the Hampstead Garden Suburb was built, it embodied Barnett's sentiments about women and the home but not her ideas that it be a place where the classes would mingle. Once in the hands of professionals, the Hampstead Garden Suburb became a middle-class, embounded enclave. The trust engaged the up-and-coming architects Raymond Unwin and Barry Parker to design the suburb. The Hampstead commission presented Unwin the opportunity to put into practice his simmering planning and architectural ideas. His plan for Hampstead included eliminating backyards, grouping cottages around a common quadrangle, doing away with linear streets, and creating a monumental square as the suburb's focal point. "There is something homely and dignified about a quadrangle" that a "mere street of cottages" could never accomplish, he declared. Unwin believed that he was in tune with the best ideas of housing advocates: "social reformers," he decreed, "are generally agreed that the people must be housed outside the congested town areas [and] it is taken as the best policy for the municipal polities to build attractive cottages on the outskirts of their towns."[153] Unwin did not get everything he wanted in the design of Hampstead, but what he achieved embodied much of the spirit of his ideas. Quadrangles became "closes" with houses built on three sides with open space in the center. Shops were located together at one end of the suburb so as not to mingle with housing. A Central Square, with a "monumental approach," contained two churches and other public buildings. Over time, new land was incorporated to extend the suburb. Although the winding streets were not as curved as Unwin had originally desired, the paucity of four-way intersections and limited access routes into the suburb all eschewed the old grid system of straight, connected streets and enclosed the suburb.

From its beginnings, Hampstead's design would embound and marginalize women. As with the Boundary Street Estate, shops were removed from much of the housing. The London underground station and railroad station at Golders Green were distant from the housing and could be reached only by traversing several large roads, circumstances that would hamper women's ability to travel out of Hampstead, especially with children in tow. The "enclosed" houses faced inward grouped around Unwin's celebrated closes with cul-de-sacs, walls of hedges or fencing separating housing from roads to maximize the concept of the private home. The original piece of the suburb built in 1907 had only one entrance road to the entire development.[154]

To support his plans, Unwin argued that "overcrowding of buildings upon the land" was not economically necessary. Rather, he felt that it would be more economically beneficial to owners and occupiers of land to take ten acres, with "housing in groups around a central area with no internal streets," and build 152 houses on it rather than to turn the same ten acres into a "grid system of housing along streets" that would hold 340 houses.[155] In Toronto, professional men praised the garden suburb movement as the antidote to the supposedly overcrowded city. An article in *Canadian Architect and Builder* declared that these schemes are the outcome of the tendency to seek the country for residence, which is just as marked as the tendency to seek the city for work. The very flow toward the city is what, by increasing the density of its population, makes it "undesirable as a place to live in." New technology, it continued, makes "suburban residence [a] natural state of affairs now-a-days."[156]

Unwin's pronouncements against overcrowding emerged simultaneously with the LCC-issued statistical reports that detailed that demolitions and street widenings had displaced thousands more Londoners between 1899 and 1902 than had been or could be rehoused. Up to 1904 more than half of the rooms in the old central areas of the city had been destroyed for purposes other than housing.[157] Such statistics enhanced the idea that only by moving more people out of the city along with providing more and cheaper transit could the housing problem be solved. The Royal Commission on London Traffic in 1903 had urged that as many people as possible be removed from the central city. Its report recommended that cheap and fast transit be provided by extending rail lines out twenty-eight miles in all directions from the center. Participants at the town planning meeting convened by the Royal Institute of British Architects in 1910 elaborated on these proposals. Architect Arthur Crow declared that "the element of distance *qua* distance, has been overcome by the increase in the speed of vehicles"; travel costs had been "reduced to a point that the question of expense no longer need keep the workmen in the town."[158] He asserted that "it becomes year by year more imperative to leave no stone unturned which may assist in fostering and promoting the commercial side of our communal life."[159] He recommended that all attention now be turned to slashing wide streets through the city and presented a map demonstrating how this could be done through the city's east end.[160] For his part, Unwin bemoaned the fact that "we find in our towns too often that the land all along the railway side and adjacent to the canal banks is crowded with cottage dwellings." He objected that these houses of workers and of the poor prevented "industrial concerns" from having "direct access to these transit facilities" and that these industries were scattered around the city, resulting in "destroying the amenities of some of the best residential areas."[161] Unwin's garden suburb ideal aimed to protect the city's prosperous areas, transfer significant numbers of the population to the periphery, and foster the business of the city.

In Dublin through the 1890s as the corporation also focused more on clearing slum areas, it too looked to move the poor to the city's outskirts by facilitating transit expansion. When the Dublin Southern District Tramways Company sought the right to extend and electrify its tramways system, the city council insisted that it guarantee that it would furnish "at least two carriages each way" every morning and evening for "artisans, mechanics, and daily labourers," by which they clearly intended male laborers.[162] The 1903 housing conference argued for building "on the outskirts" and procuring "cheap means of transit for workers."[163] And, as Andrew Beattie of the Dublin Citizens' Association proclaimed seven years later in opposition to Cook Street clearance schemes, "Generally speaking, it was not the custom of modern cities to build upon areas which were demolished. The present idea was to get people out into the country districts."[164]

Modernity required destruction of old ways of living and working. The city had to end haphazard growth to guarantee both economic prosperity and a new urban domesticity. New professional men offered both the rationales and the means to achieve these ends as they began to control the reconstruction of the four cities.

PART II

CREATIVE DESTRUCTION OF
THE DISEASED ORGANISM

The city is more than a place in space, it is a drama in time.
—PATRICK GEDDES, "Civics: As Applied Sociology" (1915)

Designing the city is like playing with the objects on
your breakfast table.
—Attributed to LE CORBUSIER

When Patrick Geddes (1854–1932) offered his naturalist, organic, evolutionary theory about cities, he set a path for constructing the modern patriarchal city. His idea that the city was a "drama in time," a living and evolving organism that could be studied and surveyed and have its disparate parts put together into a new whole, provided the theoretical foundation for a new way of thinking about the city's built environment. His proposal that a city could be studied organically in order to identify all its working parts was taken up by an emerging generation of town planners who adopted a top-down approach to ordering the city that "assumed social problems might be solved by manipulating the physical built environment."[1] Once the city was surveyed to obtain all facts of its situation, trained male professionals could then diagnose the city's diseased parts, on the basis of which men could plan how to eradicate the disease. Systematic planning could construct a new city. *Survey, diagnose, plan* became the new mantra of professional men.

The survey, diagnose, and plan approach, however, was undertaken within basic economic and cultural assumptions about the purpose of the city and the role of the people in it. The men who began reconstructing the urban built environment by the end of the nineteenth century were seeing the city's diseased parts as impeding the smooth functioning of a capitalist economy. According to Richard Dennis, creative destruction meant eradicating the "undesirable, archaic, or anachronistic elements of the old urban morphology."[2] As Max Page argues, it was through the "literal, physical destruction and creation of new buildings and natural landscapes" that we can see how "capitalism inscribed its economic and social processes into the physical landscape of the city, and then into the minds of city people."[3] For geographer Michael Batty, creative destruction and the human organism are comparable: "Just as the human body renews itself continuously through its cells, cities are continually renewing their fabric as they adjust to the wider economic context, changing preferences in location and travel, and of course, technological innovation."[4] An essential element of the construction of the patriarchal city, as the following chapters demonstrate, was the idea of creative destruction to meet economic needs.

Page also describes the urge to creative destruction as the tension between "stability and change; between the notion of 'place' versus undifferentiated, developable 'space.'" Here he draws on the ideas of French sociologist Henri Lefebvre. Space, according to Lefebvre, is mutable; it is functional and can be produced and reproduced. Space signified that the city was provisional; place, on the other hand, signified permanence.[5] The work of Octavia Hill violated this notion that the city must be constantly reproducing space to the detriment of place. Her focus on place provided another excuse to dismiss her as romantic and unrealistic, out of step with male modernism.[6] Moreover, Hill's system of female housing managers brought more women into the streets of some of London's worst neighborhoods, where they functioned outside male control.

Dolores Hayden reminds us that *place* is a slippery term, yet she and feminist scholars such as Doreen Massey argue that place signifies something more permanent than mutable space. Place encompasses a sense of belonging, of being in place, not merely as a resident of the city but as someone who owns the place and, conversely, is not out of place. As Massey argues, "Particular ways of thinking about space and place are tied up with . . . particular social constructions of gender relations." For women in the city, the problem is that "the space of modernity . . . becomes an abstract product of the masculine gaze, [and] place retains (problematically) feminised connotations of being and belonging." The tension between the two concepts, as Elizabeth Wilson concludes, is that women are constantly being made to feel out of place in the city because urban space is continuously identified as male space. "Women have lived out their lives on sufferance in the metropolis."[7]

Once men conceptualized the city as mutable, organic space rather than a place of belonging, houses became just pieces of that overall developable space. The focus on housing as an aspect of place that had allowed women such as Octavia Hill to play a public role in housing reform and to create what Elizabeth Darling calls women's volunteer housing sector would be shunted aside by the modernist concepts of space and creative destruction.[8] Late-nineteenth-century activist women had engaged in what Ruth Livesey terms that "endless process of marking place . . . through daily practice at street level."[9] When the professionally trained men of the early twentieth century steered reform efforts away from that concept of the city as a place of daily experience, toward promoting broad-based spatial reconstruction, scientific planning became the key to eradicating overcrowding and congestion and preserving the city for economic growth. Moving people—mainly families, and thus women—out of the central city, or as in Toronto and Chicago, filling in the city's empty outer spaces for middle-class residence, men rejected women's ideas about the city as a place with residents' daily needs as the city's priority.

The writings of Ebenezer Howard and John Ruskin had catalyzed earlier reform movements that rejected the large city in favor of smaller, self-contained areas. Now, the writings and publications of the new professional men envisioned the organic city as a mutable space whose physical reconstruction could minimize social problems and maximize economic development. Patrick Geddes, Patrick Abercrombie, Thomas Adams, John Nolen, Frank Lloyd Wright, Daniel Burnham, and Raymond Unwin, among others, spread their ideas quickly through the Anglo-Atlantic world, often speaking on both continents, presenting plans for these cities, and articulating the justifications for their ideas and plans. They also disseminated their ideas through new publications such as the *Irish Architect and Craftsman*, *Canadian Architect and Builder*, the British *Town Planning Review*, the American *Municipal Review*, or Unwin's massive 1909 tome *Town Planning in Practice*. They organized transnational conferences on town planning.[10] Since training in the new scientific disciplines was reserved for men, the voice of authority on cities remained male; the systematic plan was articulated in the male voice; town (urban) planning was a male discipline.

Since the men leading the new planning movement were working within culturally historical, socially constructed ideas about the proper roles and behaviors of men and women, it was virtually inevitable that reconstructing the urban built environment through planning would become, as Barbara Hooper argues, "a participant in new forms of social control directed at women."[11] Planning thus fits into Allan Johnson's argument that a core value of a "male dominated, male identified, and male centered" patriarchal culture is control and domination in almost every area of human existence.[12] Every proposed urban plan, every decision made about what, where, why, and how the city's built environment would be reconstructed intended to reserve access to urban power, resources, and public space to men. It is important to understand that this was not a conspiracy. Rather, it was the continuation of what Helen Meller identifies as the consequence of historical cultural values. Those cultural values lumped women and children together as belonging in the private domestic space of the family. The public spaces of the city were for men and were to be planned for men.[13]

Men in each city thus proposed detailed plans for revitalizing the city. Before World War I, each city succeeded to a different extent in imposing new planning, but all proposals demonstrated the truth of Hooper's and Meller's arguments. Then the crises of World War I and its aftermath reinvigorated the justification for carrying out new plans. Finally, World War II presented the next phase of this drive to plan the city as a gendered developable space. Each chapter in Part II examines the four cities separately to examine how the men in each city worked to plan and construct the patriarchal city.

5

LONDON

To Cure the Diseased Organism

In matters civic, as well as in simpler forms of science, it is from
facts surveyed and interpreted that we gain our general ideas of the
direction of Evolution, and even see how to further this; since from
the best growths selected, we may rear yet better ones.

—PATRICK GEDDES, *Cities in Evolution* (1915)

The mass of evidence shows that the British housing problem has
been cruelly over-simplified. Good housing is not the absence of
slums any more than good health is just the absence of disease. Slum
clearance in Britain is not merely a question of substituting a clean
box for a dirty one. It is not a problem which can be solved by better
plumbing.

—ELIZABETH DENBY, *Europe Rehoused* (1944)

Englishwoman Elizabeth Denby (1894–1965) held a certificate in social
science from the London School of Economics. She began her career
in housing development in 1923 as organizing secretary of the Kensington Housing Association and Trust, where she dealt directly with potential tenants and campaigned for housing reform. Denby represented opposite
ends of the spectrum from Patrick Geddes. While Geddes looked down at
the city from on high—literally and symbolically from his Edinburgh Outlook Tower—Denby experienced the daily lives and problems of urban residents. Geddes theorized the city; Denby lived it. The preceding quotes may
be from three decades apart, but the perspectives of Geddes and Denby demonstrate the ongoing, gendered contestation over the shaping and goals of
the city's built environment.

These gendered perspectives on the city were so deeply embedded that
they were never able to coexist. Because men had the power to impose their
priorities on the city's construction, and among their priorities was to recreate the privatized home with women removed from the city's public
spaces, women's ideas and activities were constantly deflected by men who
believed that women should play biologically determined and separate roles
in the city. From John Ruskin, to Ebenezer Howard, to Geddes and his fellow

professionals and future disciples, there was no possibility that urban plans would do anything other than continue to "put women, children, and the family first under a benign patriarchy," as Helen Meller so eloquently puts it.[1] This "benign" patriarchy was men's attempt to rationalize their wishes by elevating women's status to that of the domestic goddess. Hence, we have Geddes's assertion in *Cities in Evolution* that his envisioned city would see women again "effective in the kitchen and inspiring in the hall."[2] Such ideas about proper gender roles propelled planning of the Anglo-Atlantic city for decades and consolidated a patriarchal city.

EARLY PLANNING IN LONDON

The crucial role that transit concerns would play in planning London became apparent in 1903 with the appointment of an official Royal Commission on London Traffic. The testimony before the commission demonstrated that men accepted the Geddesian idea of the city as an organic space to be surveyed and diagnosed. From their own sense of professional expertise, the men appearing before the commission asserted that the city, as currently constituted, impeded its natural function as a proper economic system. It is thus not surprising that the commission was organized by men for whom transit was the city's defining problem.

Traffic and Transit

Previously, the 1884–1885 Royal Commission on Housing had identified housing as the city's worst problem. The 1903 commission decisively shifted focus to transportation, especially roads, as the key to reforming the built environment and to creating a modern city. Many of the men who had testified to the earlier housing commission had been voluntary housing reformers, religious figures, and major property owners. The men testifying before the 1903 commission, instead, were largely professionally trained architects, surveyors, engineers, and railway developers.[3] They wielded all the new terminology of modernism to promote their ideas.

Transportation for these men was the new key to establishing London's economic growth, efficiency, and financial stability. Freeing the city streets from congestion, they argued, would ensure the city's economic development. Central-area streets had to be widened and new main thoroughfares slashed through the city. More viaducts like the 1869 Holburn Viaduct to carry railroad traffic over the streets had to be constructed. Streets had to be cleared of street sellers and costermongers. Tramways had to be built along important thoroughfares.[4] The estimated 1.5 million poorer residents currently living in the congested so-called slum areas of the city needed to be displaced so that the new projects could commence. These men saw slums as composed of deteriorated and unsanitary tenements, areas of disease, not communities of people. Disease bred inefficiency. According to the commission, "prolonged journeys to and from their work, as well as residence in crowded localities amid unhealthy surroundings, seriously impair the efficiency of the population, considered merely as agents of production." Besides, the men declared, the price of land in the center made it financially impossible to build new housing there.[5]

The men advising the commission sought to demonstrate their professional expertise and ideas about the modern city. Henry M. Bates, the principal clerk of the London Corporation's Health Department, testified that widening streets would "assist [workers'] locomotion and moving about when they came in, and we could get rid of a great many of the workingmen's dwellings, or workmen would prefer to go out and live, if they could get easily into the city."[6] For Andrew Young, valuer to the LCC, there was greater value to putting new streets where property was currently inexpensive because such new streets would raise the value of the surrounding land. For Maurice Fitzmorris, the chief engineer to the LCC, new streets and widenings were the most important municipal improvements. He advocated new east-west and north-south corridors slashed through the city.[7] Charles Booth declared that better locomotion was the "only way that the evils arising from the insufficiency and dearness of house accommodation could be provided." Booth also claimed that "such shiftings involve very little hardship to a population most always on the move . . . a better home than his own becoming available for the man whose bad home needs to be destroyed." In addition, decentralizing manufacturers would increase locomotion and prevent street crowding.[8] Alfred Willis, director of the Baker Street and Waterloo Railway, assured the commission that with new transportation systems the working man would no longer see the city as the market for his labor.[9]

Transportation planning as the key to reconstructing the city also presented an opportunity for these men to advocate for their own professional expertise. The three men who constituted the advisory board of engineers to the commission were Sir John Wolfe-Barry and Sir Benjamin Baker, both past presidents of the Institution of Civil Engineers, and William Barclay Parsons, chief engineer to the New York City Board of Rapid Transit Railroad Commissioners. They recommended two new major arteries: west to east connecting Bayswater Road to Whitechapel; and north to south, connecting Holloway with Elephant and Castle. Each artery was to be 140 feet wide and contain four tramway lines. They also advocated new viaducts from Blackfriar's Bridge to Farringdon Street and Waterloo Bridge to Wellington Street and a sunken road passing under Piccadilly to relieve congestion there.[10] The civil and electrical engineer Stephen Sellon suggested that no vehicles (including those making deliveries at markets) be allowed to stop on any London street. The streets, he testified, should be for "nothing but locomotion," and not for carrying on business. He wanted no loading and unloading of vehicles—which he called a "misuse of the roads for private trading"—crawling and standing cabs, lampposts, or street trading. He labeled the Spitalfields Market a prime example of private trading causing street congestion.[11]

Few men went as far as Sellon to suggest that streets should be used only for locomotion. But their overwhelming emphasis on speeding up transit reflected the growing perception of professional men that a modern city needed some type of time-space compression that could be achieved with technological innovation. Future prime minister Arthur Balfour declared during a debate in the House of Commons that "the remedy of the great disease of overcrowding . . . is a question simply of time and space, and nothing else. . . . [Y]ou must trust to modern invention and modern improvements in locomotion for abolishing time." He added, "I sometimes dream that in addition to railways and tramways, we may see great highways constructed for rapid motor traffic, and confined to motor traffic, which would have the immense advantage . . . of taking the workman from door to door."[12] According to David Rooney, abolishing time and shrinking space through "science, technology, industry, and progress" were "powerful techno-scientific tropes."[13] In this scenario, locomotion would become the means to decentralize the population while making it possible for male workers to reach their jobs. What was to become of women isolated into the periphery did not concern these men, except that they should remain in the home.[14]

The commission agreed with LCC clerk George L. Gomme that the city now needed large planning schemes with extensive street improvements. It concluded that transportation was the cure for all the ills of the diseased organism. It was imperative, the commission concluded, "in the interests of public health and public convenience, and for the prompt transaction of business, as well as to render decent housing possible, that the means of locomotion and transportation in London and its adjacent districts should be improved."[15] The commission advocated appointing an official and permanent Board of Traffic to monitor all transportation systems in London, make recommendations for future developments, and contribute to formulating a comprehensive plan for London. The commission's report made London, as planning and transportation scholar Russell Haywood concludes, "a test bed for the development and application of planning thought about relationships between transport and urban form in the important formative period between 1900 and 1947."[16]

When the conservative London Municipal Reform League wrested control of the LCC from the progressives in 1907, Charles Booth led a delegation of thirty prominent men, including Sir David Barbour, chair of the former Royal Commission, to the council, asking it to petition the government to appoint such a traffic board.[17] In the meantime, a newly constituted special traffic branch of the Board of Trade extended the work of the previous Royal Commission. The traffic branch's 1908 report recapitulated the commission's work and supported all its proposals but brought it up to date by providing additional information from its own survey of transportation details across the intervening five years.[18] The London Municipal Reform League called for persistent and systematic planning:

> Future improvements should be effected, not haphazard and piecemeal as has been the case hitherto, but in relation to the general needs of London, and in pursuance, so far as possible of a fixed policy, which should be followed with persistent effort over a great length of time. Such a policy can only be based upon a plan which must, of necessity, involve prolonged and minute consideration.[19]

Architect Arthur Crow sketched out a massive transportation plan for London proposing a new main east-west artery of ten miles slashed through many crowded neighborhoods. The road would be 225 feet wide—considerably larger than the 140-foot-wide arteries recommended by the Royal Commission's advisory board—including a double avenue separated by a central boulevard with a double tramway running along it. He admitted that his plan would "unfortunately" tear down some buildings that were part of community life in Holburn, Finsbury, and Paddington, among other areas, as he traced his new road, section by section, through the city. The people and institutions of Holborn would be especially hard hit by Crow's plan.

> Farringdon Road is crossed and the new avenue then follows the Clerkenwell Road, which is widened on its northern side as far as Gray's Inn Road. This widening involves the removal of St. Peter's Italian Church, the Italian Evening School in Little Saffron Hill, the "Field Lane Refuges, Ragged School and Mission" in Vine Street, several blocks of "Victoria Dwellings," and "Cavendish Buildings," as well as several belonging to the Artizans,' Labourers' and General Dwellings Company, Limited, at the junction of Rosebery Avenue and Gray's Inn Road. . . . The cross streets leading to Warner Street, including Little Saffron Hill, Back Hill, Eyre Street Hill, and Vine Street, with the back streets known as Summer's Street, Baker's Row, Great and Little Bath Street and the nest of courts and alleys (mostly closed) would be cleared away.[20]

Despite his occasional expressions of regret for the destruction, Crow cavalierly dispatched people's housing, community landmarks, and the small shops and businesses that served and employed the neighborhoods. He insisted, rather, that "it becomes year by year more imperative to leave no stone unturned which may assist in fostering and promoting the commercial side of our communal life."[21] The traffic branch's own report recommended 99.9 miles of new roads and 25 miles of improved roads.[22]

As Crow and the traffic board were crafting their schemes, Parliament passed the Housing, Town-Planning, Etc., Act (1909), which removed control over existing streets from borough councils and made the LCC the local planning authority for London. Now the LCC could initiate planning measures in accordance with the Local Government Board (LGB) for all unoccupied land in the city. According to William Thompson, who chaired the LCC in 1910–1911, the act established "the important principle that the use of land for building purposes shall be subject to control in the public interest" and gave the council the power to administer the act.[23] The objects of the plan, he pointed out, were defined as "securing proper sanitary conditions, amenity, and convenience in connections with the laying out and use of the land and of any neighboring lands." To make certain that these vague objects were understood to encompass a broad range of responsibilities, the act specified "Streets, Buildings, Open Spaces (private and public), the Preservation of Objects of Historic Interest or National Beauty, Sewerage, Drainage, Lighting, Water Supply, Rights of Way, Obstructive Buildings, and any consequent works to the foregoing as being within the scope of a town plan."[24] The plan mandated that the LCC confer with the public and borough officials about any plans regarding all of the above and compensate landowners. Nevertheless, the LCC would thenceforth exercise planning power in London. Despite its official name, the act had little to do with housing beyond the earlier Housing of the Working-Classes acts. The essence of the 1909 act was its authorization for local authorities to draw up town plans for land not currently built on.[25]

Professionals Take Control

London men were neither content to wait for the LCC to act on its own nor satisfied with planning only on unbuilt land. To take more control, they constituted other groups and started new publications to promote their ideas of professional scientific town planning. The National Housing and Town Planning Council (NH&TPC), a consolidation of two earlier housing reform organizations, was now led by men such as Raymond Unwin, Henry Aldridge, and William Thompson. These men and others organized international planning conferences and constructed traveling town planning exhibits that they carried through the United Kingdom. At the 1910 Conference on Town Planning, convened by the Royal Institute of British Architects (RIBA), Arthur Crow again called for moving people out of London by building new roads and providing cheap transit. He provided maps to depict his ideas for constructing new east-west and north-south arteries (picking up the recommendations of the London traffic branch) and presented a list of nineteen roads to be widened and new ones to be built. He also called for rail terminals to be extended twenty-eight miles out from the city center.[26] The RIBA, which had its own town planning committee, suggested eleven principal guidelines for town planning—not incidentally promoting a prominent role for architects. Five of the eleven guidelines focused on roads, streets, and traffic centers; another stressed that the "exact position for business and commercial areas is perhaps of more importance than for any others"; another advocated designing "appropriate centres for governmental, administrative, commercial or educational purposes."[27]

American architect and planner Daniel Burnham's presentation at the 1910 town planning conference not only focused on planning to eliminate street congestion; he explicitly connected the well-ordered city with manhood:

> The most significant aspect of this new phase of life in the United States lies in the kind of men who are actively engaged. They are the best and strongest men of affairs we have. . . . When a cry, almost universal, goes up for good order and its consequent beauty, when men everywhere begin to demand harmonious conditions of life, it means that the race has arrived at that stage of development which in an individual would be called manhood.[28]

Crow added his concern for the virility of the British race if planning were not to be implemented. "Apart from the commercial aspects of the case, there is a question of still greater importance to the community. I refer to the physique of the rising generation. . . . [L]et us not forget that a sturdy virile race must ever be the great bulwark of a nation's prosperity."[29]

The *Town Planning Review* (1910), based in the department of architecture and civic design at the University of Liverpool, then headed by S. D. (Stanley) Adshead (fellow, RIBA), provided a new venue from which professional men, especially architects, could advocate town planning. The publication invited submissions from all professionals concerned with town planning. During its first year, essays by Adshead and Patrick Abercrombie dominated the issues, but American architect Cass Gilbert and other associates of the RIBA also contributed articles. By 1914, a Town Planning Institute (TPI) had been formed with the Scots surveyor Thomas Adams as its first president. In one of his first addresses to the institute, Adams emphasized that roads and transportation were the bedrock of planning; he wanted a comprehensive plan for London and seven of his nine essential elements for formulating a plan involved roads:

There is much inter-relation between the economic questions connected with the development of land and those relating to the provision of various classes of highway, ranging from the wide arterial
road to the narrow domestic cul-de-sac; between questions relating
to modes of transit and those relating to the width, position, and
alignment of streets; and between questions relating to the height,
character, and elevation of buildings and those relating to the width
of streets on which they have a frontage.[30]

Despite the focus of Adshead and the *Town Planning Review* on civic
design, not all architects were satisfied that the right kind of planning was
being done. Frustrated by the "inadequacies of the London county and borough councils in overseeing the future planning and development of the
capital," these men founded another organization, the London Society
(1912), to stress that planning was also the management of public taste and
that London should be planned "into a grand, neo-classical space of boulevards and monuments." This society wanted to consolidate planning work
by attracting as many professional men as possible. Adshead, Adams, and
Unwin joined, as did Geddes until he left for India in 1914. Representatives
from the RIBA, surveyors institutions, the NH&TPC, and the Garden Cities
and Town Planning Association sat on the society's council. "Having set
themselves up as self-appointed co-ordinators of the planning of London,"
according to one assessment, "members of the Society expected that a solution to many of the city's environment and amenity problems would naturally follow."[31] By 1913, the group was publishing its own review, the *Journal
of the London Society*. Through this journal, the *Town Planning Review*, the
RIBA *Transactions* of planning conferences, and a plethora of other professional organs published by engineers, surveyors, and builders, professional
men spread their gospel of planning throughout the Anglo-Atlantic World.
Dublin called on the British men for help, Thomas Adams moved to Canada,
and American and Canadian planners added their own publications to
the mix.

The professional men and their organizations were never able to get everything that they wanted in an overall plan for London. Although they
worked with the LCC, led delegations to Parliament and ministers, and attempted to convince the general public that their proposals should be implemented, the five years between the 1909 Act and entry into war were too
short to accomplish much. Nevertheless, these men had set themselves up to
be the voice of planning once the war was over. In 1914, Unwin was appointed to the newly created post of Chief Town Planning Inspector of the
LGB, which oversaw any actions proposed under the 1909 Act. The men of
the London Society spent the war years preparing "proposals for improving
the great roads of London" as suggested by the traffic branch.[32] Unwin di-

rected the preparation of this development plan; Adshead and Crow headed two of the six sections preparing the plan. The finished plan demonstrated three abiding planning principles for London's future development: thinking regionally, coordinating all road transportation, and planning done by experts according to their professional training. Unwin declared after the war that the plan was now "the standard plan for all who had to do with London improvements."[33]

Not to be outdone, the NH&TPC took advantage of the war's upheaval to propose plans for the war's aftermath. Henry Aldridge headed this group, which held a National Congress to Consider Home Problems after the War in April 1916. Its "Memorandum Relative to the Housing Preparedness Campaign of the NH&TPC" quoted the president of the LGB saying the previous year it would be a "black crime" if after all the suffering endured by the men at the front, the city "did nothing by way of preparing to ensure that when these men come home, they shall be provided for with as little delay as possible. To let them come home from the horrible water-logged trenches to something little better than a pigsty would be indeed criminal." In March 1918, the NH&TPC began to plan conferences to consider housing and town planning after the war and held its first conference that July. Such conferences, their prepared suggestions, the London Society development plan, and the assertions of groups of trained professional men that only they could rebuild London would put these men on the front lines of planning London following the war.[34]

Gender and Early Planning

By the end of the war, thus, women had been largely excluded from discussion or decisions about reconstructing the built environment. Women still had little access to the professional training that men now deemed the foremost criterion legitimating such participation. They did not belong to the various planning groups. These men also made it clear that work on the built environment was the job of men. Thomas Adams addressed the TPI in 1914 extolling the town planning act as something that creates "a new atmosphere and a new interest and breeds a new form of intellectual activity amongst our public men."[35] The men at the 1916 meeting claimed that "the chief feature of the great conference . . . was the fact that for the first time the chief range of interest of those concerned in the providing of housing accommodation was represented."[36] Put in the context of the declaration that same year of the president of the LGB, it would seem that it was all right for women to live in little better than a pigsty but not for the returning male warriors.

While men's public expressions tended to emphasize the need to make the built environment more efficient—"all congestion entails loss of time and money"; the "loss of time due to traffic delays was economically indefensible";

"good roads were a national asset of the greatest value"[37]—reengineering London's social and spatial configuration was at the heart of their plans. All schemes to create a more efficient built environment meant reconfiguring streets to limit them as socially usable spaces. Limiting road space for anything but vehicles, eliminating "refuges for pedestrians," and declaring that "almost the worst obstruction of all is the construction of public lavatories in the centre of open spaces or in congested thoroughfares through which there is much traffic" or that "every cabstand, refuge, and central standard for tramway or light purposes, and every stationary vehicle is a waster of road space" implied that streets should no longer be considered public gathering spaces.[38]

But a city's social reconstruction needed more than restricting the streets as social gathering spots. For many men, the home and its immediate surroundings had also to be reconfigured so that people could be content to stay in restricted places. Unwin was a leading advocate of such thinking. His ideas about community derived from his belief in the moral aesthetics of architecture and that social living could be planned through architecture. Living in bad or indifferent architecture, Unwin believed, left people unable to develop their own moral aesthetic. "A reciprocal and interactive relationship existed between the built environment and the community. The visual coherence of a place and a sense of community could be enhanced by the 'aesthetic control' of building materials, housing design, and layout."[39]

According to Unwin, a new form of social living could be achieved through town planning that produced good architecture:

> Though town planning powers will not change the individualistic impulses which prevail, they will for the first time make possible as adequate expression of such corporate life as exists. . . . [T]he more adequate expression of corporate life in the outward forms of the town will both stimulate and give fresh scope to the cooperative spirit from which it has sprung.[40]

For town planning to control how people lived, architects needed to have both aesthetic control for housing arrangements and the freedom to redesign the interiors of houses. Unwin told the 1910 Town Planning Conference that planners needed "to group our buildings into centres and to lay out much of the surrounding ground to be shared as recreation and pleasure grounds by the whole of the dwellers in this group."[41] Much of Unwin's designs for Hampstead are discussed in the previous chapter. Here it is necessary only to point out again that his vision of social living was one that clustered people into small groups where they would live and associate with that group rather than the larger city. It was also a vision for reengineering the domestic family life. As late as 1933, Unwin continued to emphasize good housing design for families. Speaking to the National Association of Building Societies, he encouraged builders to consider that "society was, and would long remain upon family life." There should be no letup in designing and building sufficient housing for every family, he told them.[42]

Tenement buildings, children's public play areas, lodging houses and transportation for female workers, and public facilities for women did not fit into Unwin's plans or those of other men. In one way or the another he and other professional men deemed such arrangements as detrimental to the English way of life. The social living ideas of Octavia Hill, her housing managers, Elizabeth Denby as we shall see, and other female housing activists sought ways for people, especially families, "to live in a 'modern' city" by addressing the practical "patterns of inhabitation." According to Meller, women's concerns included the following:

> How to find accommodation? How to improve on what has been found? How to bring up a family in the city and keep them all healthy? How to cope with economic vicissitudes and the vagaries of the labour market? How and where to go to buy things? How, with the technological revolutions in transport to even cross the road? . . . [A]nswers to all of them were circumscribed by the quality of the built environment.[43]

These people-centered questions reflected women's desires to make the city a home for all its residents in which people's daily experiences would be the center of attention of urban life.

Seeing the city as a home did not accord with the male vision of the city as a diseased, nonfunctioning, inefficient, congested organism. For the city to become a functioning and efficient organism, it had to be socially as well as spatially transformed through planning. With extensive and rapid tramway and electric railway systems in place, workmen would not need to live in the center city. Once families were cleared out of the city, tenements and dwellings in courts and alleys could be transformed into sites for business purposes. For Arthur Crow, living outside the city would produce "the clearer and purer mind, the greater mental vigour, and hence the greater capacity to produce works requiring thought and skill, and the greater power to produce works wrought out of muscle and sinew and bone."[44] The city, thus, would become an efficient space of production with more efficient workers. The private home on the periphery would produce the Geddesian imperative of an organic social harmony with women as the private reproducers of family and preservers of culture and men as the public producers of society.

Such "root and branch" approaches overwhelmed women's people-centered approach. Annie Hankinson, who worked with the Octavia Hill–

inspired Manchester Housing Company acknowledged that certain areas needed to be rooted out but pleaded for combining such work with a policy of making older city housing "habitable for people needing that class of accommodation at low rentals and near to their work."[45] She argued that economic exploitation resulted in bad housing:

> A living wage and an economic rent are two indispensable factors in any lasting housing reform; without these there can be no solid building up of a healthy independence and self-respect among the people housed and no solid security for the community that a sound financial basis will ultimately be attained. And how sorely this "living wage" is needed only those with close and intimate knowledge of the poor can testify.[46]

Hankinson feared that any people-centered approach was "in danger of being obscured by the larger more arresting movement for drastic clearance and rebuilding."[47]

But advocates of town planning were eager to apply their new professional tools to rationalize such destruction. As Richard Dennis observes, "once large-scale maps had been produced, revealing the narrowness or twistedness of streets and the disorderly layout of districts," city council members, engineers, and planners could imagine how they would redevelop these areas by remapping them into orderly geographic sections.[48] Charles Booth's mapping had made it possible to classify areas and people and thereby identify certain areas as slums. Planning could then eliminate whole areas.[49] Booth's maps, like large-scale geographic maps, looked down into the city from above without seeing the people who lived there. Octavia Hill, her female housing managers, and Hankinson saw the city on the ground, working personally to understand the needs of people. This street-level approach to understanding the city had brought more women into those streets, making both their ideas and their increasing public presence threats to the orderly vision of the city viewed from above.

Professional men quickly adopted the Geddesian survey method along with new precision mapping techniques. They wanted every city and town surveyed along five lines: situation, topography, and natural advantages; means of communication, land, and water; industries, manufacturers, and commerce; population; and town conditions. These survey methods promoted attention to the functionality of the city rather than to its social conditions.[50] The RIBA combined the civic survey with a recommended technical survey that would apply the new tools of mapping, including color-coding, to depict land ownership, value of land, new technological and service developments, poor and unsanitary areas, and "all features worth preserving, including well-grown trees." The RIBA, not surprisingly, recommended that the "architect's point of view" was desirable for assessing the reshaping of the city.[51]

Geddes's management of the civic survey was as gendered as his concept of women's role in the city. He sent both teams of male and female students to survey city neighborhoods, but gender determined their task. Men were to report on the quality of housing; women were "to record anything they thought interesting" in order to "learn about social engagement." Unlike the growing number of professional planners, Geddes did seek to include an understanding of social evolution, the interaction of people and place, as a factor in creating a good built environment. According to Meller, his organic vision included seeing "place and people progressing in an evolutionary way to greater perfection and happiness," but by dividing the survey between functional and social, giving the former task to men and the latter task to women, Geddes reinforced the prevailing gender ideas of men.[52] For most male professionals, the private and the instinctual played no role in a professional endeavor directed by male architects, engineers, surveyors, and politicians. When Abercrombie enthusiastically embraced the concept of the survey, he turned it into a professional tool and removed women totally from participating in surveying the city.

The 1909 Town Planning Act limited planning to developing areas, but London men were able to combine this power with powers of public health acts to justify decentralizing the working classes onto new developing lands and rebuilding the city center for business and monumentality. But the growing presence of working women in the city, whether middle- or working-class, complicated this desire. An expanding commercial consumer economy depended increasingly on women producing and shopping. More consumption meant more women in public. Women could not be banished altogether from public, but their access to public spaces could be controlled. Refusing to furnish public toilets for women was one means of exercising control.

Private Bodies in Public Spaces: Public Toilets

Moving through the city required access to toilet facilities if the city was to remain clean and sanitary. Men accessed toilets within elite private clubs, middle-class workplaces, working men's clubs, public houses, and public toilets built by the vestries and boroughs.[53] London public houses were especially numerous, convenient, and furnished with at least urinals. The *Surveyor and Municipal and County Engineer* had declared that "public urinals ought to be erected by the urban authority as a matter of convenience to the peripatetic portion of any community, and also to prevent nuisances being committed in improper places." The *British Architect* called a new men's underground lavatory in front of the Royal Exchange, around the base of the Duke of Wellington's statue, a "city improvement of a most important character."[54]

Until 1899, vestries and districts—on whose boards women had been eligible to serve—controlled provision of public services including public toilets, paying for them from the rates. Vestries had furnished public toilets for men, but most of them refused to do so for women. The few exceptions were generally those vestries where women served on the vestry boards.[55] When the vestries were dissolved in 1899 and replaced with twenty-eight metropolitan boroughs, which then controlled such decisions, women became ineligible to hold the new councillor positions. George Bernard Shaw was a lone male voice in calling for women to serve as councillors. He argued that they were needed in this capacity to help rectify women's unequal access to public toilets, including the fact that where they existed women always had to pay, while men had choices between free and paying facilities.[56]

The progressive former vestry of St. Pancras had built two public toilets for women. But when vestries were dissolved, in the new borough, women were unable to secure any more public toilets. When the St. Pancras borough did experiment with providing a wooden prototype of a women's public toilet in 1900, it provoked a backlash from the councillors and businessmen. Barbara Penner explores this case in detail, but consideration of it here helps illuminate how it was tied to ideas about the built environment and decisions about women's access to public spaces.[57]

This temporary wooden prototype was located on Park Street, almost directly opposite the existing public men's toilet at the intersection with Camden High Street. Businessmen, tradesmen, and male residents denounced the women's toilet as an affront to public decency and a damage to their economic well-being. A semi-organized protest ensued in which, as recounted a few years later by George Bernard Shaw,

> every omnibus on the Camden Town route, every tradesman's cart owned within a radius of two miles, and most of the rest of the passing vehicles, including private carriages driven to the spot on purpose, crashed into that obstruction with just violence enough to produce an accident without damage. . . . [T]he joke soon caught on, and was kept up for fun by all and sundry.[58]

The structure was hit an "incredible forty-five times," and that put an end to any permanent women's toilet.[59]

By knocking over the wooden prototype, men were able to claim that its location would be a nuisance to traffic and trade, despite the fact that a men's public toilet, as well as a pub with men's facilities, stood directly across the street. Yet the arguments men made at the subsequent council meeting demonstrate that their response was rooted in male ideas about women's use of public spaces. The men argued that a women's public toilet would "spoil a most important thoroughfare and seriously depreciate the character and value of property in the immediate vicinity."[60] A women's public toilet would symbolize women's rights to be wherever, and whenever, they wanted in the city. Their expressions against that public toilet were gendered notions of women's appropriate behavior. One opponent claimed that 90 percent of the women passing through the spot lived in the area and thus would use facilities at home. Another councillor quipped, reportedly to much laughter, that a "suitable house" could be found for the "use of [other] ladies." Still another opponent decreed that "ladies" out shopping would not be able to endure the sight of this toilet, ignoring the fact that women had been passing the men's toilet for several years. A more vitriolic opponent declared a woman's public toilet an "abomination" and that any women supporting such a structure "so far 'forgot their sex' [they] should not have anything provided for them at all." The reference to a "suitable house" clearly associated a women's public toilet with a brothel.[61] Women were expected either to use private facilities in department stores, to stay at home and not be out in public, or at the least not stay in public spaces for too long.[62] In addition, as lower-class women were considered the most disorderly, men also protested that public toilets would be used by flower sellers and street women. Men's advocacy of confining women's toilets to London's department stores had a triple purpose: it would keep so-called respectable women inside the stores rather than on the streets; it would encourage female consumerism "organized around male retail business interests";[63] and it would discourage the so-called less respectable women, who did not frequent the department stores, to stay off the streets.

Legally barred from public office, women had to continue agitating for public toilets through women's organizations. A Ladies' Sanitary Association had been arguing for women's public toilets, and in 1884 a Ladies Lavatory Company had opened one in Oxford Street "for ladies who had to spend the whole day in London."[64] The Union of Women's Liberal and Radical Associations of the Metropolitan Counties, claiming to represent "four thousand working-class women in and around London," tried to convince men to provide one free facility for women in every vestry.[65] Later, the Women's Municipal Party would remind the boroughs that they had the power to provide public toilets, which the women not only wanted but wanted to be free. The WMP also demanded that women have the right to serve on the borough councils to enforce such powers.[66] But women's demands were consistently rebuffed. A 1928 survey by London's medical officer of health found that London had furnished a total of 4,541 toilet accommodations—urinals, stalls, and water closets—throughout London for men and only 846 accommodations for women.[67] Nevertheless, the medical officer asserted that "sensitive women" found "the very public nature of

entrances on busy thoroughfares" a drawback to their use. Women, according to him, preferred railway station toilets because they were more private.
He did concede that it was unfair that women would always be charged to
use public facilities when men were not. One potential resolution for this
circumstance, he recommended, would be for "some engineer to design a
female equivalent to the male urinal" so that women would not have to
pay.[68] (See Figure 5.1 for the women's toilet that was finally installed at that
St. Pancras intersection.)

Figure 5.1 Camden High Street with Mother Redcap Pub in background and women's
underground lavatory, London, 1930. (Courtesy of the London Metropolitan Archives,
Image 106696, available at https://collage.cityoflondon.gov.uk/quick-search?q=106696.)

PLANNING THE PRIVATE HOME

"Homes for Heroes"

If London's leaders and professional men were not enthusiastic about providing women with public facilities, they were keen to provide new housing for the men returning from the war. In 1917, the LGB appointed a committee to study the problems of housing for the working classes and make recommendations for postwar building. Its report and recommendations to a great extent reflected the views of its prominent member Raymond Unwin. Named for its chairman, John Tudor Walters, this Tudor-Walters report became the bible of postwar construction of council housing estates.[69] Its adopted phrase, "home for heroes," was shorthand for Prime Minister Lloyd George's promise to provide for the heroes who won the war. While such a campaign undoubtedly reflected a social unrest among the working classes, its gendered component has been largely ignored in the literature on this campaign.[70] Designating new housing projects as homes for heroes allowed professional men to implement a new domesticity, a new way of social living, by redesigning house interiors to institutionalize the separation of private and public. The Tudor-Walters report proposed several interior design types, but whatever designs were proposed, they reflected little input from women, whose lives inside the home would be most affected. Moreover, beyond concerns about economizing in design, men's ideas about sexuality and morality were part of the discussion about appropriate interiors. The journalist T. P. Ritzema demanded that sexes be separated in bedrooms and bathrooms: "In houses without bathrooms 'males and females wash practically in the scullery exposed to each other. . . . [S]uch a habit does not tend to a natural delicacy of feeling, and the result is that subjects which should be sacred are common topics between the sexes.'"[71] At a conference of the NH&TPC, the king of England stressed the connection between housing and morality:

> It is not too much to say that an adequate solution to the housing question is the foundation of all social progress. . . . If a healthy race is to be reared it can be reared only in healthy homes: if infant mortality is to be reduced and tuberculosis to be stamped out, the first essential is the improvement of housing conditions; if drink and crime are to be successfully combated, decent, sanitary houses must be provided. If "unrest" is to be converted into contentment, the provision of good houses may prove one of the most potent agents in that conversion.[72]

Women tried to insert their voices into the house-planning process. The Women's Labour League (WLL) had spent several years trying to make the home a political issue from a woman's perspective. The league had demanded that female architects design new homes along lines desired by women. As early as 1913, the WLL had organized a conference for working women to discuss the type of homes they wanted.

> The focus for the detailed discussion in the first session was the demand for self-contained homes with sufficient water supply, a bathroom, a larder and scullery . . . discussion that was determinedly practical, considering matters which they felt male architects overlooked. . . . As important as this clear and detailed vision was the fact that all the papers in this session were given by a new recognised type of "expert": working women who had practical experience in running their own homes.[73]

One speaker at the conference made it clear that the working woman's home needed to provide a parlor (or living room), separate from the kitchen, because "however good your kitchen may be, you don't want always to be in it. I've never heard it suggested that people use an office or a workshop as a sitting-room, and the kitchen's our workshop."[74]

The WLL solicited opinions from the Women's Co-operative Guild, the Women's Municipal Party, the National Council of Women, Women Citizens' Associations, and various Women's Institutes. After holding over forty meetings and twenty-four conferences it produced *The Working Woman's House*, in which it declared that "unless the working woman's point of view is understood, no housing schemes can be really successful. From direct personal experience a housewife knows, in a way that no other sections of the community *can* know, the most pressing needs for the establishment of a healthy home life."[75] *The Working Woman's House* also demanded that more women be appointed to the local housing committees mandated by the 1919 act, and expressed doubts that "those who build only for profit will do any important work towards providing housing for the people."[76]

The Ministry of Reconstruction did organize a women's housing subcommittee composed of professional, middle-class, and working-class women (including one of the authors of the preceding publication). Its charge was to "examine houses and plans 'with special reference to the convenience of the housewife,'" and this subcommittee concurred with several of the WLL's demands. These women emphasized the need for a separate bathroom, a living room separate from the scullery, and a "regular and efficient hot water supply" because "the extra time, trouble, and expense involved when water must be heated in kettles and carried to the bath, wash tub or sink, is a serious addition to the housewife's burden." In all their recommendations, the women rejected the idea that the first consideration should be cost: "that in matters where the original money cost is weighed against such vital needs as the health and general well-being of the family, the latter must be our first consideration."[77] In part 3 of the report, the women criticized the minimum housing standards proposed by the LGB as "not compatible with the interests of the housewife," and they especially objected to the omission of a parlor from the plans. As Alison Ravetz points out, the men of the LGB were so offended that women questioned the board's house plans that they questioned "the women's ability, let alone right, to read its plans." The ministry published only a modified version of the women's report.[78]

The *Town Planning Review*'s review of the "Women's Housing Report to the Ministry of Reconstruction" on the one hand congratulated the women for suggesting new methods of cooking and heating water. On the other hand, the reviewer took them to task for not understanding that a large scullery with a large cooking range would be "an impossible arrangement unless other means are provided for heating the Living room." The reviewer most objected to women's recommendations for a large scullery because he wanted to isolate the scullery from the rest of the house: "As these ladies are very well aware, to provide a large scullery and put in it a large kitchen range is merely to encourage, even in a Parlour house, the Scullery to become the Living Room." The reviewer also declared that however good the recommendations might seem to the women, the worth of their suggested innovations such as communal hot water could not be verified by actual figures. The reviewer then dismissed the women for not understanding the needs of working women:

> We would also utter a word of warning against the tricky, ingenious, and amazingly complex suggestions which are constantly brought forward. Such, for example, as a hot-water apparatus which, firstly, can either be heated by gas or at the back of a kitchen fire; secondly, contains two storages for 5 quarts or 13 gallons. The complexities suggested by these alternative methods were probably grasped at once by the clear untroubled intellects of the ladies forming this Committee: but we wonder if they ever attempted to put themselves in the place of the working woman who is to use the house![79]

The reviewer was identified only by the initials L.P.A., but he was undoubtedly Abercrombie, whose given names were Leslie Patrick. Recognizing women as experts in designing homes because they lived and worked in them challenged the professional authority of men such as Abercrombie.

Despite one scholar's optimistic conclusion that once the issue was raised, "the nature of housework and its effects on women's physical and mental health could no longer be treated as private and rather trivial," women gained no immediate influence in the design and building of housing to meet their needs.[80] Since the 1919 act made the Ministry of Health responsible for housing and public health, with Unwin subsequently appointed the ministry's chief housing architect, this could hardly not have been the result. Unwin stressed harmony and rhythmical planning for all new housing, in which "a bedroom should be used more as a sitting room," and said that "one of the first things that ought to go out of the house was the washing, especially the rough 'sloppy' part." He declared that as "hundreds of thousands of houses [were] to be built," each would "be the home of family life for a hundred years."[81] In effect, Unwin and other professional men were planning private homes and not just housing. They intended to reconstruct family life with the woman at the center of it by designing the insides of houses along specific lines. In describing the ideal cottage, Unwin pronounced that "family life depended on one woman" so that houses could not be too large.[82] Such perspective, Clara Greed has argued, resulted in men feeling "perfectly justified in interfering in the internal design of the artisan's cottage, breaking down the internal divisions between the living room and parlour," and advocating placing the stove in the living room, among other internal designs that would give a woman no space of her own inside the house.[83]

Decentralization and Council Estates

The privatized home that men such as Unwin set out to construct could be accomplished only by decentralizing the population through planning, and this aim became another rationale for slum clearance. Rather than thinking about housing as a human need, professional men prioritized slum clearance and prioritized town planning for doing so. For C. M. (Charles Moyston) Lloyd, "town planning is not really a sub-division of the housing question, and it deserves a better fate than to be tacked on as a sort of tail to a Housing tract. . . . [I]t should be studied independently as a larger and profoundly important subject. . . . It ought to be regarded as one of the most urgent tasks of the Local Authorities."[84] The goal, as he told local authorities, was "not [to] follow the old reactionary Local Government Board by constantly insisting on 'central re-housing.'" He praised the policy of the Ministry of Health, which urged authorities to "inquire into the genuineness of claims that residence very near to the place of employment is essential, and not allow the life-long attachment of the slum dweller to his slum to override the general good."[85]

Once the LCC assumed authority to direct town planning, it adopted the policy of moving people out to new housing estates on the city's periphery. The London Society took a leading role in offering ideas about a new London. Various contributions to a published volume of essays, *London of the Future*, captured the abstract ideals of decentralization of population and fostering business and industry as principal goals of city planning. Unwin's essay demonstrated a continuity of thinking about the city across the decades among men even as their professions changed. Ruskin and Howard had wanted to reduce London's population. Unwin now advocated the same reduction: "I venture to suggest that London as a single aggregation of population is already far too large. . . . [W]e should look to the early arresting of such growth, and even to the possible diminution of the number of people already occupying the area of London itself." Dormitory towns on the periphery would separate home and work and collapse the time-space problem for workmen by coordinating the means of transport to ensure that their travel could be made in good time.[86] Adshead acknowledged that there might still be some room in central London to house working-class people who wished to live in town near to work. But he concluded that "central London is to-day no place of residence for the masses."[87]

Surveyor W. R. Davidge declared that "comparatively few Londoners live in houses of which they can be reasonably proud." He also disconnected home and work by declaring that the ideal home was "a place of which the housewife can be proud and to which the children can in after years look back with affection." The need for London was "undoubtedly for the small self-contained house . . . not in the centre of London, but on the outskirts" so that it was important for town planners to convince "the mass of the people that they can live farther from their work"—that it was not necessary for people to live in crowded tenements "in order that the bread-winner may be near his work."[88] Henry Aldridge continued to dismiss the idea that people should be rehoused near their work, specifically rejecting the European or American policy of erecting high tenements.[89]

In existing central city tenements, or block dwellings as they were generally called, working women could live near work rather than commute. Housing on the periphery not only added to that commute time; it deprived working women of close neighbors who might look after their children and deprived women who did not travel outside the home to work of close neighbors with whom to socialize during the day. In her study of time-space constraints, Mei-Po Kwan reveals how the choices of women with small children were particularly "disadvantaged in terms of job choices and location because of the space-time fixity of many child-care and household-serving tasks."[90]

In his essay on London housing, Davidge provided a typical series of maps and diagrams showing population distribution, costs of season ticket rates for London transit systems, and the proximity of railway stations within the various areas of London, all predicated on the abstract movement of men. His illustrations mapped the city without people. They display his objection to a dissatisfying aesthetic sensibility as he declared that "however useful or desirable a bay window might be, it appals [sic] one when repeated a hundred times in a hundred similar houses in a hundred similar streets." Housing had become an abstraction, mapped out in terms of density, distance, and rateable growth. While earlier photos of London streets and

housing had depicted women's public presence, standing in doorways, buying and selling, now Davidge erased women and focused solely on the aesthetics and abstraction of housing. The same contrast appeared in the before
and after photos of the Boundary Street area.[91] The self-contained house, on
the periphery, with its proud housewife inhabitant, would recreate the private-public separation of the built environment and simultaneously promote
the ideal of domesticity for women. As Marion Roberts puts it, "The provision of self-contained dwellings was seen as a method of preserving the sanc-
tity and purity of family life"—a sentiment that Davidge and Unwin, among
others, would undoubtedly have supported. Unlike some later feminist analyses, Roberts does not believe that the male proponents were necessarily
"making specific assumptions about gender roles" but rather that their "encouragement of a privatized family within a strictly managed housing project which forbade, among other things, certain types of homeworking for
women, presupposed that women would primarily take responsibility for the
domestic sphere."[92]

Roberts's analysis would seem to split hairs. When men assumed that
women would have all the responsibility for the domestic space, they were
making assumptions about gender roles. The women who compiled *The
Working Woman's House* had in fact offered a different focus on women and
women's lives beyond the house itself. Women, according to the report, were
overwhelmingly concerned with how they and their families would live in
decentralized estates and what such new housing developments would mean
for women. For instance, they wanted child care facilities near their homes,
saying, "It is not good for either mothers or children that the little ones
should always be under the care and within the sight and hearing of their
mothers. The nursery school supplies the need for both, giving freedom for
a few hours a day for the mother either to spend in her home or in other
concerns outside it, and giving to the children a better training both for
mind and body." The publication also pointed out that all women believed
that doing all the housework was a "great hardship," and that this "hardship
is being more and more felt by working women as their interest in affairs
outside their homes grows, and their desire for further education and the
widening of their outlook increases."[93] Wanting child care facilities and help
with housework signaled women's intentions to leave the home in order to
advance their own lives, which was not what the men promoting the self-
contained home on the periphery had in mind.

The Working Women's House demonstrated that women envisioned
housing according to the people-centered approach to daily life that women
had been promoting for years. When women received suffrage after the war,
the Women's Municipal Party urged women to elect women to the local
authorities who would be making decisions on housing, women, and children, believing that "surely women must have a voice on the councils that

are to decide the locality, the building, and the arrangement of their future homes." In appealing to women, the WMP spoke about civic responsibility, but they meant something different from most male professionals, who easily adopted Geddes's idea of the civic to their own ends. Women's sense of civic responsibility meant providing for people in "a more humane and a more personal system."[94] When the 1923 Housing Bill proposed to limit government monetary subsidies to only those smaller houses that lacked many of the amenities that women said they wanted in their homes, the Women's Co-operative Guild objected to this proposal's lack of attention to the reality of women's lives. "The woman's point of view in the planning of houses must be considered for it is the woman who will have to spend most of her life in the house attending to her domestic duties."[95]

Karen Hunt argues that the working women's initiatives, especially by Labour women, during and after the war were attempts to create a politics of daily life based on the home and to move the housing issue "from the private life to the public arena."[96] Such initiatives challenged existing gender relations, and if they had succeeded they would have opened new paths for women's broader public political voice. The WMP, headed by the Duchess of Marlborough and focused first on London, promoted similar objectives, although through its active political work. The WMP drew up political programs to put before all LCC and local authority candidates. It demanded many of the items that women had now been agitating for across the decades: more housing reform, free public lavatories for women, women's municipal lodging houses, the building of small houses on cleared slum lands, and an adequate supply of baths and wash houses in the city. The WMP wanted to "create a stronger civic feeling among women" and secure election of women to borough councils on which they were now eligible to serve.[97] In their pamphlet *Women and Municipal Work*, the WMP declared that

> local government is concerned with domestic and economic measures which affect the health, the education, the housing—in fact, the general welfare of the family. It deals with such questions as the health of mothers and babies, the sanitation of the home and streets, the inspection of foodstuffs and milk, and the appointment of health visitors and sanitation inspectors. Can anyone deny that these are matters which directly concern the housewife and the mother?

The pamphlet castigated men's "lack of common sense in the adoption of economy," apparently meaning on what endeavors they decided to spend or not spend money.[98] The WMP's *Third Annual Report* juxtaposed the infant mortality rate by borough against the number of municipally provided infant welfare centers. Of the twenty-nine boroughs (including the City), only eleven had municipal infant centers, while the infant mortality rate per

1,000 births ranged from a low of 64 in Chelsea to a high of 142 in Shoreditch. Mothers in every borough except the City and Greenwich had to rely on voluntary centers staffed mainly by women.[99]

Into the 1920s and 1930s, other London women continued their voluntary people-centered approach to housing. Irene Barclay and Evelyn Perry worked for the St. Pancras House Improvement Society Limited (1924), which was building new housing in the Somers Town area. Anne Lupton worked with the Fulham House Improvement Society.[100] The work of Elizabeth Denby on housing went almost unnoticed in discussions of the built environment until her contributions to housing were resurrected by Elizabeth Darling. Denby's work with the Kensington Council of Social Services located on Portobello Road in north Kensington was in a poor area of the city virtually untouched by postwar housing reform. Denby then worked for two new organizations, the Kensington Housing Association (1925) and the Kensington Housing Trust (1926), both groups run by women. House Improvement Societies were generally public utility societies that either took over the management and improvement of existing rundown buildings or built and managed some new buildings inside the city.[101]

As Darling notes, Denby's work, and by extension that of other women in the housing societies, embodied the social philosophy that a significant element of urban reform was to assist people "to develop as social beings and enable them to become citizens who took an active part in civic life."[102] For Denby, housing estates on the periphery were socially isolating for their inhabitants. She also believed that all new or rehabilitated housing schemes had to focus on the daily lived experiences of people. Social centers, nursery schools, and playgrounds as well as well-equipped kitchens had to be part of any housing schemes. As Darling also notes, Denby was "a confirmed urbanist [whose] ultimate goal was to keep people in the city and thus limit suburban sprawl."[103] Barclay and Perry, in their 1929 survey of housing in Southwark, focused on the need to redevelop that area, not merely to clear it and move people out. According to their findings, almost half of the families currently living there could not afford to live in council estates, so moving them out was not an option. The women wanted "new flats to high standards with spaces for gardens and playgrounds" built in the area.[104]

PLANNING THE DECENTRALIZED PATRIARCHAL CITY

With the few exceptions of these female housing activists, and the Home Improvement Societies that worked in the city's poorer areas, by the mid-1920s a people-centered approach to the city had been decisively rejected in favor of a top-down centralized version of creative destruction in which housing was just one element of a well-planned city. Yet the decentralization project was constantly beset with problems. Many working people could afford neither the higher rents on the estates nor the cost of travel into work. Along with giving preference to Londoners who had done war service, the LCC in 1919 had made qualification for housing in their new estates dependent on "an income five times greater than the total of rent, rates and fares" and demanded that prospective tenants demonstrate a record of cleanliness and punctuality of previous rent payments.[105] The new housing estates were often constructed without necessary amenities for daily life for the "decanted" (Denby's term).[106] The Norbury estate outside the county boundary to the south contained 716 houses in 1922 but only four shops.[107] The reports on development of the St. Helier estate, intended to accommodate forty thousand to fifty thousand people, described it as a "transference of part of London's overcrowded population to the outer fringes" and assured the public that the area would be convenient because the "City and South London Railway is only half a mile from the north-west boundary."[108] Assessments such as this were predicated, as Greed asserts, on the male workers' travel needs: home to work to home. Moving women out of the city assumed they would remain in private at home.[109]

In her collection of memories of East End residents who were moved out to the estates, Gilda O'Neill recounts women's sense of being uprooted from a community into something foreign, even if they acknowledged that their material conditions were better:

> We lived in rows of terraced houses with just upstairs and downstairs, and a few with basements [airys or areas], wedged close together. . . . We were much less private than we are today, but it built in us a feeling of comfortable community. . . . There was a neighbourliness and readiness to help those in need, from the simple cup of sugar to helping a family who had lost their home because of a fire.[110]

But beyond missing this type of community, much of a woman's previous daily life had been in the streets. There they had talked, socialized, and watched each other's children playing outside:

> It was how you passed a few pleasant hours. You'd have a talk and a laugh. Better than sitting indoors by yourself while the old man was up the pub and the kids were out mucking about in the street. . . . In the 1920s it was a wonderful experience living in the East End—you lived outside. . . . [W]e were all out in the streets, including the children, till late at night.[111]

But children playing in the streets, women congregating there, and streets used as public gathering places threatened anticongestion schemes and the search for urban order. No one forgot the dirt, disease, hunger, and cramped living conditions of the old East End. They were not wistful for returning to those conditions, but when that first generation of displaced Londoners measured living on the more anonymous council estates against the lost community feeling of the East End, they believed that they had lost something valuable in their daily lives, especially the women:

> So many people thought they were moving to little palaces when they moved out. They were going to have a fitted kitchen, with lovely hot water and central heating, which they'd never had before. In their terraced houses they'd had an outside toilet and a scullery. Them people died when they moved. They'd got nothing. What can you do in your palace? You can cook a dinner, you can go to the inside toilet, you can be warm. But you ain't got nothing. You can't sit at your door, sit there shelling peas, talking to people.[112]

Some eastenders even managed to return. "Moving to Dagenham was the worst day's work I ever did. It was a lovely little place, the house, but I didn't know a soul. It was lonely. No friendliness. I tried, but it wasn't like living up home. . . . I was glad to get back. Got myself an exchange."[113]

In fact, many people refused to move out to the estates. LCC chair Lieutenant-Colonel Cecil Levita complained in 1928 that there were empty houses on some estates. The problem was that "only 5 percent of the people either could or would leave the conditions in which they were living. They could not make the people go. In a number of cases where they cleared the people out they wanted to go back, and they did go back."[114]

In 1936, when Denby became the first woman to address a session of the RIBA, her speech titled "Rehousing from the Slumdwellers' Point of View" was not what the men wished to hear. Denby emphasized how even people who could qualify for housing complained about the expense of commuting to work from remote locations. She pointed out that beyond this expense, her interviews with people who had been rehoused on council estates revealed complaints that the estates lacked both cheap shopping centers and local tradespeople to extend credit in hard economic times—a common practice in older central city neighborhoods. She reported that her interviewees were "overwhelmingly in favour of some form of development which houses the people nearer to their work and nearer to the companionship of the centre of town." RIBA president Percy Edward Thomas bristled that he could not "imagine any mere man having the courage to stand up here and tell us that the work of our architects and social reformers is in the wrong direction."[115]

Professionalizing Patriarchy

In his inaugural address after becoming the first professor of urban planning at University College London in 1914, ironically titled "The Democratic View

of the Town Planner," Adshead articulated the patriarchal relationship between the planner and the public. He declared that the town planner "should
not only look to the convenience of the community, but also be dictator of
the arts, leader of fashion in building, and arbiter in matters pertaining to
architectural character and style." The town planner—always a *he*—should
be "able to inspire the inhabitants of a town, to excite their ambitions, and to
lead them to finer achievement, and fire their imaginations with the ideals
of a nobler life."[116]

By the mid-1920s, Adshead's ideas were being institutionalized as town
planning became a subject of study at universities. New male professionals—architects, engineers, and surveyors—were educated to prepare "widely-
considered schemes," as Adshead asserted at a 1924 town-planning conference and exhibit of plans prepared by students at University College London.
The conference opening address celebrated Great Britain's leadership in
"carrying out big housing schemes on town-planning lines. . . . [T]hese
housing schemes would always remain an example to posterity of what
town-planning really meant."[117] While serving as president of the TPI two
years later, Abercrombie reported that he was leading a group of men to prepare a "Plan of London over an area of 2,000 square miles . . . a considered
scheme, financial, administrative, and technical by which this essential work
for the well-being of London can be put in hand at once." Abercrombie's
planning scheme focused on the structures of movement and enterprise of
the built environment. "With the apparatus for a complete plan of London
in being (including besides road, rail and river traffic, the equally important
matters of zoning, housing, and open spaces)," he asserted, "it should be
possible to report upon special urgent aspects such as river bridges at an
early stage of the work."[118]

By the 1920s, the male focus on the so-called scientific objectivity of
surveys, mapping, and overall planning schemes had reduced the city to an
abstract entity of buildings, streets, and infrastructure. With this perspective
guiding planners, they could not see the city as a place of homes and daily
life. Barclay and Perry's survey of Southwark had focused on the social conditions and needs of residents living in that borough, assuming that many of
these people would remain housed there but in better housing. Denby objected that "good housing is not the absence of slums any more than good
health is just the absence of disease. Slum clearance in Britain is not merely
a question of substituting a clean box for a dirty one. It is not a problem
which can be solved by better plumbing."[119] But planners concluded that
slum areas and overcrowding were principal problems standing in the way
of creating their preferred city.

In public reports and other venues, professional men emphasized the
destruction of whole areas as scientific necessity. The *Times* reported in
late 1927 that the LCC was clearing ninety-one acres of property, now
designated as slums, displacing over twenty-five thousand people, in the

East End, Southwark, Bethnal Green, and other areas in the center of the city. At least eight thousand of the displaced were to be moved out and rehoused on council estates.[120] The people being displaced were often blamed not just for creating slum conditions but for being incapable of living in any other conditions and thereby contributing to the failure to eradicate slums. For Levita, chair of the LCC housing committee in 1925, "the dwellers in condemned areas are frequently drawn from a class which must be the despair of any housing reformer. Both from their habits and their means they are unable to adapt themselves to a higher standard of accommodation."[121] New Housing and Town Planning Acts would continue to give the LCC and borough councils additional authority to pursue slum clearance.[122] At each step toward the planned city, women's voices were ignored.[123]

Fixating on overcrowding rationalized destruction and displacement. Overcrowding could be quantified and easily fit into Geddes's tripartite concept of seeing the city. Whole areas could be surveyed with numbers of people in flats and buildings counted. Numbers would tell if the area was overcrowded, the area diagnosed as diseased, declared a slum, and planned away to rebalance the city socially.[124] In a gathering hosted by the London Society in 1924 on the subject of satellite towns, Minister of Health Sir William Joynson-Hicks declared overcrowding as the singular evil facing cities. "The question of transportation, and even of locomotion, in great cities . . . had become a most grave problem," he declared. "Congestion had reached its limit and more than its limit." It was absolutely necessary to get the people "out of the existing enormous cities," to uproot entire areas of the city into satellite towns, "complete new entities planted out in the country districts."[125] Since the men who wanted to move people out defined what constituted overcrowding, it was a circular concept rationalizing their objectives. The people who lived in the area did not need to be consulted. If earlier generations had ignored the plight of the working and lower classes, planning now made these same people pawns to be moved around by the planners so that they could reconstruct the city to their ideals. Such sentiments were echoed ten years later as presentations in the House of Lords in 1934 enthusiastically predicted a future without slums:

> A survey had been made by the local authorities of the number of slum houses that must be replaced. The next step would be a survey of the number of families now living in overcrowded conditions for whom better accommodation was required. Lastly, there was the statutory duty resting on local authorities to meet any housing needs in their areas which might remain when account was taken of the slum clearance and overcrowding schemes. . . . Therefore at the end of five years there would be . . . no more slums.[126]

Through the 1920s and 1930s, street and traffic congestion continued to preoccupy London men. To relieve traffic congestion, the LCC in 1924 proposed to remove the Covent Garden market from its existing location to an area in Bloomsbury on the grounds of the Foundling Hospital. "The plans have been drawn on the assumption that a great underground goods station will be constructed beneath the market and linked up with the principal railway termini" to create "the world's best market."[127] The London Society supported these plans in principle, saying of the Foundling Estate, "If a famous institution on the north side of the Thames were lost they had the consolation that the Bethlem [Bedlam] Hospital in the south was going to be preserved."[128] As part of the scheme, streets through that area would be widened and others closed. It was argued that removing the market from its current site would allow

> a street widening scheme extending from the north of Trafalgar-square to Aldwych, and taking in Chandos-street, Maiden-lane and Tavistock-street . . . and a new Strand could be constructed running parallel with the present Strand. An important thoroughfare could also be constructed running north and south across the present site of Covent Garden and connecting Southhampton-street and St. James-street, all of which measures would greatly relieve and facilitate traffic to and from the City; and throughout the whole of this congested district.[129]

Adshead asserted that Bloomsbury was "in the throes of a traffic problem" that "offered considerable obstruction to the continuance of east and west traffic."[130] As part of his assessment of property in the Bloomsbury area, LCC valuer Frank Hunt contended that traffic control was an important dimension of the scheme. He insisted that many buildings in the area had reached the end of their economic and physical lives. Although he was forced to admit that this kind of declaration had no measurable precedence in planning decisions, he insisted that this was a reasonable way to decide on destruction.[131]

The fate of this proposal to move Covent Garden, however, demonstrated the power of those in the city with money and position versus the poor and working class to control their immediate environment. Despite his concern for traffic congestion, Adshead belonged to the Foundling Estate Protective Association. He proposed preserving that specific site as an example of good civic space and advocated instead creating different diagonal axes through the area. The scheme to transfer Covent Garden was then abandoned.[132] Residents and property owners in Bloomsbury had the power and influence to stop the move of Covent Garden's market and to mount a spirited opposition to the LCC's overall Town Planning Scheme #5, which proposed to plan the redevelopment of the entire area in order "to secure amenity and convenience in connexion with the use of the land." The scheme's opponents, however, objected that the plans would destroy such amenity and convenience because they would increase business and commerce in an area that was primarily residential.[133] E. Guy Dawber, president of the RIBA, had supported this opposition, contending that the scheme would "destroy an example of successful town planning and civic design . . . a valuable legacy of the 18th century."[134]

Less successful in protecting their neighborhood were petitioners against the mid-1930s schemes that threatened access to housing and work in Finsbury and Poplar. Finsbury petitioners to the LCC, for example, protested that the schemes threatened access to their housing and work. The political committee of the St. Peter's (Roman Catholic Church) Men's Club noted that areas cleared of housing were being taken over by factories and warehouses, necessitating "the removal of all the local inhabitants to the suburbs." Those residents who were removed could "rarely keep their employment owing to the difficulty of finding transport. . . . [T]his misfortune can be obviated by building homes on the old sites."[135] Residents of other areas resisted the decentralizing schemes. The Poplar borough council reported that it had "transplanted nearly 1,000 families," nearly five thousand individuals, to outlying council estates at Becontree and Downham but that many residents did not want to leave and that there were also many who could not afford the expense of commuting to work, the longer travel times, and the higher rents on the estates.[136]

By essentializing women as wives and mothers, planning both reoriented the public and private spaces of the city by gender roles and reasserted control over women. Low-density housing, achieved by scientific assessment of the appropriate maximum number of houses to an acre, isolated houses from each other and isolated women into their separate dwellings. Transferring families to the periphery further isolated women from access to the city center. Refusal to build public toilets for women or to furnish municipal lodging houses structurally signaled that the urban built environment was an unwelcome place for women. Removing working-class women from the public spaces of streets, alleys, and courts, in tandem with determination to make streets function primarily for transit, helped turn streets, as Dennis concludes, into impersonal, controlled spaces where no one could feel at home. "Public streets lost their publicness . . . became less conducive to social functions."[137]

The processes of straightening and widening streets, eradicating short streets and alleys, and destroying neighborhoods and livelihoods in the process turned the city from a home for its residents into a socially engineered, exclusive, and segregated space that circumscribed the public lives of women. Women on the council estate of Watling complained that the area was a desert where they were left alone all day in their houses. Their larger houses with new consumer appliances—women were expected to contribute to consumption—increased their housework and left them with far less time to socialize than they had in their old neighborhoods.[138] Moreover, once residents were removed to the estates, differing gender experiences were significant. Ruth Durant reported that for men nothing much had changed except for the actual home. They went to their same work, with the same routines and coworkers where they spent most of their days. For women, "having changed their homes, [they] had to build up entirely new lives. Everything was not only new but also so much more difficult than previously; the shops so far away; the neighbors strange; no schools for their children. The loneliness pressed much harder on the women than on the men."[139] Such complaints from women support Wilson's argument that this was a desired, if unspoken, aim of men to reorder the city by putting women back into their rightful place in the home and off the city streets.[140]

The Scientific Abstraction of Planning: Modernity, Linearity, Geometry

For professional men, urban planning involved a "large scale, future oriented, impersonal, abstract, quantitative approach to problem solving," which, as Greed observes, excluded "women's needs from the terms of reference."[141] So beyond eradicating slums and reducing crowding, the new professional men identified other impediments to modernity. The modern and efficient built environment needed straight wide streets, lined with monumental buildings and modern housing. Such streets would speed transportation throughout the city but also make streets more orderly public spaces no longer easily used as gathering places for crowds.

The reconstruction and widening of Victoria Street between 1850 and 1916 that connected Westminster and Westminster Abbey on the northeast end with Victoria Station on the southwest end was an example of such ideas. The proponents of the new Victoria Street envisioned it as a corrective to the narrow, short, and congested streets that crisscrossed the area. It could also serve as a barrier separating the insalubrious Devil's Acre south of the abbey from the more respectable northerly area with the monarch's new London residence of Buckingham Palace.[142] Building along Victoria Street and adjacent streets cleared out small streets, destroyed the old buildings, and turned the area into a monumental, civic, and modern area populated heavily by men. By 1916, mansion flats were built to accommodate businessmen and members of Parliament who needed small London residences and to furnish offices for professional men. A new Roman Catholic cathedral on the southwest end, the Army-Navy stores for military officers and their families at the midpoint, and the Westminster Palace Hotel "with ample space for business meetings" and separate men's and women's coffee rooms replaced alms-houses, a women's prison, and distilleries.[143] Dennis concludes that Victoria Street "was perhaps the nearest that London came to a Haussmannesque Parisian boulevard."[144] It was "Haussmann . . . who imposed the logic of the straight line." The new Victoria Street also put Victoria Station into a direct line along a broad thoroughfare into Parliament Square and government offices, similar to what Georges-Eugène Haussmann had done for Paris.[145]

An obsession with speed, linearity, and the creation of order were defined as hallmarks of masculine modernity and then used to define women as the feminine antimodern. Barbara Hooper argues that "the fantasy of the straight line" is a hallmark of modernism. The straight line would divide the light from the dark, the orderly from the disorderly, and bring discipline to the city. But the straight line as both a physical plan and a metaphor when applied to the city's built environment embodied the gender ideal of separating the male from the female and the public from the private. For Hooper, the "sexist/gendered/heterosexist ordering of urban space that produced the design of male cities and female suburbs [with curving, nonlinear streets], the ideas of function and place that worked to divide the private life of the house from the public life of the street and polis" made "planners as disciplinary experts . . . participants in control of the female/female body/female sexuality."[146] For Greed, this assessment of the gendered ideals embodied the development of the planning profession:

> One can see "male" sexual allusions in the metaphors used to describe urban problems in discussions of retention and uncontrolled sprawl and denseness being associated with tenseness. Likewise, images of urban form were strongly sexualized as reflected in the planners' pre-occupation with controlling linear ribbon development, and of course, in the later fixation with high-rise building forms.[147]

Beyond the wish of planners to create wide, straight streets to control congestion, the ideology of the straight line, and its relation to a man-woman dichotomy as pursued by continental modernists such as Le Corbusier, Adolf Loos, and Otto Wagner would continue to influence reconstruction ideas for the near future. The urban disease was produced by curving, narrow streets rather than straight lines; ornamentation rather than functional architecture; unplanned difference rather than uniformity in buildings. As Wilson argues, "The city—as experience, environment, concept—is constructed by means of multiple contrasts: natural, unnatural; monolithic, fragmented; secret, public; pitiless, enveloping; rich, poor; sublime, beautiful. Behind all these lies the ultimate and major contrast: male, female; culture, nature; city, country." In every dichotomy, women were the problem—the gender that threatened the efficient functioning of the city.[148]

For Le Corbusier geometry was the mastery of man over nature. "Straight and vertical forms represent[ed] the rational, modern, and masculine, while horizontality and curves represent[ed] the feminine irrationality of primitive nature." Ornamentation was "an excess of matter. . . . [O]rnament is to architecture . . . 'what a feather is to a woman's head . . . sometimes pretty . . . and never anything more . . . [which] conceals a defect in construction.'"[149] As early as 1908, Austrian architect Adolf Loos wrote that "freedom from ornament is a sign of spiritual strength." Loos "considered the child, the 'savage' and the woman to be at a lower level of civilisation, since they took pleasure in ornamentation." Otto Wagner wanted to elevate "uniformity into monumentality."[150]

In *Urbanisme* Le Corbusier wrote, "Free, man tends to geometry. . . . The work of man is to put things in order. . . . When man begins to draw straight lines he bears witness that he has gained control of himself and that he has reached a condition of order."[151] He further stated that "man walks in a straight line because he has a goal and knows where he is going. . . . [T]he pack-donkey meanders." He proceeded in this vein, declaring that "a modern city lives by the straight line. . . . [T]he curve is ruinous, difficult, and dangerous." For Le Corbusier, straight lines "represent the rational, modern and masculine. . . . [H]orizontality and curves represent the feminine irrationality of primitive nature"—the pack-donkey. The feminine was the disorder of "fluidity, indeterminancy, and amorphousness."[152]

The preoccupation with linearity in the urban built environment is a historical trope since Plato, traveling through Vitruvius, Leon Battista Alberti, and Haussmann and onto the modernists.

> Within the built environment of the nineteenth and twentieth centuries the surprise-free city ultimately came to epitomize the Platonic-Cartesian faith in geometry and mechanics. Le Corbusier and his intellectual mentor, Tony Garnier, as the two foremost leaders in urban planning adopted the primarily Platonic notion of a remote blueprint in forging their ideal form of a city. Twentieth-century city plans by and large followed their lead in espousing a static, remote ideal blueprint for a city or parts thereof.[153]

Le Corbusier referred to Paris as "she" and described it as "old, decayed, frightening, diseased . . . [a] dismal and suppurating zone."[154] The Platonic masculinist ideal city thus could be achieved only if the city was cleansed of its disease. For millennia of Western history, men associated the feminist with the disease and the masculinist with the cure. By the 1930s, reconstructing London and other Anglo-Atlantic cities was also an exercise in modernizing the city by reclaiming it as a strong, masculinist, linear space, separated from the female suburbs of curving streets and feminine domesticity.

PLANNING GREATER LONDON: POST–WORLD WAR II

According to Darling in her recent book on British modernity, "By 1939, modernism was well established in Britain. Its principles had been associated with the resolution of some of the most significant social problems of the day and links had been made with policy makers and those with influence upon them."[155] The German bombings of 1940–1941 that razed parts of the working-class East End and the Docklands afforded these men new opportunity to reconstruct the city along modern lines and to institutionalize Abercrombie's dictate that the survey was "the essential basis of all planning."[156] The architect Clough Williams-Ellis, a rather confirmed advocate of rural life, exalted this destruction: "I had to regard the destruction not with the excitement of the eyewitnesses or the indignation of the outraged citizen, but with the cool detachment of the professional town planner.... [T]oday [our cities] are all swept away to the undisguised delight of the more enlightened citizens and of the very able architect." Speculating on rebuilding Britain, William A. Robson declared that "as site-clearing agencies [Nazi bombers] have shown themselves to be wonderfully effective."[157] New planning and creative destruction could complete the war's destructions.

In 1941, the LCC asked Abercrombie to consult with its architect J. H. Forshaw to prepare a new overall plan for the greater London area. Among its objectives would be to promote slum clearance so that the "term East End should be a simple geographic term and not one of social reproach."[158] The resulting County of London Plan (CLP) recommended removing six hundred thousand people from the city, rebuilding the East End with fewer residents in a mix of single-family housing and flats, and rehousing people in satellite towns separated from the city by a new green belt. It proposed to make London "a large number of separate communities of varying sizes and population," with new transportation systems, radial roads, and three ring roads located at intervals beyond the center. *The Times* hailed this as the "remodeling" of London by "outward movement of the population."[159]

In 1944, Abercrombie formulated a new Greater London Plan (GLP) that increased removals to one million, asserting that "a broad policy of the movement of people and work can and must be pursued," paying close attention to the "harmonizing of human and industrial movement." The GLP proposed eight to ten new towns in which to relocate industries that would "take with them skilled male labour and their families." At least one hundred thousand of the removed were to be "decentralized beyond the London influence."[160] The LCC's Town Planning Committee suggested some refinements but accepted the GLP in principle. By early 1946, the Labour-party-led LCC fully supported decentralization, envisioning reducing the population of the inner-city areas of Stepney and Poplar by 58 percent. *The Times* called the plan "the biggest and most imaginative ever put forward by any city in the world, the Council's first broad frontal attack on the squalor of the over-crowded parts of London."[161]

But popular enthusiasm for planning was muted. Seeking to convince people that planning was a democratic endeavor, planners promoted a new civic education by staging exhibitions to demonstrate the modern city.[162] Marco Amati and Robert Freestone contend that such exhibitions "capture the importance of particular planning proposals through the manner of their staging, the notables who opened them, visitor numbers and reactions, and the extent of publicity generated." The king and queen visited Aber-crombie and Forshaw's 1943 exhibition presenting the CLP.[163] Abercrombie and his co-planners hoped to stress the importance of the plan by making sure that "all different facets of London's governing elite" were represented at the exhibition's opening. W. R. Davidge, past president of the TPI and longtime advocate of planning, was an invited speaker. This exhibit "was an important part of a range of activities during the 1940s that aimed to keep afloat the public spiritedness engendered during the war and redirect it to-wards the cause of planning reform."[164]

For his part, Abercrombie quickly moved to promote the GLP. He stressed that

> our concern is primarily with the 'distribution of the Industrial Pop-ulation.' . . . [G]reat as are the difficulties of transport provision[,] . . . enormous as is the need to protect agricultural productivity[,] and vital as is the preservation of the recreative reservoir of country and pure air; nevertheless, it is the regrouping of population and industry that is the real task of this Plan for Greater London.[165]

Abercrombie's ideas and the exhibition's promotion of planning according to principles laid out by him and other men contained little room for wom-en's ideas or preferences about the built environment. In 1939, a group of women led by Elizabeth Denby had drawn up proposals and models for housing that focused on designing new types of housing. The women fo-cused on both the interiors of housing and its community setting within the city. But the priority that men gave to their preferred specific types of plan-ning, and their continual desire to move people out of the city, left little chance that professional men would pay any attention to these women.[166]

By 1947, when a new Town and Country Development Act authorized local planning to adopt the Geddesian complete survey method to support land use proposals and to control land development, women were further removed from decision making. By placing land development at the fore-front, according to Stephen Ward, "planners everywhere were able to think of land more as a neutral platform for activities and buildings rather than as a source of private gain and object of speculation."[167] For Greed this meant that planners received "increased powers to control all types of development, and to imprint their gendered beliefs on the built environment more comprehensively." Planners now "took a greater interest in aspatial issues related to economic development and social policy as part of the apparatus of the Welfare State. Planning prioritized policies related to production, which was socially constructed to emphasize 'male' forms of work."[168] Planning the built environment was predicated on "the activity patterns of men and patriarchal assumptions about the role of women."[169] Lewis Mumford proclaimed that "the first consideration of town planning must be to provide an urban environment and an urban mode of living which will not be hostile to biological survival." Planning, "by sympathetic magic," would "encourage in women of the child-bearing age the impulse to bear and rear children as an essential attribute of their humanness" and discourage them from seeking success outside the home.[170]

By the late 1930s, prevailing theories in urban sociology reinforced the planners' certainties that embounded self-contained neighborhood units were necessary to reform cities.[171] American sociology professor W. Russell Tylor declared the neighborhood to be "a basic unit of social control" and warned against its disappearance in cities. "The importance with which the neighbourhood is coming to be viewed in present-day urban and regional development lies not so much in its necessity as an area of planning operation as in the recognition of the social values inherent within it as a primary group." The breakdown of the neighborhood would lead inexorably to social chaos: "our loss is that of the social control that springs from neighbourhood opinion."[172] In England, National Council for Social Service pamphlets emphasized the need to create the neighborhood unit.[173] Abercrombie and Forshaw had pursued the idea in the CLP.[174] As Greed points out, planners had accepted the functionalist social ecology theory of the city pioneered at the University of Chicago, which implied "that major problems only existed in the deviant area" that could be eradicated or isolated and replaced with newly planned neighborhoods.[175] Wilson underscores the "supreme inconsistency" of the neighborhood-unit-planners. "They aimed to create 'neighbourhoods' and 'communities' in the new residential areas they were building, in spite of the fact that they utterly rejected the spontaneous communities of the old working-class neighbourhoods they were pulling down."[176] Rather than women being integral to maintaining neighborhood life through their access to streets, shops, watching each other's children, and going out to work, new planning ideas focused on the family unit within the embounded neighborhood unit that would isolate women in their homes, keep them from the streets, and provide them little opportunity to work outside the home.[177]

The forty-acre Barbican Estate built over the bomb-destroyed Cripplegate neighborhood in the City area of London perfected the modernist gen-

Figure 5.2 Development model for Barbican Estate, London, 1955. (Courtesy of the London Metropolitan Archives, Image 238701, available at https://collage.cityoflondon .gov.uk/quick-search?q=238701.)

dered ideal of the patriarchal built environment with its urban public-private dichotomy and the embounded "neighborhood unit." The architectural design and layout of the Barbican can be traced historically back to the Peabody Estate architecture. But the Barbican took the ideas of emboundment and gendered environment even further than earlier developments. Not only does the development face away from the streets; it is elevated above streets and away from the city's open spaces. A recent analysis of the area observes that from the outside, it "looks more like a freeway overpass than a residential development . . . a modern walled fortress." It is an "inner-city enclave for the middle-class" (Figure 5.2). Moreover, since the corporation would build and own the Barbican, it constructed it as a gendered corporate space: it was to be "a haven for young [male] executives whose employment would make them natural boosters for the City." With the Barbican, London's past industrial culture and its planning ideals, merged easily into the postwar corporate culture of the patriarchal city, which depended on (male) employees who were "expected to prioritize stability, family, and loyalty."[178] What life in the Barbican Estate was to be for women was given as little consideration as it had been for the earlier Boundary Street Estate; the main concern was that they stayed confined inside the estate. And as with Dublin's Marino Estate, which provided no play areas for children, the Barbican "tuck[ed] away play fields on the periphery of the Estate, behind shrubbery and concrete barriers."[179]

6

DUBLIN

Property, Gender, and the Civic Unit

We regret to have to report that some of the property owned by [three members of the Corporation], and from which they are deriving rents, is classed as 3rd-class property . . . or in other words that it is unfit for human habitation.
—LOCAL GOVERNMENT BOARD FOR IRELAND, *Report on the Housing Conditions of the Working Classes* (1913)

I do not think that it is slum property in [the sense of being unfit for habitation]. People have been living there for 15 years and are perfectly healthy.
—FLORENCE CONAN, Alexandra Guild (1913)

A CITY IN CRISIS

By the turn of the twentieth century Dublin had high levels of poverty and unemployment among a working class composed largely of unskilled and seasonal laborers, especially dockworkers and those in the distilling and brewing industries, whose seasonal labor and low wages produced chronic underemployment and an easy slide into poverty. A paucity of housing produced overcrowding in the poorer areas of the city, where deteriorating older housing had been subdivided into single-room dwellings often occupied by entire families. Slaughterhouses and dairy yards located in crowded districts and the city's failure to eliminate sewerage and other health nuisances from the streets and lanes produced a chronic public health crisis. In 1899, the city's mortality rate was 33.6 per 1,000. By 1906, it had dropped to 22.3 per 1,000, although in some neighborhoods the death rate was over 30 per 1,000. London's mortality rate by comparison was 15.6 per 1,000. Tuberculosis and infant mortality due to diarrhea and the inability of undernourished mothers to feed infants adequately plagued the poor families of Dublin. In 1905, the mortality rate of children under five among people classified as "hawkers, labourers, porters, &c." was 12.7 percent (1,145 deaths among a population of 89,861). The comparable statistic for the middle class was 2.7 percent (239 from a population of 87,186). By the end of the nineteenth century, Dublin was considered one of the unhealthiest cities in Europe.[1]

Because Dublin was a colonial city, its ability to control its built environment was limited by British parliamentary legislation. The 1898 Local Government (Ireland) Act gave Dublin's municipal government more authority, but the city was still subject to the Local Government Board (LGB), whose powers, including fiscal authority, were set by England and whose members represented England. This new authority, however, did give more influence to the council's Irish nationalist members, who envisioned Dublin as the restored capital of a free Ireland. As a result, the corporation and the LGB were often at odds, and the council grew increasingly confrontational with England especially since the LGB severely limited the city's borrowing powers.[2]

Groups of activist men and women agreed that the situation was serious but held different ideas about how to address it. The Alexandra Guild and the Women's National Health Association (WNHA) wanted the city to adopt a people-centered approach that focused on the housing and health needs of the poor and working class where they lived. Dublin men leaned instead toward slum clearance to create a new capital city.[3] Even though the chief medical officer of health, Charles Cameron, and the WNHA agreed that conditions of poverty, health, and housing were inextricably linked and had to be attacked in tandem, they did not agree about how to solve the problem.

Because Dublin lacked the financial means to confront the housing problem directly, the city had depended on the Iveagh (Guinness) Trust or the Dublin Artisans' Dwellings Company (DADC) to furnish new housing. When the corporation did enter directly into supplying housing, it pursued a clear-and-rebuild policy, depending on the city's sanitary officers to designate unhealthy areas to be demolished. The intent was to have new, less-crowded housing erected on the cleared land but not to build and own it. Generally, the city purchased the land and then leased it to the DADC. This process was expensive, considering that legally owners had to be compensated for loss of property and the council demonstrated a marked proclivity to compensate at high rates. The Board of Works complained that the council operated "on the basis that utter confiscation of property is too drastic a remedy, even in the case of property owners who do not keep their property in a sanitary condition."[4] Combined with the LGB's restrictions on Dublin's finances, this respect for property made the clear-and-rebuild policy a slow and unsatisfactory process. As unhealthy areas were cleared and sanitized and less-crowded housing was built, the former tenants could not afford the higher rents. The promoters of this policy hoped that renters who could pay more were presumably healthier and possessed of higher moral standards than the now-dispossessed tenants. At the same time, the dispossessed were supposedly to be uplifted morally and physically by moving into some presumably decent buildings being vacated by those who could afford the higher rents.

Such policies were constantly remaking Dublin's geography of poverty and public health without confronting it. Newcomers crowded into any derelict tenement vacated by former occupants. Charles Cameron had lobbied hard during the 1885 British government Housing Inquiry for the city to provide new healthy housing specifically for the Dublin poor, which he defined as those who "could not rise above rents of 1s or 1s 6d per week." But faced with low finances and resistance to state-subsidized housing, the city declined to initiate such a process. Cameron and some like-minded Dubliners had formed the Housing of the Very Poor Committee to promote building tenement blocks with rents below 2s per week, even if they would not be profitable.[5] They argued for municipal responsibility for housing for the very poor, acknowledging that it could never be profitable, but that it would be a public good, similar to providing municipal drainage schemes. The Dublin-based *Freeman's Journal and Daily Commercial Advertiser* generally supported the idea:

> The need for a reform of the whole tenement house system of Dublin has been sufficiently demonstrated. If such a reform is to be undertaken it ought to be undertaken very thoroughly and on a large scale; and even if, as in the case of the Main Drainage Scheme, the profit to be derived from it is to be looked for in the improved health of the citizens rather than in pounds, shillings, and pence, the present high death-rate in Dublin is a sufficiently strong argument in its favour.[6]

Although this committee did build some housing, it could not begin to solve the problem.[7]

The corporation had neither the will nor the finances to accept that housing for the poor was a municipal responsibility. Moreover, Dublin's governing men believed that property was sacrosanct, especially since a number of them were tenement-building owners or important builders who did not wish competition.[8] But by the beginning of the twentieth century, Dublin men were beginning to turn to slum clearance and decentralization as the best means for changing the housing situation. A 1903 conference convened at the Mansion House, chaired by the Lord Mayor and attended by representatives of the Dublin Corporation, the Dublin Trades Council, and Dublin's parliamentary representatives—no women were included—concluded that current measures were wholly inadequate. Only 5,394 families had to that date been rehoused from 59,263 total families in the city. The committee concluded that "it would be a fatal mistake to continue to put a premium on bad sanitation and improper housing by purchasing up, at a ruinous rate, unsanitary areas and rebuilding them. The most desirable remedy . . . is to build first on the outskirts cottages or self-contained dwellings, and to procure cheap means of transit for workers."[9]

As Jacinta Prunty writes, it was not until 1898 that the word *slum* entered into general use as a pejorative term regarding living conditions and the people housed in specific areas of Dublin. That year, a meeting of the Arran Quay Ward Ratepayers' Association used the term "slum evil" when referring to Dublin's housing problems.[10] In the aftermath of the 1903 conference, the Dublin Council approved the formation of a committee "to deal with the abolition of the slums and housing question, and to take up the work recommended by the Conference held at the Mansion House."[11] And, as was the case with London, the search was then on, through groups such as the Statistical and Social Inquiry Society of Ireland, to quantify the conditions that would define an area as a slum.

Following the 1903 conference, reference to providing good housing for everyone in the city as a public good largely disappeared as attention turned more toward the slum question, although the council did not immediately follow through with its own resolution. Parliamentary control of finances, the lack of legal authority, and the fact that adjacent areas were independent townships impeded the pursuit of the suburban solution. Instead, the council's Public Health Committee continued to close unhealthy houses that, "owing to want of proper sanitary accommodation, defective drainage, dilapidation, dampness, or other sufficient causes," make a house "unfit for occupation until the defects stated are remedied."[12] When Parliament passed the 1908 Housing of the Working Classes (Ireland) Act, the so-called Clancy Act named for Dublin MP John Joseph Clancy that removed some legal and financial impediments, the council remained cautious about changing its policies and only formed a permanent Housing Committee in 1910.[13] As the council continued to clear and rebuild, Andrew Beattie, representing the Dublin Citizens' Association's Housing Committee, described building on cleared areas as backward: "The modern idea was to get people out into the country."[14]

GENDER AND THE MODERN DUBLIN

For Dublin men, the modern idea of the suburban solution could solve two problems. It could demolish the slums and simultaneously attack the gender problem that increasingly concerned them. Ireland's steadily collapsing rural economy kept pushing more women into Dublin, where they found little economic opportunity. Dublin's dependence on general unskilled labor such as dockworkers and laborers in brewing and distilling provided few employment opportunities for women. Street selling, or dealing, was done primarily by women, and, according to Mary Daly, "the proportion of females engaged in [such] distribution in Dublin was far in excess of most other cities." Women who might find employment as charwomen or washerwomen would in most cases find that their meager earnings from such work could hardly support a family.[15] The 1911 census revealed that a higher percentage of female-headed households occupied the tenements than other type of housing.

Prostitution

Such desperate circumstances often made prostitution women's only viable option. The quartering of British troops in Dublin increased the possibilities for sex work. Although arrests for prostitution had fallen in 1910 to just under 800 from a high of several thousand per year in the 1860s and 1870s, Maria Luddy estimated that by the early twentieth century there were 1,500 Dublin women working as prostitutes. Other scholars estimated higher, but the precise number is less important than understanding how concern over prostitution was one element of a general anxiety over women's growing public presence and activities. Since prostitution often involved solicitation in public spaces, or took place in brothels, lodging houses, or other houses scattered throughout neighborhoods, prostitution enhanced anxiety about the contamination and inappropriate uses of urban space.[16]

It is impossible to disentangle attitudes toward women's public presence from Irish nationalism and religion. In late 1910, the Reverend J. Gwynn, S.J., publicly declared Dublin to be "one of the most immoral cities" of Europe. According to Gwynn, "The principal streets of London, of Brussels, of the great cities of in France and Germany had by no means that air, whatever be the reality, of looseness and depravity which invaded our main thoroughfares with the fall of night." Gwynn singled out the presence of Dublin women on the street as the source:

> What was the childhood, and what were the surroundings of those crowds of young girls who took possession of the centre of the city when the darkness comes, and whose whole demeanour by no means suggests the modesty and decorum they were wont to regard as inseparable from the Irish maiden. Foreigners had [to his own knowledge] come to our shores and gone away speaking very plainly of their impressions gained from our streets concerning what we once claimed as the special glory of our Irish girls.[17]

In response to this inflammatory charge, the council proposed that the police authorities take note of Gwynn's allegations. But several council members objected outright to this allegation and proposed an amendment declaring that "Dublin is not an immoral City, and in fact bears no comparison to the immorality of London and the Continental Cities." The council as a whole rejected that amendment and ratified the original proposal.[18] Gwynn's charge had touched two sore points. First, it compared Dublin unfavorably to London, the capital city of the colonial oppressor. Second, by singling out Dublin women as fostering the city's immorality, it implied that Dublin men were failing in their patriarchal duties not just to defend the city but to defend Irish honor. This entanglement of gender anxiety with Irish pride and nationalism underlay decisions made by Dublin men about women in public space.

Public Toilets for Women

By the late 1890s, the Dublin Council's public health committee had recommended erecting public toilets "for the use of the workmen and others engaged along the quays."[19] Between 1898 and 1901, the corporation approved sums ranging from £300 to £1,820 for new men's public toilets throughout the city, and the committee was directed to erect the following facilities: a men's underground convenience in each city ward; ten new urinals and two water closets on Bachelor's Walk at O'Connell Bridge; and a urinal for Mountjoy Street with "ribbed glass roofing."[20] Following the recommendation of the high sheriff that the council draw up a comprehensive plan for public toilets for "both sexes," the council instructed the improvements committee to investigate the "desirability and the necessity of providing proper sanitary conveniences for females in or near certain populous thoroughfares in the city." The next year, the committee declared "that the necessity for such conveniences is not of such a character as to render the building of them a work of urgent importance." Besides, it said, the corporation was "committed to a large number of other Civic schemes, which are of paramount importance."[21]

Medical officer Charles Cameron resisted building public facilities for women: "I am of the opinion that women would not use underground lavatories, or even Kiosks, placed in prominent positions." He preferred that "ladies use the lavatory accommodation provided in the confectionary establishments through the city." Cameron acknowledged that not all women could frequent such shops, so he conceded that the council might supply a few small shops with a women's toilet at back, with a female proprietor, who "might sell papers or other small articles, which would be the excuse some women might like for entering the place." Women, of course, would be charged for using such toilet facilities, although Cameron granted that one toilet in a shop might be free.[22]

The council, realizing that it would cost less to erect a facility than to supply small shops and facing pressure to provide women's toilet facilities, decided in 1907 to build a facility on Sackville Street (now O'Connell Street) adjacent to Nelson's Pillar just north of the Liffey River.[23] Since it had recently authorized contracts for erecting public urinals along the river at Merchant's and Eden's Quays, perhaps the men thought that there would be no serious objection to one women's facility along the quays.[24] As in London's St. Pancras, however, business and property owners near the proposed site strenuously objected. A group of Dublin shop owners sued the council, claiming that to erect

> in close proximity to the respective plaintiffs' premises, a building, placed overground, to contain water closets, lavatories, etc., for use by the female public [would] constitute the same a nuisance to the plaintiffs and their tenants, and an injury to the property and business of the respective plaintiffs and their tenants . . . would obstruct hitherto unrestrained flow of pedestrian and vehicular traffic . . . prevent respectable inhabitants and visitors from using the passage between Nelson's pillar and the proposed building . . . as respectable people of both sexes would naturally shrink from frequenting a crossing in proximity to a public convenience . . . and that existence of such would attract a different class of women . . . [and] would tend to divert ladies and others from the plaintiffs' premises.[25]

As in London, these men also claimed that a women's public toilet would obstruct traffic. When called to testify at a hearing on the suit in his capacity of medical officer, Cameron mildly countered the plaintiffs' concerns about respectability, saying that the toilet entrance would face the pillar and thus would be "effectively screened from public view." The plaintiffs' counsel raised hearty laughter when he wondered at this "latter day use to which Nelson's Pillar is to be put—to act as a shield for a Corporation lavatory." The court granted an injunction against building the toilet and the council agreed not to go ahead with the project in return for the plaintiffs agreeing that the council had the right to erect such facilities if it chose to do so.[26] The council was far more interested in protecting its prerogatives to decide on the built environment than it was in providing women's public toilets.

In 1911, the WNHA led a delegation to the council to plead for women's toilets. The WNHA specifically asked the council to build facilities in the working-class areas on Moore, Thomas, and Camden Streets and in other "such busy thoroughfares." Moore Street, in particular, was located in a busy street market area. Following the delegation's visit, the public health committee asked the corporation for a loan of £1,000 for a woman's lavatory, to be taken from appropriations for men's public toilets. Despite the committee's cautious assurance that "every proposal to establish a woman's lavatory would, with full details, be submitted, for approval or otherwise, to the Council," Cameron again objected and proposed instead that lavatories be constructed in the back of small shops "in which the attendant could sell papers, stationery, etc."[27] The Lord Mayor ruled the entire question out of order, so again no public toilets were provided for women.[28]

In the meantime, the council continued to authorize expenses for men's public toilets and urinals. The same year that the council again failed to fund public toilets for women, the council's cleansing committee, noting that the corporation made a profit from men's public toilets on O'Connell and College Streets, recommended providing additional urinals and water closets—which charged 1d for use—in those locations.[29] The council then built a urinal at The Slip, East Wall, claiming it was needed because this was a bathing place "frequented by close on 20,000 [evidently male] bathers during the summer months, and is adjacent to one of the principal thoroughfares of the city."[30] In 1915, following a joint recommendation of its improvements, public health, and cleansing committees, the council erected a temporary women's toilet at the southern foot of O'Connell bridge on Aston Quay with the possibility of turning it into a permanent structure. The council assured the public that this would be an inconspicuous structure, furnished with ornamental windows lined with newspapers—presumably again with the idea of disguising the building's function.[31] Businessmen and property owners again protested. A letter to the council from Hodges and Sons, Aston Quay, objected to "a structure of this class . . . in such an exposed position. We consider [that] it would largely reduce our business." These men suggested that instead some shop furnish a "ladies cloakroom . . . [with] the lavatory placed at the rere [sic] . . . where ladies would not be observed passing in and out of same."[32] Another letter of protest came from "ratepayers," who contended that such a structure would be "highly injurious to our interests . . . objectionable and an obstruction . . . that would practically hide our shop windows."[33] Without comment, the council abandoned its plan. The last mention in the council and corporation records about providing a women's public toilet came in 1921, when the council authorized £5,000 to erect such a facility on Burgh Quay. This time, the Port and Docks Board, composed primarily of businessmen, especially shippers, protested that such a facility on that site had the potential to weaken the river wall. The council agreed to stop work if it caused any weakness in the river wall, but subsequent records provide no information about the eventual outcome of this proposal.[34] (See Figure 6.1.)

As in London, Dublin men considered the use of public spaces for women's toilets to be obstructive, objectionable, a nuisance, an inconvenience, and an injury to the property and business of the city's businessmen. But behind such objections lay men's desire to control women's public presence. Women were more than welcome to shop in stores along the streets, but access to public toilets might make it possible for "respectable" women to stay on the streets rather than going home immediately after shopping and might attract the wrong class of women into the city center. Controlling women's respectability, no matter of what class, was an important facet of men's control of the city, so the council also refused to build women's toilets in the

Figure 6.1 Map of men's and proposed women's public toilets in Dublin.

working-class areas of the city where the WNHA wanted them provided, even though the council was erecting them for men in working-class areas. And businessmen along the quays do not seem to have objected to the various men's toilet facilities that were erected along the quays and O'Connell bridge; nor did they object to the council spending money to erect such facilities in working-class areas.

GENDER, NATIONALISM, AND OWNERSHIP OF THE CITY

The issue of public toilets for women, connected as it was to concerns about the public morality of the city and women's presence on the streets, could not be disentangled from the city's nationalist movement. In that sense, the struggle over Dublin's built environment differed from that of other cities. As Dublin men sought to limit women's public presence, they simultaneously wanted to establish their authority to order the city against that of the colonial occupier.[35] In such a situation, women's ideas on a range of issues stood little chance of consideration.

The Female Perspective

Beyond the issue of public toilets, small groups of Dublin women were pointing out Dublin men's failure to confront other social problems in the city.

Lady Aberdeen (Ishbel Hamilton-Gordon), wife of the Lord Lieutenant (Viceroy) of Ireland, had founded the WNHA shortly after she and her husband arrived in Dublin. She was especially concerned about the virulent presence of tuberculosis in Ireland, and the WNHA first pursued a public health campaign to educate people about the causes and prevention of this disease. Under Lady Aberdeen's leadership the organization's work expanded into attacking the poor state of Dublin's overall public health and conditions of daily life. Frances Carruthers, in her Ph.D. dissertation on Lady Aberdeen, notes that she and the WNHA moved from their original position as philanthropists to social reformers because they realized that "an array of social problems were the fault of society and its lack of support for the poor, who were striving against great odds to survive in an extremely hostile environment of poverty, ignorance, lack of all types of facilities and other deprivations."[36] The WNHA began to directly attack how these problems affected women and children, raising subscriptions to pay for district nurses; operating a pure-milk depot; feeding poor women and children; organizing Babies' Clubs staffed with female nurses; funding boot, dental, and coal thrifts; arranging home visits by nurses for mothers and sick babies; and organizing, in 1916, the city's first school medical clinic.[37] The WNHA published its activities and reports in its monthly magazine, *Sláinte* (Health).

The city council rarely responded to WNHA appeals to support its work. The council's housing committee refused its request to provide a recreation hall and working boys' building in its Ormond Market plans. Its public health committee turned down another request for a recreation hall "for the respectable young people of the city."[38] It took three years and severe wartime shortages for the corporation to support the WNHA's pure-milk depot.[39] So, as was the case in London, women had to rely on women's voluntary work and subscriptions to carry out their work.

Moreover, the council always sought to control women's activities, as the earlier experiences of the Alexandra Guild demonstrated. In 1916 the WNHA proposed a cooperative scheme with the council's public health committee for fostering infant health through enforcement of birth registrations under the recently passed Notification of Births (Extension) Act. The women wanted the WNHA, the Infant Aid Society, and the public health committee to coordinate activities toward this end. The committee agreed to the proposal but demanded control over all activities. "Your Committee is of the opinion that the work can best be done on the likes presented in this report"; that is, both societies would be put under the committee's supervision and its officers "are to have the right to examine the books of the various Clubs [i.e., the WNHA Babies' Clubs] whenever it is considered advisable, and to have power to attend the usual meetings of the committees controlling the Clubs." The public health committee also demanded that three of its members be appointed to represent the city government on the WNHA and

IAS committees, whose role would be advisory to the public health committee.[40]

The WNHA also suffered from nationalists' suspicion that Lady Aberdeen was not truly concerned with the health and well-being of the Irish
people. Being British (Scots, actually) and representing the British crown
made her suspect to many nationalists, who accused her of seeking to keep
the working classes loyal to the crown.[41] Anyone working with Lady Aberdeen was accused of sycophancy. Although as Carruthers notes, three nationalist women—Maud Gonne, Madeleine ffrench-Mullen, and Dr.
Kathleen Lynn—later organized schemes to feed schoolchildren and to provide hospital aid for children with tuberculosis, the types of social reform
measures that Lady Aberdeen had championed.[42]

Dublin men kept control of the city by rejecting women's ideas and requests. At the same time, P. C. Cowan, the LGB chief engineer, did not, or
could not, comprehend the motives of women's organizations. Addressing
the 1911 Town Planning and Housing section of the Public Health Congress,
he expressed his opinion that "some of the newer organizations, notably the
WNHA, will prove powerful agencies for the cultivation of self-reliance and
individualism which are so vitally important in the improvement of the well-
being of a nation."[43] But the women of the WNHA were not cultivating individualism for the sake of the nation. They were working instead to have
government improve the conditions of all people while simultaneously making it possible for people to take better care of themselves and their families.
None of the WNHA activities were part of the cult of individualism that
Cowan promoted. Whether Cowan just did not get it or deliberately miscon-
strued women's ideas to suit his purposes cannot be answered. But the
WNHA's vision of what the city and its residents needed clearly differed
from that of most Dublin men.

Reasserting the Male Perspective

Because the WNHA was so concerned about overall conditions in Dublin,
Lady Aberdeen used her access to the new professional men outside Ireland
to help raise public awareness of Dublin's precarious situation. In spring
1911, she and the WNHA planned a health exhibit in Dublin and invited
Patrick Geddes to bring his Cities and Town Planning Exhibition to the city.
She then organized the Public Health Congress and invited Geddes to address its Cities and Town Planning section.[44] Then, in the distressed aftermath of the 1913 strike and lockout of the Irish Transport and General
Workers Union—led by James Larkin—and the fatal collapse of two tenement buildings in Church Street, Lady Aberdeen and the WNHA led a delegation to the Chief Secretary for Ireland, Augustine Birrell, to demand an
official housing inquiry, more government subsidies for housing, and broad

citizen representation on any body constituted for such an inquiry. The Irish Women's Suffrage and Local Government Association, the council's housing committee, the Dublin Trades Council, and the Dublin Citizens Association, among other groups, supported this request. The delegation wanted an independent viceregal committee that they presumably believed would represent the interests of Dublin. But Birrell, who was also president of the LGB, instead constituted a committee of four men, three of whom were inspectors on the LGB, and the fourth was on its staff. The LGB's chief housing expert, Cowan, was not even included. Birrell originally decided that testimony before the committee would be taken in private, despite the Lord Mayor's objection that this was obstructing the will of the people. In the end, Birrell agreed to public meetings.[45] The committee solicited testimony from men, the only exception being Sarah Harrison, who was also the only woman currently serving on the Dublin City Council. Harrison presented statistics on the housing situation and testified that the number of badly housed Dubliners had increased between the 1901 and 1911 census. Harrison had previously objected in the council against the composition of the committee, proposing a resolution that it be a larger committee of people more expert in housing issues and not directed by the LGB.[46] Her motion was carried by the council, but the inquiry went ahead directed by the LGB. When asked by the committee what she thought of the working class, Harrison told them "that if people were treated like animals much could not be expected from them but on the whole she had the highest respect for the unskilled labourers of Dublin." She also testified that she believed that housing for the poorer classes should be provided in combination by the corporation and the state.[47]

As the Birrell Committee was conducting business, the Irishwomen's Reform League held a public meeting, presided over by (Miss) Louie Bennett, to discuss the housing crisis. Bennett urged that action replace talk. She also asserted that housing "was especially a question for women and could only efficiently be dealt with by the help of women" and that it was "very difficult to keep men up to the question of housing." Florence Conan from the Alexandra Guild Tenement Company pointed out that there were in fact empty rooms in the city.[48] A few months later, the group held another public meeting on the subject, with Bennett again stressing that "housing was essentially a women's question."[49]

The Birrell committee refused to consider most of the demands of the citizens' groups who had wanted an inquiry that would produce ways to move forward with bettering the housing situation. Instead, it issued a report blaming the corporation for failing to carry out its duties to guarantee the sanitary conditions of the city's housing, focused attention on the corporation men who owned dilapidated housing, and declared that slum housing produced the low social conditions of Dublin's poorer residents. It also accused members of the Dublin government of corrupt dealings with landlords to protect the latter's property. The report emphasized that Dublin could expect no additional monies for its housing efforts. As summarized by Daly, the final report reflected more reliance on gathering statistics than on advocating solutions.

> When the report strayed from the path of detailed financial and demographic calculations it displayed an extraordinary faith in the deterrent powers of stringent local enforcement of sanitary legislation, combined with a touching belief in the ability of private enterprise to adequately house the working population—ideas which would seem to have been thoroughly discredited by 1914.[50]

The council rejected this blanket charge of incompetence and possible corruption and attempted to reassert its control over the housing situation. The council's housing committee rebutted almost every point made by the inquiry board. It pointed out that of the four men on the inquiry board, only one had even a nodding acquaintance with "the housing, sanitary, and general work of the city." The housing committee further accused the inquiry board of having never intended to make any comprehensive inquiry into the corporation's housing and sanitation efforts and countered that "facts demonstrate how conscious the Corporation has been of its obligations to the working classes."[51] While the inquiry had concluded that "the plea of the Corporation in regard to the insufficiency of their power would have considerably more force were it supported by evidence of a right administration of existing powers," the committee rebutted that the corporation could not do more unless it had more government financing.[52]

The housing committee also rejected the board's implication that the corporation failures had caused much immorality among the working classes and poor. The committee accused the board of reaching this conclusion because it had listened to too many clergymen who were concerned about open doors and unlighted hallways in tenements. As for the inquiry's failure to credit the corporation efforts to reduce the city's mortality rates, the committee rather caustically charged that the board had "deliberately ignored the repeated testimony of witnesses of absolute independence on that point, and based a general charge on the circumstances that the corporation had not pulled down enough tenements, and driven a sufficient number of families into the streets."[53]

The inquiry and its report further exacerbated the tensions between Dublin's nationalists and the British government. The (London) *Times* coverage of the inquiry focused on the committee's charges against the corporation, especially the extent of ownership of tenement properties by members of the corporation.[54] Of the inquiry committee's final report, the English paper concluded, "it is obvious that the Corporation as at present constituted is quite unfitted to deal with the housing question."[55] The LGB report put the corporation into an almost untenable position. It blamed the corporation for the situation but promised no additional monies toward resolving it. Rather, the report favored decentralized housing built by private enterprise.[56] Seizing on using the report for their own priorities, according to Daly, British officials declared that the results of the inquiry were demonstrable proof that Irish nationalists were not ready for home rule.[57]

Several Dublin men's organizations were operating outside these official channels by moving toward adopting the ideas of town planning and decentralization being promoted by the British Town Planning Association and men such as Abercrombie. Following the 1911 exhibition, a group of men organized a Housing and Town Planning Association of Ireland (HTPAI), and under its auspices they organized a local housing and town development conference. Their purpose was to convince the city to adopt a professional city planning approach to resolve all municipal problems. Other groups of men were promoting the same idea. Dublin Trades Council vice president William J. O'Brien had told the housing inquiry that he supported decentralized housing, "built on virgin soil," although he wanted it built by the corporation.[58] E. A. Easton, a leading figure in the Dublin Citizens Association, "called for the development of 'plantations for city workers in convenient rural areas.'"[59] The Presbytery of Dublin appealed to the council "for this matter [housing] to be dealt with on thorough and business-like lines" with all information gathered by "a body of competent persons either experts alone or comprising both experts and local representatives."[60] In light of the growing support for planning and decentralization, the council and corporation began rethinking their objectives. They charged the housing committee in 1913 with undertaking a comprehensive city survey "with detailed facts and figures and estimates" with the idea of moving toward formulating a citywide plan for housing.[61]

The unsympathetic report from the 1913 housing inquiry gave town planning advocates the opportunity to move their ideas to the forefront of proposals for reconstructing the city's built environment. Urged by Patrick Geddes and the Civics Institute of Ireland (formed in 1914 along lines being advocated by Geddes), Lord Aberdeen sponsored a £500 award for a town planning competition to be judged by Geddes, American planner John Nolen, and Dublin city architect Charles J. MacCarthy. The charge was to design a comprehensive plan for the greater Dublin area—that is, beyond the city boundaries—focused on communication, housing, and metropolitan improvements. Proposals for communication were to consider road, rail, and canal systems; all existing and proposed industrial locations; and main existing and proposed streets and thoroughfares. Housing ideas were to be directed toward recommending preferred number, type, and location of dwellings; specifying what the population density should be; and relocating

the various institutions from the city center to the suburbs. Recommendations were to be made about preserving and expanding existing public institutions, including building a new art gallery and a new cathedral.[62]

Abercrombie and his collaborators, Sydney Kelly and Arthur Kelly, ultimately won the competition with a proposal titled "Dublin of the Future: The
New Town Plan." Their plan's housing section was concerned with statistical
calculation. They defined "a standard of permissive density per acre for
health purposes" calculated as 75 people per acre. They asserted that Dublin
density was currently 95.8 per acre, and therefore "a surplus of 59,750 inhabitants must be extracted from their present dwellings" and "rehoused on
extra-urban land." The men pointed out that the suburban solution had
three advantages: it was less expensive than acquiring land inside the city;
large tracts could be purchased in bulk in the extra-urban areas; and "the
moral and exemplary effect of these large tracts of suburban planning on the
most up-to-date lines would be incalculable."[63]

As the competition proceeded, however, the council's housing committee sought to keep matters more firmly under its control. The council invited
Geddes and Raymond Unwin to inspect several of the city's neighborhoods
and comment on the council's proposed schemes for these areas. The committee was disappointed when Unwin and Geddes declared that its schemes
to continue clearing tenement areas and rebuilding on central city sites were
fatally flawed. They dismissed the council's plans for the center-city Spitalfields area, which the council had declared an unhealthy area and where it
had proposed to acquire all its property, clear the entire site, and build "upon
the same of houses suitable for the working classes."[64] Unwin and Geddes
declared that this area needed "more extensive improvement than present
plans show. . . . [E]ven living in such a neighbourhood could not be favour-
able to anyone seeking steady employment."[65]

The two men also specifically rejected the council's decade-long scheme
for the Ormond Market area; among the proposals for using that space had
been the WNHA's request for a children's playground.[66] Unwin and Geddes
now proposed that "for the present [the area] be cleared and leveled as an
Open Space, retaining only such building as may be useful as shelters, &c.,"
contending that the area needed a planning scheme to recognize its potential
as a grand civic space. The men recommended that no further plans be made
for the area until the town planning competition was settled.[67] According to
Unwin and Geddes, Dublin's housing problem could be solved only if "a
considerable proportion of the population of Dublin" were removed "to better houses built on cheaper virgin land on the outer areas within the city
boundary." They argued, as men had argued for London, that many working-class and poor residents would choose to live outside the central city "if
they had the chance." And, not incidentally, they declared that living outside
the center would make "healthier, and therefore more efficient workmen."[68]

The housing committee complained that the "suggestions of the Housing Experts were almost entirely devoted to Town Planning" and that the men had "looked at the matter from the point of view of Garden Cities." The committee moreover believed that most Dublin workers wanted to live in the city. It had hoped that Unwin and Geddes would give further encouragement and insight into building small cottages within the city, rather than focusing as they did on garden suburb development.[69] The committee also rejected the report's conclusion that solving Dublin's poverty had nothing to do with solving the housing problem. The committee feared that "if we exclude the poverty problem, and build only for the economic class, which is the only conclusion we can draw from the report, a serious responsibility would rest on your Committee, which we apprehend the present members are unwilling to bear."[70]

Certainly, the members of the housing committee would not have appreciated the report's almost complete dismissal of its plans. And coming from two British men whose focus on monumental buildings such as the Four Courts rather than on housing Dublin's poor, it had to exacerbate nationalist feelings. As Andrew Kincaid suggests in *Postcolonial Dublin*, buildings such as the Four Courts adjacent to the Ormond Market were symbols of British hegemonic colonialism.[71] But there was a deeper disconnect at play. The council's housing committee and Unwin and Geddes were indeed working from different visions. Unwin and Geddes represented the new professionals of town planning. One of the report's specific suggestions was that a "main line of meeting the Housing difficulty is by proceeding with the erection of one or more Garden Suburbs." It proposed that if this were done for the Marino area (this area is further discussed later), it would be a "Garden Village" second to none anywhere "on grounds of accessibility, economy, and beauty alike."[72]

Geddes's traveling Cities and Town Planning Exhibition had also focused on planning in which housing was just one element of civic uplift through orderly planning.[73] His idea of the city as a diseased organism that could be cured only through radical and systemic uprooting and replanning was spreading deep into the planning movement and replacing housing as a primary focus. American architect, planner, and competition judge John Nolen lectured Dubliners in March 1914 that planners were "doctors of cities, civic improvers [who] could do nothing for Dublin unless the ways and means were found through the medium of town planning to extend the character and business significance of the city."[74] At the 1913 annual meeting of the Architects Association of Ireland, its chairman had emphasized the city as a diseased organism. He spoke glowingly of plans "to open up a broad central highway connecting Dame Street and Mary Street, thus forming a new artery through the present diseased heart of the city."[75] Razing the tenements of Dublin and relocating their residents out to the periphery would clear the city center and make way for planning a city focused on business development and civic beauty.

As the competition concluded, and Unwin and Geddes submitted their report, the outbreak of war precluded pursuit of any systematic town planning or housing reform for Dublin. Abercrombie's award was not even given until 1916. In the meantime, the cost of war blocked the attempts of the Dublin Council to extract money from the English government. A 1914 Housing Act had been extended to Ireland, but the LGB, controlled by the British Treasury, declined to appropriate money for Dublin housing, despite the housing committee's plea in September 1915 that recent demolitions of derelict buildings had left 1,212 families without shelter.[76] Then the 1916 Easter rebellion further complicated matters and brought Unwin back to the Dublin planning scene.

SURVEY, DIAGNOSE, PLAN

When Irish nationalists occupied the General Post Office on O'Connell (Sackville) Street on Easter Sunday, 1916, the British response was swift and brutal. British artillery destroyed significant portions of the city's economic center along O'Connell Street and the northeast section of the quays. While Dubliners were appalled by the destruction and the imposition of colonial military control on the city, leading figures in the architectural, building, and planning fields saw it as their opportunity to reconstruct the city. R. M. Butler, editor of the *Irish Builder and Engineer*, declared that a "wonderful and unlooked for opportunity has arisen in Dublin, a city that has long prided itself on the beauty of its streets and buildings. . . . [O'Connell] was a street of which any nation might be proud."[77] William A. Scott, chair of the department of architecture at University College Dublin, and who had worked in the LCC's architects' office before returning to Dublin, believed that the reconstruction of O'Connell Street gave the city "an opportunity rare in the history of cities" to formulate a unified urban plan. Ruth McManus notes that Butler was "principal of one of the busiest private architectural practices in Ireland."[78] In an ironic twist for the O'Connell Street merchants who had campaigned against a women's public toilet being placed in front of Nelson's Pillar, not only were their establishments now either gone or badly damaged, but Butler suggested removing the pillar itself from the street and constructing new monumental buildings along the street.

With rebuilding now necessary, men such as Butler and Scott hoped that their visions could come to the fore. The Civics Institute of Ireland reported that Lord Aberdeen was ready to finalize the award from the 1914 competition, but the outbreak of World War I and the 1916 Easter Sunday uprising delayed the award. The Royal Institute of Architects of Ireland expressed its frustration at the delay, but by September 1916, Abercrombie and his associates were acknowledged as the winners. Then the Irish rebellion following World War I deferred the plan's publication until 1922.[79] Abercrombie's plan, however, would become a model for reconstructing Dublin after the founding of the Irish Free State.

"Dublin of the Future" exhibited all the survey-diagnose-plan ideals being promoted by professional men. "Before entering on the general details of the Report," the planners declared,

> it must be stated that any recommendations are to be looked upon as tentative, and that no work should be commenced without a thorough system of investigation by means of a Local Civic and Regional Survey to provide the necessary information that was not available to the competitors. . . . This survey, among other things, would deal with the density of traffic, both vehicular, pedestrian, tramway, and railway, its location and direction at various hours in the day; population, density, and vital statistics; physical features; historic growth; industrial development, etc.[80]

Despite advocating survey first, the plan made sweeping proposals that, if adopted, would have significantly changed the city. It proposed a new traffic pattern that carved a new road system of widened radial streets of 60 feet, three super-radials 120 feet wide, and three new circular roads. A crucial element of this new system was to be a traffic center that would move traffic directly from the north circular road to Upper Ormond Quay, in the process destroying much housing in the poorer areas of the city, especially those in the streets surrounding the Ormond Market, where many of the area's current residents also worked. The market itself was to be remodeled into a Central Place and Mall, depriving those currently living in the area of both homes and livelihood (Figure 6.2).[81] The plan advocated new railway terminals, moving the docks farther east along the river away from the Custom House, and relocating factories and industry away from the river. Under such a scheme, the Liffey's role as a working river would be downplayed while that of road and railroad transport could be elevated. Shifting the docks farther away from the city center would also make it possible to incorporate the river into the vision of a monumental and civic space to be laid out for the north side of the city. A central feature of the plan was to create a new monumental center for the city, with new streets, monumental buildings and other structures as focal points on the north side of the Liffey. "It cannot be denied," the report concluded,

> but that the route from the Custom House [east] (with its restored circus and its true relation to the centre of the town re-established by the destruction of the railway bridge) to Phoenix Park [west] would

be one of great grandeur. O'Connell Street must first be crossed with its vista beyond the Nelson Pillar towards the National Theatre, then Capel Street, down which would face the huge front of the new Cathedral; a gradual widening leads into the open central square with the Four Courts on the left and the tower of Christchurch seen across the Bourse across the river; in front is the wide, tree-planted mall dominated by the obelisk, leading past the busy market-place, the tree-enclosed Art Gallery, finally to end up at the entrance of the superb central "*allée*" of Phoenix Park.[82]

References to continental cities were scattered throughout the plan. It proposed that the new cathedral be a basilica-type akin to Rome's St. Paul outside the Walls (San Paolo fuori le Mura), with a round tower placed in its courtyard rising above the church to be the spiritual center of the city. The new National Theatre would be Dublin's Opéra de Paris; the new art gallery should be placed on the site of the former royal barracks, positioned to resemble the Parisian setting of the Grand Palais and Petit Palais.

To complete this monumental city, Abercrombie recommended that the Rotunda Maternity Hospital at the top of O'Connell Street be removed to "the country air," having had "a long and honorable career." The Rotunda structure, he declared, could be "restored to nobler uses" and with a new

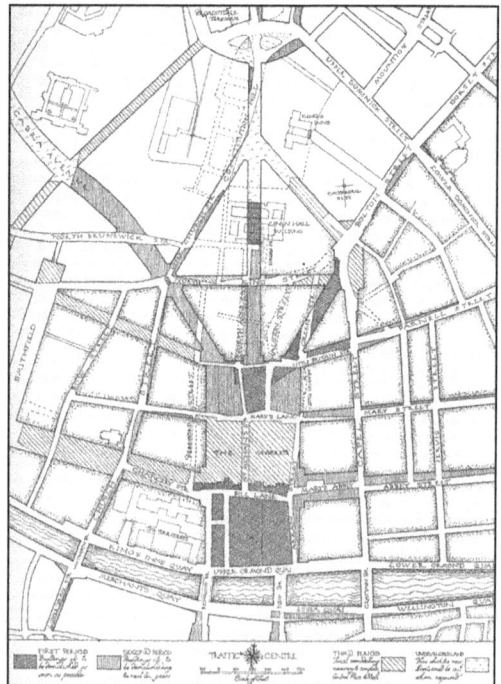

Figure 6.2 Proposed Dublin traffic plan. (Patrick Abercrombie, Sydney Kelly, and Arthur Kelly, *Dublin of the Future: The New Town Plan* [Liverpool: University Press of Liverpool, 1922], plate xxvii.)

wing built onto it to serve as a Music Auditorium, and a City Restaurant to face the Rotunda Gardens, which itself should function as a "town garden for sculpture, like the *Volksgarden* at Vienna."[83] The Rotunda was the only one of Dublin's three maternity hospitals on the north side of the Liffey. That Abercrombie blithely suggested removing it from the city and putting the structure to "nobler uses" implies that women delivering babies is not a noble use of a building while it simultaneously dismisses women's and children's needs for health care in the city. As with the refusal to provide women's public toilets, Abercrombie's proposal would render women's bodily functions invisible in the new civic city of men.

The plan recommended moving about sixty thousand people out of the city into new extra-urban areas. The recommendations for types and layout of new housing always referenced men and property. According to the plan's authors, whether to provide a garden or simply some open frontage should take account of the fact "that the man who is not fond of gardening, but who likes living in these suburban conditions, [will not be] burdened with garden space which he does not want; whereas his neighbor who may be an enthusiast, can take up his share." Creating housing for the "satisfactory type of workingman" in more hygienic conditions would help workers afford "larger and more capacious houses . . . who will be able to contribute their quota to the Exchequer."[84] Besides the idea for the Rotunda and the idea that any neighborhood parks should have croquet lawns for "older women," the plan did not mention how replanned Dublin would affect women lives.[85]

War and civil unrest precluded any immediate adoption of Abercrombie's plan, and the Rotunda Maternity Hospital remains in situ to this day. But between 1916 and the plan's official publication in 1922, Dublin men moved toward accepting the plan's major ideas as the way to reconstruct Dublin. Planning advocates were heartened by passage of the Dublin Reconstruction (Emergency Provisions) Act in 1916 after the destructions. The corporation formed a Reconstruction Committee and authorized it to consult with architects to determine how rebuilding should be done. Unwin traveled back to Dublin to draw up recommendations on the O'Connell Street reconstruction. All recommendations focused on rebuilding for future economic growth and development, with finances and concerns of building owners integral to the decisions.[86]

By 1918, the corporation was moving slowly toward adopting the ideals of the Abercrombie Plan, if not all its details. That year, the council's housing committee authorized a complete civic survey of the city before proceeding with major changes to the built environment. Acknowledging that "in this matter we are faced with the problem comprehending the alternatives of demolition, improvement or drift," the committee now agreed with the 1914 Unwin and Geddes report.[87] The survey, issued as the "North City Survey," actually covered only the city's north side streets, where some of the worst housing existed. But there it recommended acquiring and clearing eighty acres of so-called slum property in the area and building two thousand new houses.[88] LGB engineering inspector P. C. Cowan, however, warned that building new housing in the center would "mar the dignity and beauty of the Metropolis [and] ruin the city socially, commercially and industrially and make the prospects of a restoration of health and economic conditions in the greater Dublin hopeless." He recommended possible sites in suburban areas for twelve thousand new houses.[89]

Prunty notes that the survey now used the words *tenement* and *slum* interchangeably, so that housing in certain areas of the city was no longer classified as unhealthy or even overcrowded but as slums. The report declared that "sanitary standards are no longer central to the debate; it is taken as granted that scullery and WC for the 'sole use of each family' will be installed and that dwellings should be 'of sufficient size to prevent overcrowding and to admit of the separation of the sexes.'"[90] Thus, once an area was designated a slum because it did not meet internal housing arrangements decided on by men, that area became expendable and its residents and their desires became pawns to be moved around at will. Between 1918 and the mid-1940s the Dublin government adopted the rhetoric of slum clearance for razing tenement housing and accepted the assertion of planners that new housing should meet the preceding criteria.[91]

PLANNING THE CIVIC UNIT

Once housing was subsumed under planning and slum clearance rationalized the destruction of any area, the rhetoric of constructing the city as a civic unit became an accepted trope. In 1922, Horace T. O'Rourke, the city's newly appointed chief architect and former editor of *Irish Architect and Craftsman*, told the *Irish Independent* "that the idea of the city as a unit of life and culture was emerging after a period of unconsciousness, during which the civic unit had been obscured by haphazard development and national politics. Town improvement was the outcome of a new recognition of the importance of the civic unit."[92] O'Rourke found common ground with other professional men who were ready to push ahead with new developments using the rhetoric of planning the civic unit to promote slum clearance, decentralization, and economic development.

The Civics Institute of Ireland had absorbed the HTPAI in 1916. After that, the institute acted as an umbrella organization for men pursuing housing and town planning initiatives. The institute wrote the preface to the Abercrombie Plan, in which it claimed that it wanted the plan's publication to educate a well-informed citizenship because such "is the first and most essential force for the proper correction of the defects of community life." The institute wished "to arouse the historic and traditional spirit of Civic pride . . . and to revive that native genius which will place Dublin in its proper position as one of the world's best Capital cities."[93] Such expressions, and the fact that few Dubliners would ever read this volume, meant that the institute clearly had a limited vision of who possessed civic pride and what was the purpose of a plan for Dublin.

Although Abercrombie's plan had won the competition, the judges had praised another entry submitted by the English architects Charles Ashbee, a former resident of Toynbee Hall, and G. H. Chettle, for its emphasis on the civic unit. The strength of their entry, "New Dublin: A Study in Civics," according to the judges, was that "no other report expresses a fuller and more comprehensive grasp of civic problems."[94] Although "New Dublin" was never published and the outbreak of war prevented Ashbee from even submitting a final version, his text to the plan demonstrates how professional men were now seeing the city as a blank canvas on which they could imprint their ideas of the civic unit. Ashbee wanted his plan "to stimulate Dublin opinion and fix the attention of thoughtful people upon the city of the future."[95] Such recommendations as decentralized population "on a large scale," decentralized hospitals, "increased investment in fixed infrastructures" such as new wide roads, more public buildings, and expanded open spaces especially around all railroad stations were all abstract elements that could be imposed on any city regardless of its history and culture. Ashbee advocated a new university to enhance the civic life of Dublin. By "the decanting of the tenement population," the city would be able to use its "most beautiful eighteenth century streets and 'make of them University settlements.' For him, the university 'takes its constructive idealism into the City slum' . . . and helps transform slum dwellers and slums."[96] For Ashbee, as had been the case for Toynbee Hall and Toronto's University Settlement, well-educated men would lead the people into the correct ways of living in the city.

Once Dublin had weathered the violence of the Irish war of independence and the ensuing civil war years, the city's government and professional men moved quickly to implement new plans. In 1923 O'Rourke and the Civics Institute undertook a new expansive survey of the city. The *Irish Times* advocated such a survey "as necessary to a town plan as a physician's diagnosis is to his prescription."[97] The following year, the corporation initiated a Greater Dublin Commission to recommend reforming local government to foster more systematic growth for Dublin and incorporating suburban townships into a Greater Dublin. The concept of creating a Greater Dublin was to plan regionally rather than locally as the most efficient means to separate home and work and foster the city's economic progress. In a power struggle with the national government, the corporation was temporarily suspended in that year, and the idea of forming a greater Dublin was sidelined.[98]

The Dublin Civic Survey Report, completed and issued in 1925, was intended to be the complete city survey such as Abercrombie was now recommending as the means for constructing a civic society and the preliminary requirement for preparing a town plan.[99] Abercrombie wrote the report's foreword, proclaiming that Dublin was now ready to move forward. The report declared the civic survey as "the statistical and graphical representation of things as they are in a community," and repeated the phrase that "it was as necessary to a town plan as is a physician's diagnosis is to his prescription."[100] The report had almost nothing to say about the social nature of housing and as an element of a civic community. Instead, it focused on resolving the city's housing situation by separating housing and commercial areas. Referring to housing solutions in England, the report declared that "housing in suburban areas," along with new transit facilities, had "changed the subject of housing from a hopeless study into a wonderful science . . . a step toward the social millennium."[101] For Dublin, the "practicable solution [for housing] appears to be a combination of the central, on a limited scale, and the suburban methods, with the ultimate hope of eliminating the former."[102] The report declared that "the artisan of to-day desires to bring up his family in a fresher atmosphere, amid more attractive surroundings than are to be found in the heart of the city" and that carefully planning new suburban areas "would protect these areas from ever reaching slum conditions." Moreover, central city housing was surrounded by "the public house and street corner, and the paved thoroughfare as a playground for the children. Contrast these surroundings with those obtained in suburban areas, where the father has a little plot for gardening, the mother a space for drying clothes, and the children in the garden are immune from traffic dangers. The first environment is a slum, the second is a home."[103] By the time of the civic survey, Dublin women's concerns for what was necessary to foster a good community and life for all people in the city were no longer considered by the men leading Dublin.

The new housing developments begun in the 1920s reflected the report's recommendations. They aimed either to provide for property ownership or at minimum to allow the better-off working and lower-middle classes to rent single-family homes. New middle-class suburban areas were the target. These areas were often built by public utility societies, which functioned through a combination of private and public cooperation; the corporation leased to the societies land on the outskirts that already contained roads and other infrastructure, with favorable rent rebates and rates concessions.[104] As Ruth McManus concludes, the new national government in the 1920s was composed of "conservative revolutionaries . . . almost exclusively drawn from the ranks of the middle class" whose immediate objectives were to provide new housing for the middle class. The Housing Acts of 1924 and 1925 gave grants to entities building owner-occupied housing of a larger dimension than the working class could ever afford, let alone the poor.[105]

Such policies would reinforce a class-based geography, a feature of Dublin's reconstruction on which Dublin literature has focused.[106] But this literature rarely considers what these developments meant for women.

Marino: The Middle-Class Solution

The planned housing scheme at Marino to the northeast beyond the original city boundary became a model for Dublin's middle-class suburban development.[107] The scheme was officially underway in 1924, although Unwin had begun developing plans for the area in 1914. Marino's layout shares its conception with British planning ideals. It is interior-focused and laid out in the hub-and-spoke style, as was London's Boundary Street Estate, although Marino contains single-owner housing, not flats. There are only four direct entrance roads into Marino—Unwin's original sketches had referred to creating "gateways" into the area—each of which leads into an open central circle. These streets run through smaller open areas called crescents around which houses are arranged. As at Boundary Street and Hampstead, all social interaction is directed away from the street. Every street looks identical, every crescent has the same layout, and once you reach the center green, if you do not remember from which spoke street you entered, you are unsure as how to get back to where you first entered (Figure 6.3).

Figure 6.3 Ordinance survey map, Marino scheme, Dublin, 1938.

Even today, the layout is totally disorienting to a stranger. It discourages strangers from entering it and wandering around. Moreover, it isolates residents inside the area. Marino is encircled by a ring road, and spaces outside that interior are hemmed in by larger, busier streets. Access to the nearest Dublin Area Rapid Transit (DART) station today requires crossing busy streets, and the only designated children's play area is across Fairview Road, a multilane road with few traffic lights. Neither the central green area nor the crescents are provided with any play facilities for children. Within the area, walking is definitely discouraged because there is nowhere to go. Shops are located only on the periphery roads.

In the 1920s and 1930s, women living in Marino would have felt even further removed from the life of the city because most of them would not have had cars. Existing and planned tram systems were designed to carry workers and businessmen into the city center, not to facilitate circulation through local neighborhoods. Until 1938 there was only one tram line in Marino, on the edge of the area. The area's DART transit station was not built until the 1990s. James Killen concludes that Marino and other suburban development were "always conceived of as catering for individuals who would find employment and seek services in the city centre. It is notable . . . [that] provision of shops and employment opportunities received scant attention."[108] It is hard to imagine that women living in Marino could have felt part of Dublin as a civic unit, yet without expressing it in those terms, neither the men promoting the civic survey nor those of the Civics Institute thought about women as public participants of the civic unit. Rather, as stated in the civic survey, they rejected central area housing because they believed it bred crime, danger, undesirable behavior, and undermined appropriate gender roles.[109]

Subsequent suburban housing schemes followed the Marino pattern and continued to isolate Dublin women from the life of the city and close them into their houses. Drumcondra to the west of Marino built some housing grouped around cul-de-sacs; some houses were even closed off from the street by a spiked chain strung between concrete pillars. Such features might be considered an "attractive feature" from a planning perspective, but they also embounded women. McManus points out how this aspect of the Drumcondra scheme resembled London's Becontree council estate. In both Dublin and London, postwar suburban developers adhered to Unwin's ideal of housing grouped around closes.[110] His use of the term *closes* could be seen as a metaphorical representation of closing women into their immediate surroundings.

Slum Clearance: The Poor and Working-Class Solution

Dublin's preoccupation with suburban development for the middle class and attention to "assisted private enterprise" also meant that the city did not focus on the housing needs of Dublin's poorest residents, whose central city housing conditions were desperate. Members of the city government, including the Lord Mayor and several aldermen and councilors still owned tenement properties in the 1920s on some of the city's worst streets. A 1923 public health committee report specifically noted the complaints against the tenements on Upper Rutland Street owned by Alderman Thomas O'Reilly and listed other council members as tenement owners.[111] The 1925 civic survey showed Upper Rutland Street located in one of the most densely populated areas of the city's north side. But property rights continued to influence council decisions, trumping concerns about public health beyond tenements. In 1925, the public health committee extended the license for a horse slaughterhouse on Henrietta Lane on the city's north side, noting that the license had been held since 1896 and that the medical officer of health had no objection.[112] Thus, a privately owned slaughterhouse was licensed despite the existence of a municipal abattoir on the far northwest edge of the city.[113]

Along with promoting suburban housing, the city was focusing much of its energy on replanning O'Connell Street, using the powers it had gained in the 1916 Dublin Reconstruction Act and the 1924 Dublin Reconstruction (Emergency Provisions) Act, while claiming that it did not have the financial means to provide better housing for the poor.[114] In 1923, the council's reconstruction committee had recommended O'Connell Street as a city priority, suggesting that the council begin buying up property along the perpendicular Gloucester Street, "a decaying street, the majority of houses being occupied as tenements," so that the city would profit from rebuilding.[115] Two years later, the council authorized spending £28,532 to continue the work of extending Gloucester Street to intersect with O'Connell and to widen Cathedral Street where it led into O'Connell. The council justified the expense because it "will tend toward the betterment of the district."[116] Using the powers of the 1924 Reconstruction Act, Horace O'Rourke directed the reconstruction work, following the advice of a committee of architects appointed by the Royal Institute of Architects of Ireland (RIAI). Most of the properties that had been destroyed in the civil unrest of 1916 and 1921–1922 were privately owned, but O'Rourke and his consultants wanted to prevent property owners from rebuilding on their own. The professional architects wanted to implement a harmonious architectural style for the area. *Irish Builder and Engineer* warned that Dublin should not become an ugly city that failed to develop a style of street architecture.[117] In late 1924, Abercrombie returned to Dublin to confer about developing a complete town plan for the city and region. For a variety of reasons, including financial ones, official town planning would not commence until the 1930s. But under O'Rourke, the O'Connell Street reconstruction was accomplished using funds made available through the reconstruction acts.

On the other hand, both the city government and the new Irish State rejected calls for better housing in Dublin contending they lacked the funds to do so. In 1923 Alfie Byrne, a former alderman, member of the Dáil (Irish parliament) representing north Dublin, and future Lord Mayor of Dublin, asked the Minister for Local Government "whether he was aware 'that many thousands of Dublin citizens are now sheltering in rat infested basements of slum property'" and that he please clarify the state's housing policy. The minister replied that "unsettled conditions," financial debts, and high building costs rendered it impossible to fund any municipal schemes.[118]

By the early 1930s, however, the Dublin government could no longer ignore the central city housing situation. The medical officer of health, Dr. Matthew J. Russell, detailed severe overcrowding, concluding that such conditions were unfit for human habitation. On the city's north side, the Railway Street area bounded by Summerhill, Buckingham, and Marlborough Streets and rail lines on the south, housed 308 families (1,187 people). The Townsend Street area just south of the Liffey was said to contain 206 families (836 people).[119] In 1934 the council's housing committee simultaneously declared that "the new phase of housing envisages the complete abolition of the slums" while admitting "the impossibility of all dwellers in these slums being in a position to pay for new accommodations commensurate with their family needs."[120] Among the impossibilities was the fact that if neighborhoods were designated slums to be cleared, rehousing the displaced created a crucial problem because the city's leaders wished to adhere to the ideal of low-density housing. While slum clearance was the accepted rhetorical device to rationalize moving people out of existing housing, it could not be easily squared with reality. There were arguments on both sides about whether to build more cottages on the periphery or to tear down the tenements and build flats on the cleared land. Proponents of suburban housing promoted property ownership and the single-family home. A Catholic clergyman urged "one house, one family." Multiple-family flats were deemed "not a proper home for human beings." No architect, he claimed, could "obviate the moral dangers of the common staircase." Flat life was an "unnatural thing . . . a smashing blow at a fundamental instinct of humanity, the instinct to guard the family by isolation." Property ownership was deemed an integral need for sustaining the nation. "The more men you deprive of even the minimum of property represented by a garden and a really private entrance, the more you are weakening throughout the State that clinging to and respect for property that is the expression of man's desire for liberty." The only mention of women in this article was to promote the single-family home because "above all for the poor woman and her children, the home is ninety per cent. [sic] of their existence."[121] Dublin's Anglican archbishop John Gregg also advocated suburbanization, contending that "the welfare of the city, morally and physically, is bound up closely with the housing of its citizens of every class and their ready access to fresh air." In suburban housing, families would be able "to live healthily and with decency."[122] As Daly demonstrates in an essay on gender and sexuality in Ireland, the Irish, especially the Catholic Church, remained preoccupied with preventing the state from interfering in the family.[123]

In the end, financial considerations determined Dublin's decision on working-class housing. The corporation continued to build suburban housing schemes pushing farther out from the city center, but rents in these developments were generally too high for poor Dubliners. So "block schemes" of flats were built on cleared slum areas. The choice for these people was to leave their neighborhood for housing that they could not afford or to live in cheaply built flats. The residents of Dublin's tenement neighborhoods were subjected to professional men's ideals of slum clearance and planning to remove people from the city. These men never consulted the residents as to their needs, desires, or ideas of community.

Moving as many people as possible out of the city center effectively removed women from its streets and satisfied the male vision that the street "was an essentially male domain."[124] At the same time, it spatially separated the reproductive and the productive spaces of the city. The presence of women and children on the streets produced messy social and economic relations. Street selling disrupted the even flow of traffic, but it also encouraged people to occupy the street, which violated an "orderly social geometry" and interfered with the planning of straight wide streets intersecting as much as possible at right angles.[125] The replanning of O'Connell Street that had extended Gloucester Street (now Cathal Bruga Street) into O'Connell and had widened Cathedral Street implemented such geographic symmetry. The professional men and business leaders desired hegemonic control of economic and property interests and had absorbed, at least to some significant measure, the ideals of professionals and theorists such as Abercrombie and Le Corbusier. Lynne Walker argues that because architecture "defines the public and private spheres: to allow women access to the design of architecture therefore threatens patriarchal control of spatial definitions, which are essential to maintain the social, economic and cultural *status quo*."[126] Dublin's women assuredly wanted better housing. They wanted their children to survive into adulthood. But they were not consulted about their preferences and needs. The struggle was over whether the city was foremost a place where people lived, worked, played, and were present in public, or whether it was foremost the place of business, order, and a public presence controlled by men to achieve their ends. As Elizabeth Darling and Lesley Whitworth remark, women exhibited a "startling . . . capacity to elide the public and the private in the pursuit of their goals."[127] Men, on the contrary, wished to keep the public and the private as separate as they could.

Dublin, Women, and Gender in the New Irish State

The founding of the Irish Free State had freed Ireland from the English Protestant culture that had devalued Irish Catholicism. For Dublin women, the new free state would further limit their ability to function as public figures, because the nationalist project had linked Irish identity with Catholicism and made women's domesticity and purity a cornerstone of the state's identity. Rev. Gwynn's charge in 1910 linking women's public presence to the outsider's perception of Dublin as one of the most immoral cities in Europe was not an isolated instance of this preoccupation. The superiority of Catholicism vis-à-vis English Protestantism relied heavily on rhetoric about the "purity" of Irish women. It also contributed to the Irish Free State's reluctance to pursue certain types of social welfare measures lest they result in "excessive" or "unwarranted" interference with the family.[128] Such an attitude was heavily gendered both as to women and as to ideals of femininity and masculinity. Women were to be kept and protected inside the feminine domestic sphere. Men were to be the masculine protectors of that domestic realm, with only minimal state legislation interfering with male control of the family.[129]

Aside from the Alexandra Tenement Guild women, Dublin never possessed female housing managers such as London women who had inherited Octavia Hill's work and ideas.[130] Yet Dublin women often expressed similar ideas. In 1925, Mrs. Greville, a rent collector for the Alexander Guild buildings, for example, noted the difference between viewing housing as a personal, human, and community need and the professional men's expressions of housing as a way to increase civic pride. In Greville's presentation to the guild's central housing committee, she reported that she "always tried to know the people and their requirements and to take an interest in them, going into the houses and talking to the women."[131] Perhaps the women in these houses resented this middle-class woman as an intruder. We do not know because we do not have their voices recorded. But if we extrapolate from evidence that we do possess from London, we can see how that city's female rent collectors and building residents engaged in mutual negotiation over the definition of housing, with the rent collectors having to take as much as they gave.[132]

Cultural differences also precluded Dublin women from producing professional women to challenge the male professional outlook. Dublin had no equivalent to London's housing consultant Elizabeth Denby, who promoted "mixed development schemes" that included laundries, shops, and schools and whose goal was to keep people in the city, not move them out to the suburbs. Dublin had no professionally trained women such as Dorothy Braddell, who designed "labour-saving modern kitchens" in the 1930s, or a Women's Co-operative Guild to agitate for better housing for working-class women.[133] Male professionals who planned and controlled London developments restricted these English women's efforts, but they continued to promote a different vision of housing that represented a women-centered ideal about daily life in the city that contested the ideas of the professional men.

For Dublin's poor and working-class women, slum clearance policies restricted choices. One woman who grew up in the old south side Liberties area described the conundrum:

> With the passage of time the tenements in the surrounding streets were depleted and demolished, the families were banished to the outskirts of the city to housing estates where there were no facilities whatsoever. . . . In one way the families were better off, in that they had proper houses with toilets, water on tap, bedrooms and gardens, but their relations, friends and neighbours weren't there, the shops, schools, churches, the dealers, pay shops, hustle, bustle, atmosphere, bumping into people they knew all their lives, the cinemas, theatres, dance-halls, factories, yards and offices, the security of community life was gone. The Corporation housing schemes gave them houses, but it stripped away the fabric of their lives.[134]

She was not alone in mourning the lost sense of neighborliness. Another woman who had grown up in the tenements acknowledged that "it was a hard life" but declared:

> I wish I was back in it again, in the tenement again. When they started tearing the old tenements down it was like tearing *us* apart. It tore *me* apart. It broke me heart. We were all one family, all close. We all helped one another. If I had a tenement house now I'd go back and live in it . . . yes, I would.[135]

Another former female tenement resident expressed her sense of loss of a way of life that the civic reformers abhorred:

> You'll often hear people say now, "God be with the tenement houses." Everybody was generous to one another. Doors was always open, no lock nor keys nor bolts. No robberies or nothing in the tenements. And you'd know every foot that went up the tenement stairs. Everybody was generous to one another. Knockabouts would come into the halls and sleep on the stairs and all the tenants would bring them out a cup of tea in the morning.[136]

Women who were moved out of the tenements lost more than that sense of neighborliness. They had previously earned money and supported their

families through street selling. One woman described how with unemployment so high among men, "the women traders they held the families together. . . . My mother and grandmother sold on Parnell Street, sold
vegetables and fruit and fish." Other women had worked as "tuggers," scour-
ing the suburbs for old clothing and other items they brought back to be sold
in the used-clothing-and-goods markets that dotted the tenement districts.[137]
Old photos of the streets in the tenement areas demonstrate the presence of
women on the streets, selling, shopping, moving from place to place. Riddell's Row, which ran perpendicular to Moore Street, which itself lay west of
O'Connell between Parnell and Talbot Streets, for example, was once such a
street for selling secondhand clothes and footwear and thus was always
crowded with women.[138] Moore Street was also one of the streets on which
the WNHA had demanded that the council build a women's public toilet.
This area was not a locale for those middle-class women that Dublin men so
worried would be shocked by the sight of a woman's public toilet. Nonetheless, the council had refused to build such a convenience there. One could
say they did this despite the overwhelming public presence of women, but
that could have been precisely the point: slum clearance also removed street
markets such as the ones on Riddell's Row and thus also removed women
from the public streets of the city center. Since O'Rourke did not retire until
1945, he bore much responsibility for the planning and reconstruction of
Dublin for more than two decades.

No women wanted to return to the poverty, hunger, disease, and lack of
sanitation that poor Dublin tenement residents had endured. What they
missed was a sense of community that could not be reproduced in the new
planned areas that intentionally closed them off from each other and embounded women into the home and off the city streets. Oral testimony from
a man who had lived in the tenements illustrated the gender difference: "It
was funny, you could move a man ten miles out and on a Saturday night he'd
come back into the old pub for his drink."[139] Women did not have similar
freedom to hold on to old attachments, friends, and neighbors. They had to
stay at home with the children. They could no longer spend evenings in windows or doorways talking with their neighbors or watching each other's children. What the planners saw as clean and orderly living, women often saw
as a sterile environment that virtually eliminated community life in favor of
the organized civic unit.

STILL SEEKING DUBLIN OF THE FUTURE

In 1934, a new Town and Regional Planning Act gave the Dublin government the authority to draw up a complete planning scheme for the city, defined as a "scheme made in accordance with this Act for the general purpose
of securing the orderly and progressive development of a particular area,

whether urban or rural, in the best interests of the community and of preserving, improving, and extending the amenities of such area."[140] The council constituted a new town planning committee to follow the act's recommendation that a local authority prepare a planning scheme that "should
be guided at all stages by expert advice." This committee named a subcommittee of four members who, despite the animosity of the Irish Free State
toward Britain, were directed to go to there to study the planning of cities.
The subcommittee subsequently recommended that Dublin employ Abercrombie and Sydney Kelly to provide a substantive planning scheme for Dublin "from its inception to its ratification."[141]

Working now with Irish architect Manning Robertson, Abercrombie
and Kelly in 1939 presented a Sketch Development Plan (SDP) for Dublin.
Along with a subsequent refinement in 1941, the SDP reflected Abercrombie's preoccupation with regional planning, building satellite towns, and
embounding neighborhoods inside the city. Embounded neighborhoods
and satellite towns were to assume functions that previously might have
been done in the city center.[142] The 1941 refinement of the SDP emphasized
that the recommended "satellites are not 'dormitories' for the primary city,
but they have their own churches, schools, factories amusements. They depend upon the primary [larger city] for major centralised activities such as
universities, museums, and so on. It is essential, however, that the satellites
should be separated from the primary, and from each other, by a wide open
belt." The SDP also wanted these satellites to limit their population to sixty
thousand. It focused on transportation, relieving traffic congestion, laying
out new roads including three new ring roads, and erecting grand buildings along the quays.[143] The plan recommended that rural migration into
Dublin be stemmed so that the city's population would be controlled to
seven hundred thousand to eight hundred thousand residents. The council's general purposes committee approved the plan with a few amendments, but the council did not move to carry out the plan.[144] In its report
on the SDP, the Town Planning Committee acknowledged that, again, financial constraints would prevent the city from undertaking all the recommendations.[145]

Yet by the late 1930s the city's failure to solve its housing situation, including its traditional reliance on private enterprise, had created such a massive problem that it was difficult for it to undertake a general planning
scheme such as that offered by Abercrombie. According to Joseph Brady's
recent analysis of Dublin from 1930 to 1950, the housing problem, by the
early 1940s, was so far from being solved that "the authorities were simply
'running to keep still'; a plan was seen as a luxury or even a threat."[146] Even
while Abercrombie and his associates had been formulating comprehensive
plans, in 1939 the council fell back on directing the Ministry for Local Government and Public Health to begin a new housing inquiry to investigate

"how the housing of the working classes can best be expedited without undue burden on the ratepayers."[147]

Housing and planning in Dublin were constantly enmeshed in concerns about gender across the 1930s. The Irish Free State was still struggling to build a postcolonial identity clearly distinguished from Britain and was preoccupied with the place of women in that new state. The national government enacted new restrictions on women's public presence to "restore the traditional order and hierarchy" of gender relations so that the respectable Irish woman "would become a badge of respectability for the new state."[148] As Irish women confronted legislation stripping them of equal citizenship rights, reconstructing Dublin was in the hands of the men controlling the city whose plans pursued the patriarchal private-public divide. Men assumed that city center living was not "conducive to proper formation of the family, with its overlapping of public and private spheres, and the blurring of family boundaries implicit in the tenement life." Dublin's growth as the commercial and industrial center of the country magnified fears that a crowded and poor inner city "posed a moral and a social problem for central and local government," as it "upset the balance of the urban nuclear family [and] lessened the scope of its traditional functions."[149]

Dublin leaders had valued housing built by the public utility societies because suburban development of single-family cottages was a financial and social means to solidify proper gender relations and traditional family values. The societies built 48 percent of all new housing on the periphery for the middle class, stressing home ownership as a stabilizing social factor.[150] Alison Ravetz's conclusion about the gendered dimension of British council housing decisions pertains also to housing decisions in Dublin. "The suburb," she contends, "was more than a place, it was a culture in which the dominant influence was the home, physically and conceptually isolated from other urban activity and the public spheres. It served new patterns of marriage where housework and care of children were not counted as 'work.'"[151]

Despite the work of the public utility societies and the government's drive to create a home-owning city, Dublin had a low percentage of home ownership even among the middle classes who had remained in the city. Even worse, in some central city wards, the percentage of renters in the overcrowded and deteriorating buildings reached over 90 percent. As Joseph Brady concludes in his recent book *Dublin, 1930–1950,* "The pressure on housing and incomes was such that the lower end of the market [the lowest rents] produced a significant income for owners," who thus had little incentive for upgrading their property. With land cheaper in unoccupied suburban areas than in the city center, and neither private enterprise nor public utility societies able to supply a sufficient amount of affordable housing, the city had by the late 1930s embarked on its own suburban housing schemes supported by subsidies from the state.[152] The appointed Housing Inquiry favored building single-family suburban cottages that it deemed more suitable for family living than inner-city flats. It rejected the argument that workers needed to live near their employment as "well-established custom rather than a necessity."[153]

But it remained financially impossible to move all the city's poor and working-class residents into cottages on the periphery. The two thousand new flats built by the city up to 1939 had not come close to satisfying housing needs, so that it needed to resort to compulsory purchase of inner-city tenements, intending to recondition these areas with multitenant rental flats.[154] The Alexandra Guild properties of Summerhill succumbed to this process. McManus observes that inner-city blocks of flats for people who could not afford to move to the suburbs was "a tacit acceptance that social segregation was inevitable" and effectively institutionalized Dublin as a class-segregated city by the 1940s.[155] The Fatima Mansions in Rialto, erected between 1949 and 1951, for example, were an example of such isolated housing. They were built between two major roads and configured to face inward, "physically and symbolically [isolated] from the surrounding neighborhood."[156]

But a focus on class-based segregation does not account for the gendered results of clearing the so-called slum areas and erecting such projects as the Fatima Mansions. Every account of tenement life in Dublin emphasizes the roles that women had played in supporting their families, often by street selling and trading and in managing small shops.[157] Both suburban housing and new flat developments physically removed women from the streets and the opportunity for at least marginal employment. In houses and developments that stressed the embounded neighborhood and the nuclear family of male worker and female housewife, women were further removed from the civic life of the city. Coupled with state legislation restricting women's rights of citizenship, Dublin's built environment became a safe zone for male economic development.

7

Toronto

Saving "Toronto the Good"

This is a subject, however, which must be examined into with the greatest care and thoroughness in order that every scientific detail may be fully comprehended to eliminate any possible question as to the future purity of our water supply.

—Mayor John Winchester, "Mayor's Inaugural Address" (1908)

Women are accused of jumping at conclusions, we are told that men reason. If they reason to come to a conclusion[,] when may we reasonable [*sic*] expect them to arrive at a decision regarding the water supply?

—Florence Huestis, Toronto Local Council of Women vice president (1907)

In the early twentieth century, Toronto was drawing its drinking water from Lake Ontario. But it also dumped industrial waste into the lake, and household waste flowed into it via the sewer system that emptied into Toronto Bay and out into the lake. The women of the Toronto Local Council of Women (TLCW) wanted the city to build a filtration plant to protect the health of city residents. City leaders had been dithering for quite some time about the issue, claiming they needed more scientific study before committing to spending for such a project. The women claimed that the provincial bacteriologist reported that thirty million gallons of sewage flowed daily into the bay, with around nine hundred cases of typhoid reported in 1907. Exasperated by the city's stalling, the TLCW organized a public meeting to discuss the problem. There, Florence Huestis told the audience that "civic rulers have taken thirty-three years to think over this problem." "Water," she declared, "is a prime necessity of life."[1] She asked women to keep making noise about the water and appealed to their sense of a common welfare. Huestis urged women to "keep it before the authorities that through the merciful intervention of Providence, we, the people, are still alive."[2] The annual reports of the city engineer in the early twentieth century made no mention of pollution; they merely focused on statistics of sewer pipes laid, the amount of water being pumped through city water mains, and the like.[3]

The clean water issue captured a differing vision of a good city. After Mayor William Howland's moral crusades in the late 1880s against saloons, gambling dens, and brothels, boosters had declared the city to be Toronto the Good. But between 1891 and 1911, Toronto's unregulated growth and sprawl threatened this supposed good city. The population more than doubled in that time from 181,220 to 381,383. An influx of new, and poorer, immigrants resulted in chronic housing shortages and overcrowding. The worst housing was in the city center bounded by Queen, College, University, and Yonge Streets. This was the so-called shantytown St. John's Ward. The ward housed mainly Italian and Jewish immigrants living in "a collection of streets and laneways, full of run-down single-family dwellings."[4] The presence of the ward threatened both the city's image and its economic expansion. The new city hall, which had cost $2.5 million (in Canadian dollars) had been built on the southeast edge of the ward. The Eaton and Co. department store, destined to become one of the city's largest emporia, was expanding just to the east and north of the city hall.

Population and commercial growth was accompanied by unmanaged sprawl that had increased traffic and communication problems and multiplied infrastructure problems. Working-class residents who could not afford housing in the center city had migrated outward and erected self-built housing.[5] The city did not control these township areas, and their very presence impeded Toronto's systematic growth. In 1907, the same year in which the TLCW was demanding a water filtration plant, the editor of the *Toronto World* laid out the idea that the city's first priority should be to expand government control over these townships for "three great public reasons": to control the water supply, transit, and sewers and sanitation. Doing so would create a Greater Toronto.[6]

Toronto's leading men were striving to remake Toronto into an orderly commercial and monumental city. By early 1900, the city had replaced the centrally located Western Cattle Market with the new Union Stockyards in Toronto Junction, northwest immediately outside the city proper, which had its own slaughtering facilities. This new location eliminated the previous practice of driving cattle through the city streets to the slaughterhouses on the periphery.[7] A modern city could not have cattle moving through its streets, or other dirty industries in its central city, if it wanted to foster commercial development and attract new men and investments into it. Systematic planning was deemed the solution for the future.

ENVISIONING TORONTO THE GOOD

Beginning at the turn of the century, Toronto men started putting concerted effort into deciding what would make Toronto a good, modern city for the future. In 1901, the men of the Guild of Civic Art (later renamed the Civic

Guild) and those of the Ontario Association of Architects (OAA; formerly Toronto Architectural Eighteen Club) began their quest to plan Toronto into that modern city following three basic ideas: the city was a body to be cured of disease; curing that body was the job of professional experts; and the city should be foremost the site of economic development.

Invited to speak before the Eighteen Club in early 1901, Philadelphia architect Albert E. Kelsey impressed on the gathering that the city was like a body. The modern city, he claimed, "involves first circulation" because it "represents the anatomy of a city, the transit facilities above, below, and on the surface of the ground, the life arteries."[8] Following this talk, a delegation from the OAA and the guild then met with the city council to urge that money be allocated to employ a "competent person to prepare plans for the general improvement of the city" and to ensure that all planning "should be done under the direction of an expert of wide experience."[9] Without using the word *decentralization*, W. A. Langton, architect and OAA president, stressed that the city was foremost a place of business and commerce. Factories and their workers clogged the city's arteries and circulation. "The use of a city," he asserted in a speech to the OAA, "is not as a place to make things in, but as a place to carry on the transactions resulting from the transfer of things made." For Langton, "the factory space, the factory smoke and the operatives are all external matters introduced into city life only to clog its simplicity and ease of action."[10]

Just as Toronto men were beginning to promote planning, in spring 1904 the city suffered a serious fire. It began on the evening of April 19 and spread across an area extending south along Bay Street toward the lakefront. The area was crammed with wholesale shops and light manufacturing in wooden buildings, including open wooden staircases and flammable goods stored in warehouses, and the flames quickly destroyed around 100 buildings. In the immediate aftermath, the men of the OAA responded as Chicago men had after the 1871 fire, and as would many Dublin men after the 1916 destructions. The event was an opportunity for creative destruction. For *Canadian Architect and Builder*, "there is now an opportunity such as will probably never occur again of improving the character of buildings for business purposes. The opportunity should not be lost."[11] The city council passed new regulations against rebuilding with wooden constructions, and the mayor praised the "determination and courage of our merchants" in rebuilding. But no further planning was undertaken at the time.[12]

In 1906, Byron E. Walker, general manager of the Canadian Bank of Commerce, raised the issue. He presented a plan prepared with cooperation of the OAA, the guild, and the Engineers Club to lay out the principles of planning that should guide Toronto's development. First, Walker focused on circulation, a problem he contended would be cured by building new diagonal thoroughfares crisscrossing the city. According to Walker, one of the "serious troubles of modern cities . . . [was] the incoming of people from where they live and the exit at night—we have to go out now in zigzag fashion." Planning could halt the proliferation of streets at right angles to each other and provide long, wide thoroughfares as great vistas that would make moving through the streets more enjoyable. Second, Walker stressed that Toronto men needed to understand that they were competing with Montreal for "supremacy of trade." For Toronto to win, its planning had to "involve making all the leading men interested in Toronto." Finally, Walker again emphasized that professional experts must take charge of planning. Experts could control planning funds raised through a tax levy free from control by the city council to ensure that "no incoming council can divert this particular item" into other expenditures. Walker exhorted the people of Toronto to recognize that the time was ripe for building a modern city:

> It is really a question of whether the people of Toronto at the present time are going to join the movement which is taking place all over Canada—there is a larger movement in railroad building, in banking, in the distribution of goods, a larger feeling from one end of the country to the other—whether the people of Toronto have got into this movement and into this larger wave of action enough to do the thing for their own city, which is not only eminently reasonable but is to the last degree necessary.[13]

The city council again failed to prioritize planning, but the guild persisted and offered another plan in 1909, again advocating the need for diagonal thoroughfares to connect the city center with the northwest and northeast corners of the city. When Langton presented this new plan to the guild, he pronounced the existing gridiron street plan a "waste of time." He acknowledged that "the saving in time to the population of the city, regarded as a body of workers, might well have a place" in diagonal streets, but that was not his primary concern. Rather, he believed that these long, diagonal roads would be profitable for business, with new buildings erected on them and old, nonprofitable businesses eliminated. The result would be a rise in land values. Running new surface transit lines along such wide new corridors, he continued, would make Toronto "a much pleasanter and more profitable place to live in." It would introduce variety "into our uninteresting street plan when every street north of Queen Street is crossed by one of the diagonals, making pleasant irregularities, striking building sites, small open spaces, places for monuments, fountains, and seats under trees." For Langton, the cost of buying land and properties to achieve these diagonals was also "a business opportunity from which there would be no hanging back in the commercial world, and there is no reason why the citizens of Toronto should be afraid of it."[14] The council again refused to undertake such drastic action.

The following year, however, the council changed its focus and urged Mayor George R. Geary to appoint a commission composed of city council members and citizens to investigate municipal conditions with regard "to the preparation and carrying out of a comprehensive plan for beautifying and improving the city." The council also proposed to create a Toronto Civic Improvement Trust "which shall have power, at the request of the City Council, to acquire, lay out, construct, extend, or improve any park, garden, playground, boulevard, avenue, street, building or other public work deemed necessary for the benefit of the City and the citizens."[15] The Board of Control, which oversaw municipal finances, rejected this recommendation.[16] If no overall planning was yet underway, Toronto men had now identified the three issues of both public and private space that would, they believed, be necessary to foster the good city: halting the building of apartment houses, preventing the proliferation of public toilets, and keeping housing a private enterprise. Each of these issues intersected with ideas about women's place in the city.

The Dangerous Lure of the Apartment House

Toronto men had always been keen to promote their city as a city of homes. The 1901 official guide to the city declared it to be "correctly described as a city of homes . . . a city of beautiful residences."[17] A 1903 booklet asserted that of all the large cities on the continent, Toronto "has been justly described as 'the City of Homes.'"[18] Now they were troubled by the growing numbers of women who were seeking, or preferring, housing other than the single-family home.

New technology that was enabling the construction of a new style of multiunit building, the apartment house, confounded this ideal and threatened the public-private divide. Men began to view the apartment house as damaging the link between home ownership and domesticity. In a 1903 essay in *Canadian Architect and Builder*, Langton declared that "home is a place which shuts off the world at the street door." Apartment ownership was not real ownership, since it did not sink its roots into the ground. Langton was even more concerned that since an apartment was a "flat," it disrupted private domesticity. In an apartment house, women would need to pass bedrooms while moving through the apartment. "A delicate woman is apt to become an indelicate woman in the matter of appearances in *deshabille*, which the comparative privacy given by the levels of a home should prevent."[19] Moreover, he warned, the apartment house was threatening women's nature in ways that would ruin the city.

> The happiness of a woman does not seem to exist now, as it did in the early days of the world, in being the mother of children. Domestic life has ceased to be her necessary field of work. Men, much as they hate work, do seem to acquire a sort of enthusiasm for the proper

fulfillment of it; it is their life. But women do not seem to regard domestic duties as their life, but as an irksome addition to their life.... They incite one another continually to desire greater freedom from care. The woman who is most envied is she who has the least care. Not only is pride in their families vanishing but pride in their housekeeping as well; and apartment life will complete the process. With no families and almost no housekeeping—for, with soup in paper boxes and fried potatoes in a bottle, a woman has little to think of now if she has credit and a telephone—with nothing to do at home, women may fulfill their ideal; but will they also not fulfill the warnings of St. Paul and "learn to be idle, wandering about from house to house; and not only idle, but tattlers also and busybodies, speaking things which they ought not."[20]

Of course, it is impossible to know exactly how many men shared Langton's opinion. But new technology was often feared as threatening women's proper role because it allowed them more freedom. (See Figure 7.1.) A few years before Langton's screed, a Toronto clergyman had railed against electric lighting "as an instrument of evil which threatened to 'release girls from honest toil to wander the streets and fall prey to the wiles of Satan.'"[21]

Figure 7.1 Women in an automobile in front of Alexandra Apartments, University Avenue, Toronto, 1906. (Courtesy of the Toronto Public Library.)

For Toronto men, a city predicated on a property culture of home owner-ship with the private family inside that home could satisfy fears about im-morality. In 1911, medical officer of health Charles Hastings emphasized this connection: "Toronto is a city of homes, and it is in the best interests of the city, physically, morally and socially, that it should remain a city of homes."[22] Moreover, people living in apartment buildings were tenants, not property owners, a situation that violated the belief that good property owners made good citizens. Linking property ownership with morality and good citizen-ship characterized all Toronto housing efforts for the coming decades. The men of Toronto's Bureau of Municipal Research, organized in 1914, would declare that "usually ownership has a determining influence not alone on the conditions of homes but on the stability of the population, the standards of citizenship, and self-respect."[23] But apartment houses were not the only threat that men perceived to Toronto the Good. They were worried about women and public toilets.

Public Toilets and Public Space

By 1900, Toronto had built a men's ground-level public toilet in the middle of the street at the intersection of Adelaide and Toronto Streets opposite the main post office (Figure 7.2). In 1904, medical officer of health Dr. Charles Sheard urged the city to supply more such amenities.[24] Mayor Thomas Urqu-hart responded that the Board of Control was considering more public toi-lets, and men's toilets opened in early 1906, one at the intersection of Yonge and Cottingham Streets and another at the intersection of Spadina Avenue and Queen Street.[25] The Toronto city council resisted furnishing public toi-lets for women even though—or perhaps because—the number of Toronto women moving through the city was increasing every year, especially in the city center. By 1901, 56 percent of employed Toronto women worked in the city center as opposed to 47 percent of employed men. By 1911, the average distance traveled between home and work for women was 1.7 kilometers, and for the women employed in the Eaton's stores and garment factory, the average was 2.1 kilometers. Yet these working women had no access to pub-lic toilets going to and from work.[26] Meanwhile, a new underground men's toilet was built at Adelaide and Toronto Streets (Figure 7.3).

When the TLCW constituted a public health committee in 1908, it lob-bied the city council to provide public toilets for women in the downtown area. The women reported that the city council had assured the women that it would erect women's facilities in the "downtown" area as "land became available" for such sites. But in 1912, the women reported that the council had taken no further action on the matter.[27]

Between 1908 and 1920, the council refused to build public toilets for women and was even reluctant to add to the number of them for men. Pre-

Figure 7.2 Men's toilet, Adelaide and Toronto Streets, Toronto, 1900. (Courtesy of the Toronto Public Library.)

Figure 7.3 Men's underground toilet, Adelaide and Toronto Streets, Toronto, 1912. (Courtesy of the Toronto City Archives, Fond 1231, Item 1657.)

sumably a public site of bodily functions clashed with their image of Toronto the Good, but also the city council prioritized spending its money on other public improvements. When the city did propose building public toilets, almost none of the potential sites was in the city center where the TLCW was seeking women's lavatories. Instead, it proposed new public toilets located east, west, and north of the downtown area.[28] In 1910, when controller J. J. Ward muted the possibility of more centrally located facilities at College and Spadina Avenues, he wanted them installed not on the streets, but in the basements of shops in buildings owned by the city, which could bring rental revenues into the city coffers. A ladies' section, he thought, could be disguised by including manicure and hairdressing facilities. Presumably this would protect middle-class women's sensibilities while at the same time making it an inhospitable or perhaps unaffordable place for working-class women. Other men rejected even this modest suggestion, declaring that there was no need for public toilets in that location.[29]

Unlike in London and Dublin, however, Toronto's rejection of public toilets for women was rarely discussed. Ward's suggestion of disguising a woman's toilet in the basement of a shop seems to have been one of the few instances where Toronto men even raised the issue of women's public toilets. Overall, public toilets in the center of the city countered the image of Toronto the Good, even though they were being furnished for men. One aldermanic opponent to the proposed public toilets at College and Spadina declared that such a facility would disturb young people going to the nearby Broadway Tabernacle. Another opponent declared that any public toilet in the center of streets was "always objectionable."[30] Even the board of the new public library Riverdale branch at Broadview and Gerrard Streets in the eastern section of the city objected to furnishing a public toilet inside the building.[31] The gendered conceptualization of Toronto the Good thus both precluded furnishing women's public toilets in the city center at all and even limited, although never excluded, providing these facilities for men.

Housing for Profit and Domesticity

Toronto men had two goals for planning and building housing. They wanted to keep the processes in private hands so that money could be made from building and selling it, and they sought to use housing as a way to make women conform to male ideals of both private and public patriarchy. With its abundance of surrounding land, Toronto was a perfect site for suburban development, where new, single-family homes could be erected. Building such homes in new areas could also provide the opportunity to rearrange domestic living spaces to separate work and home, the public and the private, and reembound women into a new domesticity.

Toronto men never lost sight of housing as a private enterprise, but they faced a quandary with the apartment house: if they blocked developers from erecting apartment houses on their own property, they were violating the tenets of private property and enterprise. Providing housing was an enterprise for making a profit, and "apartments were built because they made money." But Toronto men resolved their quandary by claiming that apartment buildings housing multiple families stopped other people from making money by building single-family houses.[32] In 1912, real estate agents petitioned the council to limit "the erection of new buildings or the conversion of existing dwellings for anything other than a dwelling house for one family."[33] Owners of single-family homes also asserted that apartment buildings in their neighborhood lowered property values. Being sympathetic to these types of appeals, the council passed new legislation in 1912 that forbade apartment houses being built all the way to the sidewalk and another act that forbade their building at all on residential streets. Thenceforth they could be constructed only on main commercial streets.

But the vacant land surrounding the city offered an even better opportunity for profit and sustaining the city of homes. In 1911 the Board of Health recommended that congested and overcrowded areas in the city could be reduced by building "suburban garden cities with rapid transportation facilities" as well as a "proper scheme of city planning."[34] The next year, the health board noted approvingly that a garden city scheme was underway and that "capitalists who feel disposed to aid the poor by means of self-help" now had an excellent opportunity to do so. The board recommended appointing a small housing committee composed of a physician, an engineer, an architect, a real estate expert, a building expert, and a social worker.[35] The Board of Trade promptly agreed to join a committee that "had in mind a scheme which will stand on a firm financial basis, so that the revenue on a co-partnership basis . . . will practically carry the investment."[36] Under co-partnership both private investors and potential tenants would buy shares in a housing company, with the money being put toward building the houses and tenants ultimately able to purchase their home. The Board of Control, however, refused to sanction a new housing committee or any housing schemes that might impose on municipal finances.

In his 1913 inaugural address, Mayor Horatio Hocken proposed to solve the housing problem by recommending that the city annex unincorporated sections to the west and east of the city. He looked "to this further annexation as the very best means within our reach at this time for solving the housing problem." Hocken also wanted to request authorization from the provincial government for privately built garden suburbs and transit lines.[37] Nothing could have better pleased Toronto men. Vincent Basevi of the *Toronto News* advised G. Frank Beer, president of the Canadian Manufacturers' Association, that since "every slum is a breeding ground for vice, crime, and purposeless living . . . the easiest solution is to be found in the formation of a company to build, on a large scale, houses for clerks, artisans, and other small wage-earners."[38] Beer agreed and initiated the Toronto Housing Company (THC) in 1913, which he envisioned as a co-partnership arrangement under which all shareholders would receive an annual dividend of 6 percent. Once the provincial government passed the Ontario Housing Accommodation Act in 1913, under whose terms cities were empowered to guarantee up to 85 percent of a housing company's bonds and limit dividends to 6 percent, the THC could use the invested money to acquire suburban lands on which to build new housing, and respectable tenants would ultimately be able to buy their dwellings.[39]

Sean Purdy's study of the THC asserts that Beer believed that "a combination of limited government assistance, individual self-reliance and beneficence, and strict business sense was key to solving urban housing problems."[40] In its first annual report the THC optimistically, and rather immodestly, declared that "from the first the objective of the Company was not to rehouse the slums, nor was it to meet the demand of any class for housing accommodation; it was to seek a solution for the whole housing problem."[41] While the *Toronto Daily News* lauded that "the company has proved its contention that the housing business can be coordinated in the interest of citizens . . . on an economic basis which affords the capital invested a reasonable return,"[42] as early as January 1914 Beer was discouraged. The rising cost of living was increasing the price of land and raising rents to a point making it difficult for the working classes to ultimately buy their houses and "discouraged the building of cheap housing."[43] The THC had to resort to renting its buildings rather than depend on investments and selling houses. By the end of the decade, the emphasis on profitability had undermined the company. Summarizing the THC's work decades later, the *Toronto Globe and Mail* reported that by 1918 the THC was turned over to the Trust and Guarantee Company, rents were raised, and "an official of the company official later stated that there was no longer any idea of housing improvement or public service. It had degenerated into a real estate enterprise."[44]

Other Toronto men were also pursuing suburban development. Wilfrid S. Dinnick, president of Dovercourt Land Building and Savings Company, had drawn up suburban housing schemes as early as 1907 modeled on the garden suburb ideal. His plans for Lawrence Park (in the northeast bordered by Yonge Street and Lawrence Avenue) called for circles, crescents, a central circular garden, winding streets, and so on, all of which resembled English garden suburb plans. When ultimately completed, Lawrence Park was scaled back from the most idealistic of these plans, but it still resembled the 1920s layout of Marino in Dublin.[45] Dinnick proclaimed that his goal was "to make Toronto a city of gardens" in which "all the land within ten miles of Toronto will be equipped with good roads, good transportation, and settled with good suburban homes."[46] Dinnick claimed that the "[housing] situation in Toronto can be helped only by private enterprise, and . . . any project providing living accommodation that can only be rented and not purchased is unpopular with the people."[47]

But the TLCW wanted more public initiative for housing inside the city of the type that violated the single-family home ideal. The women recognized that housing was needed for a variety of living situations and asked the city to create a municipal housing committee to consider, among other goals, building temporary municipal lodging houses for newly arrived immigrants and ultimately permanent municipal lodging houses for both women and men.[48] The women noted that many people could not afford to buy property and were left at the mercy of landlords. The TLCW did not wish to eliminate rentals—renting, for example, was the only way that most single women could afford housing—but since 1908 they had been asking the city to compel landlords to keep their properties in decent condition.[49] The women also continued to agitate for building a home for working mothers with accommodations that would rent for an average of $1.75 per week, include a central nursery, provide a hot meal at noon for children, and staff a free employment bureau for the women, among its other amenities.[50] There is no evidence how, or even if, the council responded to the women's requests. The city certainly never provided municipal lodging houses for women. By 1912, it was clear that the city had no interest in providing housing for single women.

The women were still hoping to find a way to accommodate single women at the lowest possible rents at something more permanent to their Women's Welcome Hostel. The numbers of women being temporarily accommodated at the hostel made it clear that there was a dire shortage of housing for women. They were also continuing to support and solicit donations for the endeavor of the Central Neighbourhood House settlement to establish a women's residence "where women could room and have part of their meals."[51] In the absence of securing such housing, the TLCW took advantage of the THC's inability to sell its properties to secure more housing for women. Although it was a more costly arrangement that could be afforded only by more highly paid single women, the TLCW leased buildings being erected on Bain Avenue from the THC for five years with these premises to be rented by "self-supporting women."[52]

But women had neither the power nor the resources to prevail on decisions about housing. Rather than providing for women in the city, plans such as those of Dinnick and the THC consciously set out to ensure separation of the public and the private by keeping women as much as possible in their new home. Planners and home builders put much thought into constructing homes with new domestic arrangements that they proclaimed would make women's lives easier and happier in their homes. Their new housing arrangements would include compact kitchen arrangements with increased numbers of amenities to increase the efficiency of cooking and cleaning. Front and back parlors would be collapsed into one large sitting and eating room, separated from the kitchen but in an adjoining room to facilitate the housewife-cook moving back and forth as she served meals. The reality of the compact kitchen stuffed with new amenities also meant that food preparation would no longer be a family task because the space was too small to be shared. Not only were women to be isolated inside the home; they were to be isolated in the kitchen. Sean Purdy presents a benign analysis of the THC's kitchens, pointing out that the addition of amenities such as shelf spaces to the kitchen "promised to outfit the domestic environment with an orderly means to store food and cleaning supplies and to assist in tidy meal preparation, proficient laundering, and other necessary chores."[53] On the other hand, as Suzanne Mackenzie points out, new household commodities and an emphasis on scientific domesticity through use of these new commodities would solidify women's role as full-time housewives and keep women confined to "an increasingly specialized, spatially separated, and single gender world."[54]

Private development companies could not always build only single-family houses, but even a development of two-family flats such as the Riverdale Courts enhanced women's isolation. In these buildings, each flat had a separate entrance, "angled in such a way that parents could watch their children play [outside], out of sight of neighbors in adjacent units."[55] One can use the plural *parents*, but the assumption was always that it would be the mother in the house watching the children and not interacting with her neighbors. Suburban living such as that of Riverdale Courts was intended to ensure the reproduction of the family in the private domestic sphere by keeping women attached to the home. The very word *home* had acquired a gender-freighted meaning in Toronto. Beer had declared "that we all know that the morals of a community are moulded largely by home environment." He sounded the alarm that "the very existence of the family life upon which we pride ourselves is dependent upon decent housing. . . . Slums produce inefficiency—inefficiency begets poverty and poverty of this character means disease and degradation."[56] Medical officer of health Charles Hastings declared that "there is no more sacred word in the English language than 'Home'; and on the retaining the sacredness and significance of our homes depends the future of our municipality and of our nation."[57] Home to Hastings meant the single-family home. "All municipalities," he asserted, "must have a keen sense of the social and national significance of the term 'home' as being of one-family dwellings."[58]

PLANNING TORONTO THE GOOD

By the second decade of the twentieth century, Toronto's leading men were set to reconstruct the city with housing built as much as possible by private enterprise, designed to foster a new domesticity and make the family home the moral center of society. Along with those aims, all reconstruction would be designed to promote economic development. Such objectives pursued by men who had the power to accomplish much of what they wanted left Toronto women with little means to prevent the reconstruction of the city's built environment as anything other than an organic, male-oriented, patriarchal space.

Housing Remains Private

Despite their lack of power, the TLCW kept trying to make men listen to their ideas about what would make Toronto a people-centered city. In 1921, the women formed a new housing subcommittee to urge the municipal government to take more responsibility for housing. They asked the city council to request that the provincial government extend to the municipality its recent guarantee to back up to 85 percent of the cost on bonds issued "for the purchase of land and the erection of houses" by a private company. The women wanted the "municipality itself to build houses for sale or rent" and to create a municipal department of housing that would acknowledge municipal responsibility.[59] Throughout that year and into the next, the TLCW emphasized that "adequate and proper housing" was essential for individual and social good. The women urged the council to "avail itself of some of the $25 million of federal government loans for housing" that were now being promised to cities. The TLCW continued to focus on the need for good rental housing and asked the council to pass a fair-rents bill.[60]

Yet by 1921, it was manifestly clear that men were unwilling to listen to women. In 1918, the provincial government had constituted an Ontario housing committee and passed acts to make it more financially feasible for local governments to support housing development. No women were appointed to serve on the committee. Women responded acerbically to this failure. They protested that "men have been telling us for years that our place was in the home" but appointed no women to a housing committee and asserted that there was a "need for women's brains and experiences in planning homes."[61] Not only did the committee ignore omen's protests, brains, and experiences; the men of the committee simply asserted that they knew better. One of the committee's first actions was to ask "what constitutes a house" and answer its own question. For the committee, the first of eight essential features was "sufficient land to give each family privacy and plenty of air." Then it declared that "the working man's wife, with a family of small children, will appreciate the saving in steps which such an [new house's internal] arrangement will ensure."[62] As with the Tudor-Walters postwar report in London, men defined a home and told women what they needed and wanted in their homes.

The city council refused to create a municipal department of housing with power to decide on where and what kind of housing would be built and declined to enact a fair-rents bill. Instead, in the face of the failing THC, the city organized a new entity, the Toronto Housing Commission, whose members were to include the municipal commissioners of finance and works, the city architect, and that staunch advocate of the single-family home, Charles Hastings. The main operating principle of this commission was the idea of co-partnership, with all applicants for housing to provide a down payment to help finance new building, which would subsequently be applied to buying the homes through monthly payments. The commission also wanted employers to provide 25 percent of the money required for purchasing land and building on it, with bonds issued for the other 75 percent. One newspaper account of the commission's initial meetings reported that the commissioners gave "a decided cold shoulder to the proposition that the city itself build houses." They feared it "would increase the load of the already heavily burdened taxpayer. . . . If the city is to attract new manufacturers, merchants, and population and if encouragement is to be given to people to own their own homes, to builders to construct and to investors to purchase and loan on real estate the tax rate must be brought down to a reasonable point."[63] Such a perspective, as well as depending on co-partnership housing that required a down payment, would always disadvantage women, especially single working women.

The new commission members assumed the task of investigating the state of housing in the city center. They were disturbed to find that of the 13,547 houses they inspected, only 4,835 of them were occupied by one family. They judged this situation to be "obviously an undesirable tendency, since the future greatness, stability, and welfare of any city depend on the number of inhabitants who own their own residences."[64] Despite this obvious need for housing, and the fact that multifamily buildings could provide it, the commission rejected a suggestion that large centrally located houses be divided into three-family flats.[65]

The commission very quickly encountered a situation similar to that of the THC. Applications with down payment for its preferred type of housing were limited, and with their charge being not incurring municipal financial loss, the commission reported that it was at an impasse: "Having studied the situation from all viewpoints . . . [we] strongly recommend the City to cease building houses; but should the City see fit not to act on our recommendation, we will be forced to decline to go on with operations, which, in our opinion, will mean serious loss to the citizens and a further increase in an already high Tax Rate."[66] When the commissioners resigned in early 1920, alderman W. R. Plewman suggested constituting a new commission of five, to include one woman and one member of the working classes. But other council members wanted to continue their cautious assessment of the housing situation before moving forward with any new commission. By later that year, the council still had not settled on any type of new housing scheme, so building was almost at a standstill.

Frieda Held of the hybrid public-private Neighborhood Workers' Association lamented the commission's lack of positive action. She asserted that families living in many of the investigated houses experienced a much higher rate of infant mortality than families in other areas of the city. She also pointed out that a number of people in the area who had bought houses hoping to escape high rents now found themselves unable to meet their monthly payments. High rents being charged by property owners made it increasingly difficult for residents of limited income to live decently. At the least, she wanted the city council to publish the names of landlords who did not keep up their property.[67] But the council made no specific new plans. It merely asked the housing commission to have the city architect draw up plans and specifications for new small houses. Simultaneously it rejected a motion to have a new building program formed under a Civic Commission that would be composed of the city architect, the council's Committee on Finance, and its Assessment Committee.[68]

Harbor Development

With the housing question left more and more to private enterprise and suburban development, Toronto's leading men had been able to focus specifically on promoting the city's economic growth. The *Globe* had wanted Toronto to become the Pittsburgh of Canada by developing the existed marshland at Ashbridge's Bay along the eastern part of the waterfront into "the site of one of the great iron and steel plants in America. . . . It will soon be the biggest producer in Ontario of the basic material of twentieth-century prosperity—iron and steel."[69] But Toronto's leading men were no longer interested in bringing dirty industries to the city. The Board of Trade, instead, focused on developing the city's natural harbor as the best means for securing economic growth. In 1911, the Canadian parliament had granted the board's request to authorize creation of an independent Toronto Harbour Commission. The board argued that such a new entity, separate from the municipal government, would remove it from political interference. An independent commission would guarantee urban development by "'right-thinking,' disinterested individuals, whose decisions were independent from political processes."[70]

The Canadian Manufacturers' Association, the Retail Merchants' Association, and the District Labour Council joined the Board of Trade in a campaign to convince voters in a referendum to adopt the commission, arguing that economic growth would be assured by such a new commission. The commission's advocates told voters that beyond refurbishing and managing the harbor, the commission would systematically improve and develop existing undeveloped land within the city, direct the harbor on a businesslike basis, and make Toronto "one of the greatest industrial centres on the continent."[71]

The marshlands along the waterfront were a health hazard, but by turning this piece of the waterfront into a commercial site, it would simultaneously make it profitable. As Paul Jackson claims, for the Board of Trade, a healthier city could be achieved through "'positive'—that is profitable—

enterprises."[72] A healthier city, not necessarily all healthy people in it, promised continued investment in economic growth. With the support of Mayor Geary, the city readily ceded the marsh land to the commission. The men on the Commission, particularly R. Home Smith, had the banking connections to help attract national and international investment in the project. Women, of course, had neither the power to convince the city government to undertake their desired reforms nor connections to attract financing.

Between 1912 and 1920, the commission developed a Toronto Waterfront Plan that involved significant landfill along the lakefront, dredging, building new dock walls, and other major work. The commissioners quickly published a pamphlet, "Toronto, A City of Opportunities," to give readers all the statistics they believed were needed to demonstrate that Toronto, a "City of Churches . . . City of Homes . . . City of Factories," was well situated for future industrial economic growth.[73] The vision of harbor commissioner Smith, who also happened to be a land developer, was that by developing its harbor, "our undoubted future is to be populous and wealthy . . . a chief metropolis of the British empire, a world's centre of politics, [unreadable], science, amusement, and society."[74]

At the sixth annual National Conference on City Planning, harbor commissioner Robert S. Gourlay (former Board of Trade president) reiterated the need of waterfront development for commercial use, tied it to new transportation networks through the city, and promoted Toronto's harbor development as a blueprint not only for Toronto but for other cities to emulate: "A city possessing a water front has a heritage of incalculable value for every citizen." Gourlay declared that the harbor commission's plan was aimed "at removing some of Toronto's disabilities" by constructing a new 130-foot-wide east-west "commercial business highway" and bringing rapid transportation with radial service "to the heart of our business, market, and dock facilities." The city, he said, had given the commission property valued at an estimated $9 million.[75]

Transit and Communication

As the Board of Trade focused on harbor development for economic growth, the Civic Guild envisioned an overall plan that reordered the city's transit and communication lines as essential for securing that growth. The guild's plan subcommittee declared that "numerous and intricate as are the questions involved in a comprehensive plan for a rapidly growing Capital city like Toronto, the basic problem is transportation . . . so that in expenditure of time and effort, transportation, alike of people and commodities, shall be as economical as possible."[76] At its second Toronto Improvements Conference, the guild declared that "at the present time in Toronto the subject of street widening is all important." Representatives from business, members of ratepayers organizations (all male), and neighborhood groups, all of whom were said to be mainly concerned with such street issues, attended this conference.[77]

Success with harbor development boosted optimism for securing a new overall city plan. At the first meeting of a new provincial town planning congress in December 1912, Civic Guild president C. H. Mitchell laid out the guidelines for the appropriate means to plan the city. He drew on the conclusion of Mayor Geary's civic improvement committee that

> civic planning may be divided into three general divisions as affecting the city or town within its boundaries. . . . These are as follows:
>
> 1. The first division concerns the circulation and transportation problems within the city, and embraces streets, railways, waterways, and all means of communication
> 2. The second division concerns all other public areas and buildings not devoted primarily for circulation . . . such institutions as municipal buildings, schools, post offices and Government buildings, hospitals, libraries, museums, churches, public halls, theatres . . . parks, gardens, highways, boulevards, playgrounds, amusement parks, cemeteries, etc.
> 3. The third division related to all of the remaining or privately owned lands within the city . . . particularly the character of their development

Mitchell lauded the guild, the Board of Trade, and ratepayers organizations as being the most effective and impartial voices for securing useful action and legislation toward such planning.[78]

He mentioned housing only to encourage the building of garden suburbs. He exhorted employers to provide such housing "to ensure their workpeople being contented and efficient." According to Mitchell, "'Garden Suburbs' for working men can be readily organized and should be attractive and worth while."[79]

With groups of Toronto men lined up behind street and transit improvements, the municipal government now began prioritizing reconstructing the built environment through improved streets and transit systems. The *Toronto Star* reported in spring 1911 that the city "is undertaking over one million dollars worth of street widening besides a number of street extensions. . . . One of the most important of the civic works being undertaken is the improvement of Bloor street from Dundas street westward to High Park avenue . . . estimated at $133,000."[80] This sum was more than four times the estimated $30,000 it would have cost to build three public toilets. By 1912, extensive street-widening proposals were making their way through the City Council. There were proposals to widen Terauley Street either to sixty-six feet or to eighty-six feet. The civic works committee estimated that the cost for the sixty-six-foot widening would be significant. The council ultimately approved the immediate widening of Terauley at the cost of $1.25 million in early 1914, although the work was then delayed by the outbreak of war.[81] In the 1920s, Terauley was renamed Bay Street, as the existing Bay Street was extended north along the line of Terauley.[82] If not a new diagonal street, this extension did help satisfy professional men's desires to have more long, continuous streets, rather than the discontinuous streets that previously had led out of the center of the city to the periphery. Danforth Avenue was also widened, as it was regarded "essentially a business street."[83] Other street projects were also delayed until after the war. The North Toronto Ratepayers Association had petitioned that the "widening of Yonge Street, Toronto's main thoroughfare, is a matter of utmost importance to every loyal citizen having the welfare of our city at heart." Again, the exigencies of war caused the council to rescind the bylaw it had previously passed to widen the street, although the group continued to protest its need.[84] The optimistic predictions of Wilfrid Dinnick that before 1919 Toronto would spend $350 million on public improvements would also be thwarted because of the war.[85]

Nevertheless, there was probably no more important transportation-communication scheme undertaken during the war years than the Bloor Street Viaduct (bridge) over the Don River and Don River Valley in the northeast section of the city. While voters (primarily male, as the only women with the municipal franchise were unmarried property owners) had previously rejected this scheme in referenda in three previous years, in 1913 the voters changed their minds and approved the project. When finished five years later, the cost of the project totaled over $2 million.[86] The *Toronto Star* boasted that the viaduct was "an epoch-making enterprise. . . . [I]ts effect upon the natural tendencies of the city's growth will be revolutionary."[87] By January 1916, the *Toronto* Star reported that the "Don Section" of the viaduct would be open by the end of 1917, and the city engineer was assuring that the entire viaduct would be completed within the proposed time limit.[88] The decision to build the viaduct helped put an end to any further discussion of driving new radial streets connecting the old center to the suburbs.

The Bloor Viaduct (also called the Prince Edward) gave the city a new east-west extension to the north away from the previous center close to the harbor. The decision to fund such an expensive work demonstrated the priority the city was giving to suburban development. The viaduct would cross over the Don River and extend Bloor Street to the east of Yonge Street, an area that geographer Richard Dennis characterizes before the viaduct as a "polite residential backwater."[89] Connecting the east-west sections of the city would facilitate the modern economic progress desired by Toronto men to make the city the chief metropolis of the British Empire. As a new city, Toronto accomplished this feat without needing to destroy much of the existing street patterns or move masses of people from their dwellings.

PLANNING MODERNITY

The viaduct was a symbol of modernity for Toronto. It might not have quite the import of the Brooklyn Bridge in New York, but for many Toronto men it symbolized that Toronto was a city growing in importance not just in Canada but on the continent and even the world.[90] As the celebrated Holburn Viaduct in London had conquered the Holburn/Fleet Valley, easing east-west access in that city, the Bloor Viaduct conquered the steep ravines of the Don River Valley. Moreover, the viaduct demonstrated the capability of engineering to conquer nature, placing Toronto on a plane similar to London and other important cities. It would also close the time-space gap by speeding up traffic. According to the superintendent of construction, once finished the viaduct "will take seven minutes by streetcar to go from Bloor and Yonge to the near end of Danforth. At present it takes about half an hour to forty minutes. I think that alone declares in a nutshell the problem the viaduct will solve."[91]

Efficient City, Efficient Citizenship

Toronto's businessmen believed that a modern city required both efficient government and efficient citizenship. To achieve both types of efficiency, a group of Toronto businessmen organized the Bureau of Municipal Research (BMR) in 1914. The BMR was almost exclusively a male organization. The nine men who agreed to contribute either $500 or $1000 to underwrite its work constituted its Provisional Executive Council. The BMR functioned through monetary subscriptions that came overwhelmingly from men and businesses; in general, the subscriptions ranged from $25 to $100. Very few women were ever subscribers. The treasurer's report of November 1925, for example, listed small subscriptions from two women, one for $10 and the other for $15. Five years later, a report listed only four women and the Women's Teachers Association of Canada among the close to five hundred subscribers.[92]

One of the BMR's first objectives was to have an extensive civic survey that included a survey of all municipal departments to ascertain their efficiency, including budgets, accounting systems, financial reports, and so on.[93] The BMR's *First Annual Report* declared that the organization was dedicated to establishing a "scientific form of budget."[94] Focus on efficient, scientific governance meant that surveying conditions in St. John's Ward, as the Central Neighbourhood House and the Public Service Division of the Health Department requested of the BMR in 1915, was not on the men's immediate agenda.[95] The bulletins and reports of the BMR through the following years comprehensively detail all municipal functions with an emphasis on efficiency. The close relationship between the businessmen of the BMR and the men in municipal government, even if they did not always agree, allowed the BMR to assume a prominent role in diagnosing Toronto's problems and suggesting solutions for its built environment. The same year that the BMR was founded, for example, the city council had rejected a motion to drop the property qualifications for election as mayor, controller, and council members, so all decisions about the built environment were still carefully controlled by the city's leading professional and political men.[96]

New Planning Initiatives

As the BMR was beginning its work, the Commission of Conservation of Canada (CCC), an organization founded in 1909 and charged with providing expert advice to government about the conservation of both human and natural resources, was drafting legislation to authorize forming a central planning authority with powers to develop an overall city plan for Canadian cities. G. Frank Beer was a member of the commission's committee on town-planning legislation. The Scottish planner Thomas Adams, who had come to work in Canada and advise about town planning, praised the commission's work for following, even bettering, the British legislation in its conception of the city as an organic entity needing an organic approach to planning. Since Adams was also the town planning advisor to the commission, he would have a profound effect on city planning throughout Canada.[97]

Under the CCC's auspices, representatives from across Canada, who were overwhelming male (including Horace Brittain, director of the BMR), met in Ottawa in 1915 to discuss forming a Civic Improvement League. Beer presented the assembly with the draft of a town planning proposal that included constituting a league to "be formed with the general object of promoting the study and advancement of the best principles and method of civic improvement and development and to secure a general and effective interest in all municipal affairs."[98] There was no opposition to forming such a league, but the few women who were present objected that the specific objectives of the league gave no attention to social issues. Their complaints, as usual, had no traction. The men endorsed Montreal's Dr. J. J. Guerin's understanding of the league's general rationale being for civic improvement:

> The Civic Improvement League, as we all know, is something that is calculated to improve the surroundings and conditions of our fellow citizens. It is by improving the homes, and consequently the municipalities, that we can make people happy. When a person is in a state of contentment, and his environment is agreeable, then he will

be satisfied with his conditions, and that person will be a loyal citizen of Canada. Consequently our effort is toward the creation of loyalty and contentment among all the citizens of this country.[99]

Beer reinforced this emphasis on citizenship by introducing an amendment to his original motion, adding the words "and to encourage and organize in every community all those social forces that make for an efficient Canadian citizenship."[100] Securing efficient citizenship could be accomplished through eight objectives.

1. The application of sound economic principles to the administration of municipal government
2. Preparing town planning schemes for providing sanitation, convenience, and amenity in developing land
3. Replanning old districts, removing slums, widening public thoroughfares, and other reconstruction schemes
4. Conservation of industrial and physical resources of the city, housing conditions, health of the citizens, and adequacy and efficiency of public services
5. Preservation and increase of natural and structural beauty
6. Preparation of civic surveys, maps, investigations into housing, transportation, and industrial conditions
7. Promotion in school and college courses of civics and civic design
8. Increasing production from the soil[101]

This list and each point were vague and somewhat innocuous, which was precisely what troubled the few women at this meeting. Mrs. Adam Shortt (married women were always referred to by their husbands' given name),[102] from Ottawa and a member of that city's Local Council of Women, asked what objective would address such things as "mortality and public health. Would it not be well to have another clause which would cover public health in regard to municipal affairs?" Thomas Adams responded that objective number four would cover those issues, so there was no need to be specific.[103] But Mrs. Smillie from Ottawa pursued the issue: "Would it not be well to put in the words 'child welfare'? Then it will be easy to coordinate the actions of the Women's Council and other organizations that are taking special steps in regard to child welfare." Now Beer rejected these questions, stating that "a general statement is always stronger than a specific one."[104] And Adams objected that any statement specifying child welfare "would put child welfare as something different from the general health of the citizens."[105]

At the second meeting that officially launched the league, Thomas Adams set the tone and the agenda for the league's work. For housing he claimed that "it is difficult to deal with in the form of a general recommendation."

Rather, he suggested that the league constitute a committee to collect statistics on housing. As to public health, he dismissed any concerns by calling it
"a matter which is being well taken care of. . . . Our machinery to deal with
that is fairly up-to-date. . . . [H]owever, there is a need for more accurate and
more comprehensive statistics."[106]

Shortt now demurred from Adams's optimism about the state of municipal well-being. She again demanded that the league specify more concrete examples of the reforms to be undertaken, especially ones that would
gave more attention to the condition of women and children. "I feel, and I
fancy that others, particularly the ladies, feel that Mr. Adams is perhaps just
a little too optimistic about the physical well-being and conditions of our
cities." She wanted to see more practical and effective consideration of "the
physical problems in our cities." Shortt claimed that cities needed municipal
abattoirs, fire escapes on all apartment houses, official factory inspectors,
and enforcement of bylaws on garbage collection and smoke nuisance. All
were problems that the Ottawa Local Council of Women had been trying
without much success to remedy, because, she pointed out, for every issue
the women had encountered the intransigence of male property rights and
financial interests that overrode the solution. In confronting what she saw as
the gendered difference, she asserted that "our mothering instinct goes out
to the problems that affect the physical well-being of our growing children.
I am sure that you will admit that we have not been successful in the past,
and that we need some way of making greater progress." "Where," she asked,
"did we get our housing problem, our feeble-minded problem, our tuberculosis problem? . . . Why the disgrace that not more than one-half the children
born into the world ever have a chance to grow up? Are these not the big
things? Are not the physical features of city life of primary importance?"[107]

But men pursued a different vision of what was important. When W. H.
Hanna, the Ontario Provincial Secretary for Canada, expressed his idea
about citizenship in specifically gendered terms, the women may have had
even more cause for alarm. "Civic problems are largely solved," according to
Hanna, by providing for the Canadian *boy*. The boy needed, among other
things, "a home with sunshine and fresh air on all sides." He needed garbage
disposal, sewerage, fire equipment, supervised playgrounds, occasional visits
of the country, manual training, a school savings bank to learn thrift, public
libraries open on Saturdays, movie censorship, and compulsory military
training. Girls needed to learn "mothercraft, cooking and sewing" and to
have "some practical education" in case they needed to be wage-earners.[108]

In asking where the problems came from, and why they were allowed to
exist, Shortt confronted the problems that had always bedeviled the TLCW
in its efforts to create a more people-centered city. As she herself had answered: male politics and vested economic and property interests determined the city. Fair rents, municipal built housing, municipal lodging

houses for single women, housing for women with children, and public toilets for women all would have interfered with private enterprise and property rights and necessitated spending from municipal finances. Gathering statistics about the housing needs of single working women, let alone of working mothers with children, would not have led to better housing and health for them without accepting the idea that their needs should be taken care of. And if the best place for women and children was cloistered in the single-family home, there was still the question of what would happen to those people unwilling or unable to relocate to the suburbs.

When the BMR finally decided to pay attention to the conditions of St. John's Ward in 1918, it did not attempt to answer that question but surveyed the area statistically to demonstrate the harm it was causing the city. Congestion was determined to be a primary culprit for the ward's condition: "60% of the available area is covered with buildings in comparison with 40% in an ordinary thickly populated residential district." Such congestion led to lack of open spaces, which "causes the streets to become [the residents'] place of amusement with a consequent loss of health and decency, and it does not create an atmosphere likely to raise the already too low standard of living of the foreign resident or make for good and efficient citizenship." The BMR calculated that the ward contained "71 people per acre in comparison with 21 per acre in the city as a whole." The BMR had to admit the area could not be considered a true tenement district, such as that of Cleveland with its 208 people per acre, but it abhorred the idea that "many of the houses are occupied by several families."[109]

The BMR was most concerned that the ward was creating burdens on the city—"hospital burdens, unemployment burdens, health department burdens and educational burdens." It contended that "at least 4% of the Public Health Nursing in the city is caused through the needs of 'the Ward' population." According to the BMR, the needs of the ward disproportionately engaged city sanitation and housing inspectors; meat and food inspectors; and medical, dental, and quarantine services. Infant mortality in the ward was higher than in the city overall—38 percent to 28 percent for children under age two—while the report concluded that 9.19 percent of the city's foreign population (who lived mainly the in the ward) accounted for 23.6 percent of Toronto's feeble-minded and insane population.[110]

Yet the report contained almost no recommended measures to change the conditions of the ward. The report suggested giving the city more power to demolish buildings and have better planning for shifting balances between residential and business neighborhoods. It asserted that the city needed "garden suburbs with rapid transportation facilities, such as they have in England." The report also scolded the city for allowing so many foreigners to live together "without the adoption of effective measures to socialize them." The real focus of the report was to warn the city what it needed to do to prevent these conditions from developing elsewhere in the city. Toronto needed to plan, replan, initiate tax reforms, and enhance its powers of condemnation. As the report concluded, "the foregoing pages show what has happened to what was, at one time, an inviting section of the city. It shows what is about to happen, or is already in the process of happening in other widely distributed areas."[111]

The BMR report did not suggest that the ward be demolished as a slum, just that its worst excesses that caused the city financial expenditures should be eliminated. Efficient citizenship would result in efficient municipal management of resources. For the BMR, the ward was the example of what not to allow to happen in the rest of the city. By extension, the BMR was advocating how to safeguard and foster its ideal built environment for the city. If twenty-one people to the acre were to be taken as the norm, then the city could sprawl out with single-family housing. If tax exemptions were given to all who improved their land—one of the recommendations—then male property owners would be encouraged to keep up their property to high standards. If there was a city planning commission to advise the municipal government about how to foster development in all parts of the city, then better living and working conditions would be secured because these men—and they intended them to be male experts—would make the correct decisions.

The BMR was keenly concerned about linking home ownership with efficient citizenship. The report decried the fact that 85 percent of the ward's residents were renters, as opposed to 15 percent in the rest of the city. According to the BMR, this situation was a problem because "usually ownership has a determining influence not alone on the condition of the homes, but on the stability of the population, the standard of citizenship and self-respect."[112] Twenty years later, the BMR would still be concerned that property ownership, especially home ownership, was the key to efficient citizenship. The group feared that declining home ownership then was causing a drop in the number of voters. In a white paper titled "A Home Owning Citizenship," the men exhorted property owners to come out and vote. "The vital interests of property owners and property users with regard to economic government coincide," the men argued. "They are not divergent."[113] And women could be reordered into the single-family home, with the home defined as the "place in which the moral content of life could be controlled and the wife/mother and children could be safe and content." According to Jill Delaney, with men having linked their idea of the home so resolutely to the fate of the city and the nation, the social disruptions of World War I "served to heighten this idealized image." Thereafter, men would respond by seeking to create "an even greater separation between work and home, both physically and socially."[114]

The Efficiency of Social Provision

Beyond its concern for the ward's inefficiency and economic burden on the city, the BMR began to exert its control over social issues and provision of social services in the name of efficiency. In late 1915, the BMR director spoke to school nurses on how the work of school nurses could be made more efficient.[115] In 1916, it celebrated the fact that the Social Service Commission led by a small group of businessmen, organized in 1912 to manage municipal charity services more efficiently, had helped the city relief officer secure "partial payments amounting to $8,561.05 from patients at the various city hospitals and had blocked admissions to undeserving applicants after investigation."[116] The BMR decried what it called haphazard as opposed to planned philanthropy, and in 1917 it solicited the Social Service Commission to update the BMR on a variety of social services, especially their financing. Among these services asked of the commission was to "make careful investigation of all parents to ensure that they are entitled to use charitable creches."[117]

The social concerns expressed by the women attending the formation of the Civic Improvement League and those of the TLCW, that public health, housing, and child welfare should be at the forefront of Toronto's municipal initiatives, were steadily overwhelmed by ideas about efficient government, efficient citizenship, and economic and business growth. The concept of efficient citizenship did not square easily with the idea that it should be a municipal responsibility to foster a socially just citizenship.

The BMR never acknowledged that it was primarily a group of a segment of Toronto men. The BMR proudly reported that it had the backing of the citizens:

> Since the Bureau's inception it has been in constant communication with individual citizens. . . . Professional men write that they place all of the Bureau's literature in their waiting rooms for the use of the public. . . . The head of at least one secondary school uses the Bureau's publicity in the preparation of material for his classes. Educational experts, a judge of the Supreme Court, heads of University departments, heads of public service corporations, editors, Members of Parliament and businessmen have written expressing their approval.[118]

Lacking a voice on the Civic Improvement League (and the CCC was abolished in 1921), with no realistic representation on the BMR and no representation at all in the municipal government, Toronto's women were effectively blocked from having their ideas about what made a good city incorporated into any planning for the city.

NEW PLANNING INITIATIVES

By the mid-1920s, the men of the BMR were lamenting the lack of a city plan, which they deemed necessary "if Toronto is to continue to be the home of business and industry; if it is to continue to be a city of homes something will have to be done quickly and thoroughly to put the conduct of the city's business on a higher plane of policy forming and administrative efficiency." City planning through careful study and survey of the city, they believed, would lead to planning that was "a method of controlling a city's growth so as to secure for the city the greatest service for the least money and for the citizens the greatest amenity for the least tax burden." City planning, the BMR concluded, could also implement zoning, which, among other results, "preserves thee home character of single and two-family residence districts by segregating types of residences into districts where they are appropriate."[119]

Street Reconstruction

With efficiency, economic growth, and business desires dominating men's ideas about the built environment, street planning became increasingly synonymous with city planning. In 1915, the BMR had asserted that

> all agree that the transportation question is the most vitally important city-planning question which must be answered by the city within the next four or five years. The only way it can be answered effectively is by careful and continuous inquiry and planning by a special body appointed for the purpose and made up of men whose training and expertise fits them particularly for the work.[120]

As automobile traffic increased, Toronto men grew ever more concerned about congestion of the city's arteries.

The possibility for more systematic street planning arrived in 1928 when the provincial government gave the city the power to appropriate land specifically to extend University Avenue south. The mayor then appointed an Advisory City Planning Commission—composed of himself and six "experts," including R. Home Smith and three members of the BMR: E. L. Cousins, J. H. Gundy, and H. H. Williams. Williams was a major real estate dealer in the city; Cousins was a harbor commissioner.[121]

A few council members objected to the commission's composition, believing that these men already exercised too much control over the city's development. City controller Albert Hacker pointed out that Smith, Williams, and Gundy each had financial and property interests in expanding University Avenue, and that Smith and Cousins were already on the harbor commission. "I am one of those men," he said, "who believe that Mr. Smith and Mr. Cousins should not be on the board owing to their connections with the harbour board and their connection with the improvements in the west end of the city." Alderman James Cameron also wanted Cousins removed and suggested that a woman from the TLCW be appointed in his place. Only three members of the council supported this suggestion. A woman had been nominated for the commission, but Mayor Sam McBride refused to consider her, saying that the proposed commissioners were chosen by him, not nominated by anyone else. Alderman James Stewart wanted the commission to have a membership more representative of the "important organizations of the community," including labor and women's organizations.[122]

Despite such dissent, the council easily agreed to the original proposed composition of the commission. Alderman Joseph Gordon assured his fellow council members that "these men are too big to be influenced by any private interests they have in the city. They have large property holdings that show their faith in the city."[123] Gordon apparently did not see the irony in his statement. It was precisely on the basis of their property that these men were most interested in planning the city to foster their interests. For these men, their economic interests and the interests of the city were the same.

The commission's plan, issued early in 1929, clearly reflected the connection between businessmen and planning. First, the plan encompassed only the area bounded by College Street, Spadina Avenue, the waterfront, and Parliament Streets, an area of about 2½ square miles. The commission justified these limits by asserting that "within this zone lies the commercial, financial, wholesale, retail, theatre, and administrative centres" of the city. Within this area, the plan recommended carving out new streets and widening and extending others, including University Avenue, which would be extended south from Queen Street to reach the new Union Station on Front Street and named Queen's Park. The plan called for a new monumental civic space as a memorial to Canadians who had died in the war and a traffic circle to be named Vimy Circle, also to commemorate the war. The cost for the proposed plan was $13 million. When questioned as to whether Toronto voters would approve such an expenditure, commissioner Smith replied, "Yes. This is a great city with the finest quality of citizenship on the continent." Toronto, he continued, "will never lag behind or lack courage in solving its own problems. . . . This city will be true to its opportunities and destiny and within five years will be the talk of the world." Commissioner Ross claimed that the report was a "constructive, unselfish movement that will do much for the public welfare."[124]

The commission's focus on street planning alluded to the city as a body. "Your commission is convinced that the primary need of the city is the development of a series of through arteries for motor traffic free of car tracks." This area was the heart of the city and its arteries needed to be unclogged for the free flow of its commercial lifeblood—traffic. The built environment also needed to be opened up and cleansed through street reconstruction to impress visitors with Toronto's greatness. "No street [yet] exists of which the stranger sightseeing between trains can unhesitantly say, 'This street undoubtedly leads to the centre of things. Toronto is no mean city.'"[125] The heads of the city's civic departments supported the recommendations. "The need for opening and extension of great arterial thoroughfares in the downtown section of Toronto cannot fairly be questioned." Doing so "would provide a permanent means for the facilitation of traffic, and at once afford opportunity for commercial and aesthetic development along profitable lines." These men wanted no delay in carrying out all of the commission's recommended projects because "the stimulation to general business, to the building trades, in fact, to every department of city life, from such a programme will be certain and profound. . . . When completed the City will have a downtown section which in beauty and dignity, ease of traffic flow, business utility, will be equal to that of any city on the continent."[126]

As the report made its way through the council, with the mayor asking for passage of a bylaw to raise the money for the commission's plan, the actual figure for the proposed work was increased to $19 million. Some aldermen suggested that rather than agree to the plan as a whole it be broken into its various proposals with each piece considered separately. But the city's department heads had insisted that the recommendations could not be considered separately. They were "constituent parts of a composite whole, embracing the embodiment of a splendid vision, the material attainment of which is vitally requisite to the present and future development and well-being of Toronto."[127]

The council, with some opposition, passed the requested bylaw and put it to a referendum. The campaigning and publicity for the bylaw's approval stressed the economic value it would bring to the city. The Board of Trade and the Trades and Labor Council were said to be firmly behind the plan, the latter group because it would provide jobs for its members. Although the president of the TLCW and the chair of its housing and town planning committee were listed in publicity as members of the Honorary Committee of the Citizens' Committee for a Greater Toronto, I have found no explanation of why they supported the bylaw or whether the TLCW generally agreed.[128]

Despite the optimism of the bylaw's vocal supporters that voters would recognize the need to carry out the proposed reconstructions, the voters narrowly rejected issuing the necessary bonds. Denton Massey, a plan supporter, a member of one of the city's leading manufacturing families, and himself an engineer, was philosophical about the defeat. "The citizens have voted against spending $19,000,000 on the downtown area because, I think, they felt there was too much to be done outside of it." He advocated that new plans should include improvement such as new arterial streets that would benefit more of the residents. "It must be recognized that the constructive work to be done is city-wide."[129]

Despite this setback, works commissioner R. C. Harris continued to push for the extension of University Street and the widening of York and Queen Streets.[130] University Street would be extended and widened as a local improvement, but other proposals to create southeast and northeast diagonals from the extension were not accepted despite the works commissioner's support for them. The City Plan Commission, now headed by Tracy D. leMay—formerly the city's chief surveyor—kept working to draft a master plan for the city that would satisfy opponents of the bylaw's focus on downtown. Amid much discussion in the council, with some aldermen lamenting that the proposal neglected the downtown area, the proposal was passed onto the works committee.[131] Debate continued on the widening, extension, and straightening of various streets, with the council at times rejecting the recommendations of the works committee. Yet crafting an overall planning scheme for the city was dead until the next decade.[132]

Housing, Again

Toronto's leading professional and business men had been overly optimistic in their certainty that other city residents agreed with them about what the city most needed. Timing was undoubtedly a factor in the bylaw's defeat as Toronto was experiencing the effects of the international economic downturn. Ironically, for men who had wanted Toronto to be the city of single-family homes, their failure to address squarely the housing situation as a central aspect of developing a good built environment kept the city falling behind in that endeavor. As the population increased, so did its multiple households. In 1901, 4.9 percent of Toronto households had contained more than one family. By 1931, that percentage stood at 23.2 percent with a total of 31.6 percent that had more than one family, a lodger, or both. The city's population had increased from 522,000 to 631,000 between 1921 and 1931, but it had increased by greater numbers between 1911 and 1931, so it was not just more people that accounted for the multiple-family situations. Economic necessity and the lack of sufficient housing for residents who could not afford the single-family homes pushed more Toronto residents to seek housing they could afford.[133] Moreover, women kept challenging the patriarchal desire to embound them into single-family, male-headed homes. Between 1914 and 1930, the percentage of female heads of households living in apartments had increased by 20 percent to 39 percent, with 57 percent of those women being single, never-married women.[134]

By failing to confront the city's housing crisis, Toronto men had left themselves open to the scathing criticism of the city by Ontario lieutenant governor Herbert Bruce that it had done nothing substantive to eradicate slums. Bruce, who had headed a provincial investigative committee on housing conditions in Ontario, produced a report in 1934 that castigated the city for not sufficiently decentralizing its population. This was a critique not of Toronto men's planning ideas but of the fact that they had not undertaken large-scale slum clearance to move more people out of the city.[135]

Morality was again the focus of the Bruce report. The report focused on the so-called public immorality of bad housing, asserting a direct correlation between bad housing, juvenile delinquency, sex delinquency, and the breakup of family life. "Overcrowding conditions in the homes lead the children to use the streets for playgrounds. It is natural for children to form play-groups or gangs, but in these districts, because of the lack of proper guidance either from the home or the community, these natural gangs become the breeding place of juvenile crime." The report also claimed that "the whole plane of sex morality is likely to be lower in districts of poor housing. The breakdown in self-respect due to lack of privacy and indiscriminate intermingling of the sexes results in a general increase in sex delinquency." The report submitted potential slum clearance plans for rebuilding areas of the city with housing facing inward from the streets, grouped around open courts, thereby eliminating many of the small, narrow streets that currently ran through the neighborhoods.[136]

Mayor James Simpson responded that the city would "place human rights above property rights" to counter the housing problem. "Where it is necessary to subordinate property rights for the good of our people we will do it," he declared. But council members were stung by the report's implication that they had been lax in attacking the housing problem and resisted the mayor's call. Alderman W. G. Ellis called the report self-aggrandizing and unrealistic: "I am of the opinion that Dr. Bruce's social splash on slumming has received far too much attention already. . . . The question is one of expenditures of city moneys." Alderman F. J. Conboy objected that not enough investigation had been done to ensure that "no action should be entered on till every aspect of the situation has been examined." Alderman J. R. Beamish rejected the report's recommendation that the city build working-class apartments, preferring a plan in which builders and home owners make low-cost repairs to existing buildings "to bring them up to 100 per cent efficiency." Alderman Robert Leslie agreed that housing conditions in the city "are really deplorable. They must be relieved, but at the same time the taxpayer must be considered."[137]

Across the following years, there was sporadic discussion about slum clearance based on the Bruce report, but little action was undertaken. The city kept waiting for the provincial government to come up with money for any such schemes. The council discussed a potential slum clearance bill for

$2 million in 1937, but there was no clear consensus on whether to put it to the voters. One faction in the council wanted it submitted to voters, amended to state that the money would be used for slum clearance, demolishing old housing and replacing it with low-cost housing. Not only could the council not agree how, or whether, to proceed with a housing plan; Mayor William Robbins declared that while he supported a housing scheme for the city, he would not support anything that did not have substantial sums of money coming from both the federal and provincial governments. Robbins also favored a housing scheme only as an unemployment scheme, for which he believed the city should not have to bear the entire burden.[138]

The Bruce report had urged the city to adopt a unified city planning agency to direct control of the built environment rather than relying on various municipal departments to undertake individual projects. According to the report, "There is no citizen who does not stand to profit, in the long run, from a beautiful, orderly and conveniently planned city."[139] But the economic depression of the 1930s and then Canada's entry into World War II diverted attention for a time from the housing issue and from devising an overall planning scheme.

A City of Planned, Healthy, Happy, Purposeful Neighborhoods

The Board of Trade, however, refused to give up its desire for comprehensive planning. In late 1941, it attempted to secure a new regional master plan that would address the city's economic and social development. According to Helen Jarvis, preoccupation with a master plan stemmed from "a supremely masculinised belief system that places a heavy emphasis on the male-dominated sectors of economic activity in the city . . . [and] effort to force fluid socio-cultural complexity into neat compartments and orderly processes." The master plan was associated with "competitiveness and growth as the dominant purpose of development."[140]

The board asked the Board of Control to constitute a Toronto City Planning Board whose appointees would not be responsible to the council but would work with Tracy leMay on planning for the city. The board hoped that such a body would "prevent 'patchwork,' improvements by evolving a broad, general plan, applicable over the years."[141] Mayor Conboy concurred, expressing his hope that the members of such a board would be "selected with only one idea in mind, 'efficiency, capacity.'"[142] In 1942, leMay was charged with formulating a new city plan. As city surveyor, leMay had primarily focused on traffic patterns. His appointment now promised that planning for the city would concentrate on traffic flow. Speaking to the young men's section of the Board of Trade in early 1939, leMay had asserted that it was time to build express highways rather than continue extending and widening existing streets. "Eliminating intersections is the answer to slow traffic," he stated. "If we build more streets we only create more intersections and aggravate the problem."[143] The proposed 1943 Master Plan focused on "regional land use planning," envisioning new areas with a population density of ten thousand per square mile—half the current density of the existing city. It also recommended building new superhighways and a focus on creating the neighborhood units in reminiscence of the plans of Ebenezer Howard.

The 1943 Master Plan for the City of Toronto (MPCT) closely resembled Abercrombie's proposals for London and Dublin. It was regionally focused with a reliance on population decentralization and rapid traffic movement. As a recent analysis of the MPCT put it, the "plan reflected the latest thinking of the day [of other Canadian planners]. . . . [T]hey thought lower densities were better than the existing densities of the city. . . . [T]he plan opted for a settlement much more spread out, as though the existing city was too crowded." The plan provided no reasons for its ideal population density of ten thousand per square mile; nor did it present any rationale for its recommendation to build five superhighways, "perhaps because it was thought that none was needed." Professional highway engineers were quite enthusiastic about superhighway plans. The plan's introduction declared that it was "a people's plan aimed at meeting the crisis created by the necessity of building a modern city on the framework of the old pre-machine town."[144] The city council endorsed the plan but did not give it official approval because it wanted more assurance of regional cooperation from surrounding municipalities before committing to the plan.[145]

The Board of Trade nevertheless promoted the plan and attempted to secure public support in early 1945 by staging an exhibit of the plan. The *Toronto Star* declared that the "outstanding feature of the display is that it defines a democratic community. This is not merely a place where an individual 'resides,' works, eats and sleeps, but where he has his home. . . . When a person realizes that his home 'is more than a parcel of real estate in a block, that it is a vital part of a neighborhood, depending on the neighborhood for its continuing value and future,' he has become a citizen." With the plan, according to the newspaper, "tomorrow, Toronto can be a city of planned, healthy, happy, purposeful neighborhoods."[146]

Political wrangling among various city officials; their reluctance to take advice from a citizen-constituted planning board, even one that they had agreed to support; and the difficulties inherent in attempting to focus on the broader region prevented the plan's implementation. Nonetheless, elements of it, including some of its regionwide proposals such as developing greenbelt areas and superhighways, would reappear in later planning. The ultimate result would be the creation of the Metropolitan Toronto area later in the century.

As city leaders continued to reject public funding for housing despite the incapacity of private enterprise and housing companies to meet housing needs, war workers flooded into the city. The mayor's advisors on the housing shortage suggested such measures as erecting fifty houses on Muggs Island that then could be used as summer houses after the war's end, converting stores into dwellings, and relaxing housing codes to convert large houses into multiple dwellings. The advisors also concluded that one thousand housing units were sufficient to meet the current need.[147] Within a year, Dorothy Denison, manager of the Toronto Housing Registry, declared that 1,100 families needed housing and that "nine out of 10 families coming to us have children, and practically every landlord makes it quite clear that children are not wanted."[148]

The gendered legacy of accepting the professional, expert planned vision for the built environment continues to reverberate in Toronto. Like London and Dublin, by the 1940s planning the built environment was now the province of professional men. Women's decades-long work to secure sufficient and decent housing for all the city's residents had fallen victim to men's reluctance to focus on this need as a primary responsibility of the city. And, as in those two cities, by the 1930s women had virtually disappeared from public discussions of the built environment despite their continued concerns. The TLCW maintained a housing and town planning committee, but it was reduced mainly to having male experts give it talks on what the men were recommending. One of the mayor's advisors, and a participant in designing the Master Plan, Eugenio Faludi, had told a meeting of the TLWC in late 1942 that "the future was in mail-order, pre-fabricated houses. . . . If we find our house isn't big enough we shall be able to telephone the store and say send us a no. 5 bedroom or a no. 7 sunroom."[149]

Women's decades-long concern that the city provide sufficient and decent housing for Toronto's people, especially for families, children, and single women, could not compete against the fanciful plans of architects such as Faludi or with men's focus on the single-family home with women embounded in it. As Sylvia Novac asserts, housing policy in Canada "has ignored women; gender is rarely a variable in the statistics. Women are invisible, subsumed within a framework of 'family'; the particular family form in housing policy is that of the patriarchal, privatized nuclear family."[150]

8

CHICAGO

City of Destiny

Perhaps the real reason we do not attack the housing problem in the city with more ability is that we do not really feel the responsibility of it. . . . The city is no better than the poorest individual man in it.
—ANITA (MRS. EMMONS) BLAINE, housing activist (1912)

The housing problem is exceedingly complex. It is bound up with land and land capitalization, with the organization of industry and commerce and their profits, processes and wages.
—CITY CLUB HOUSING COMMITTEE, *Final Year's Report* (1916)

When John S. Wright arrived in Chicago from Massachusetts in 1832, it was a small collection of buildings huddled along the Chicago River. He had come west seeking economic opportunity and believed that this new town would provide such opportunity. Wright made and lost fortunes speculating mainly in real estate, but setbacks never dampened his faith in the city's boundless economic possibilities. In 1868 he predicted future greatness for Chicago as the "emporium" of the upper midwest. When he died in 1874, Chicago's population was over three hundred thousand, the city had been rebuilt after the tragic 1871 fire, and it was now the railroad center of the nation.

Almost six decades later, University of Chicago geography professor J. Paul Goode labeled Chicago a "City of Destiny." He was convinced that its geographic location and its hardworking residents had made Chicago into Wright's emporium but that it had barely scratched the surface of its economic potential. "Chicago is now a great merchandising focus, one of the greatest that the world has ever known. But when we run the gamut of all the advantages focusing upon this city site, we will realize that we have barely begun to grow." He concluded, "We [the people of Chicago] have brains enough, and energy enough, and wealth enough. . . . There is not a shadow of a doubt but that when we put our shoulders to the wheel, we will accomplish marvels in civic, social, aesthetic, and spiritual ways. We need only to invoke the 'I Will' spirit of Chicago to accomplish our hearts' desire."[1]

Such optimism and hubris had carried Chicago through the 1871 fire. Two decades later, to showcase the city's accomplishments, businessmen secured the 1893 World's Columbian Exposition for the city. A cadre of architects led by Daniel Burnham designed the exposition's monumental architecture, earning it the nickname "the White City." Throngs of visitors were awed by exhibits of the city's manufacturing and technological prowess. But Chicago was a rather grimy industrial city with a dark and violent side. Industrial conflict and anarchist activity threatened business control of the city. The strike against the McCormick Reaper Works in 1886 had led to a violent confrontation, called the Haymarket Massacre, after which eight prominent anarchist leaders were tried and convicted of murder, shattering the movement.[2] The day the exposition closed at the end of October, a disappointed office seeker assassinated Mayor Carter Harrison I. An estimated one hundred thousand unemployed workers now haunted the city, victims of a massive economic depression. Then in July 1894 workers struck the Pullman Palace Car Company, owned by the prominent businessman George Pullman. Mayor John Hopkins and Illinois governor John Peter Altgeld supported the strikers, who refused to obey a legal injunction to halt the strike. Pullman appealed for help to President Grover Cleveland, who sent in federal troops to break the strike.

By the 1890s, homelessness, a high infant mortality rate, lack of housing and sanitary regulations, and other social problems also characterized life for many of the city's more than one million residents. Yet the city's leading men were not ready to confront these problems. Instead, their main goal was planning the city's lakefront into an aesthetic public space that would showcase the beauty of the city and bring economic investment and tourist money.

PUBLIC SPACES AND GENDER

Planning the Lakefront

The Real Estate Board had convened a meeting in 1893 to discuss lakefront development. The next year, representatives from the Real Estate Board, the Builders and Trades Exchange, the Illinois chapter of the American Institute of Architects, the Chicago Society of Artists, and the Western Society of Engineers constituted the Chicago Municipal Improvement League (CMIL). They invited a group of "prominent citizens" to formulate a plan "to secure for our city such an arrangement, design, and adornment of our public buildings and grounds, streets, boulevards, and other public works as shall most contribute to the convenience and enjoyment of the public; shall stimulate a public appreciation of art and give to the city a fit expression of its greatness."[3] Daniel Burnham presented a plan to turn Lake Park into a public park extending from the current easternmost street (Michigan Avenue) 1,300 feet to the shore of the lake (Figure 8.1).[4] Burnham's plan also included construction of a new city hall and a natural history museum to join the recently completed Art Institute on Michigan Avenue, as well as an exposition building, amusement and parade grounds, boat basins, and a bevy of monuments, fountains, and statues. Burnham asserted that he wanted to make Chicago a "Lakeside Paris." He also proposed to extend the park south along the lake to 67th Street with interior lagoons and "five stations for heroic monuments."[5]

Burnham's proposals found much support among the city's leading businessmen. At a meeting of the Commercial Club in late 1894, dedicated to promoting the plan, the club's chairman, William T. Baker, called the current state of the lakefront "a positive disgrace to the city of Chicago."[6] The packinghouse magnate P. D. Armour declared that "the [Lake] park will be an excellent thing for Chicago. . . . I believe that Burnham's plan is entirely satisfactory."[7] Other supporters claimed that Burnham's plan would make Chicago the "greatest city in the world." A magnificent lakefront, it was said, would demonstrate this greatness if "greatness be counted by heads and commercial importance."[8] Burnham declared that "the best welfare of the City demands that the town should immediately put on a charming dress and thus stop our people from running away, and bring rich people here, rather than have them go elsewhere to spend their money."[9]

Burnham's reputation had been burnished by his designs for the 1893 exposition. He was now connected to leading men in the city, including James Ellsworth, the head of the South Park Board—which exercised author-

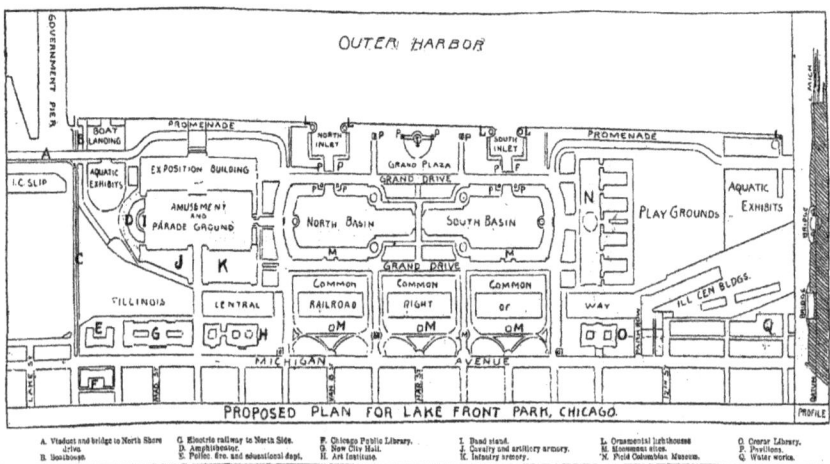

Figure 8.1 Sketch of 1895 Burnham plan for Chicago lakefront from *Chicago Daily Inter-Ocean*, August 10, 1895.

ity over this piece of the lakefront.[10] Burnham's father-in-law was a commissioner on this park board and would succeed Ellsworth as its president.[11] Designating themselves an "assembly of citizens," the members of the CMIL predicted that Burnham's plan would "produce a park and water front that will have no equal in the world." Chicago men praised the plan's classical antecedents, claiming that the proposed parade ground was "similar in plan to the Circus Maximus of Constantinople." They enthused that Burnham's overall layout resembled a "grand court" flanked by monumental structures that would mimic the Court of Honor of the recent Columbian Exposition. Burnham told business luminaries such as Marshall Field and George Pullman that his park plan "will contribute to their [the people's] health and happiness more than anything which is in the power of the city to do."[12]

The CMIL asserted that "the plan is expected to do justice to all interested parties. We have considered first the general public to give the city the kind of park it needs."[13] When a new municipal ordinance was passed to facilitate building the lakefront park, the *Daily Inter-Ocean* concluded that "public opinion has gained a great and signal victory. . . . Seldom has any project met with more cordial, popular support."[14] In April 1897, at a banquet attended by the city's prominent businessmen, the men resolved, "By citizens here assembled representing many organizations of a public nature . . . that the creation of a lake-front park is of the highest importance to this and future generations."[15] Although Burnham's plan was never fully realized, he would have another chance to redesign the lakefront in the next decade. And the lakefront today is still visually and concretely identified with the city's earlier prominent businessmen.[16]

The CMIL's claims to popular support were greatly exaggerated. Groups of Chicago women, for example, immediately objected that the lakefront should be a social space providing for public welfare rather than a grand monumental space. Beginning with their challenge to men's leadership after the fire, Chicago women had been pursuing a public role in the city's affairs, engaging in direct investigation of the city's conditions.[17] In 1892, they had founded the Municipal Order League (MOL) to pursue a citywide campaign for a cleaner and more orderly city, headed by Ada Sweet, a federally appointed head of the United States Pension Agency. Settlement house residents, several female physicians, and some of the city's wealthier women joined the MOL. The women followed the practice of direct investigation that they had begun after the fire and that would characterize their public activities from then on. The MOL instructed each member to investigate and report on conditions in her local precinct, especially to uncover the conditions of streets in poor neighborhoods. MOL member Florence Kelley reported that streets and alleys were clean and tidy in prosperous areas of the city and totally neglected in poorer areas.[18] Now the MOL argued that health and sanitation should be the focus of lakefront development. The women wanted the lakefront to have a central bathhouse, additional bathhouses, and a public laundry. Rather than a great monumental lakefront, they believed the lake was an amenity that should belong to the people of the city.

Public Baths

Dr. Sarah Hackett Stevenson led the MOL campaign for public baths. She declared that "air, water, and sunshine are the common property of mankind" and that "the greed of a few has robbed a large part of our population of these things." She wanted the city to furnish "floating bathhouses all along our lake shore in the summer."[19] In the summer of 1892, Stevenson pleaded in an open letter published in the *Tribune* for donations to help the MOL support one free public bath, saying that "it is useless to go to the city authorities for an appropriation for this purpose. 'No money' is the cry from every official's door."[20] She reported that the MOL had established a free bath along the lake at the foot of Chicago Avenue that had been used by thirty-one thousand bathers in just two months.[21] In the summer of 1893, the women reported that they had enough money on hand to reopen this bath for one week, but their goal was still to secure municipal responsibility and funding for bathhouses all around the city.[22] The MOL divided the city into north, south, and west sections and designated Stevenson, Dr. Julia Lowe, and Dr. Gertrude Wellington to conduct investigations into the neighborhoods in most need of such facilities.[23] The women's agitation convinced the city council to erect the city's first municipally built free public bath in January 1894.[24] Ironically, despite women's role in securing this bath and the others that followed, they were all named after men.[25] Chicago's male leadership thus symbolically and concretely erased women's efforts to bring about better health conditions from public memory.

The MOL disbanded in 1895, believing that the newly constituted, male-led Civic Federation could exercise more influence over many of the league's issues. A number of women objected to this move, especially since they had earlier not succeeded in having men join their efforts. Led by Gertrude Wellington, these women reorganized into the Free Bath and Sanitary League (FBSL) to continue to work for public bathing facilities.[26] The FBSL ultimately persuaded the council and park commissions to open lakefront beaches north and south along the lake and to build some neighborhood swimming pools.[27] But the city never built public baths or laundries along the central lakefront.

Public Toilets

Stevenson and the MOL also wanted the city to provide public toilets, at first stressing that such amenities would keep men and boys out of saloons.[28] But the women's attention shifted to a broader public need that included public toilets for women. The city council was not interested in furnishing public toilets, even when the *Chicago Tribune* urged that it build underground lavatories as alternatives to saloons for men and boys.[29] Only when other men began to debate the issue did it even receive a public hearing. In 1907, Thirty-fifth Ward alderman Frank Race proposed that the city architect recommend locations for public comfort stations in the downtown district. Race's interest, however, was purely economic. He hoped that such amenities could lure the 1908 Democratic and Republican conventions to the city.[30]

Once a man had made public toilets a public issue, more open discussion about them followed, although most Chicago men resisted constructing such facilities. Several male civic clubs organized a committee to study whether providing public toilets was an appropriate municipal responsibility. No women were invited to participate.[31] The city council had previously appropriated $5,000 for an experimental public toilet but had diverted the money to the sewer department. In 1909, the city's assistant engineer proposed fifteen suitable locations in downtown, and Race again requested an appropriation for such facilities. Only in 1911 were two municipally furnished public toilets built in the basement of the new city hall at the corner of LaSalle and Washington Streets.[32] Despite one of these facilities being for women, City Hall was an overall male space that many women might have felt uncomfortable entering, especially descending into a basement.

Over the following years, Chicago men deflected the possibility of municipally furnished public toilets by suggesting that the park districts provide them in the parks. They made a show of gathering statistics on public toilets from other cities but then did nothing.[33] Diverting calls for public toilets to the restricted spaces of parks, where women could presumably go either with children or accompanied by a man, and placing the first woman's toilet in the basement of City Hall, kept the city's downtown commercial and political districts safe from the sexual disorder of women's presence. The council even rejected the 1913 offer of the downtown main public library on Michigan and Randolph Avenues, where women were frequent patrons, to provide a space under the sidewalks at that intersection for public toilets. The council would have been obliged to build and maintain it.[34]

By 1910, organized Chicago women had made public toilets—primarily, but not exclusively, to accommodate women and women with children—a central concern. The Chicago Woman's Club (CWC), the Woman's City Club of Chicago (WCC), and Chicago Woman's Aid (CWA) led the struggle for public toilets across the following years. The women circulated pamphlets through the city and petitioned the city council. The mayor promised to furnish a women's facility inside the library, but the council failed to act. Public toilets were finally constructed inside the library. Even then, only through persistent lobbying efforts did the women force the city's Health Department in 1923 to erect a public sign pointing to its location.[35]

By 1916, the newly created Department of Public Welfare—staffed primarily by women—surveyed Chicago and other cities on the provision of public toilets. The department then produced what it described as "the most comprehensive piece of work of its kind ever accomplished in the United States."[36] The department recommended building public toilets in each of the city's thirty-five wards. One of the investigation's findings was that even when public toilets had been furnished in parks, there were always more facilities for men than for women.[37] In light of their constant pressure on the council, women succeeded in having a bond proposal for $150,000 for public toilets placed on the ballot for the 1917 elections. That year, women were also working to connect public toilets to new street-widening projects for the city that were under way as part of a larger citywide plan. When the bond passed, the WCC proclaimed it a "signal victory" and congratulated women for their hard work on the issue. The women believed that now they would be consulted about where to locate such facilities. "We will be privileged to assist in the planning of at least six additional stations, two of which, due to the unceasing demands of your [beaches and public comfort stations] committee, will be included in the Twelfth Street widening plans," the WCC assured its members. Shortly after, however, the WCC leadership informed members that there was no progress in having public toilets incorporated into the plans and warned that "unless these stations are built forthwith, the widening will be completed without proper provision for the comfort stations."[38] Despite promises that three public toilets would be incorporated into widened Michigan Avenue, by midsummer 1918, no facilities had been erected either on Michigan Avenue of Twelfth Street.

In its July and August *Bulletins*, the WCC dramatized the discouraging situation in the form of a movie script. In the script, Jennie Purvin, chair of the organization's bathing beaches and public comfort stations committee and former president of the CWA, trudges from floor to floor in city hall inquiring about the lack of progress in spending the $150,000 and asks to see the plans. She shuttles among the public works, health, and sanitary departments and the city architect's office; each office sends her elsewhere and assures her that the plans must be in another office. She leaves the building, counting "how many months have elapsed since the city council began to spend money on paper, for comfort stations; she reaches sixteen, heaves a sigh of regret, and proceeds on her way." In the script's second episode, Purvin repeats the process, and after again being sent from office to office, she is asked why she is concerned. Was it a personal concern, one of the men wanted to know? She replies no, that the WCC had been trying for seven years to secure public toilets in the city. She leaves after being assured that the women should keep working on the matter. She muses about how long it will be "before her committee may rest from its efforts. She decides that it would be easier to guess when the war will end."[39]

In summer 1918, alderman John Lyle of the Thirty-Second Ward proposed that the council consider building public toilets—if financially feasible—in elevated railroad stations. He was mainly concerned about the situation of soldiers in wartime. "Such [public comfort] stations are of particular importance at this time because of the large number of soldiers and sailors coming and going out of Chicago on Saturday afternoons and Sundays when so many public buildings are closed." Lyle reasoned that it was the city's duty "to protect the health and administer to the comforts of soldiers and sailors passing in and out of Chicago, and likewise our duty to our own citizens, who reside here." The council never considered the proposal.[40]

The WCC continued to lobby for municipally erected public toilets. The women demanded that all new plans for the built environment incorporate public toilets, especially in all street improvement plans so that they were available for "the community at large instead of local patrons only." They advocated for public comfort stations to be built at 35th and 47th Streets in the city's African American neighborhood. The WCC firmly rejected the council's idea that public toilets had to be "self supporting through the rental of space for news and fruit stands, etc." Every time, the women thought that they were making progress, such as in 1922 when the WCC committee believed that it had secured the cooperation of the current Plan Commission and the Board of Local Improvements to incorporate potential sites into planning, or in 1923 when the WCC committee reported that it had finally persuaded the city council to solicit bids for building public toilets. But the women were always disappointed. The WCC informed its members in 1925 that few public comfort stations had been built with the bond money.[41] Relying on the park boards to build public toilets did not bring much success either. The WCC had to keep lobbying the boards to erect conspicuous signs directing pedestrians to any public comfort stations in the parks. Moreover, the park boards were as reluctant as the city council to finance public comfort stations unless they could be profitable or self-sustaining. In early 1926, for example, the West Park Board authorized a public toilet but required that it be self-supporting through "news, candy, tobacco, and ice cream stands to be operated in the same building."[42]

Burnham's Chicago Plan

By the middle of the first decade of the twentieth century, Chicago's leading men had moved from focusing on the lakefront to developing a complete general plan for the city. The idea for such a plan originated with the Commercial Club and Merchants' Club, the city's two leading businessmen's organizations. The younger businessmen of the recently organized Merchants'

Club initiated the planning process, convening a meeting in October 1906 to pledge money to fund the project, to approach Daniel Burnham to create a plan, and to select men to work with him as a Plan Committee. The two clubs merged in 1907 under the Commercial Club's name. The Commercial Club, whose early members were some of the city's leading commercial and industrial giants, had never seen any distinction between their members' economic and property interests and those of the city.[43] Now they and the younger businessmen feared that without a more orderly city focused on transportation and communication networks, new men and money would not flow into Chicago. A Plan Committee was duly organized, and in a memo of a meeting of April 1, 1907, the committee reported that the progress on the plan would be delivered at "a closed meeting of Commercial Club." The committee specified that only a "carefully prepared statement should be given out to the newspapers not going into detail and above all things, not using all of our ammunition at this time."[44] The men specifically directed that any publication of the plan "should emphasize the fact that the Plan is a business proposition."[45] An array of politicians and male professional and business organizations, including the American Institute of Architects, the Western Society of Engineers, the Real Estate Board, newspaper executives, and the men of the city's park boards, among others, rallied to the idea of a general city plan.[46]

Once a plan was drawn up and ready for consideration, Mayor Fred Busse appointed a commission of more than three hundred men to study it. One hundred fifty men attended the commission's first meeting, where Busse declared that the plan's designers were "hard-headed businessmen" concerned with enhancing the city's commercial assets and real estate values. The plan, he said, would make Chicago "the greatest and most attractive city of this continent." He also claimed that the commission was "as representative as possible of every element of our population." Commission chair Charles Wacker assured the men that it was "composed of truly representative and public-spirited fellow-citizens."[47] Of course, this commission represented, at best, every element of white businessmen and politicians. The head of the Chicago Federation of Labor, John Fitzpatrick, declined to participate, citing his dissatisfaction that the plan included no provisions for taking care of workers: "It is time we of Chicago should be seriously concerned with a 'Chicago Plan,' but one having as an object a better life, a better home, a better future for human beings."[48] Numbers of the city's ethnic businessmen served on the commission, as did African American city council member Robert R. Jackson, although all aldermen were members of the commission.[49]

The conspicuous absence of any women on the Plan Commission alone reveals the patriarchal nature of planning. But when a photo of the planning committee at work in 1908 sitting around a well-set dining table is compared with two 1871 sketches following the fire, we have a visual representation of decades of urban patriarchy. The first 1871 sketch shows men seated around a table poring over reports as they discussed how to distribute aid money. The second sketch depicts well-dressed young women cutting bread on a rough plank "ministering" to the barefoot children gathered around them.[50] Men were to make the decisions; women were to be helpers.

The only woman who seems to have been queried about the plan was Jane Addams, presumably because the Hull House settlement's position on Halsted Street would be affected if that street were to be widened. According to Carl Smith, Addams responded that she did not oppose the street widening "if it were a part of a well considered scheme for the general improvement of the city."[51] What Addams had in mind as a well-considered scheme is not known.

The plan that emerged implied that Chicago was a diseased organism. First, the city suffered from a circulatory disease. The narrow and clogged arteries of the city's economic center hampered the free flow of traffic and threatened to slow economic growth and efficiency. The absence of radial streets made it difficult to circulate around and throughout the city. The lack of modern bridges spanning the river compounded the circulatory problems. Second the city lacked a heart, a central node that would organize the entire city and pump its lifeblood. Third, the city had weak lungs. The lakefront was failing to provide sufficient respiration, fresh air, and breathing space for the city's residents and for tourists. Finally, disorder sickened a city as it sickened a physical body. Only a comprehensive plan that embodied much creative destruction could cure the diseased organism. The improvements to the city brought about by such planning, according to the planners, would "increase the comfort of the people, provide outdoor recreational facilities, and serve to reduce nervous tension, thus improving the general public health. Congestion and disorder are conducive to discontent and crime. . . . [R]educing congestion and substituting order for disorder" would be "a great social service."[52]

Circulation and Arteries

For Burnham and his businessmen supporters, traffic circulation was the most troubling disease that had to be eradicated or the city's economic growth would stagnate. Major replanning of the city's streets, railroad facilities, and river crossings was necessary. Charles Wacker underscored this goal by appealing to masculine leadership and pride. "The men behind the guns in shaping this work were hard headed business men whose interest and welfare are bound up with the industrial and commercial growth of Chicago." He also echoed Burnham's earlier idea that Chicago should be beautified to attract tourists: "It is stated that American tourists spend in Europe every year $500,000,000. We want some of this business."[53] Commercial Club president John V. Farwell assured the club members that the plan would promote such growth and compared a great city to well-rounded men:

The Plan of Chicago is not only a Commercial Club project, but it is also in every sense a commercial project, for the very foundation and aim of the whole idea is to develop the enduring prosperity of Chicago; and in order to do that all the elements which go to make up a great city must be considered, just as all exalted characters must be well-rounded men, men who are developed on all sides of their character, physically, mentally, morally and spiritually.[54]

Wacker declared that "the entire scheme of the Chicago plan is based upon the most vital questions confronting every metropolitan community today—traffic in all of its relations. . . . It is plainly a duty of the city as a matter of foresight and justice to exercise a guiding hand in improving conditions that are actually harmful to the city's business interests." The commission agreed that street widenings and the extension of main arteries were the "solution of the city's internal transportation problem."[55] The geometric ideals of the linear, wide street and symmetrical layout dominated the recommendations. By 1919, twelve major street reconstruction projects were under way. The east-west artery at the south end of the downtown, Twelfth Street (today Roosevelt Road), had been widened and extended with new viaducts and bridges crossing the river and passing over railroad tracks. Michigan Avenue was also widened and extended to cross the river north over a new bridge, creating a new major north-south axis through downtown that linked both sides of the river. One of Burnham's more fanciful proposals to turn parts of Michigan Avenue into a double-deck thoroughfare never came to pass, but a new double-deck bridge crossing the river was ultimately built. The Twelfth Street constructions cost over $8 million; the Michigan Avenue expense was estimated at $14 million but rose to $16 million by the mid-1920s.[56] Creating Michigan Avenue as a great thoroughfare was promoted as of "tremendous importance to the entire city," an artery that would give Chicago equality with avenues such as the Champs-Élysées in Paris and Berlin's Unter den Linden and lure travelers to Chicago as did those great European arteries.[57] The commissioners later asserted that once the work on Michigan Avenue was completed, the reconstructions had repaid the expenses "six times over in increased property values."[58]

Circulatory System

The plan's next strategic recommendation was for a new heart that would enhance the circulatory system of the city. Burnham designed a system of diagonal streets to form a quadrangle radiating from a newly proposed civic center "to form the foundation of the entire streets circulatory system" and "cement the whole city." At the commission's 1913 meeting Walter Moody compared this ideal to Vienna's Ringstrasse.[59] The diagonal street plan and the new civic center were never implemented, so downtown remained the heart of the city. To bring a more orderly circulatory system around and through this central node, streets leading in and around downtown had to be replanned. Planners moved Burnham's quadrangle idea to inside that district, where main streets were to be widened, extended, and connected with new bridges across the river. Viaducts across railroad tracks were to be widened to connect east and west sides of the quadrangle. Inside the quadrangle, the bend in the south branch of the Chicago River west of downtown was straightened to facilitate water traffic. The first segment of a planned double-deck road along the river—named Wacker Drive—was opened in 1926. The planners had hoped to erect a new main railroad station south of Twelfth Street to remove some railroad traffic from the heart of downtown. But railroads resisted this plan in favor of a site nearer to downtown. The compromise was a new Union Station constructed just west of the river at Jackson Street that helped alleviate some of the circulation problems.[60]

Respiration: The Lakefront, Again

To turn the lakefront into the lungs of the city, Burnham reprised his 1895 plan, only on a grander scale. He proposed locating the Field Museum of Natural History on the south end of the former Lake Park (now Grant Park) to anchor the park as a monumental civic space. He also recommended that the city landfill the lakeshore to create a waterway five miles long and six hundred feet wide between Grant Park and Jackson Park on the south end. The area would include bathing beaches and accommodate regattas, rowing, boating, skating, and two motorboat racing courses along a government-built breakwater.[61] Jane Addams urged Burnham to plan the lakefront for the benefit of the public, arguing that centralizing civic and cultural institutions such as the Field Museum downtown to join the Art Institute would take such cultural amenities away from neighborhoods and impede access for the majority of Chicagoans. Addams, however, could not compete with ideas such as Walter Moody's that "placing the Field Museum centrally is what has been termed 'capitalizing a city's luxuries'" so that it would become one of the city's "famous places talked about by its visitors."[62] For Burnham, the lakefront was also "luxury, tourism, and commercial attraction." He wrote, "Imagine this supremely beautiful parkway with its frequent stretches of fields, avenues, playgrounds, and groves. . . . When this Parkway shall be created our people will stay here and other people will come to dwell among us—the people who spend time and large amounts of money in Paris, in Vienna, and on the Riviera."[63]

The WCC pleaded with the commission to build a children's playground on the south end of this "supremely beautiful parkway." The women argued that there was no children's playground in the city's lakefront First Ward, where approximately ten thousand children lived.[64] But Burnham's plan saw the lakefront functioning as a monumental breathing space, not as a children's playground. The planners also ignored women's pleas for erecting small neighborhood parks or playgrounds throughout the city.[65] Instead, the Plan Commission focused on moving recreation out of the city to forest preserves on the periphery, where the recently created Cook County Forest Preserve District could acquire land. According to the plan commissioners, "The worth of forest preserves to a community is so well established as to scarcely require mention here. The humanitarian and commercial value of these country playgrounds is beyond computation."[66] Charles Wacker was a board member of the Forest Preserve District.

The existence of a Small Parks Commission, created in 1899 to consider building small parks and playgrounds throughout the city,[67] left the planners free to design the lakefront as a grand leisure and ornamental area that would attract tourists and promote Chicago as a city on the scale of monumental European cities. The booklet explaining the plan as originally presented by the commission, for example, contained numerous illustrations of what had been done in Europe, making it clear that the commissioners wanted to emulate European cities. Putting the costs for outlying forest preserve districts onto a separate governing body meant that the commission could finance its desired improvements without needing to spend money on recreation inside the city.

Patrick Abercrombie hailed Burnham's plan as "the most complete and sumptuous proposal for re-creating a town that has yet appeared in America."[68] Carl Smith's recent book on the plan called it "one of the most fascinating and significant documents in the history of urban planning . . . [whose] fascination arises from the imaginative and visual appeal of its stirring prose and stunning illustrations."[69] Although many of the plan's most ambitious recommendations were not realized, the elements of it that were undertaken significantly reordered traffic circulation in the city. What was not achieved at the time would set the tone for future ideas about planning the city. Moreover, enough had been done by 1919 that the Plan Commission grandiloquently declared that "the destiny of Chicago is assured. The door of its future is open. Our city has crossed the threshold and will never step back over it. The die has been cast. . . . [N]either war, nor pestilence, nor panic, nor time will serve to efface that which has already been started or prevent the complete realization of that which is proposed."[70]

HARBOR DEVELOPMENT

Burnham had not intended to extend his lakefront plan north across the Chicago river except to connect the north and south sides of the Loop with new bridges. He had, however, planned for two new piers extending into the lake, and this proposal coincided with ideas to build a new centrally located working harbor. In early 1908, Mayor Fred Busse had appointed a Harbor Commission of five businessmen, men "well-equipped for the important undertaking," to study the potential of such development. The *Chicago Tribune* declared that the "commercial supremacy of Chicago is the goal" of this harbor.[71] When a new state law gave cities more power to determine development of their water resources, the city council subcommittee on harbors, wharves, and bridges began drawing up plans for a working harbor north of the river. After consulting an array of professional men, including several engineers and men from the Association of Commerce, the subcommittee recommended that plans for such a harbor "can be arranged and developed to dovetail perfectly with the scheme of the Chicago Plan Commission, so that the harbor construction work can be made to form an important step in the development of the lake front plan."[72]

The council's proposed plan for harbor development envisioned several new ship docks and a large offshore anchorage site to accommodate additional ships. The men of the City Club expressed "unanimity of opinion" with the view of Lyman Cooley, former chief of the sanitary district, that "for the industries of Chicago you want waterfront by the mile, for the industrial element is the largest element in the population. The next is the commercial element."[73] The Association of Commerce and business luminaries such as Marshall Field and John Farwell favored the proposal. Mayor Carter Harrison II supported the proposed harbor and urged the council to appropriate the necessary finances.[74] But the council believed that both state and federal funding would be needed, and that the federal government would need to allow building a new breakwater to protect the harbor. The city also did not own all the land along the lakefront, and several individuals claimed title to parcels of lakefront land for which they demanded compensation. Moreover, there were competing business interests at work pursuing a plan for the sanitary district to build a harbor south of the city at the mouth of the Calumet River. Chicago men considered this a ploy to take control of the harbor away from the city and enrich the property of a few industries south of the city.[75]

In the end, legal, technical, and financial impediments, along with political infighting, blocked central harbor development. Only one piece of Burnham's original plan, Municipal Pier 2 (later Navy Pier), opened in 1916, but it accommodated recreational outings rather than industrial shipping. Wacker and Moody, however, now wanted the city to construct southside working harbors between 16th and 31st Streets and to have the entire stretch between 16th and 47th Streets planned for both recreational and commercial purposes.[76] The Illinois Central Railroad held a right of way for its tracks along this part of the lakefront, and other land was owned by the South Park Board, so these plans also never materialized.[77] By the late 1920s, the Commercial Club had proposed a new plan for a southern lakefront harbor development to connect the lake's commercial traffic with the city's railroads. For the *Chicago Tribune*, this proposal was "drawn up with much understanding of Chicago's industrial and commercial requirements and of the requirements of traffic moving through Chicago."[78] By the 1930s, however, the federal government was focusing its funding for harbors and waterways on the southern end of the lakefront at Calumet Harbor.[79]

PLANNING AND SOCIAL ISSUES

The Chicago Plan Commission vision for distributing benefits and of what kind throughout the city was as limited in its social responsibility as had been the 1890s ideas about the lakefront. After their ideas were generally ignored by men, more women had begun to organize to confront Chicago's social problems. In March 1896, representatives from forty women's clubs met to organize a day-long public meeting to discuss all issues that concerned the health and rights of children. At the meeting in May, the women argued that it was the city's responsibility to provide better schools, more health measures and recreation facilities, and more legal protections and social justice for children. This was a public meeting, publicly advertised, and included an evening session in the city's Central Music Hall that the women hoped would attract a large audience. Very few men attended the gathering.[80]

Now the Plan Commission, after ignoring women's requests for a children's playground along the lakefront, public toilets, and small parks and playgrounds distributed throughout the city, also rejected women's ideas for the municipal pier. A delegation from the CWC met with the harbor commissioners to ask that the pier include social amenities such as public toilets, a public library, a children's nursery, and space for concerts and dancing. Women organized a joint committee representing the CWC, the WCC, the Juvenile Protective League, and the Political Equality League (PEL) to lobby the commissioners and the council's Public Works Committee to keep the pier clean, orderly, and under public, not private, concessions and to make sure that there was "adequate street car access" to the pier.[81] I have never found any information to demonstrate that the women's requests were honored, and bids were put out for private concession owners.[82]

Planning Does Not Include Housing

At the Fifth National Conference on City Planning in 1913, Charles Wacker neatly divorced social issues from planning. "The Chicago Plan Commission," he asserted, "cannot enter into administrative functions, such as the inauguration of hygienic measures, or measures for the amelioration of living conditions of our people. In all its educational efforts it persistently calls attention by word and by picture to the importance of relieving congestion, facilitating transportation and providing means for the preservation of life."[83] Among those issues not to be included in planning was one of women's most significant demands: housing.

As soon as the plan emerged, Chicago women had objected to its focus. In 1912, Anita (Mrs. Emmons) Blaine—daughter of the wealthy industrialist Cyrus Hall McCormick—asserted of the plan that "as fine as it is, it ought to be Volume II, Volume I should be 'The Housing of the People.'"[84] Mary McDowell, the head of the University of Chicago social settlement, had pleaded with the plan commissioners to include better housing in the plan, explaining that "the housing problem is of central importance in any scheme of city planning. It requires competent, impartial public control, and immediate action must be taken."[85] In 1912, at a Civics Associations' Night organized by the City Club, a frustrated Blaine remarked that "perhaps the real reason we do not attack the housing problem in the city with more ability is that we do not really feel the responsibility of it. At bottom we feel that it is not our responsibility; that every man's home is his castle; and that if we invade that with activities of our own, we are interfering." But, she went on, "the city is truly the great home of everyone who has adopted it, and those that manage the affairs of the city are the delegated housekeepers. The city is no better than the poorest individual man in it."[86] Here was a fundamental difference in vision about the welfare of the city. Wacker had asserted that "the Commission believes that such meritorious and far-reaching questions as the proper regulation of tenements and the housing of the poor are in themselves so important as to demand special consideration as separate and distinct measures." In the commissioners' 1919 publication, housing was mentioned in only one sentence, stating that the commissioners gave "continued support and encouragement of the important housing question."[87]

To abdicate any responsibility for housing was extreme vis-à-vis planning efforts in London, Dublin, or Toronto. Surveying and diagnosing the diseased built environment in those three cities had included an understanding that the housing situation must be dealt with to make the city healthy, even if, as with Abercrombie's plan for Dublin, housing ranked below traffic circulation. Moreover, Chicago had a severe housing crisis. As McDowell had told the Plan Commission, in her Twenty-Ninth Ward there were "hundreds of families existing in dark, unventilated rooms in cellars," and such conditions existed in other parts of the city.[88]

Women continued to see providing decent housing as one of the city's most important responsibilities. In 1912, the CWC surveyed housing conditions in the near west side Twentieth Ward (immediately adjacent to Hull House's Nineteenth Ward) and reported 1,644 sanitary violations to the Sanitary Bureau. After then reporting that 945 such conditions remained or had even worsened since the survey, the women decried the city's lack of attention to housing conditions. They wondered:

> What civic ideal could be more inspiring than that of comfortable, healthful homes for all citizens and their children[?] The so-called "City Beautiful" of parks and ornamental waterfront and boulevards on the outside, if achieved, with a great rotten core of slums teeming with suffering and misfortune, so far from being beautiful would not even be moral. . . . It is high time to co-ordinate these energies and turn the impulse to perpetual good and make Chicago in its homes a model city.[89]

Charles Wacker, on the other hand, believed that planning the city would produce a civic ideal by "building civic character and inspiring civic spirit in the youth of Chicago . . . a perfectly arranged city will produce . . . a higher, mental, moral and physical people."[90]

After women failed to elicit any agreement from municipal authorities that the city should assume responsibility for housing, in 1916 several women's organizations formed their own Housing Council and organized a city-wide Housing Conference hoping "to stimulate public concern, and to act as a clearing house for ideas and methods of housing betterment."[91] The *Chicago Tribune* announced this plan but gave no coverage to its proceedings. The unwillingness of the Plan Commission and the city government to confront the housing crisis had previously compelled McDowell to seek private investors for building and maintaining model tenements on the model of housing initiatives such as the Peabody and Guinness buildings. She pleaded that "if we can do this on a business basis others will follow our example. Then this house may be a type of help in giving the best to the most needy." She appealed to Chicago businessmen to seize this as a "psychological moment when a successful concrete example of housing for wage earners built on a business basis will be stimulus towards standardizing housing in Chicago." Even such a modest proposal did not interest Chicago's businessmen, one of whom admonished McDowell not to "mix business and philanthropy."[92]

Focus on private property ownership and the city as an economic growth machine also determined much of the men's attitude toward housing. At a housing conference held by the City Club in January 1921, settlement house leader Harriet Vittum pleaded that "without decent homes people cannot live decent lives." She called on the city to "build and work as well as think and talk about the problem." Every male speaker at the conference either emphasized the need to expand financing options and reduced costs of building materials or declared that more housing needed to be built because bad housing led to "crime, labor turnover, bolshevism, unAmericanism" and

produced moral defectives who were physically and mentally unfit.[93] Emphasizing housing as a human need, not decrying bad housing as producing
crime and moral defectives, separated Vittum and other Chicago women
from most of the city's male leaders.

Defending the Color Line in Housing

Racial prejudice and residential segregation complicated all of Chicago's
housing issues. Large numbers of black southerners had begun migrating
into northern industrial cities during World War I. Although Chicago was
not legally segregated as were southern cities, de facto segregation confined
black residents to a small area on the city's near south side colloquially called
the Black Belt. Wacker's and Moody's ideas about developing the south side
lakefront for recreational purposes would not have enhanced the neighborhood. Beaches and recreational facilities along the lake were informally racially segregated. An invisible but inviolable line was drawn at 29th Street,
south of which the beaches were for white Chicagoans only. The men's suggestions for harbor development between 16th and 31st Streets not only
would have produced more industrial congestion in the area; they would
have virtually eliminated any beach areas for black Chicagoans.

Housing in this area steadily worsened as more black migrants settled in
the only neighborhood available to them. High demand allowed landlords
to charge high rents for substandard housing; landlords became adept at
subdividing available apartments into smaller one-room units called kitch-
enettes for entire families.[94] Housing conditions for thousands of poor and
working-class whites were also dire, as was the case with McDowell's ward,
but racial politics and economics made the situation worse for the city's
black population. When African Americans moved into a previously white
residential area, for example, white residents moved out and landlords usually increased rents about 25 percent for desperate black tenants. No new
housing was being built in the area, and upkeep of existing buildings was
minimal.[95] Severing housing from planning the built environment allowed
the commission to avoid addressing the city's racial segregation. At the same
time, the Real Estate Board was drawing up a restrictive covenant for property owners' associations to use to deny housing to "undesirables" in white
neighborhoods. William MacChesney, a member of the Plan Commission's
Executive Committee, was drafting the covenant as a legal document.[96]

Working through the University of Chicago School of Civics and Philanthropy's Department of Social Investigation, several Chicago women had
also undertaken a massive house-to-house canvass of the city's housing conditions. They included the black neighborhoods in the survey even though
the Health Department told Sophonisba Breckinridge "that the areas weren't
worth canvassing."[97] Breckinridge and her colleagues ignored such attitudes

and issued a devastating report on housing in the city's black neighborhoods that also argued that the problems of housing there affected all the city:

> The Negro's economic and social limitations have brought peculiar-ities of living conditions in the colored sections of the city which are the concern of the white sections as well as the colored. For this rea-son it was believed that an intensive study of the housing conditions in the two largest colored districts would throw light, not only upon the general conditions under which the Negro lives, but upon the larger housing problem of Chicago.[98]

When the women compared the housing conditions in black neighborhoods with those in the city's poor, immigrant, and working-class areas, they con-cluded that conditions were always worse in the former areas. Black tenants, for one example, paid $12 a month for a four-room apartment, while white ethnic immigrants paid $8.50 for a similar sized apartment. This state of affairs stemmed solely from racial prejudice.[99] Breckinridge asserted that "a decent home . . . in a respectable neighborhood and at a reasonable rental" was one of three indisputable rights of black Chicagoans that needed to be protected by law and by the city.[100]

Relying on private enterprise to build housing was especially pernicious for Chicago's black residents because business resisted investing in housing for the area. Even white philanthropist Julius Rosenwald, who was very con-cerned about the dismal state of housing for the city's black residents and proposed to build a model apartment building in the so-called Black Belt, could envision this project only as a business proposition. He believed that it would be good for the city because better housing in the area would help maintain the color line. When he discovered that he could not be assured of a sufficient return on his investment, he dropped his plans.[101]

As the crowding in the Black Belt increased at the end of World War I, a group of the city's prominent black and white businessmen met in June 1919 to discuss organizing a mixed-race commission to come up with a plan "to eliminate unfit buildings and rebuild in their places wholesome apartments" in the Black Belt.[102] Before these men could take their ideas any further, and even as the plan commissioners were lauding their reconstruction of major streets and future plans for the built environment that would keep Chicago a city of destiny, serious racial rioting erupted between white and black youths along the lakefront. A black youth who had inadvertently drifted into the white beach area south of 29th Street drowned after rocks were thrown at him. This incident followed a series of bombings of black property across the previous six months. White property owners and real estate agents, par-ticularly in the Hyde Park–Kenwood area just south of the Black Belt, who were railing against any incursion of "undesirables" into their neighborhood, had undoubtedly inflamed racial antagonism. A spokesperson for both the Kenwood Improvement Association and real estate interests told Chicago newspaper reporter Carl Sandburg that he had told representatives from the black community that "you people are not admitted to our society." Getting perhaps to the nub of white racism, he went on to say that "improvements are coming along the lake shore. . . . [W]e can't have these people coming over here. . . . They injure our investments. They hurt our [real estate] values."[103] Now the young man's death sparked five days of frenzied violence that increased attacks on African Americans and fire-bombings of their property but also saw black Chicagoans fight back against the attacks.[104]

The racial rioting occurred nine months before the men of the Plan Commission congratulated themselves on their work and declared that this marked an "epoch in the history of the Chicago Plan Commission" in which "[almost] all of its recommendations have been provided for."[105] These men had not been moved by the racial tension revolving around the housing crisis. Now Mayor William Thompson, a Republican with strong support from the city's black voters, appointed a biracial, all-male Chicago Commission on Race Relations to investigate the causes of the 1919 rioting and make recommendations. The commission issued a six-hundred-plus-page exhaustive report in 1922 as to causes but produced no structural solutions. The report instead suggested more vigorous use of police power against violence and better behavior on the part of the citizenry. It exhorted black Chicagoans to promulgate "sound racial doctrines" and discourage "propaganda and agitators seeking to inflame racial animosity and incite Negroes to violence." White Chicagoans were encouraged to "seek information from responsible and representative Negroes as the basis of their judgments about Negro traits, characteristics and tendencies and thereby counteract the common disposition . . . to regard all Negroes as belonging to one homogeneous group and as being inferior in mentality and morality, given to emotionalism, and having an innate tendency toward crime, especially sex crime." At best the report encouraged more social organizations to become involve in race relations and urged that "all white citizens energetically discourage [predatory practices in housing] and either cooperate in or start movements to solve the housing problem by constructive and not destructive methods."[106]

The commission declared its work to be "epoch-making." Yet its focus was so specialized on investigating the social context of racial thinking that it made no significant suggestions that the city should take responsibility for confronting the white prejudices that fostered segregation. Instead, the report perceived black and white residents as two separate forces in the city that could not live together but perhaps could coexist in some kind of amiable segregation. Even before the report was published, the African American paper, the *Chicago Defender*, charged that "the thousand and one committees appointed by the Chamber of Commerce and a score of other civic bodies, to look after the housing conditions of our people have done little more than make a lengthy report." Moreover, according to the paper, none of these organizations had tried in 1917 and 1919 to persuade the Armour family not to tear down flats along Federal and Dearborn Streets without replacing them with new housing.[107] By 1925, the paper reported that "the housing situation is steadily growing worse. . . . [F]lats meant to accommodate eight people are giving shelter to as many as 30 persons."[108]

McDowell and the WCC had organized a Committee on Race Relations and Civic Betterment in the wake of the rioting. McDowell challenged the notion that there could be any kind of civic sense when any group was not treated equally. "The race riots last summer brought to the consciousness of thoughtful, unprejudiced citizens the fact that it is not possible to have a well governed city with a segregated group of any kind within its boundaries." The city's black residents "are here, they are citizens of our city. . . . Civic patriotism demands that for the welfare of the city as a whole, race prejudice must be lost in a constructive program to provide proper housing, full recreational privileges, and increased educational opportunities [f]or where they are now lacking." McDowell noted in particular the lack of decent housing for black Chicagoans and the exorbitant rents they were required to pay for substandard housing.[109] By the end of 1920, the WCC reported that sixty-seven black and white women's clubs with over nineteen thousand members were working as an Inter-racial Co-operative Committee to foster "intelligent co-operation for civic betterment [and] to encourage equal opportunity irrespective of race, color, or other artificial distinctions."[110] On the one hand, trying to undermine racial antagonism through cooperative activities in the face of more powerful political and economic forces did not necessarily lead to its eradication or to better living conditions and equal opportunity for black Chicagoans. And despite now having suffrage, women had no political power to force change. On the other hand, the Commission on Race Relations had failed to confront the effects of racial thinking by making only tepid calls for "White Members of the Public" and "Negro Members of the Public" to examine their behavior.

Housing remained in control of private landlords who continued to exploit the situation in the Black Belt. The determination to keep housing as private enterprise meant that any plans for new housing in that neighborhood changed little over the coming years. The Association of Commerce and the Real Estate Board proposed to form a real estate improvement corporation to build up the Black Belt. It was to be a corporation "for profit." The board's president declared, "If we can settle the housing problem satisfactorily it will dispose of 90 percent of the race difficulties." The men envisioned making a profit by confining black Chicagoans to one area of the city, hoping that if they built housing in the neighborhood, offering them opportunity "to have homes of their own," they would solve the city's racial issues. These white leaders believed that they could protect racial segregation by offering "industrious Negroes" the chance to own property. As the board president put it, the corporation would raise money "with which the industrious Negroes can buy small homes and pay us back on the installment plan."[111] Underlying such thinking were two firmly embedded conceptions of the city that owning property created a stable male citizenship and that only "industrious" hardworking men deserved to be considered good urban citizens. The leaders of the city's black community were not immune to the culture of property ownership, although they were admittedly probably aided by a resignation that conditions could not be bettered within the confines of the Black Belt. The *Chicago Defender*'s editors by 1925 were urging their readers to move out of the city to become a "home-owner instead of a home-renter."[112]

Promoting the reconstruction of the built environment as both the means and the end of civic spirit was a male conceptualization of the city, but in Chicago it did not necessarily apply to the city's African American community. Wacker's proclamation that the plan would build civic character and civic spirit among the city's youth could hardly have convinced Chicago's black residents that a perfectly arranged and orderly city would mean better housing and employment for them. Men's appeal to the civic conscience of the community as the means to resolve racial discrimination and avoid future racial clashes tacitly accepted the white ideal of a segregated built environment.

Unfortunately, racial prejudice was deeply embedded in white civic consciousness, and when combined with the profit motive in housing, the city's color line would remain intact and black Chicagoans would continue to be excluded from the civic welfare. Even women who were very concerned about the inclusion of black Chicagoans in all housing considerations often accepted that racial segregation would persist. In the context of American racism of the time, few white Americans believed that the color line should be, or could be, breached. These women can be justly castigated for not directly attacking racism, but they did believe that black Chicagoans were a part of the civic fabric of the city whose needs and rights to decent housing should be considered along with those of white Chicagoans.

SURVEY, DIAGNOSE, ZONE

Chicago's business and professional leadership had grasped Patrick Abercrombie's ideal in his Dublin plan that housing was "a matter of regulating future growth."[113] This ideal separated human need from planning. Now men found further justification for this separation in academia.

Impersonalizing Social Needs

Led by Robert Park, Louis Wirth, and Ernest Burgess, the University of Chicago Department of Sociology offered a sociotheoretical framework for understanding the city. These men pushed the Geddesian organic idea to define the city as an ecological organism to be investigated as an abstract social and cultural phenomenon. Park theorized that the city should be seen

> not as a mere congeries of persons and social arrangements, but as an institution . . . a section of corporate human nature plus the machinery and the instrumentalities through which that human nature operates . . . as something more than a mere collective entity. We may think of it as a mechanism—a psychophysical mechanism—in and through which private and political interests find corporate expression.[114]

Viewed this way, the city could be examined impersonally, as "a laboratory or clinic in which human nature and social processes may be most conveniently and profitably studied."[115]

Female social scientists such as Sophonisba Breckinridge believed that inquiry and social responsibility could not be separated. In their practices, these women pursued a bottom-up, experiential, personalized microperspective approach to understanding social issues. The men of the Chicago school were moving academic social sciences away from seeking practical solutions to everyday life that linked "scholarly inquiry and social responsibility." Instead, they wanted to use "scholarship to advance both knowledge and civic-mindedness"[116] through what Helen Jarvis describes as the "'macro' grandstand views of the city."[117] In advocating for a new social science curriculum at the university, Burgess advocated attacking "social problems from the standpoint of a social psychology which seeks not merely to state social problems, but to explain them."[118] The conclusion was that "reform could be advanced only by the most rigorous, logical, and scientific investigations."[119]

Social scientists such as Breckinridge and Edith Abbott had used social science techniques to uncover specific problems and recommend specific social actions. In the face of new male academic ideas, they and all other female social scientists who had formed an intellectual core of the University of Chicago's department of sociology were pushed out of the department and gathered into a School of Social Services Administration. They continued to work to formulate social welfare policy and advocate the importance of social knowledge, but social welfare as a fundamental right to be applied to thinking about the built environment was now cast as a gender-specific woman's idea, severed from the supposedly rational, impartial scientific approach of professional men. Abbott lamented that "some of our social science friends are afraid that we cannot be scientific because we really care about what we are doing and we are even charged with being sentimental."[120]

Zoning Is the Answer

The rational, scientific focus of planning made dividing the city into zones of activity a logical outcome. Zoning had not been the focus of the Chicago Plan, but the City Planning Committee of the City Club had been working since 1917 to secure state legislation giving cities the power to enact zoning. The men of the club believed that zoning was necessary for "the conservation and proper development of the economic and social interests of urban communities." In a long essay in 1919, American planner John Nolen added zoning to the city planning arsenal, declaring that "districting or zoning of a city is, or should be, one of the three fundamental parts of every comprehensive city plan." Zoning, he contended was a low-cost procedure that only required study and preparing a plan but could "afford not only stability, but additional income to property owners, and also to the city."[121] Once the requisite legislation had been secured from the state legislature, the City Club constituted a committee on zoning (subsequently folded into the City Planning Committee) to work with the city council to write the city's first zoning ordinance.[122] In mid-December 1919, Chicago men organized a Citizens' Zone Plan Conference to discuss and plan zoning. All the citizens were male. The Real Estate Board sponsored Scots city planner Thomas Adams, who was currently serving as planning and housing adviser to the Commission of Conservation of Canada, as the featured luncheon speaker for the gathering.[123]

Planners on both sides of the Atlantic were emphasizing that no zoning plan should be enacted without conducting a complete survey and diagnosis of the city. The *Town Planning Review* described the appropriate process:

> The study before zoning is long and laborious, entailing detailed civic and regional survey work. . . . Personal inspection of ground and outlying districts is necessary, together with detailed notes of buildings and streets, physical characteristics, and the immediate environment of every block. Aeroplane photographs have been employed with great success on this type of survey work. . . . All this is indispensable to the determination of the number and characteristics of various kinds of districts.[124]

In his analysis of Harland Bartholomew, one of the most prominent planners in the United States from the 1920s, Joseph Heathcote argues that professional men saw the city as a laboratory that could be scientifically planned.[125] Once again, women who had little access to what men decided was the requisite scientific training, and who did not see the city as a laboratory, would be excluded from this process.

In summer 1921, Mayor Thompson appointed a commission to write a new city zoning ordinance. Real estate interests and leaders of the older Plan

Commission were well represented on this new body. Charles Wacker—who now declared the city's "haphazard growth . . . a crime and a waste"—was appointed to the commission, and previous plan commissioner E. H. Bennett was named its director of zoning work. Four of the nine private citizens appointed to the commission were real estate agents. There was one black representative, Charles S. Duke, an engineer, but no women.[126] As the new commission commenced its work, its advocates echoed Nolen's ideals. Bennett declared that zoning Chicago would "create conditions favorable to industrial enterprise, to the protection of business, and the improvement of working conditions." Zoning, he asserted, would save the city $1 billion by preventing property depreciation and by raising property values.[127] Sanitary Bureau head Charles B. Ball promised that zoning would enhance the value of the city. "Zoning sells a town. . . . [A]n unzoned town is like a dead stock of goods on the shelves."[128] According to Wacker, zoning would solve everything:

> City planning and zoning are interdependent. . . . The concurrent development of city planning and zoning will mean a saving in taxes, improved standards of living, stabilized and increased property values and the safeguarding of our homes, playgrounds, parks, and schools from undesirable encroachments, thus opening the way to a solution of the vitally important housing problem.[129]

In the spirit of scientific surveying and diagnosis, the Zoning Commission began a long and laborious process of using the city as a laboratory, an activity that was much more expansive than Nolen had claimed. It commissioned a staff of forty architects, engineers, and planners to undertake a "scientific management of urban space." They were instructed to survey the existing condition of all building development in the city: its use, height, area, and state of depreciation of all property. They were to record the data and produce color-coded and symbol-coded maps. The minutiae of information to be gathered was astounding. Surveyors were directed to count how much front footage was used for private residences, apartment buildings, retail businesses, and factories. They were to count the number of apartments in buildings as well as the number of residential apartments that were located above stores. The surveyors were instructed to ascertain what each factory manufactured; how much space it occupied; how many workers it employed; the condition of its buildings and yards; the manufacturing and shipping processes of each entity; and how it affected the property around it. The commission assured the city that "the entire work throughout is being conducted on a highly technical and scientific basis and with the most exacting standards for accuracy, by men trained in the zoning field."[130]

Real estate interests saw zoning as the means to rezone the so-called tenement districts—both white immigrant and black residential areas—for

commercial and industrial growth. While zoning plans did not endorse racial segregation, they did not include any attention to providing better housing for black Chicagoans or to ending racial segregation. By 1925, the Real
Estate Board declared that the housing shortage was over because higher-
end and single-family housing was fully supplied. On the other hand, other
surveys revealed that "decent housing which poorer workingmen, white or
black, could afford had not really increased."[131]

Organized Chicago women did not oppose planning and zoning per se.
But the women approached it from a different perspective, something that
men again either willfully misunderstood or simply construed to their own
liking. For example, when the head of the WCC committee on housing and
zoning, Madge Headley, addressed a 1921 conference on small home problems, the *Chicago Tribune* depicted her as an enthusiastic supporter of zoning because it would protect private property. According to the *Chicago
Tribune*, Headley "lauded" zoning as "a great aid to home building" that
would result in a "stability to home owning."[132] Speaking to the WCC just
before that, however, she had stressed her belief that "a zone plan provides
for the healthy growth of children in comfortable homes" and that it should
be a priority for the city to provide them. "The test of a city is not its show
places in public buildings, in museums, in hotels. It is the number of healthy
families in comfortable homes," she told the women. Spending millions on
streets, bridges and transit, she continued, while neglecting to protect homes
did not lead to a good city.[133]

Whether the *Chicago Tribune* simply plucked what it wanted from Headley's speech is impossible to know without a transcript. But her emphasis to
the WCC on the benefit of zoning to home and children indicates a gendered
perspective on the purpose of zoning for the built environment. Women
perceived no public-private divide on this issue But in a presentation to the
WCC titled "City Zoning and the Home," planner Harland Bartholomew
stressed a different perspective by mentioning housing only in the context of
congestion. The architect's vision, transportation, transit, zoning, public recreation, and civic art, he said, were

> the physical makeup of the city and must all be considered in a com-
> prehensive workable city plan. It is the zone plan which ties them all
> together. Housing is a different proposition. But the zone plan does
> touch on housing in that it attempts to regulate the worst of the hous-
> ing evils through regulation of the height of buildings, the area of the
> lot, etc. . . . [I]f the congestion of population is controlled a great share
> of disease and crime is also prevented.[134]

I have never found any evidence that Chicago's male zoning advocates
discussed the advantages of zoning for home and children. Their rhetoric

always stressed the benefits to property ownership and protection that zoning would bring to the city. The cover of the zoning committee's 1922 pamphlet emphasized how a new zoning ordinance would "protect private residence blocks against apartments and stores; apartment house blocks against stores and public garages; shopping streets against warehouses, public garages and laundries; commercial and light manufacturing streets against offensive industries; and manufacturing against fear of molestation."[135] The *Chicago Tribune* praised the commission's work for its promise to protect property values. "Every person who invests in business or residential property will do so with the assurance that his investment will be protected and improved by any building which goes up in his neighborhood" and no property owner will need to fear "encroachment of undesirable neighbors."[136] While the commission and its supporters always stressed how it invited the contribution of women, what they really wanted was for women to support whatever it decided. The pamphlet stressed that "the commission seeks to make [the ordinance] the expression of every community in the city and to have it voice the desires of the home builder, businessman and manufacturer so that this ordinance will be in truth a 'people's ordinance.'"[137] Very few women were the people of the zoning commission's communities.

Most of the city's black residents also did not constitute one of these communities. When the commissioners stressed that property owners would guide zoning decisions, the Second Ward's residents, the majority of whom were renters, feared additional threats to their neighborhood. The *Chicago Tribune* reported that the problem of zoning the Black Belt had "baffled" the commission. Property owners along the railroad tracks on the western edge of this area wanted it rezoned as a manufacturing district; they would profit considerably from selling this land. Residents asked, "If our homes are torn down to make way for factories, where will we go?" The commission evaded the problem by declaring that it was open to "constructive suggestions."[138] The commission's one black member, Charles Duke, supported city planning in general and the zoning plan as financially beneficial to the city as a whole; the *Chicago Defender* publicized it as a protection for property owners.[139]

The commission's optimism that zoning regulating height, usage, and so forth of property would ultimately solve housing had a conspicuous flaw: it could not be applied retroactively. That meant that existing deteriorating property and overcrowding in some areas of the city would not be helped by zoning. Even worse for the people living in those areas, they could be forced out if their neighborhood was rezoned for manufacturing. Women's organizations objected to the commission's focus on zoning for manufacturing and commerce to the detriment of the amount of land rezoned for single-family homes. The latter, they claimed, would "make the entire plan of greater value." In a letter to the Zoning Commission, signed by the WCC, CWC,

CWA, Chicago Federation of Settlements, Chicago Federation of Women's Clubs, the South Side Catholic Women's Club, and the Woodlawn and Englewood Women's Clubs, the women argued that the "frontage" allotted for such areas in the plan would be exhausted within three years.[140] A sketch in the WCC *Bulletin* compared the mileage extent of the different zones if they were stretched along a straight line. The zoned areas for manufacturing would stretch from Chicago to Butte, Montana; that for commercial development from Chicago to Houston; and that for single-family homes from Chicago to Toledo. Chicago men were now planning for two-family apartments, the mileage for which stretched to Key West, Florida; for multiple-family apartments, the mileage stretched to Denver (Figures 8.2 and 8.3).[141] The so-called City of Homes was to become a city of apartment dwellers to provide sufficient area for economic development.

The commission's plan was to divide the city into five use districts—residential, apartment, business, commercial, and manufacturing—and five volume districts—regulating height of and amount of land any building could occupy.[142] Despite some unhappiness that the plan allowed some nonconforming uses to continue, the zoning proposals pleased the Real Estate Board and men's organizations. They agreed that zoning the city would guarantee its economic future and construct a built environment that would always promote business and the property of the city's leading men. The

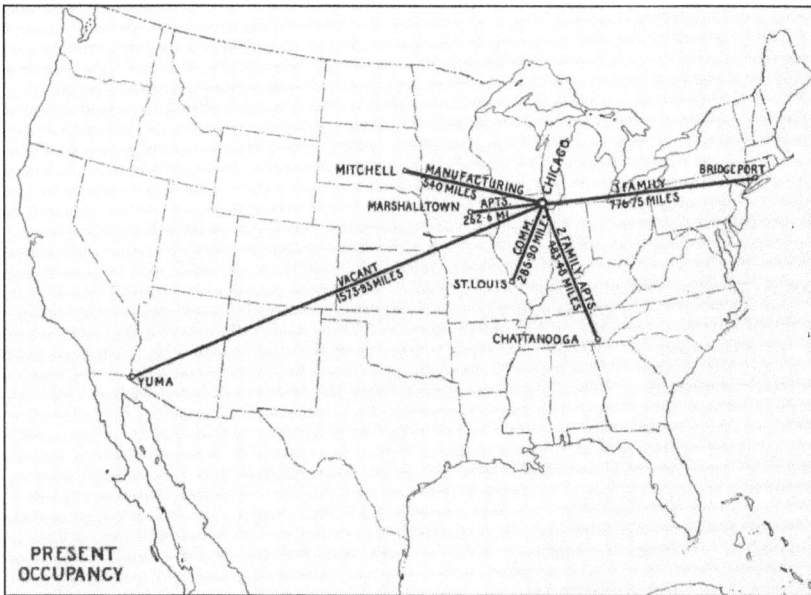

Figure 8.2 Prezoning mileage sketch from Woman's City Club of Chicago, *Bulletin*, March 1923.

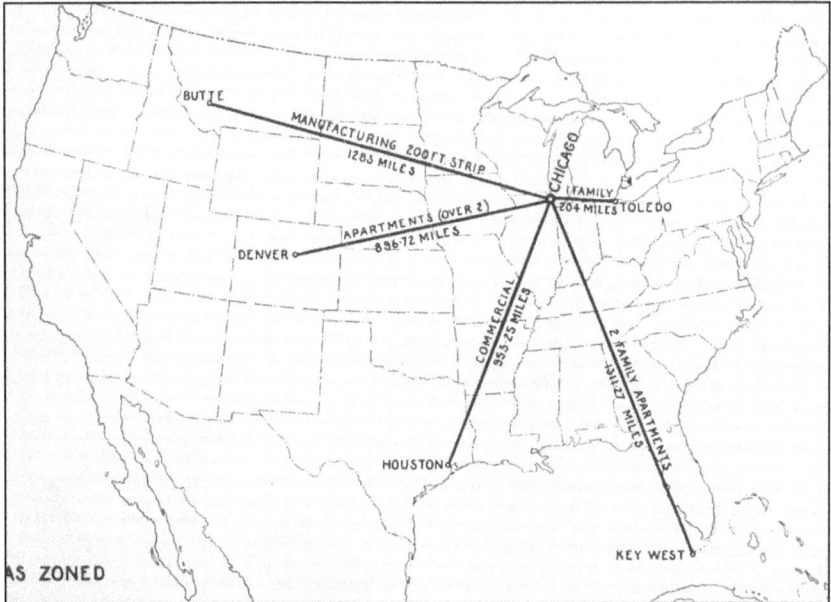

Figure 8.3 Postzoning mileage sketch from Woman's City Club of Chicago, *Bulletin*, March 1923.

council passed the new zoning law, and the *Chicago Tribune* called it a "big advance for Chicago."[143]

Buoyed by this success, the City Club moved to consider regional planning as the next step in the city's economic development. At a luncheon in 1923, attended by around two hundred men and three women (one representative each from the WCC, CWA, and Outdoor Art League), Jacob L. Crane, the Real Estate Board's zoning consultant, offered a resolution to organize the Chicago Regional Planning Association to plan highways, parks, and utilities for the region.[144] At this point, advocates of zoning ceased to worry about the state of existing housing and resisted any attempts to have the city assume responsibility for housing its residents. As one study of housing in Chicago acerbically put it, this "commission made no little plans, and regarding housing it continued to make no plans at all."[145]

PROPERTY AND GENDER

As they were working toward enacting zoning for the city, Chicago men had continued to link the idea of property ownership with good citizenship. In 1919 a group of wealthy businessmen formed the Chicago Housing Association (CHA; not to be confused with the later Chicago Housing Authority) advancing the money to capitalize the Housing Association at $600,000.

They expected a return of their money plus 6 percent profit. McDowell, Vittum, and Breckinridge belonged to the association, although McDowell called herself a reluctant participant, but most of its members were "major figures in commerce, industry, finance, and construction." The association was led by wealthy businessman Benjamin Rosenthal. Its stated goal was to build ten thousand model homes.[146] The City Club called the CHA a "million dollar corporation . . . with the purpose of relieving housing conditions . . . and supplying the worker of moderate income the opportunity of buying his own home."[147] The *Chicago Tribune* praised the association's focus on home ownership and its relation to citizenship:

> Owning a home has a moral as well as an economic result. It tends to reduce unrest and make for a substantial citizenship. Such a citizenship is interested in good government. It has something at stake and will exercise care in its use of the ballot and its daily contact with its fellows. It appreciates property rights and property responsibilities. It strengthens the city and the nation.[148]

Focus on home ownership as the means to good citizenship ensured that women's ideas on how to improve housing conditions throughout the city continued to fall on deaf ears. Nevertheless, Chicago women kept trying. Several women's organizations, including the CWC, WCC, and PEL formed the Chicago Housing Council (CHC) to function as a clearinghouse for discussing and disseminating ideas on how to improve housing conditions in the city. The CHC and the housing committees of various women's clubs turned to the state legislature to secure measures to bring about better housing. They sought a state housing code that would compel municipal health departments to enforce compliance of minimum standards on issues such as water supply, sewage, light, ventilation, heating, and fire escapes. The women believed that a municipal health department empowered to enforce regulation was the best way to guarantee the health and welfare of all Chicago residents. When the so-called Kessinger Bill to provide standards for sanitation and safety in buildings was introduced in the state legislature in 1919, the WCC supported it, although women were disappointed that the bill would merely set minimum standards and not mandate higher ones. The city's health department supported this bill, but real estate and building industry interests opposed it, warning that its provisions were so onerous they would stop all private building. Over the coming years, these interests continued to block any proposed housing legislation as impeding new building or putting a burden on property owners.[149]

Beyond its lax housing codes, Chicago suffered a serious homeless problem, especially during the cold winter months. Limited housing supply and high rental prices virtually guaranteed a homeless population. The city had always refused to make any provisions for lodging homeless women. With the exception of the Mary Dawes Hotel for Working Women, women's groups continued to shoulder the burden of providing shelter for homeless women. But women saw the general issue of homelessness as a municipal responsibility. In 1921, the women of the WCC's Second Ward committee led by African American activist Elizabeth Davis petitioned the mayor to open a municipal lodging house for the ward's unemployed men.[150] As commissioner of public welfare, McDowell had made her department one of the few official agencies concerned to lodge the homeless, although her department had no funds for operating lodging houses. In 1924, McDowell managed to persuade Mayor William Dever to supply some money for a men's lodging house, and over a period of three months the lodging house accommodated 4,219 lodgers.[151] McDowell believed that homeless men were part of the city's civic life and not a shiftless population. She asserted that "since 40 per cent of the men [lodged] have been in Chicago a year or more, they have a legal and moral claim upon the community," for assistance. "Most of the applicants," she declared, "have no other wants than a job or temporary shelter and food."[152] Her attitude was unlike that expressed a few years earlier by alderman Robert Mulcahy, who wanted a municipal lodging house as the means to keep homeless men under surveillance.

As women struggled to find shelter for the homeless, McDowell and other women also continued to argue that the city's small-wage earners needed decent housing. McDowell's department allied with the Illinois League of Women Voters to survey living conditions among this segment of the city's population. Their investigations revealed that between 1914 and 1925, rents in "even the poorest houses" in which Chicagoans lived had almost doubled. African American and Mexican residents faced the worst housing conditions, being able to find housing only "in the most outworn and insanitary houses which the city keeps." The women concluded that "in spite of the great activity in building, almost no new houses have been erected in Chicago to rent for prices these small-wage families can afford." The chief cause, McDowell argued, was that "the profit-making enterprise in building devotes itself chiefly to the erection of high-priced apartments."[153]

As the city's director of public welfare, McDowell organized yet another Housing Conference that met on April 16, 1926, hoping "to stimulate interest in the serious lack of proper living quarters for the small-wage-earning families in Chicago, and to focus this interest to effect some continuous effort to improve generally the housing situation in Chicago."[154] She assembled a conference committee of women and men who had been working on the housing problem, including a few plan commissioners. The African American community was represented by banker and businessmen Jesse Binga, activist and clubwoman Irene Goins, and A. L. Foster, executive secretary of the Chicago Urban League. Foster had urged McDowell to assemble this conference.[155] The conference resulted in persuading the city council and Mayor Dever to designate a special Housing Commission. As usual, this commission was composed largely of men: "thirty-five business men, labor leaders, club officials, and sociologists." Six women including McDowell were appointed to the commission to represent women's clubs and Foster represented the African American community.[156]

By the time of its first meeting, the commission had expanded to forty members and was chaired by Joseph K. Brittain, president of the Real Estate Board and head of the Chamber of Commerce's real estate division. Other members included representatives from some of the city's largest businesses: Illinois Bell Telephone; Western Electric; Swift and Company; Armour; and Hart, Schaffner and Marx, among others. Given this composition, it was hardly surprising that the men would adopt the drawn-out method of survey, diagnose, and planning for deciding on housing. Brittain outlined a four-step procedure: gather all expert data; determine which areas of the city are dedicated to low-rent housing; determine conditions of ownership and "the effect of existing laws upon improvements in these areas"; and "develop plans of a practical character to encourage the investment of capital . . . to take care of the problem." While women's groups wanted more immediate attention and resolution of housing conditions, the men's preferred process would take time and persuasion. Willoughby Walling, president of the Chicago Council of Social Agencies, who was leading the commission's first efforts, accordingly told the commissioners that the "task may take years." He advised them that they "should be prepared for long service."[157]

The WCC, along with McDowell, Vittum, and Addams, scheduled another housing symposium in October 1927 to which they invited representatives of the city's prominent male and female civic organizations. At the symposium women again focused on the personal hardship bad housing imposed on residents, especially women.[158] But Albert F. Allen, who was then chairing the housing commission, reported that "the housing commission has not yet given out its policies or conclusions and that it has not had sufficient funds to do effective work." He also reiterated the businessmen's ideal that the project of housing should be "a work of profound business sense."[159]

Focus on professional planning removed women further from direct access to decision making. A 1931 conference of the housing commission even seems to have excluded women. At this conference, Crane, who was a former city planning engineer, recommended that bad housing should be torn down and replaced with parks rather than build new housing in the city. "It is clear," Crane declared, "that good new housing for the worst 'blighted areas' would then make much of the city not now called blighted look like slums. . . . A large part of the worst blighted areas should never be reconstructed, but should be cleared and made into parks and playgrounds." And he specifically rejected following any European housing standards as being "probably not good enough for us."[160] Presumably Crane was reacting against the social housing policies that were being directed by social democratic governments in continental Europe.

By the end of the decade, the city's housing situation had worsened as the population grew from 2.7 million in 1920 to 3.37 million in 1930. But professional men and businessmen focused on planning and zoning and saw housing only in terms of what kinds of houses should appear in which zones. They wanted a professionally planned city that would "meet the competition" of other midwestern cities for economic prominence.[161] As the *Chicago Tribune* had declared earlier, the "city must be opened up," which meant that into the 1930s the focus of planning remained heavily on traffic. New street widenings and new traffic arteries (so-called superhighways) were proposed to eliminate "all cross traffic and pedestrians from the pavements" so that automobiles could travel quickly and unimpeded from the city's boundaries to the downtown business district.[162] By 1933, the Plan Commission was advocating construction of an airfield on the lakefront to make Chicago the center of air traffic as it had been the center of rail traffic across the previous decades. When A. A. Sprague was appointed to head the Plan Commission in 1935, he declared that building such an airport and a west side elevated superhighway were two of the city's most critical needs.[163]

SLUMS AND BLIGHT

While the Plan Commission was focusing on transportation, a new term—blight—was added to the vocabulary of slum clearance that would further marginalize women's ideas on housing. The formation of a new private housing agency, the Metropolitan Housing Council (MHC), directed the conversation on housing toward eradicating blight. Slum clearance was no longer sufficient; now whole areas in the city were to be designated as blighted. The so-called blighted areas were not yet considered slums but areas to be saved from becoming slums. A neighborhood that "had once been suitable and attractive for residential purposes" but was "no longer desirable" could be designated as blighted. As a rhetorical trope, planners could now argue that neighborhoods had to be rehabilitated by tearing down old housing to save them from turning into slums.[164] While women had focused on the pernicious effects of bad housing on poor, working-class, and African American and other migrant individuals and families, the ideas of slum clearance and blight designated whole neighborhoods to be destroyed. The *Chicago Tribune* celebrated the beginnings of this policy in 1934 when Mayor Ed Kelly wielded "a silver pickax" in a campaign to rid the city of bad housing. Not surprisingly, the first buildings destroyed in the campaign were those of African Americans living along South Federal Street in the old Black Belt. The *Chicago Tribune* article declared that the cleared property was to be turned into playgrounds or gardens, not to be used for new housing, a type of plan-ning that Crane had advocated.[165] The cleared area indeed remained vacant until after World War II, when public subsidized buildings, the Dearborn Homes, were erected on parts of it under the auspices of a new federal hous-ing program. To build the Dearborn Homes, an additional 406 housing units were demolished, including the Douglas Hotel, one of the few residences in the city for single black men.[166] A large section of this area remains vacant today.

The executive director of the MHC, Elizabeth Wood, understood that clearing slums and blighted areas was not a housing policy but rather a pol-icy for restructuring the built environment. She asked the WCC for assis-tance in working on a plan to replace the housing stock in cleared areas. "We have realized that no fundamental change in the housing conditions in the enormous slum and blighted areas can be effected until it has become per-fectly clear that such areas shall have low-cost residential usage perma-nently," she wrote. Wood even expressed amazement that the original Chi-cago plan had paid no attention to housing.[167] Yet clearing neighborhoods, whether they were designated slum or blighted, was never paired equally with new housing starts, especially in African American neighborhoods where one third of the housing demolition occurred in the years following 1934. Chicago's Building and Health Departments used new police powers to demolish bad housing, but the city continued to rely on the private mar-ketplace to build new housing. The MHC had to report that between 1929 and 1939 about twenty thousand housing units were destroyed, while only a little over ten thousand new ones were erected.[168]

New state and federal housing legislation enacted in the 1930s further impeded Chicago women's ability to influence the direction of housing. This legislation officially severed housing from overall considerations for recon-structing the built environment, as it focused as much on restarting the col-lapsed private housing market as on seeing decent housing as necessary for human welfare. Women's organizations that had struggled for so many years to make this latter vision the guiding one for resolving the housing crisis were again shunted aside when the Illinois legislature established a state housing commission in the early 1930s. The legislators appointed only one woman, Edith Abbott, to the commission. Although Chicago women con-tinued to hold conferences to discuss the housing problem and to share in-formation about the use of state and federal funding, they were effectively shut out of decision making. The MHC constituted a women's division that was purely advisory to the men in charge.[169]

The official denouement for women's direct participation in reconstruct-ing Chicago's built environment would begin with passage in 1937 of the nation's first federal housing act. The act established the principle of a fed-eral-local partnership with new money coming from the federal government, but the contest over which side would exercise more control inevitably drew attention away from finding a true solution to housing. To benefit from the new programs and money, a semipublic entity—the Chicago Housing Authority—was established in early 1937. This CHA (not to be confused with the older, private CHA) possessed the authority to decide on the location of public housing as well as to build and manage it. Mayor Kelly appointed five professional men as CHA commissioners, with Wood as the authority's executive secretary.[170] The CHA had a dual mandate to provide housing for the city's poorest residents who could not afford market-based rentals and to clear the slums. But the men running the authority had neither the desire nor the clout to confront directly the results of decades of enforced racial segregation in housing. The CHA learned very quickly that white Chicagoans resisted moving into public housing alongside black Chicagoans. The CHA thus used its condemnatory powers to prioritize slum clearance, a policy that ultimately produced construction of high-rise tower blocks for poor black Chicagoans that would keep them segregated and embounded into specific spaces of the city's built environment for decades to come.

The creation of separate authorities such as the CHA made it possible for the city to keep the housing and racial problems from interfering with planning the built environment along the lines desired by professional planners and the city's economic leaders. Professional men were freed to focus on rezoning the city, building highways, and regional planning for economic development. Moreover, the CHA was not an agency within the municipal government, so by the late 1930s Chicago's government was relieved of any direct responsibility to provide new and sufficient housing for its people.

Chicago Pursues the Master Plan

In 1939, Mayor Kelly introduced an ordinance to reconstitute a Chicago Plan Commission (designated CPC2 here) as an official municipal authority, not merely an advisory board, to craft "the official plan of the city."[171] The original eleven appointed members of the executive committee were businessmen and bankers. They were to be assisted by a large advisory board of civic leaders, among whose 180 members were only 8 women. Only one African American man was appointed. In late 1940, the CPC2 hired city planner Theodore T. McCrosky, former director of New York City's master plan division, as executive director.[172] The new CPC2's work and its resulting 1943 plan sought, as David Pinder explained of modern planning, to construct a harmonious and pure space that would also institute "a regulatory regime to control spatial form and the movements and presence of "bodies in space or body space."[173]

The CPC2 conducted a massive land use survey, led by its chief engineer, Hugh E. Young. It published its results in 1941 in two massive volumes, *Re-*

port of the Chicago Land Use Survey. The publication stated that the survey's purpose was to "provide an inventory of the physical, economic, and social characteristics of every use of land in the City of Chicago."[174] Its proud claim to be the first survey in the country "to tabulate and map land use by individual parcels" exemplified Pinder's explanation that modern planning was about categorizing and sorting.[175] The work also sorted groups of people, advising that certain of them were a danger to designing a good neighborhood. It warned that "an abnormally high percentage of the population in the older age brackets or a disproportion in either sex are warning signals to the analyst" and advocated that neighborhoods should now be rated "by the characteristics of the inhabitants themselves."[176] In other words, the perfect neighborhood should be composed largely of families.

The resulting 1943 *Master Plan of Residential Land Use* recommended "demolition and complete rebuilding" of over nine square miles surrounding the city center, the economic heart of the city. Doing so would demolish nearly 25 percent of the city's housing stock. In total, the plan recommended demolishing or redeveloping twenty-two square miles of designated blighted or near-blighted areas and presented specific definitions of what constituted blight and near blight.[177] Mayor Kelly urged that buildings in these areas, housing almost nine hundred thousand people, should be "demolished and replaced by new buildings for a new type of development." He conceded that there was no current solution for rehousing all those displaced but hoped that "such a solution might be forthcoming."[178] The CPC2 chair declared that the "decay of the neighborhoods near the central part of the city must be arrested if real estate and business values are to be maintained."[179]

All the CPC2 proposals would socially reengineer the city by moving people around and relocating them in their proper place. A CPC2 booklet, *Building New Neighborhoods: Subdivision Designs and Standards,* declared that "people have shown conclusively that they want to live in comfortable homes in well-designed neighborhoods of good environment rather than in congested, drab surroundings." The CPC2 advocated using Chicago's still vacant tracts of land to build new subdivisions inside the city boundaries that could be the Community of Tomorrow. These communities could be curvilinear areas of distinct neighborhoods with limited traffic on residential streets. The CPC2 envisioned twenty-three square miles of blighted and near-blighted city neighborhoods rebuilt along such lines, even referring to the possibility that they could be "garden spots." One proposal called for building two thousand housing units in a neighborhood that currently housed about ten thousand residents.[180]

The new neighborhoods would eliminate shopping along streets in favor of centralized shopping centers, a spatial innovation very much contingent on using cars for shopping. The shopping center proposals focused on traffic congestion, parking possibilities, and the perceived shopping convenience that would mean "increased profits to the merchants." Centralized shopping would be difficult for women, the primary shoppers, if they did not have access to a car and would also inhibit their ability to shop with children. If Raymond Unwin had been alive (he died in 1940), he might well have celebrated the plan's proposals as the fruition of his earlier twentieth-century ideas. The elements of the CPC2 Community of Tomorrow would institutionalize the private-public divide and embound women. It envisioned centralized shopping separated from residences and closed neighborhoods ringed by express highways. Inside the neighborhood, residential streets would be designed "in such a manner as to discourage through traffic from entering." The street plan's call for curvilinear streets, reflecting the supposed feminine nature of nonlinearity expressed by Le Corbusier, signaled that the Community of Tomorrow was the place of reproduction not production. In Clara Greed's critique of this idea of planning on the "neighborhood unit," daily life for women would be not only isolated and less convenient but based on a "sentimentalized ideal of community."[181]

Beyond planning new neighborhoods, CPC2 surveys and plans continued to pay special attention to slum and blight clearance. The CPC2's 1946 *Housing Goals for Chicago* recommended that the city adopt a "comprehensive city plan . . . whereby all land within the city may be developed or redeveloped according to its best social and economic use."[182] According to this idea, twenty-two square miles of blighted or near-blighted districts should be "rebuilt because of their economic influence upon the entire city." According to the CPC2, preventing their spread was "essential for Chicago's continued prosperity." So-called slum and blighted districts were "cancerous growths [that have] already formed a ring around the central business district."[183] Slum clearance and removal of current inhabitants would also solve social problems of crime and juvenile delinquency and other dangerous conditions.[184] The CPC2 asserted that "the re-housing of low-income families in other low-rent structures . . . need not, however, take place within the same areas as the ones where those people are now living." Instead, blighted areas could be "redeveloped to house a higher economic group" and "attract the type of occupancy that can bring back to the central city a well-balanced distribution of families in every economic group."[185]

Slum clearance in Chicago especially targeted the African American neighborhoods. The segregated overcrowded so-called Black Belt was now designated the most blighted area in the city. It also happened to be close to the city center that businessmen and politicians wanted cleared out and redeveloped for economic purposes. The bodies of black Chicagoans were to be banished to undeveloped land, such as the far southside Altgeld Gardens housing project (1943), "built on an isolated tract . . . far from any residential development . . . but within reasonable distance from" factories that would employ black workers. Since those black workers were predominantly male,

Altgeld Gardens' 1,500 housing units would become an embounded neighborhood for the women living there. Public housing of the 1940s aimed to
reform poor, black families by relocating them into model housing environments where their behavior could be overseen and controlled. Public housing was to be as embounded and family-oriented as the white neighborhoods
of the Community of Tomorrow, except poorer, more crowded, higher, and
still segregated.[186]

A newly constituted body, the private South Side Development Board,
redeveloped a significant part of the old Black Belt with private-built housing
projects that catered to middle- and upper-class families. These new developments were internally focused and surrounded by fences.[187] As a recent survey of Chicago planning describes it, the massive redevelopment in this area
"created a modernist—almost Corbusian—landscape . . . that followed the
'neighborhood unit' of planning that had guided the profession since the
start of the century, with its desire to coordinate shopping, schools, and
other community facilities." The authors conclude that the result "was an
uninspired and ultimately vacuous area with little sense of neighborhood or
community."[188] The process of clearing out and redeveloping areas of the old
Black Belt, renamed Bronzeville, continues to this day.

Focusing on the neighborhood unit in Chicago, by designating areas as
slum, blighted, or even near-blighted, satisfied the prevailing theories of
planning and urban sociology that the city could be made orderly and controlled by breaking it down into smaller units. The CPC2's 1946 housing
goals advocated that the city should be planned into fifty-nine neighborhoods, each with six thousand to eight thousand residents, with these neighborhoods then grouped into fifty-nine communities. The ideal was that each
small city would contain fifty-thousand to eighty thousand residents. Every
community would include a high school, a large park, an athletic field, a
major shopping center, and "other services that may not be available within
the neighborhood."[189]

Half a century later, the ideas of Ebenezer Howard resonated in the
minds of Chicago's planners. Order and control could be imposed by replanning the built environment to create new patterns of urban living. Creating
garden cities was no longer the goal; now planners sought to reconfigure
cities. Focusing on neighborhood centers with a self-contained populations
could determine where and how shopping would be done and regulate how
people interacted inside the neighborhood and with anyone outside it. As
part of the process, women could be embounded in these new neighborhoods or in new suburban areas. And in Chicago, order and control through
slum clearance and isolated neighborhoods could preserve the color line.
The city, theoretically, would be safe for economic development.

Conclusion

The Patriarchal City Consolidated

Many members will remember that whenever Raymond Unwin, our beloved second president, addressed us he was accompanied by his wife who used to sit, serenely knitting, listening with rapt attention to every word that fell from her famous husband's lips. Her presence added grace to our meeting.[1]

It would be hard to imagine any more damning statement attesting to the patronizing attitude of professional men toward women. Every word that fell from Unwin's lips was golden, while his wife (unnamed—not even Mrs. Unwin!) sat knitting and enraptured. Women's presence was to add "grace" to the men's meetings, as Toronto's mayor said about women in 1908. They were not to be the "abnormal" single women of W. R. Greg's 1869 polemic. Across eight decades, men had not merely refused to accept women's view of the city and its needs. They had purposefully reconstructed the patriarchal city where its public spaces were for men, and where women were supposed to remain in the private place of the home. A growing number of professionally trained men, bolstered by theories from new social scientific disciplines, had allied with politicians and businessmen across these decades to reconstruct, as much as possible, the urban built environment as a physically, socially, and psychologically patriarchal space. In doing so, they did not merely dismiss women's ideas about the city as a home for all people in which daily experience should be a significant factor in decisions over the built environment. They patronizingly rejected that women could even understand the needs of the city and its residents.

The Patriarchal Vision Consolidated

The attitudes of men toward the city and their determination to reshape and control it begins with the disgust that John Ruskin and his cohort such as William Morris had for London. But Ruskin's anger with Octavia Hill because she did not agree with him revealed the underlying gendered visions of the city that propelled men to focus on reshaping and controlling the city to continue its public-private dichotomy. Women's increasing public appearance and their demands to have a voice in the city threatened male control of both the public realm of the city and the private domestic home. Women were the disorderly and uncontrolled presence in the modern city.

The urban utopian patriarchal vision of Ebenezer Howard's garden city and the scientific rationalism of Patrick Geddes's organic metaphor offered both the means and the rationales to initiate reconstructing the city of the male public and the female private. For both men, the city was a disorderly mess. Howard wanted to create new cities, while Geddes proposed a new way of looking scientifically at cities. Although their proposals differed, they both believed that there was a man-woman dichotomy. The city would function best if it were organized to give women, who possessed a so-called feminine nature, private roles in the city that would complement and not compete with the masculine world of men.

In all four cities, architects such as Raymond Unwin in London turned theories into realty. Academic planners such as Patrick Abercrombie—who credited both Howard and Geddes as his inspirations[2]—were called on to redesign cities and eventually to help inspire the idea of the master plan. Tracy leMay in Toronto and the men of the various Chicago commissions sought to formulate new master plans, aided by planners such as John Nolen, who extolled the virtues of the zoned city. By the 1940s, the modernist utopian visions of Le Corbusier, the Congrès Internationaux d'Architecture Moderne (CIAM), and Maxwell Fry and the Modern Architectural Research group (MARS) in England proposed to create cities as harmonious, pure spaces without contradictions and antagonisms. An underlying characteristic of so many of these men and their cohorts was a dislike of the city. In analyzing planners in Toronto, for example, John Sewell concluded that not only did these men possess a "straightforward belief that cities are bad, in and among themselves"; they decided that existing cities were "physically, socially, aesthetically, and morally" unhealthy and bad for family life. "The city and its buildings required replacement by something more fitting for the times."[3]

None of these men or groups exercised any singular control over reconstructing the urban built environment. But they were part of an international cohort of professionals who influenced the creation of a modern city. That modern city, as David Pinder contends, was to be "a regulatory regime" that would "control spatial form along with the movements and presence of bodies in space or body space."[4] Regulating the bodies of women became an important element for reconstructing the modern built environment. In rebuilding the city and designing new types and locations of housing, professional men sought to embound women into these private places and thereby limit their disorderly intrusion into the city's public spaces. Such ideas and goals allowed professional men to shun, even patronize, women's ideas and activities. New transportation systems, wide roads, slum clearance, suburban single-family housing, protection of the central business district, a new monumentality, and creative destruction were to be the hallmarks of urban modernism, designed to protect men as the public actors in the city while pushing women back into the home.

Professional men were able to exercise so much control over the built environment in the face of women's activities because they controlled the professions and the entrance into them. As architects assumed professional control over the design and building of housing, for example, they generally refused to accept women as equal colleagues with worthy ideas about housing design or urban planning. A trained architect such as Jane Drew, the wife of MARS leader Maxwell Fry, was a distinct minority in the profession.[5] Elizabeth Denby had worked with Fry in the 1930s to design two blocks of flats in London: R. E. Sassoon House and Kensal Flats. In both developments, Denby had worked to "combine material and social reform" by including social clubs, a nursery school, a playground, and a tenants committee to manage the daily needs of the flats. According to Elizabeth Darling, these flats "could not have been more different from the LCC's brick-built, five-storey blocks of flats." Denby, she asserts, was "a confirmed urbanist" whose "ultimate goal was to keep people in the city and thus limit suburban sprawl." Denby proposed to form a professional relationship with Fry, but he refused her proposal. Fry, according to Darling, "equated design with form-making alone and saw Denby's role as helpmeet rather than partner." He was the professional "form-giver," and Denby was merely the helper who could suggest adjustments. He was never able to "to conceptualize her contributions to the making of these projects as anything more than help: adjustments to what he as the form-giver had ordained."[6]

Planning historian Clara Greed argues that male professionals had to consistently mute the voices and ideas of urban women because the men's ideas were embedded in "assumptions about the need for the gendered organization of space to express public/private dichotomies." She further asserts that since city form is "a reproduction over space of social relations," it can act "as a constraint on the nature of future societies living in that city because of the restrictions of its layout, street pattern, design, and subculture."[7] Once the men in these four cities had accomplished much of this type of restructuring, once the city was spatially rearranged, and as men remained in professional and political power, for the decades to follow, it would be virtually impossible to rethink the form and purpose of the Anglo-Atlantic city. Moreover, men did not wish to rethink it because they wanted to maintain the patriarchal city. As Helen Jarvis contends, even in the face of late-twentieth-century economic crisis, as some cities included groups of women into their urban projects, "this inclusion was always subordinate to the overriding priority of unrestrained economic growth without which there could be no development-as-modernity.[8]

Direct links between past and present are easy to identify once one acknowledges the gendered vision of urban patriarchy. In 1915–1916, when discussions took place about constituting a Civic Improvement League for Canada, the few women at these meetings had wanted any plans to spell out in specific detail what were to be the means to secure better housing and health, especially for children. Thomas Adams and G. Frank Beer had objected to anything specific along these lines, contending that general statements were better. At the same time, however, Beer had detailed the specific means for securing efficient citizenship.

More recently in Britain, when female planners tried to include provisions for public toilets and creches in shopping center developments in policy statements for planning, they were denied such inclusion on the basis that a development plan was "no place for such detailed quotas and standards." Yet, as Greed notes, male planners had no such hesitation in detailing car parking standards.[9]

In all four cities, women had worked, and continue to work, to better the everyday experiences of urban life. London women's "voluntarist" housing sector did influence professionals such as Fry to think in terms of building housing with a moral purpose.[10] But, as Greed argues, women were always disadvantaged by assumptions that "might be so deeply embedded in people's minds, and in western civilization as whole, that demolition, bombing, or the imposition of a revolutionary plan will not eradicate the tendency to revert to a particular type of urban form."[11] Moreover, as politicians agreed with the professional men's ideas for the city, and the state assumed a central role in decisions over housing and social welfare measures in general, professional men and the state formed an almost unbreakable partnership in making these decisions that had further marginalized women's ideas and voices in each city by the 1940s.

For centuries of urban development in the Anglo-Atlantic world, men had controlled cities politically and economically for their benefit. They believed that the purpose of the corporate city was to foster economic growth and saw little or no distinction between the progress of the city and its benefits to themselves. Once they began to fear an assault on their control of the city, they had to establish new means to reassert that control by identifying the nature of the threat. The disorder of women became a chief threat to male control. Despite specific historical circumstances or cultural differences among them, in each of these cities men reconstructed the city in a similar fashion. They identified what was wrong with the city, they created the new terminology of modernism to suit their aims, and they envisioned women as a profound disorderly threat. They consolidated their control over the city by creating a regulatory regime of material modernity that privileged the lives and work of men and fostered the private-public divide.

An integral element of material modernity was reshaping the relationship between the home and the city so that the city could be the masculine space of production and the home could be the feminine space of reproduction.

Men such as Howard and Geddes idealized women as having a natural role to play in the city that was complementary to and not competitive with men. By idealizing and sentimentalizing women as the civilizing gender, whose appropriate sphere was in the home, men were able to deflect women's ideas and activities and simultaneously control their disruptive, disorderly public appearance. The idea that there were two diverse, dichotomous gendered natures in the city had to be managed to privilege men so that the supposed emotional and sentimental, not to mention sexual, natures of women would not threaten the masculine, dynamic, modern city that men desired.

It has taken the work of feminist social scientists to set out a path for urban historians to follow to investigate the construction of the patriarchal city. Social construction of ideas about race, ethnicity, and class, among others, have all been used to explain the history of cities. Without negating that such ideas have influenced urban development, it is strange that ideas about gender have been so little examined except for the fact that most urban history is written by men who do not perceive their own gendered assumptions. Here is a rhetorical question: How many male urban historians would read the quotation that begins this Conclusion and think nothing of it? Statements such as that quotation have been presumed normative, as have the values and behaviors of men in interpreting the construction of the built environment.

The built environment itself is a social construction in that there is a direct relationship of spatial layout, types of buildings, forms of architecture, and planning to the social relationship of its residents to their city. Helen Jarvis suggests that the gendered nature of the built environment becomes apparent if we look both historically and in contemporary times at the "infrastructure of everyday life."[12] The distribution and affordability of urban amenities determine who is able to do what in cities, and whose needs are met and whose are either unmet or made more difficult to attain. In planning the modern city, men prioritized transit and traffic. They decided where to lay out transit lines and roads, drew up schedules, and designated the location of stops. They attempted to eliminate as much as possible city streets as social spaces, leaving streets free for traffic and economic purposes but decreasing their safety, especially for women, and depriving children of places to play right outside their homes. Measures other than the convenience of women who did most of the shopping determined the distance to, availability of, and location of shopping areas. Along with moving people out of the city, creating the isolated suburban home and atomized neighborhoods, failing to provide basic public services such as accessible toilets, ignoring issues of women's safety in all public spaces, and implementing zoning that separated home from work and groups of people from one another, all these factors and more demonstrate that the modern Western city has been built by and for men.

The ideas of women decades ago that the city had to function for every-one in it, that the infrastructures of everyday life were key to constructing a good city, were systematically rejected by men who had the power to impose many of their ideas on the city. As Helen Meller points out, from the late nineteenth century, as men began to think about reconstructing the city, they thought about infrastructure as any concrete manifestation of the city: drains and sewers, roads, bridges, viaducts, railroad tracks, monumental structures, civic buildings, and so on. These were the infrastructures that were needed for economic development and modernizing a city that worked to foster it. Infrastructure for men also meant building to demonstrate the modernity and progress of the city to the rest of the world. The latest archi-tectural designs, the newest engineering techniques, the most up-to-date technological innovations were to be applied to the built environment in an urban competition to demonstrate a city's superiority.[13]

Thinking about the infrastructure of daily life, of who was able to do what, when, and where—what Jarvis proposes as "what is possible given the closely bound nature of spatial arrangement and temporal ordering"[14]—was not part of the male conceptualization of the city. Their concerns about spa-tial arrangement and time, which were recurring themes in all four cities, were always about men, production, and economic growth. The whole idea of the master plan, as demonstrated in all four cities, is predicated on male economic needs and desires. How the spatial arrangements of the master plan would affect women and children and the needs of reproduction are not part of the equation, except perhaps in the idea expressed by John Nolen: "Good city planning would lead to better and earlier marriages by produc-ing cities in which having a child would be 'an adventure to be classed and compared with the alternative adventures of travel, or the search for a good time.'"[15]

THE PERSISTENCE OF URBAN PATRIARCHY

Once the patriarchal city was consolidated, even if men were not always able to get everything they wanted, it persists today in all four cities. Women have never stopped challenging the patriarchal city, but theirs remains a difficult struggle against both the city's structures and the gendered ideas that under-pin their persistence. Contemporary examples from Toronto and London illustrate this persistence.

In the 1980s and 1990s, groups of Toronto women actively challenged the city's plans for the redesign and maintenance of High Park, one of the city's largest parks. A 1987 city user survey demonstrated that women feared park usage far more than did men (93 percent versus 7 percent). But as the city planned to renovate the park, it patronized women, saying that their fears were more imagined than real.[16] The Metro Toronto Committee on Public

Violence against Women and Children (METRAC, formed in 1983) offered
fifty-five "explicit and extensive" recommendations in "Planning for Sexual
Assault Prevention: Women's Safety in High Park" (PSAP), many of which
focused on infrastructure for daily use. They emphasized such elements as
the placement of benches, lights, location of directional signage, and ideas for
programmed activities. The official revitalization committee simply ignored
all of these recommendations. In the process, it also shifted discourse away
from women's safety issues. Whereas the PSAP had stated that "women's use
of the public space is deeply affected by the pervasive threat of sexual assault," the final safety recommendations of the Parks and Recreation Department, arrived at after spending $40,000 on consultants, declared that "the
objective of the comprehensive safety program is to reduce concerns for personal safety of all park users." The one need not cancel the other, but in effect
the department eradicated women's particular fears of sexual violence from
the public discourse. Throughout the 1990s, officials continued to ignore
women's complaints about attempted sexual assaults in the park, although
several gay men were arrested for having consensual sex in the park. As Carolyn Whitzman observes in her account of the struggle over High Park, apparently "the police, politicians, and park staff" seem to have difficulty
"distinguishing between consensual sexual activity and sexual assault."[17]

Women's safety issues in Toronto were also trumped by economic decisions. In the mid-1980s, Toronto women persuaded the Toronto Transit
Commission (TTC) to implement more safety measures in mass transit and,
for a time, the TTC incorporated some of the women's demands into its
planning. Even while doing so, however, the TTC framed its moves as a business decision—its customers were heavily female—not as an acknowledg-
ment of women's legitimate safety concerns. By conceptualizing its policies
as good business, the TTC easily changed its policies when a new conservative government and new professional leadership promoted running transit
on a cost-benefit analysis that ignored women's particular concerns. As
Gerda Wekerle states, since the TTC had not institutionalized women's concerns into the system, "those aspects of feminist discourse that were congru-
ent with the prevailing business discourse were adopted; other gender needs
were ignored."[18]

In London, the voluntary Women's Design Service (WDS; 1983) similarly encountered the persistence of the male professional control of the patriarchal city. The WDS had been organized to publicize women's belief that
"what passed for gender-neutral in the built environment in fact excluded or
obstructed women." The WDS worked from the premise that "most of those
in decision-making positions relating to the built environment are male,
white, able-bodied and middle class, and the decisions they make tend to
reflect their particular priorities."[19] Attempting to counter this situation, the
WDS promoted research into issues of gender and the built environment,

but to do this work the WDS needed financial support from local government. Across the 1980s and 1990s shifts in government priorities and understandings of the concept of gender always determined funding and what effect the organization could have on planning. The lack of any specific attention to gender in the 2004 strategic regional plan of the newly constituted Greater London Authority demonstrated the continuing reluctance of those in positions of authority to accept women's concerns as legitimate. Even while racial and disabled groups were represented as stakeholders for determining planning, women were not. The document contained no references to women or gender.[20] A new Chicago Plan for the twenty-first century has exactly the same focus. It has a chapter on addressing race and poverty, buts none of its recommendations for the future of the city ever consider gender, even when addressing the issue of safety in public transit.[21]

The urban agendas of activist women in both London and Toronto at the end of the twentieth century were constrained by the power and focus of the men controlling the government. When Ken Livingstone was mayor of London in the early 2000s, he supported women's concerns, particularly about safety, and women made some headway in having their concerns addressed. Yet in the Greater London Plan of 2004, even Livingstone put economic growth first: London's future depended on "enhancing 'its economic and business efficiency . . . accompanied by strong improvements in the quality of life and environment and greater social and economic inclusion.'"[22]

When social objectives are those that will "accompany" the primary objective of economics, they can always be minimized when necessary to achieve the primary objective. When the governing structure of Metro Toronto was reorganized into an amalgamated City of Toronto in 1998, according to Sylvia Bashevkin, attention to municipal feminism "virtually disappeared." "Women as a group were rendered invisible within amalgamated Toronto's highly fragmented focus on 'diverse communities.'"[23]

As Helen Jarvis concludes, "Cities assume a semi-permanent spatial arrangement and material culture, filtered through the psychological architecture of belief systems in a constant state of flux. Over time these cultures sediment in the form of buildings, monuments, [and] political and administrative systems, which in turn come to symbolise and reinforce powerful regulatory norms and stereotypes."[24] The barriers that women continue to face in trying to break down these "powerful regulatory norms and stereotypes" that have concretely shaped the city into a site of gender inequality have been so reified that they demonstrate the persistence of Greed's conclusion that professional planning has rendered women's lives irrelevant. "The process of defining the terms of reference [for planners], and creating realities for how the problem and solution are seen, often renders women's existence irrelevant, and therefore cloaks over their 'real' needs and problems; the female world is blotted out by the world created by the planners."[25]

The built environments of London, Dublin, Toronto, and Chicago have been historically and continuously reconstructed to exclude or obstruct women from equal movement into and through the city's public spaces and to contain them as much as possible in the private place of the home. Women's concerns have never been institutionalized in these cities, always leaving women's groups and their needs at the mercy of those in power. It is indicative of the historical continuity of ideas about planning and the built environment, and of the power of groups of men, that the recent Chicago Metropolis 2020 project was financed by the civic committee of the Commercial Club.[26] Unless urban planners, architects, other professionals and politicians acknowledge their underlying gender perspectives, the modern Western city will continue to be the patriarchal space from which women's ideas and needs are largely ignored, despite the ongoing efforts of women to have a voice in shaping the city.

Notes

INTRODUCTION

1. For examples of their cross-Atlantic sharing, see Royal Institute of British Architects, *Town Planning Conference, London, 10–15 October 1910: Transactions* (London: Royal Institute of British Architects, 1911), available at https://babel.hathitrust.org/cgi/pt?id=pst.000033919294;view =1up;seq=9; "Cities and Town Planning Exhibition, May 24th to June 7th, 1911," Miscellaneous Pamphlets, Dublin City Archives, Pearse Street Public Library, Dublin; and "11th Annual Conference on City Planning (United States and Canada)," *American City*, May 1919, p. 501. For an analysis that deems the sharing more Anglo-Atlantic than Anglo-Continental, see William Whyte, "The 1910 Royal Institute of British Architects' Conference: A Focus for International Town Planning?" *Urban History* 39, no. 1 (2012): 149–165. For a discussion of the International Federation of Housing and Town Planning, originally formed largely by British planners, which spread to the continent but had little participation from the United States and was largely confined to building garden cities, see Michel Geertse, "The International Garden City Campaign: Transnational Negotiations on Town Planning Methods, 1913–1926," *Journal of Urban History* 42, no. 4 (2016): 733–752.

2. For a recent comparative study of the urban environment that draws conclusions about the impact of shared ideals on "theories of urbanism and actual practices of city building," see Harold L. Platt, *Building the Urban Environment: Visions of the Organic City in the United States, Europe, and Latin America* (Philadelphia: Temple University Press, 2015), 14.

3. Allan G. Johnson, *The Gender Knot: Unraveling Our Patriarchal Legacy*, rev. ed. (Philadelphia: Temple University Press, 2005), 5.

4. Lynn M. Appleton, "The Gender Regimes of American Cities," in *Gender in Urban Research*, ed. Judith A. Garber and Robyne S. Turner (Thousand Oaks, CA: Sage, 1995), 44, 47. For Judith Bennett's clarification that patriarchy "might be everywhere but it is not everywhere the same," see Judith M. Bennett, *History Matters: Patriarchy and the Challenge of Feminism* (Philadelphia: University of Pennsylvania Press, 2006), 54.

5. Michael Kimmel defines public patriarchy as referring to "the institutional arrangements of a society, the predominance of males in all power positions within the economy and polity . . . as well as the 'gendering' of those institutions." See Michael Kimmel, *Misframing Men: The Politics of Contemporary Masculinities* (New Brunswick, NJ: Rutgers University Press, 2010), 146. See also Jeff Hearn, *Men in the Public Eye: Critical Studies on Men and Masculinities* (London: Routledge, 1992), 39. Feminist scholars have used the concept of public patriarchy to explore distinctions between a private patriarchy of suburbanization that restricted women to the home and a public patriarchy of the city wherein women had more freedom of movement and choice of labor but still functioned within attempts to enforce social conformity through means such as land-use controls. See, for example, Judith A. Garber, "'Not Named or Identified': Politics and the Search for Anonymity in

the City," in *Gendering the City: Women, Boundaries, and Visions of Urban Life*, ed. Kristine B. Miranne and Alma H. Young (Lanham, MD: Rowman and Littlefield, 2000), 29–30.

6. The bibliography of work on the urban environment is cited throughout the book. For brevity here, I offer a few examples: Ruth McManus, *Dublin, 1910–1940: Shaping the City and Suburbs* (Dublin: Four Courts Press, 2002); Jacinta Prunty, *Dublin Slums, 1800–1925: A Study in Urban Geography* (Dublin: Irish Academic Press, 1998); Carl Smith, *The Plan of Chicago: Daniel Burnham and the Making of the American City* (Chicago: University of Chicago Press, 2006); Alison Isenberg, *Downtown America: The History of the Place and the People Who Made It* (Chicago: University of Chicago Press, 2004); Lawrence Solomon, *Toronto Sprawls: A History* (Toronto: University of Toronto Press, 2007); Richard Dennis, *Cities in Modernity: Representations and Productions of Metropolitan Space, 1840–1930* (Cambridge: Cambridge University Press, 2008); Gordon Cherry, *Cities and Plans: The Shaping of Urban Britain in the Nineteenth and Twentieth Centuries* (London: Edward Arnold, 1988); Richard Dennis, "Modern London," in *The Cambridge Urban History of Britain*, vol. 3, ed. Martin Daunton (Cambridge: Cambridge University Press, 2000); Harold L. Platt, *The Electric City: Energy and the Growth of the Chicago Area* (Chicago: University of Chicago Press, 1991); Joel Tarr and Gabriel DuPuy, eds., *Technology and the Rise of the Networked City in Europe and America* (Philadelphia: Temple University Press, 1988); Martin Melosi, *The Sanitary City: Urban Infrastructure in America from Colonial Times to the Present* (Baltimore: Johns Hopkins University Press, 2000); and Michael Doucet, "Politics, Space, and Trolleys: Mass Transit in Early Twentieth Century Toronto," in *Shaping the Urban Landscape*, ed. Alan Artibise and Gilbert A. Stelter (Ottawa: Carleton University Press, 1982), 356–381.

7. For some examples, see Gilbert A. Stetler and Alan Artibise, eds., *The Canadian City: Essays in Urban and Social History*, rev. ed. (Ottawa: Carleton University Press, 1991); James R. Barrett, *Work and Community in the Jungle: Chicago's Packinghouse Workers, 1894–1922* (Urbana: University of Illinois Press, 1987); David R. Green, *Pauper Capital: London and the Poor Law, 1790–1870* (Farnham, UK: Ashgate, 2010); and Joseph V. O'Brien, *Dear, Dirty Dublin: A City in Distress, 1899–1916* (Berkeley: University of California Press, 1982).

8. Appleton, "The Gender Regimes of American Cities," 47.

9. Jane Darke, "The Man-Shaped City," in *Changing Places: Women's Lives in the City*, ed. Chris Booth, Jane Darke, and Susan Yeandle (London: Paul Chapman, 1996), 88. For more on patriarchy and women's economic segregation, see L. Benería and Martha Roldán, *The Crossroads of Class and Gender: Industrial Homework, Subcontracting, and Household Dynamics in Mexico City* (Chicago: University of Chicago Press, 1987), 11–12.

10. Helen Jarvis with Paula Kantor and Jonathan Cloke, *Cities and Gender: Critical Introductions to Urbanism and the City* (London: Routledge, 2009), 13.

11. Peter Arnade, Martha Howell, and Walter Simons, "Fertile Spaces: The Productivity of Urban Space in Northern Europe," *Journal of Interdisciplinary History* 32, no. 4 (2002): 545. For discussion of London markets specifically, see Kay E. Lacey, "Women and Work in Fourteenth and Fifteenth Century London," in *Women and Work in Pre-industrial England*, ed. Lindsey Charles and Lorna Duffin (Bechenham, UK: Croom Helm, 1985), 25. For a discussion on regulating private property, see Martha Howell, *Women, Production, and Patriarchy in Late Medieval Cities* (Chicago: University of Chicago, 1986); and Vanessa Harding, "Space, Property, and Propriety in Urban England," *Journal of Interdisciplinary History* 32, no. 4 (2002): 549–569.

12. Leon Battista Alberti, *The Family in Renaissance Florence*, trans. Renée Neu Watkins (Columbia: University of South Carolina Press, 1969). The book was originally published in 1439.

13. Jarvis, Kantor, and Cloke, *Cities and Gender*, 12.

14. See Edward Soja, *Postmodern Geographies: The Reassertion of Space in Critical Social Theory* (New York: Verso Books, 1989); David Harvey, *Social Justice and the City* (Baltimore: Johns Hopkins University Press, 1973), wherein Harvey assumes that social justice for the working class will produce social justice for the greater populace so that patriarchy never enters into his calculation; David Harvey, *The Condition of Postmodernity: An Inquiry into the Origins of Social Change* (London: Oxford University Press, 1989); David Harvey, *The Urbanization of Capital* (London: Blackwell, 1985); David Harvey; *Consciousness and the Urban Experience* (Baltimore: Johns Hopkins University Press, 1985); Ira Katznelson, *Marxism and the City* (New York: Oxford University

Press, 1992); and Charles Tilly, "What's Left of the City?" *Journal of Urban History* 14, no. 3 (1988): 394–398. Charles Tilly shifts analysis to the role of the state, critiquing the Marxist analysis for failing to acknowledge any role played by the state in the processes of urbanization, but in shifting from the local to the national, he does not question the Marxist structural analysis. Andrew Merriman analyzes the legacy of the Marxist interpretation on the city and admits that "Marxist ideas . . . have essentially been propounded by men" who see the city fulfilling "a functional role not only for capitalism, but for Marxism as well." Andrew Merriman, *Metromarxism: A Marxist Tale of the City* (London: Routledge, 2002), 6–7. For a similar critique of the Marxist analysis, see Rosalyn Deutsche, "'Men in Space,'" in *Gender Space Architecture: An Interdisciplinary Introduction*, ed. Jane Rendell, Barbara Penner, and Iain Borden (London: Routledge, 2000), 134–139.

15. Doreen Massey, *Space, Place, and Gender* (Minneapolis: University of Minnesota Press, 1994), 221.

16. Merriman, *Metromarxism*, 6, 114–120.

17. Liz Bondi and Linda Peake, "Gender and the City: Urban Politics Revisited," in *Women in Cities: Gender and the Urban Environment*, ed. Jo Little, Linda Peake, and Pat Richardson (New York: New York University Press, 1988), 21–22. See also Manuel Castells, *The Urban Question: A Marxist Approach*, rev. ed. (Cambridge, MA: MIT Press, 1979). The book was originally published as *La question urbaine* (Paris: F. Maspero, 1972). When scholars use Castells's conception of collective consumption, women are ignored. See, for example, Diane Davis, *The Urban Leviathan: Mexico City in the Twentieth Century* (Philadelphia: Temple University Press, 1994), which never considers women's roles in the development of Mexico City. Katherine Bliss, *Compromised Positions: Prostitution, Public Health, and Gender Politics in Revolutionary Mexico City* (University Park: Pennsylvania State University Press, 2001), demonstrates how this perception of the city's built environment changes when gender is considered.

18. Lynne Walker, "Women and Architecture," in Rendell, Penner, and Borden, *Gender Space Architecture*, 254. For similar observations about professional practices, see Jarvis, Kantor, and Cloke, *Cities and Gender*, 12–13; Marion Roberts, "Introduction: Concepts, Themes and Issues in a Gendered Approach to Planning," in *Fair Shared Cities: The Impact of Gender Planning in Europe*, ed. Marion Roberts and Inés Sánchez de Madariaga (Farnham, UK: Ashgate, 2013), 2–3; and Clara Greed, *Women and Planning: Creating Gendered Realities* (London: Routledge, 1994).

19. Chapter 4 discusses more thoroughly what the term and the idea of *modern* meant to groups of men and women in the city across this time period.

20. Helen Meller, "Urban Renewal and Citizenship: The Quality of Life in British Cities, 1890–1990," *Urban History* 22, no. 1 (1995): 68.

21. See Daphne Spain, "Octavia Hill's Philosophy of Housing Reform: From British Roots to American Soil," *Journal of Planning History* 5, no. 2 (2006): 106–125; and Octavia Hill, "Four Years Management of a London Court," *Macmillan's Magazine*, July 1869, pp. 219–226.

22. Lord Shaftesbury, "The Housing of the Poor," *The Times*, June 27, 1885, p. 10.

23. Dennis, *Cities in Modernity*, esp. 86–94, discusses a number of such writings.

24. John Ruskin, *The Crown of Wild Olive* (London: Smith, Elder, 1882), 28.

25. Elizabeth Wilson, *The Sphinx in the City: Urban Life, the Control of Disorder, and Women* (Berkeley: University of California Press, 1991), 8, 157.

26. Industrialization was slower in Dublin, a colonial city. The city was somewhat anomalous vis-à-vis the other four cities in this book because Ireland's foremost industrial city was Belfast. Yet to the Irish, Dublin was the capital and the most important city with a thriving port drawing rural male and female migrants. Jacinta Prunty's analysis of migration patterns reveals that in 1881, 31 percent of Dublin's population had migrated from elsewhere in Ireland, with more women than men migrating into Dublin from some counties. See Jacinta Prunty, "Mobility Rate among Women in Nineteenth Century Dublin," in *Migration, Mobility and Modernization*, ed. David J. Siddle (Liverpool: Liverpool University Press, 2000), 131–163.

27. Helen Meller, "Gender, Citizenship and the Making of the Modern Environment," in *Women and the Making of Built Space in England, 1870–1950*, ed. Elizabeth Darling and Lesley Whitworth (Aldershot, UK: Ashgate, 2007), 17, 16. For a few examples of this focus, see *History of the Alexandra Guild Tenement Company, Ltd.* (Dublin: Alexandra College Archives, 1958);

"Report of the Alexandra Guild Tenement Company," *Alexandra College Magazine*, December 1900; Toronto Local Council of Women, *11th Annual Report*, 1905, Gerritsen Collection of Aletta Jacobs (GCAJ), available at http://www.proquest.com/products-services/gerritsen.html; Toronto Local Council of Women, *12th Annual Report*, 1906, GCAJ; Toronto Local Council of Women, *16th Annual Report*, 1910, GCAJ; Toronto Local Council of Women, *21st Annual Report*, 1915, GCAJ; and "Minutes of Monthly Meeting," November 1909, Box 805-MU6362, Toronto Local Council of Women (TLCW) Fonds, Archives of Ontario (AO), Toronto, Canada.

28. Sharon Haar, "The Hull House Settlement and the Study of the City," in *Embodied Utopias: Gender, Social Change, and the Modern Metropolis*, ed. Amy Bingaman, Lise Sanders, and Rebecca Zorach (London: Routledge, 2002), 111. The Toronto Local Council of Women proclaimed that one of its goals was to have women extend their concern "for the home and family . . . outside their own domestic sphere to embrace the community." Toronto Local Council of Women, "Historical Sketch," TLCW Fonds, AO.

29. As this book focuses on how ideas about masculinity and femininity produced ideas about the proper place of men and women as perceived at the time, it does not investigate the potential effect on other gender identifications. For examples of place-making for specific urban LGBTQI communities, see George Chauncey, *Gay New York: Gender, Urban Culture, and the Making of the Gay Male World, 1890–1940* (New York: Basic Books, 1994); Marc Stein, *City of Sisterly and Brotherly Loves: Gay Philadelphia, 1946–1972* (Philadelphia: Temple University Press, 2004); and Frank Mort, "Archaeologies of City Life: Commercial Culture, Masculinity, and Spatial Relations in 1980s London," *Environment and Planning D: Society and Space* 13, no. 5 (1995): 573–590. For a recent collection of essays on planning and LGBTQ spaces, see Petra L. Doan, ed., *Planning and LGBTQ Communities: The Need for Inclusive Queer Spaces* (New York: Routledge, 2015), including Catherine J. Nash and Andrew Gorman-Murray, "Lesbian Spaces in Transition: Insights from Toronto and Sydney," 181–198, and Curt Winkle, "Gay Commercial Spaces in Chicago and the Role of Planning," 21–38.

30. See Massey, *Space, Place, and Gender*, 255–257, for an extended discussion of these dichotomies.

31. Wilson, *Sphinx in the City*, 7, 157, 87.

32. Ibid., 7–8.

33. Dennis, *Cities in Modernity*, 51.

34. Elizabeth Wilson, "Culture and Gender Concerns in Spatial Development," in *Women in the City* (Paris: Organisation for Economic Co-operation and Development, 1995), 41.

35. Wilson, *Sphinx in the City*, 7. See also Elizabeth Wilson, *The Contradictions of Culture: Cities, Culture, Women* (London: Sage, 2001). For more on middle-class women in London, see Erika Rappaport, *Shopping for Pleasure: Women in the Making of London's West End* (Princeton, NJ: Princeton University Press, 2000). For discussions of London working-class men and African American men in Chicago accepting ideas about masculinity and patriarchy, see, respectively, Martin Daunton, *House and Home in the Victorian City: Working-Class Housing, 1850–1914* (London: Edward Arnold, 1983), esp. 265, 272; and "Side Lights on Primary Day," *Chicago Defender*, February 27, 1915, p. 2.

36. Barbara Hooper, "Urban Space, Modernity, and Masculinist Desire: The Utopian Longings of Le Corbusier," in Bingaman, Sanders, and Zorach, *Embodied Utopias*, 61. Hooper traces the analogy of the female body and the monstrous to as early as Aristotle and as underlying the conceptions of the modern city by modernists such as Le Corbusier.

37. For examples, see Daphne Spain, *How Women Saved the City* (Minneapolis: University of Minnesota Press, 2001); Miranne and Young, *Gendering the City*; Little, Peake, and Richardson, *Women in Cities*; Roberts and Sánchez de Madariaga, *Fair Shared Cities*; and Bingaman, Sanders, and Zorach, *Embodied Utopias*.

38. Jane Rendell, *Pursuit of Pleasure: Gender, Space and Architecture in Regency London* (London: Athlone Press, 2002), 21–22.

39. Wilson, "Culture and Gender Concerns in Spatial Development," 40.

40. Massey, *Space, Place, and Gender*, 233.

41. Clara Greed, "Women and Planning: Progress or Promise?" *Planning Perspectives* 22, no. 1 (1996): 10.

42. Meller, "Gender, Citizenship," 16; Michael Batty, "The Creative Destruction of Cities," *Environment and Planning B: Planning and Design* 34, no. 1 (2007): 2. See also Roberts, "Introduction: Concepts, Themes and Issues," 3.

43. Roberts and Sánchez de Madariaga, *Fair Shared Cities*.

CHAPTER 1

1. This concept derived from ancient Roman law. Cary J. Nedermann, "Confronting Market Freedom: Economic Foundations of Liberty at the End of the Middle Ages," in *Continuity and Change: The Harvest of Late-Medieval and Reformation History; Essays Presented to Heiko A. Oberman on his 70th Birthday*, ed. Robert J. Bast and Andrew C. Gor (Amsterdam: Brill, 2000), 3.

2. Philip Withington, "Two Renaissances: Urban Political Culture in Post-Reformation England Reconsidered," *Historical Journal* 44, no. 1 (2001): 252.

3. Richard Holt and Gervase Rosser, introduction to *The English Medieval Town: A Reader in English Urban History, 1200–1540*, new ed. (London: Routledge, 2014), 8–9; Phil Withington, "Citizens, Community and Political Culture in Restoration England," in *Communities in Early Modern England: Networks, Place, Rhetoric*, ed. Alexandra Shepard and Phil Withington (Manchester, UK: Manchester University Press, 2000), 139. For contestation over the extent of liberties in English towns in the fifteenth century, see Lorraine Attreed, "Urban Identity in Medieval English Towns," *Journal of Interdisciplinary History* 32, no. 4 (2002): 571–592.

4. R. B. Dobson, "Admission to the Freedom of the City of York in the Later Middle Ages," *Economic History Review* 26, no. 1 (1973): 2, 22. Dobson analyzed the town's Freeman's Register.

5. Between 1272 and 1500, only 138 York women were admitted to freedom; between 1432 and 1441 only 31 of the 1,030 enfranchised persons were women. For additional information on women, work, and medieval guilds, see Maryanne Kowaleski and Judith Bennett, "Crafts, Gilds, and Women in the Middle Ages: Fifty Years after Marian K. Dale," *Signs: Journal of Women in Culture and Society* 14, no. 2 (1989): 473–488. The authors note that even where a few guilds of skilled female workers existed, these women were excluded from "participation in civic government" (483). S. D. Smith notes that in 1693, the first woman in 130 years was enabled as a master draper and that future admission of women into the company was in the context of a decrease in the supply of male labor, the female population of the town beginning to outnumber the male, and an increased demand for female clothing products. See S. D. Smith, "Women's Admission to Guilds in Early-Modern England: The Case of the York Merchant Tailors' Company, 1693–1776," *Gender and History*, no. 17 (April 2005): 99–126.

6. For more on the need for community approval in medieval Wells, status levels among the citizens, and change over time, see Philip R. Hoffmann, "In Defence of Corporate Liberties: Early Medieval Guilds and the Problem of Illicit Artisan Work," *Urban History* 34, no. 1 (2007): 76–88; and David Gary Shaw, "Social Networks and the Foundation of Oligarchy in Medieval Towns," *Urban History* 32, no. 2 (2005): 200–222. For later centuries, see Andy Coll, "Street Disorder, Surveillance and Shame: Regulating Behavior in the Public Spaces of the Late Victorian British Town," *Social History* 24, no. 3 (1999): 250–268.

7. "Calendar of Ancient Records," Pre-1840 Collection, Dublin City Archives, Pearse Street Library, Dublin.

8. Jon Teaford, "City versus State: The Struggle for Legal Ascendancy," *American Journal of Legal History* 17, no. 1 (1973): 51–65.

9. The earlier corporation of the City of London resisted conforming to the legislation. Thus London sprawled geographically outside its boundaries, multiplying overlapping governing agencies until finally drawn together in 1889 with creation of the London County Council. The 1835 act would be repealed and replaced in 1882.

10. Alan DeGaetano, "The Birth of Modern Urban Governance: A Comparison of Political Modernization in Boston, Massachusetts, and Bristol, England, 1800–1870," *Journal of Urban*

History 35, no. 2 (2009): 273; see also 268, 269. See also Jon Teaford, *The Municipal Revolution in America: The Origins of Modern Urban Government, 1650–1825* (Chicago: University of Chicago Press, 1975).

11. Sam Bass Warner, *The Private City: Philadelphia in Three Periods of Its Growth*, 2nd ed. (Philadelphia: University of Pennsylvania Press, 1987). The 1789 Philadelphia charter, written by a merchant-artisan coalition, restricted the franchise to propertied men and pledged $5 million in municipal funds to finance a privately built intercity railroad line.

12. Robin L. Einhorn, *Property Rules: Political Economy in Chicago, 1833–1872* (Chicago: University of Chicago Press, 1991), 28. Voting restrictions for black men fell in 1871.

13. For more on London's government in the second half of the nineteenth century, see John Davis, *Reforming London: The London Government Problem, 1855–1900* (London: Oxford University Press, 1988).

14. John Ruskin, *The Crown of Wild Olive* (London: Smith, Elder, 1882), 28.

15. David Dickson, "Death of a Capital? Dublin and the Consequences of Union," in *Two Capitals: London and Dublin, 1500–1840*, ed. Peter Clark and Raymond Gillespie (London: Oxford University Press, 2001), 111–131.

16. James Whitelaw, quoted in Jacinta Prunty, *Dublin Slums, 1800–1925: A Study in Urban Geography* (Dublin: Irish Academic Press, 1998), 91.

17. Jacinta Prunty, *Dublin Slums*, 46. Until 1864, Ireland did not have its own registry of birth, deaths, and marriages, so surveys had been conducted by going building to building, counting and quizzing residents.

18. "To the Electors of Toronto," 1834, available at https://torontoist.com/wp-content/uploads/2014/03/20140306electionposter.jpg.

19. Raphaël Fischler, "Development Controls in Toronto in the Nineteenth Century," *Urban History Review* 36, no. 1 (2007): 24.

20. For an overview of Toronto's economic growth, see Peter Goheen, "Currents of Change in Toronto, 1850–1900," in *The Canadian City: Essays in Urban History*, ed. Alan Artibise and Gilbert Stetler (Ottawa: Carleton University Press, 1977), 54–92.

21. Einhorn, *Property Rules*, 38.

22. See ibid., 57–60, for a discussion of bridges and throughout the book for the special assessment system.

23. Ibid., 1.

24. Ibid., 136–139.

25. William Bross, *History of Chicago, Historical and Commercial Statistics, Sketches, Facts and Figures* (Chicago: Jansen, McClurg, 1876), 97–100.

26. Maureen A. Flanagan, *Seeing with Their Hearts: Chicago Women and the Vision of the Good City, 1871–1933* (Princeton, NJ: Princeton University Press, 2002), chap. 1. The businessmen heading the Relief and Aid Society controlled all the fire donations and paid themselves nearly $350,000 for their businesses selling supplies to the society. See Flanagan, *Seeing with Their Hearts*, 28, 229n65.

27. "Pay or Get Out," *Chicago Tribune*, January 7, 1872, p. 4.

28. Ian Archer, Caroline Barron, and Vanessa Harding, eds., *Hugh Alley's Caveat: The Markets in London in 1598* (London: London Topographical Society, 1988), 23, manuscript V.a.318, Folger Shakespeare Library, Washington, DC.

29. Barbara Hooper, "The Poem of Male Desires: Female Bodies, Modernity, and 'Paris, Capital of the Nineteenth Century,'" in *Making the Invisible Visible: A Multicultural Planning Reader*, ed. Leonie Sandercock (Berkeley: University of California Press, 1998), 230. See also Elizabeth Wilson, *The Sphinx in the City: Urban Life, the Control of Disorder, and Women* (Berkeley: University of California Press, 1991).

30. Teaford, "City versus State," 61.

31. W. R. Greg, *Why Are Women Redundant?* (London: John Childs, 1869), 5, 38. The French historian Jules Michelet wrote that the natural order of the world demanded that women not be single: the "worst destiny for woman was to live alone," and "woman cannot live without man." Jules Michelet, *La Femme* (New York: Carlton, 1867), 32, 50. See also Mary Poovey, *The Ideological Work of Gender in Mid-Victorian England* (London: Virago Press, 1988).

32. Elizabeth Wilson, "The Invisible Flâneur," in *The Contradictions of Culture: Cities, Culture, Women* (London: Sage, 2001), 85–86.

33. Hooper, "The Poem of Male Desires," 244.

34. Ibid.

35. Richard Dennis, *Cities in Modernity: Representations and Productions of Metropolitan Space, 1840–1930* (Cambridge: Cambridge University Press, 2008), 38.

36. Italo Calvino, *Le Città Invisibili* (Milan: Mondadori, 2010), v, 45–46. The work was originally published in 1972.

37. Leonore Davidoff, "Gender and the 'Great Divide': Public and Private in British Gender History," *Journal of Women's History* 15, no. 1 (2003): 22, 16.

38. Wilson, *Sphinx in the City*, 8. See also Elizabeth Grosz, "Bodies-City," in *Sexuality and Space*, ed. Beatriz Colomina (Princeton, NJ: Princeton University Press, 1992), 241–254, esp. 250.

39. Ruth Livesey, "Women Rent Collectors and the Rewriting of Space, Class and Gender in East London, 1870–1900," in *Women and the Making of Built Space in England, 1870–1950*, ed. Elizabeth Darling and Lesley Whitworth (Aldershot, UK: Ashgate, 2007), 101, quoting "The Glorified Spinster," *Macmillan's Magazine* 58 (1888).

CHAPTER 2

1. Letter from George Peabody to his trustees, January 29, 1866, in *Second Trust*, ACC/3445/PT, Peabody Trust and Related Organizations, ACC Collection, London Metropolitan Archives (LMA). Words and phrases such as "working men," "blameless," and "cost within his means" are important to keep in mind as the results of the Peabody Trust buildings are described later in this chapter.

2. Anthony Wohl, *The Eternal Slum: Housing and Social Policy in Victorian London*, 2nd ed. (London: Transaction, 2002), 162.

3. "Memorandum to Cabinet by R. A. Cross," January 28, 1875, reprinted in Eric J. Evans, *Social Policy, 1830–1914: Individualism, Collectivism, and the Origins of the Welfare State* (London: Routledge, 1978), 178.

4. Wohl, *Eternal Slum*, 107. According to Eugenie Birch and Deborah S. Gardner, British and American model dwellings companies promised anywhere between 3 and 5 percent return, percentages that "were only a point or two less than what could be earned in conservative investments at the time." Eugenie Birch and Deborah S. Gardner, "The Seven-Percent Solution: A Review of Philanthropic Housing, 1870–1910," *Journal of Urban History* 7, no. 4 (1981): 406.

5. Wohl, *Eternal Slum*, 142.

6. Evans, *Social Policy*, 144, 162–163; Susannah Morris, "Market Solutions for Social Problems: Working-Class Housing in Nineteenth-Century London," *Economic History Review* 54, no. 3 (2001): 525–545.

7. Ernest Ritson Dewsnup, *The Housing Problem in England* (Manchester: Sheratt and Hughes, 1907), 206.

8. Morris, "Market Solutions," 526.

9. Quoted in Wohl, *Eternal Slum*, 150.

10. Ibid., 145, 156.

11. John Davis, *Reforming London: The London Government Problem, 1855–1900* (London: Oxford University Press, 1988), 11–12, 25–26; David Owen, *The Government of Victorian London, 1855–1889: The Metropolitan Board of Works, the Vestries, and the City Corporation* (Cambridge, MA: Harvard University Press, 1982); Timothy B. Smith, "In Defense of Privilege: The City of London and the Challenge of Municipal Reform, 1875–1890," *Journal of Social History* 27, no. 1 (1993): 59–83.

12. Wohl, *Eternal Slum*, 250.

13. Mary E. Daly, "Housing Conditions and the Genesis of Housing Reform in Dublin, 1880–1920," in *The Emergence of Irish Planning, 1880–1920*, ed. Michael Bannon (Dublin: Turoe Press, 1985), 82, 78.

14. Mary E. Daly, *Dublin, the Deposed Capital: A Social and Economic History, 1860–1914* (Cork, UK: Cork University Press, 1984), 297.

15. Jacinta Prunty, *Dublin Slums, 1800-1925: A Study in Urban Geography* (Dublin: Irish Academic Press, 1998), 118-127; Daly, "Housing Conditions," 94; Daly, *Dublin, the Deposed Capital*, 291-292. See also Murray Fraser, *John Bull's Other Homes: State Housing and British Policy in Ireland, 1883-1922* (Liverpool: Liverpool University Press, 1996), 71-72.

16. "Dublin," *Freeman's Journal and Daily Commercial Advertiser*, August 24, 1884, p. 4.

17. "Intolerable," *Freeman's Journal and Daily Commercial Advertiser*, February 13, 1900, p. 4. For more information on the DADC, see Daly, "Housing Conditions," 98-101; and Daly, *Dublin, the Deposed Capital*, 298.

18. Prunty, *Dublin Slums*, 146-147.

19. "Report of the Artisans' Dwelling Committee," *Reports and Printed Documents of the Corporation of Dublin* 2, no. 72 (1890): 484.

20. Daly, "Housing Conditions," 101.

21. "The Dwellings of the Working-Classes," *Freeman's Journal and Daily Commercial Advertiser*, September 27, 1884, p. 3. I believe that M'Mahon was the E. M'Mahon of that company developing the Phibsborough suburb.

22. Robin L. Einhorn, *Property Rules: Political Economy in Chicago, 1833-1872* (Chicago: University of Chicago Press, 1991), 139-141. Only after a new state constitution in 1871 prevented Chicago from issuing municipal bonds for sewer extension was the city forced to levy a citywide property tax for such a system, one of the first recognitions that there was a larger public good in such improvements.

23. For the most comprehensive discussion of the fire limits controversy, see Christine M. Rosen, *The Limits of Power: Great Fires and the Process of City Growth in America* (Cambridge: Cambridge University Press, 1986), esp. 95-109. See also Margaret Garb, *City of American Dreams: A History of Home Ownership and Housing Reform in Chicago, 1871-1919* (Chicago: University of Chicago Press, 2005), for Chicago's mania for home ownership.

24. Citizens' Association of Chicago, "Report of the Committee on Tenement Houses," 1884, pp. 10, 18-19, Citizens' Association of Chicago Manuscript Collection, Chicago History Museum (CHM).

25. *Hull-House Maps and Papers: A Presentation of Nationalities and Wages in a Congested District of Chicago, Together with Comments and Essays of Problems Growing out of the Social Conditions, by Residents of Hull-House, a Social Settlement at 235 South Halsted Street, Chicago, Illinois* (New York: Crowell, 1895); Robert Hunter, *Tenement Conditions in Chicago* (Chicago: City Homes Association, 1901).

26. Thomas Adam, "Transatlantic Trading: The Transfer of Philanthropic Models between European and North American Cities during the Nineteenth and Early Twentieth Centuries," *Journal of Urban History* 28, no. 2 (2002): 343-344. Goldwin Smith was a historian and journalist born in England and immigrant to Toronto.

27. Quoted in Eric Arthur, *Toronto: No Mean City*, 3rd ed. (Toronto: University of Toronto Press, 1986), 169.

28. Toronto City Council, *Minutes* (Toronto: Toronto City Council, 1893), vol. 1, app. A, pp. 79, 101, Toronto City Archives (TCA).

29. Toronto City Council, *Minutes* (Toronto: Toronto City Council, 1894), vol. 2, p. 71, TCA.

30. David Owen, *English Philanthropy, 1660-1960* (Cambridge, MA: Harvard University Press, 1964), 508.

31. Wohl, *Eternal Slum*, 184. See also Anthony S. Wohl, "Octavia Hill and the Homes of the London Poor," *Journal of British Studies* 10, no. 2 (1971): 105-131, reprinted in Wohl, *Eternal Slum*, 199; and Jose Harris, "Victorian Values and the Founders of the Welfare State," *Proceedings of the British Academy* 78 (1992): 165-182.

32. Wohl, "Octavia Hill and the Homes of the London Poor," 130.

33. Wohl, *Eternal Slum*, 195; Elizabeth Darling and Anne Anderson, "The Hill Sisters: Cultural Philanthropy and the Embellishment of Lives in Late Nineteenth-Century England," in *Women and the Making of Built Space in England, 1870-1950*, ed. Elizabeth Darling and Lesley Whitworth (Aldershot, UK: Ashgate, 2007), 33-48.

34. See Adam, "Transatlantic Trading," 333.

35. Lord Shaftesbury, "The Housing of the Poor," *The Times*, June 27, 1885, p. 10.

36. See Robert Whelan, ed., *Octavia Hill and the Social Housing Debate: Essays and Letters by Octavia Hill* (London: St. Edmundsbury Press, 1998), 68.

37. For accounting of donations in which those from women far outweighed those from men, see Octavia Hill, "Letter to My Fellow-Workers," ACC/3445/WHT, Westminster Housing Trust, ACC Collection, LMA. By 1874, Hill was managing fifteen blocks of buildings in London's poorest areas that housed between two thousand and three thousand tenants.

38. Octavia Hill, "Blank Court; or, Landlords and Tenants," *Macmillan's Magazine*, October 1871, p. 457.

39. Octavia Hill, *Homes of the London Poor* (London: Macmillan, 1875), 27.

40. Anderson and Darling, "Hill Sisters," 40–41.

41. Hill, *Homes of the London Poor*, 28.

42. Ibid. To this criticism Hill replied, "Are not the great masses made up of many small knots? Are not the great towns divisible into small districts?" Ibid., 29.

43. Thomas Blashill, "Unhealthy Areas and Municipal Rehousing," 1899, p. 29, pamphlet HD7/349, London School of Economics (LSE).

44. Richard Dennis, "Modern London," in *The Cambridge Urban History of Britain*, ed. Martin Daunton (Cambridge: Cambridge University Press, 2000), 3:12–13.

45. John Tarn, *Five Per Cent Philanthropy: An Account of Housing in Urban Areas, 1840–1914* (Cambridge: Cambridge University Press, 1973), 46.

46. Adam, "Transatlantic Trading," 332.

47. Ibid., 337.

48. Wohl, *Eternal Slum*, 164–165.

49. Martin Daunton, *House and Home in the Victorian City: Working-Class Housing, 1850–1914* (London: Edward Arnold, 1983), 12–13.

50. William Smart, "The Housing of the Poor in London," 1889, pp. 12–13, pamphlet HD7/276, LSE.

51. Guinness Partnership, "Living at Guinness," available at http://history.guinnesspartnership.com/living-at-guinness (accessed August 14, 2017). See also Sarah Wise, *The Blackest Streets: The Life and Death of a Victorian Slum* (London: Random House, 2008), 255–256.

52. Letters from George Peabody to his trustees, February 19 and April 16, 1869, in *Second Trust*, ACC/3445/PT, Peabody Trust and Related Organizations, ACC Collection.

53. Caroline Morrell, "Octavia Hill and Women's Networks in Housing," in *Gender, Health and Welfare*, ed. Anne Digby and John Steward (London: Routledge, 1998), 102.

54. Octavia Hill, "Why the Artisans' Dwelling Bill Was Wanted," *Macmillan's Magazine*, June 1874, p. 85.

55. Letter from Octavia Hill to secretary of the Ecclesiastical Commissioners, March 1887, in *Life of Octavia Hill as Told in Her Letters*, ed. C. Edmund Maurice (London: Macmillan, 1913), 475.

56. Octavia Hill, Document 543, in *British and Irish Women's Letters and Diaries, 1500–1900* (Alexandria, VA: Alexander Street Press, 2013), 560–561.

57. Quoted in Anderson and Darling, "Hill Sisters," 44. The gardens were destroyed in the 1950s but restored and reopened recently. The cottages and hall were constructed between 1884 and 1889.

58. Women were not accepted into formal horticultural training until 1891 at the Swanley Horticultural College in Kent. Sieveking was the college's treasurer. Helen Blackburn, ed., *Handbook for Women Engaged in Social and Political Work* (Bristol, UK: Arrowsmith, 1895).

59. Hill, "Letters to My Fellow-Workers," letter of 1888.

60. Octavia Hill, "Space for the People," in *Homes of the London Poor*, 2nd ed. (London: Macmillan, 1883), available at http://www.victorianlondon.org/publications/homesofthelondonpoor-7.htm.

61. Stephen P. Walker, "Philanthropic Women and Accounting: Octavia Hill and the Exercise of Quiet Sympathy," *Accounting, Business, and Financial History* 16 (July 2006): 179; Hill, "Letters to My Fellow-Workers," letter of 1888.

62. In mapping the poverty of Dublin, Jacinta Prunty located these two streets as ones with numerous households receiving relief between 1895 and 1900 from the Ladies' Association of

Charity of St. Mary's Parish. See Prunty, *Dublin Slums*, 312–313, fig. 8.7. These designations are of civil parishes. For guild purchases, see "Report of the Alexandra College Guild Tenement Co. Ltd.," *Alexandra College Magazine*, June 1903, pp. 22–24. "Alexandra Guild Tenements Company Limited," *Irish Times*, June 30, 1899, p. 9, noted that Octavia Hill was going to train a member of the guild in housing management.

63. "Report of Fifth Annual Meeting of the Guild Tenement Company," *Alexandra College Magazine*, December 1903, pp. 38–39; "Report on Tenement House Activities," *Alexandra College Magazine*, December 1904.

64. Maryann Gialanella Valiulis, "Toward the 'Moral and Material Improvement of the Working Classes': The Founding of the Alexandra College Guild Tenement Company, Dublin, 1898," *Journal of Urban History* 23, no. 3 (1997): 303. For additional information, see "History of the Alexandra Guild Tenement Co. Ltd., 1958," Alexandra College Archives, Alexandra College, Dublin, and annual reports in the *Alexandra College Magazine*.

65. Morrell, "Octavia Hill and Women's Networks in Housing," 102.

66. "Report on Tenement House Activities," *Alexandra College Magazine*, June 1903, pp. 22–24; "Report on Tenement House Activities," *Alexandra College Magazine*, June 1904, pp. 21–25; "Report on Tenement House Activities," *Alexandra College Magazine*, June 1910; "Report on Tenement House Activities," *Alexandra College Magazine*, June 1911. Baroness Burdett-Coutts had provided a children's play area in her Columbia Road flats.

67. See An Act to Empower the Right Honourable the Lord Mayor Aldermen and Burgesses of Dublin to Acquire the Inclosed Space Known as Mountjoy Square in the County Borough of Dublin, and for Other Purposes (also known as the Mountjoy Square, Dublin, Act, 1938), available at http://www.irishstatutebook.ie/1938/en/act/prv/0002/index.html.

68. F.H.A. Aalen, "Health and Housing in Dublin: Past, Present and Future," in *Dublin City and County: From Prehistory to Present*, ed. F.H.A. Allen and Kevin Whelan (Dublin: Geography, 1992), 299.

69. See Daly, *Dublin, the Deposed Capital*, 288–289.

70. "Report on Tenement House Activities," *Alexandra College Magazine*, June 1903, p. 24.

71. "Report on Tenement House Activities," *Alexandra College Magazine*, June 1908, pp. 41–42.

72. "The Housing of the Very Poor," *Freeman's Journal and Daily Commercial Advertiser*, June 28, 1899, p. 4.

73. William Lawson, "Remedies for Overcrowding in the City of Dublin," *Journal of the Statistical and Social Inquiry Society of Ireland*, no. 12 (1908–1909): 237–238.

74. "Housing of the Working Classes," *The Times*, May 8, 1885, p. 10.

75. Hill's testimony appears in "Report by Statistical Officer of the Council on the Re-housing of Persons of the Labouring Classes, Displaced by the London, Brighton, and Southern Coast Railway," Section IX, London City Council Printed Documents Collection, LMA. See also Hill's testimony and that of others in *First Report of Her Majesty's Commissioners for Inquiring into the Housing of the Working Classes* (London: Eyre and Spottiswoode, 1889), 55, 86, 88.

76. By 1900, estimates were that in Chelsea private enterprise and philanthropic housing building efforts had displaced 7,000 residents while rehousing only 1,500. Testimony on the Peabody Trust and Chelsea estimates is from Wohl, *Eternal Slum*, 170–171.

77. See Wohl, *Eternal Slum*, 239, for a list of men appointed to the commission and which constituency they each represented.

78. Prunty, *Dublin Slums*, 144–145.

79. Anthony Wohl, "Unfit for Human Habitation," in *The Victorian City: Images and Reality*, ed. Harold Dyos and Michael Wolff (London: Routledge, 1973), 2:613.

80. *First Report of Her Majesty's Commissioners*, 22.

81. Ibid., 23.

82. "The Housing of London Workmen—Not in the Slums" (part 1), *Pall Mall Gazette*, January 31, 1884, pp. 11–12. The editor of the *Gazette* at the time was the reformer William T. Stead.

83. "Housing of the Working Classes," 10.

84. Andrew Mearns, *The Bitter Cry of Outcast London: An Inquiry into the Conditions of the Abject Poor* (London: Clark, 1883). See also Wohl, *Eternal Slum*, 240.

85. Prunty, *Dublin Slums*, 146.

86. Quoted in Lawson, "Remedies for Overcrowding in the City of Dublin," 241.

87. "Housing of the Working Classes," 10.

88. "The Housing of the Working Classes in Ireland," *The Times*, August 14, 1885, p. 8.

89. See, for example, Ruth Livesey, "Women Rent Collectors and the Rewriting of Space, Class and Gender in East London, 1870–1900," in Darling and Whitworth, *Women and the Making of Built Space in England*, 87–105; and Chicago Woman's Club Civics Committee, "Tenement Housing Conditions in Twentieth Ward, Chicago," 1912, available at https://archive.org/details/tenement housingc00chic.

90. "Report on Tenement House Activities," *Alexandra College Magazine*, June 1909. For activities of the WNHA, see the 1909 issues of its magazine *Sláinte* at the National Library of Ireland. The Dublin Corporation agreed in 1911 to rent one small patch of vacant land and gave the WNHA use of another to build children's playgrounds. The corporation reserved the right to repossess both patches of land "if required, or if it ceases to be utilised for the purposes specified." See "Report of the Estates and Finance Committee," *Reports and Printed Documents of the Corporation of Dublin* 3, no. 187 (1911): 227–228.

91. Residents of Hull-House, *Hull-House Maps and Papers: A Presentation of Nationalities and Wages in a Congested District of Chicago* (New York: Crowell, 1895), 13–14.

92. Rima Lunin Schultz, "Introduction," in *Hull-House Maps and Papers: by the Residents of Hull-House* (Urbana: University of Illinois Press, 2007), 3, 18. See also Sharon Haar, "The Hull House Settlement and the Study of the City," in *Embodied Utopias: Gender, Social Change, and the Modern Metropolis*, ed. Amy Bingaman, Lise Sanders, and Rebecca Zorach (London: Routledge, 2002), 105–106.

93. Toronto Local Council of Women, "Historical Sketch," Toronto Local Council of Women Fonds, Archives of Ontario (AO). In their own documents, the organization shifted between identifying itself as the Toronto Local Council of Women and the Local Council of Women of Toronto. I use the former designation.

94. Toronto Local Council of Women, *14th Annual Report*, 1908, Gerritsen Collection of Aletta Jacobs, available at http://www.proquest.com/products-services/gerritsen.html; Toronto Local Council of Women, *Monthly Meeting Minutes*, November 10, 1909, and March 8 and May 10, 1911, Box 805-MU6362, Toronto Local Council of Women Fonds, AO. See more about the Evangelia and other Toronto Social Settlements in Chapter 4.

95. Chicago Association of Commerce Housing Committee, "The Housing Problem in Chicago," 1912, CHM.

96. Toronto City Council, *Minutes* (Toronto: Toronto City Council, 1911), vol. 2, app. A, pp. 1821–1822, TCA.

97. "National Labourers' Dwellings and Sanitary Association," *Freeman's Journal and Daily Commercial Advertiser*, December 31, 1889, p. 5.

98. C. M. Knowles, *The Housing Problem in London* (London: London Reform Union, 1899), 18, pamphlet HD7/D101, LSE.

99. See Helen Meller, "Women and Citizenship: Gender and the Built Environment in British Cities, 1870–1939," in *Cities of Ideas: Civil Society and Urban Governance in Britain, 1800–2000*, ed. Robert Colls and Richard Rodger (Aldershot UK: Ashgate, 2004), 233; Helen Meller, "Gender, Citizenship and the Making of the Modern Environment," in Darling and Whitworth, *Women and the Making of Built Space in England*, 16–20; and Elizabeth Darling and Lesley Whitworth, "Introduction: Making Space and Re-making History," in Darling and Whitworth, *Women and the Making of Built Space in England*, 9.

100. Toronto Local Council of Women, "Historical Sketch," 1.

101. Peter G. Mackintosh, "Scrutiny in the Modern City: The Domestic Public and the Toronto Local Council of Women at the Turn of the Twentieth Century," *Gender, Place and Culture* 12, no. 1 (2005): 32.

102. Haar, "Hull House Settlement," 111, 113.

103. Ishbel Aberdeen, "President's Address to International Conference," *Alexandra College Magazine*, June 1906.

104. House of Commons, "Report from the Select Committee on Artizans' and Labourers' Dwelling," *Parliamentary Papers* 232 (1882): 159; Simon T. Abernethy, "Opening Up the Suburbs: Workmen's Trains in London, 1860–1914," *Urban History* 42, no. 1 (2015): 71.

105. Abernethy, "Opening Up the Suburbs," 87.

106. Ibid., 84.

107. Ibid., 87.

108. Ibid.

CHAPTER 3

1. Joan M. Jensen, "'I'd Rather Be Dancing': Wisconsin Women Moving On," *Frontiers: A Journal of Women Studies* 22, no. 1 (2001): 1.

2. For an example of this type of thinking, see "Unsafe Buildings," *Chicago Daily Inter-Ocean*, February 19, 1888, p. 5.

3. "The Lodging-Houses of London," *London City Mission Magazine*, August 1845, pp. 3, 5.

4. "Destitution in Bristol," *The Times*, February 4, 1851, p. 7; "Letter to the Editor," *The Times*, April 8, 1851, p. 7; "Lodging-Houses," *The Times*, April 11, 1851, p. 7; "Common Lodging Houses Bill," *The Times*, June 25, 1851, p. 2; "Lord Shaftesbury Has Resumed in the Upper," *The Times*, July 10, 1851, p. 4.

5. Henry Mayhew, *London Labour and the London Poor*, vol. 1, *The London Street Folk* (London: Griffin, Bohn, 1861), 253, 255.

6. "Rowton Houses," *The Times*, May 29, 1896, p. 11; "The London County Council and Lord Rowton," *The Times*, August 1, 1899, p. 12.

7. "Rowton Houses," 11.

8. "Mr. John Burns and Lord Rowton," *The Times*, June 2, 1899, p. 12; "The London County Council and Lord Rowton," *The Times*, August 4, 1899, p. 9.

9. "Shelters and Philanthropic Lodging Houses" letters to the editor, *The Times*, November 2, 3, 4, 5, 8, 10, 14, and 15, 1904.

10. "The International Housing Conference," *The Times*, August 6, 1907, p. 10.

11. Joint Report of the Public Health and Housing of the Working-Classes Committee, "Model Lodging Houses for Women," November 1898, LCC/CL/PH/01/269, LCC Collection, London Metropolitan Archives (LMA); London County Council, *Minutes*, January 1901–December 1902, Cases 66–77, Loose Documents, LMA.

12. "Report of the Public Health Committee," in London County Council, *Minutes*, February 9, 1904.

13. "The London County Council," *The Times*, October 16, 1901, p. 8. For additional information on willingness of council to spend money on other types of housing, see "The London County Council," *The Times*, December 3, 1902, p. 8.

14. London County Council, *Minutes of Proceedings*, December 2, 1902, document 21, p. 1820. See also London County Council, *Minutes of Proceedings*, October 28, 1902, document 34, p. 1565, and November 25, 1902, document 35, p. 1757.

15. "London County Council," *The Times*, January 27, 1909, p. 4. See also London County Council, *The Housing Question in London, Being an Account of the Housing Work Done by the Metropolitan Board of Works and the LCC, between the Years of 1855 and 1900, with a Summary of the Acts of Parliament under Which They Have Worked* (London: London County Council, 1900), esp. 273.

16. Tissie Sparrow, "In a Woman's Doss-House," *New Review* 11, no. 63 (1894): 182, 183.

17. Women's Industrial Council, "Housing of Educated Working Women in London," 1900, pamphlet HD7/D489, Archives and Manuscript Collection, London School of Economics.

18. "Women's Lodging-House in Bell Street," *The Times*, February 26, 1906, p. 3. See also "The Shaftesbury Institute's Mission," *The Times*, June 29, 1907, p. 5; and "Lodging Home for Homeless Working Women," *The Times*, March 2, 1908, p. 8.

19. Shirley F. Murphy, "Desirability of the Council Establishing a Lodging House for Women," February 9, 1910, in London County Council, *Printed Reports* (London: London County Council, 1910), LMA.

20. Mrs. Hylton [Marianne] Dale, "The Necessity for Provision of Municipal Lodging Houses for Women," in London County Council, *Printed Reports*, LCC/HSG/GEN/02, Housing/General/ Miscellaneous, Housing of the Working-Classes, LMA. Married women were almost always identified by their husband's name in official documents and newspaper accounts.

21. Quoted in National Association for Women's Lodging-Homes, "Report of the Proceedings of the National Conference on Lodging-House Accommodations for Women," May 17, 1911, p. 15, Women's Library, London School of Economics.

22. Ibid., 14.

23. Ibid., 11.

24. Quoted in National Association for Women's Lodging-Homes, "Report of the Proceedings," 29. For more on Higgs, see Mary Higgs, *Glimpses into the Abyss* (London: P. S. King, 1906), esp. "Three Days in Women's Lodging Houses"; and Rosemary Chadwick, "Higgs, Mary Ann," in *Oxford Dictionary of National Biography*, vol. 27 (Oxford: Oxford University Press, 2004).

25. Quoted in National Association for Women's Lodging-Homes, "Report of the Proceedings," 31.

26. Quoted in ibid., 62–63.

27. Women's Municipal Party, "Leaflet Aims and Programme of the Women's Municipal Party," 1914, pp. 3–4, and Women's Municipal Party, *Second Annual Report* (1915), 12, Women, War and Society Collection, Imperial War Museum, London. The second report recorded the party's membership as 1,023 and contains a list of all members (see pp. 14, 33–43). This group would participate in women's attempts to provide advice on new housing after the war. See Chapter 5.

28. "Mrs. Lewis-Hill's Will," *The Times*, November 17, 1906, p. 13.

29. Ada Lewis Women's Lodging House, *Minute Book*, LMA/4318/B/02, Ada Lewis Trust Papers, LMA. See the March 3, 1913, entry for the name change decision and the January 12, 1914, entry for the NAWLH decision. That year the charge for lodging was 3s to 5s. "The First Levee," *The Times*, February 17, 1914, p. 8.

30. "Queen Alexandra and a Women's Hostel," *The Times*, November 24, 1913, p. 5.

31. Mary Higgs, "The Housing of the Woman Worker," 1915, pp. 9–10, Women's Library, London School of Economics.

32. Ibid., 1.

33. "Letter to the Editor," *The Times*, December 15, 1926, p. 12.

34. "Homeless Women in London," *The Times*, February 3, 1927, p. 9.

35. "Common Lodging Houses in London," *The Times*, February 28, 1927, p. 14.

36. "Homeless Women in London," *The Times*, April 8, 1927, p. 11.

37. "Women's Lodging-House Fund," *The Times*, May 21, 1927, p. 16.

38. Cecil Houses, "Women's Public Lodging House Fund" (undated flyer), Women's Library, London School of Economics.

39. Cecil Houses for Women, "First Annual Report," *The Times*, October 10, 1928, p. 21. See also "Cecil Houses for Women," *The Times*, January 19, 1928, p. 15; and "Assisting Homeless Women," *The Times*, April 29, 1937, p. 9.

40. Cecil Houses, "Fifth Annual Report, 1932 December," Women's Library, London School of Economics.

41. For accounts of this issue as discussed in the city council, see "The Corporation," *Freeman's Journal and Daily Commercial Advertiser*, November 29, 1883, August 11, 1885, and April 27, 1888. For details of proposed buildings, including the inclusion of a men's lodging house, see "The Corporation," *Irish Times*, September 2, 1884, p. 3.

42. "Corporation of Dublin," *Freeman's Journal and Daily Commercial Advertiser*, October 9, 1889. See also this journal's accounts under same title on March 5 and 28, 1890; July 10, 1890; and June 1, 1891.

43. "Artisans' Dwellings in Dublin," *Freeman's Journal and Daily Commercial Advertiser*, January 12, 1899.

44. For more information on lodging house facilities, see Joseph V. O'Brien, *Dear, Dirty Dublin: A City in Distress, 1899–1916* (Berkeley: University of California Press, 1982), 169–171; for more details on financial impediments and housing, see chap. 5.

45. "National Labourers' Dwellings and Sanitary Association," *Freeman's Journal and Daily Commercial Advertiser*, December 31, 1889.

46. These asylums were not the infamous Magdalen Laundry Asylums, whose purpose was to reform "fallen women."

47. Maria Luddy, *Women and Philanthropy in Nineteenth Century Ireland* (Cambridge: Cambridge University Press, 1995), 44–45. The letter was also published in the *Freeman's Journal*, March 12, 1881.

48. "Alexandra College Guild: Women and Universities," *Irish Times*, May 6, 1911, p. 4.

49. "A Working Girls' Hostel," *Irish Times*, December 16, 1912, p. 6; "Alexandra Working Girls Hostel: The Need of Help," *Irish Times*, February 21, 1913, p. 8; "Working Girls' Hostel," *Irish Times*, March 7, 1913, p. 5. "Hostels for Girls," *Irish Times*, November 17, 1915, p. 7, gives a list of other women's accommodations that were all sectarian.

50. "Alexandra College Guild: Working Girls' Hostel," *Irish Times*, November 16, 1915, p. 4.

51. For additional details on the hostel, see Eileen Reilly, "Women and Voluntary War Work," in *Ireland and the Great War: A War to Unite Us All?* ed. Adrian Gregory and Senia Pašeta (Manchester, UK: University of Manchester Press, 2002), 59, 61, 71.

52. Lawrence Solomon, *Toronto Sprawls: A History* (Toronto: University of Toronto Press, 2007), 20.

53. For reports on the hostel, see Toronto Local Council of Women, *11th Annual Report*, 1905, *12th Annual Report*, 1906, *and 13th Annual Report*, 1907, Gerritsen Collection of Aletta Jacobs (GCAJ), available at http://www.proquest.com/products-services/gerritsen.html.

54. Toronto Local Council of Women, *12th Annual Report*, 36.

55. Toronto Local Council of Women, "Minutes of Meetings of the Executive Committee," November 10, 1909, and April 19 and May 10, 1911, Box 805-MU6362, Toronto Local Council of Women Fonds, Archives of Ontario; Toronto Local Council of Women, *19th Annual Report*, 1912, GCAJ. In this last report, the TLCW cited a building with such amenities recently erected in Rome, Italy, demonstrating that these women knew what was happening in cities outside the Anglo-Atlantic world.

56. Toronto Local Council of Women, *19th Annual Report*.

57. "Will City Locate Lodging House on Main Thoroughfare," *Toronto Star*, November 7, 1912, p. 12; "Residents Object to Lodging House," *Toronto Star*, November 7, 1912, p. 4.

58. "City Lodging Houses Badly Overcrowded," *Toronto Star*, August 13, 1913, p. 3.

59. "Dr. Hastings Talks of Civic Lodgings," *Toronto Star*, August 14, 1913, p. 2.

60. "Would License All Lodging Houses," *Toronto Star*, January 16, 1913, p. 2.

61. "Dr. Hastings Talks of Civic Lodgings," 2.

62. "General Hospital as Lodging House," *Toronto Star*, August 14, 1913, p. 4.

63. For mention of a municipal lodging house in the 1920s with lodgers put to work, see Greg Marquis, "The Police as a Social Service in Early Twentieth Century Toronto," *Social History* 25, no. 50 (1992): 344. When a group of unemployed men had asked the city to build such lodging houses, the mayor replied that the House of Industry "serves the purpose of a lodging house." "To Get Work for Idle Men," *Toronto Star*, January 14, 1909, p. 3.

64. *Report of the Social Survey Commission, Presented to the City Council, October 4th, 1915* (Toronto: Carswell, 1915), 41.

65. Toronto Local Council of Women, *20th Annual Report*, 1913, GCAJ; "Work of the Hostel," *Toronto Star*, January 24, 1913, p. 8. The hostel was still open in the mid-1920s, but the TLCW had transferred the property to the Council of Girls' Friendly Societies. "Property Transfers," *Toronto Star*, November 2, 1920, p. 10.

66. Toronto Local Council of Women, "President's Report," in *22nd Annual Report*, 1915, GCAJ.

67. "Georgina House," *Toronto Star*, April 25, 1911, p. 10.

68. "Lucky Are Girls Who Reside in Georgina House," *Toronto Star*, May 16, 1914, p. 10.

69. "Refused Applicants at Georgina House," *Toronto Star*, February 27, 1922, p. 14. See also the small archival collection on Georgina House, Fonds 1009, Toronto City Archives.

70. "Home for Unemployed Women," *Toronto Star*, January 18, 1915, p. 8.

71. For a report of its receipt of $200 from the Georgina House Association, see "Georgina House Had Most Successful Year," *Toronto Star*, February 28, 1922, p. 14; for a report of a donation of the proceeds of a dance held by the Toronto Suffrage Association, see "Suffrage Association," *Toronto Star*, December 5, 1914, p. 12.

72. "House Club for Girls Now a Reality," *Toronto Star*, January 30, 1917, p. 2. In 1910 the Canadian Manufacturers Toronto Branch had proposed to build a home for working girls along similar lines, with a potential for a 4 percent return to investors. See "Lodging Houses Are Criticized," *Toronto Star*, April 19, 1910, p. 1.

73. "Girls' Friend and Guide Is in Charge of New Club," *Toronto Star*, February 3, 1917, p. 8.

74. "Hotel for Working Men," *Chicago Tribune*, July 14, 1891, p. 7.

75. "Opening of the Friendship Hotel," *Chicago Tribune*, October 1, 1891, p. 9.

76. "Lodgers at a Feast," *Chicago Tribune*, December 1, 1893, p. 11. For a more extensive description of the hotel, see "Dollars and Cents," *Chicago Tribune*, December 4, 1892, p. 33. The proprietors, W. J. Foy and Albert Lamorris (his name is variously spelled Lamaris, Lammaris, or Lammarris), owned three additional such model lodging houses.

77. See Joanne Meyerowitz, *Women Adrift: Independent Wage Earners in Chicago, 1880–1930* (Chicago: University of Chicago, Press, 1988), 47, 79–84, for her discussion of ethnic and religious houses and boardinghouses, such as the Norwegian-Danish Young Women's Christian Home Society, the Catholic Guardian Angel Day Nursery and Home for Girls (Polish) in the stockyards neighborhood, and the Jewish Josephine, Ruth, and Miriam Clubs.

78. Lucy Flower, "For Working Women," *Chicago Daily Inter-Ocean*, July 24, 1887, p. 7. Noted female activists Sarah Hackett Stevenson and Julia Holmes Smith supported the home. See also "Home for Self-Supporting Women," *Chicago Tribune*, May 11, 1887, p. 10; "Home for Self-Supporting Women," *Chicago Tribune*, May 26, 1887, p. 11; "Home for Self-Supporting Girls," *Chicago Tribune*, July 2, 1887, p. 9.

79. "Formal Opening of the Home," *Chicago Tribune*, June 5, 1890, p. 3.

80. "In a Pleasant Home," *Chicago Tribune*, July 17, 1892, p. 34; "Safe Harbor for Working Women," *Chicago Tribune*, February 22, 1894, p. 8.

81. "Woman Aids Her Sex: Model Lodging-House," *Chicago Tribune*, December 16, 1894, p. 10. "New Corporations," *Chicago Tribune*, April 12, 1895, p. 8, reported that Stevenson, Jane Addams, Julia B. Shattock, Ida E. Keen, and others had incorporated the lodging house. The lodging house subsequently moved to 253 Ewing Street, then to Eldredge Court, and finally to 2412 Prairie Avenue. The house no longer exists, as the entire near south side area of the city has been redeveloped. See also "Women Are the Lodgers," *Chicago Tribune*, April 4, 1896, p. 16.

82. "Anniversary of Welfare Home Will Be Feted," *Chicago Tribune*, November 7, 1937, p. F3.

83. Henriette Greenebaum Frank and Amalie Hofer Jerome, *The Annals of the Chicago Woman's Club* (Chicago: Chicago Woman's Club, 1916), 169. The CWC also gave $100 to the Phyllis Wheatley Home for African American women. See ibid., 370–378, for the club's financial accounting across these years. For women's clubs that were supporting the lodging house, see "Open the New Women's Home," *Chicago Tribune*, May 20, 1899, p. 9.

84. "City Shelter for Poor," *Chicago Tribune*, January 27, 1900, p. 8.

85. "Municipal Lodging House," *Chicago Tribune*, November 24, 1900, p. 12. See also "A Municipal Lodging-House," *Chicago Tribune*, December 19, 1901; and "Lodging-House Guests Rest while City Needs Men to Shovel Snow," *Chicago Tribune*, February 10, 1901, p. 8.

86. "Paying for Lodging," *Chicago Tribune*, December 25, 1901, 12. See also "City Opens Its Lodging House," *Chicago Tribune*, December 22, 1901, 8; "Four Score in Free Beds," *Chicago Tribune*, December 23, 1901, p. 3; and "Must Work for Free Bed," *Chicago Tribune*, December 24, 1901, p. 6. From its December opening, the lodging house had accommodated 6,625 lodgers who had contributed 1,869 hours of work on the city streets. See *Journal of the Proceedings of the City Council of Chicago*, April 7, 1902, p. 32.

87. "The Uses of the Lodging House," *Chicago Tribune*, May 11, 1902, p. 18.

88. "Homeless Flock to New Shelter," *Chicago Tribune*, January 9, 1908, p. 5; "Approves Relief for Unemployed," *Chicago Tribune*, February 2, 1908, p. 8; "Demands Growing Heavier at Tribune Lodging House," *Chicago Tribune*, March 1, 1908, p. 7; "Shut Tribune Lodging House," *Chicago Tribune*, March 29, 1908, p. 6. The men of the City Club of Chicago held almost annual discussions of this issue, but always in terms of unemployment rather than about a municipal responsibility to provide housing. See, for example, City Club of Chicago, "Outline of the Municipal Lodging House System," *Bulletin*, February 5, 1908, pp. 366–368, and "The Homeless Unemployed," *Bulletin*, February 6, 1909, pp. 271–278, for a lengthy presentation by James Mullenbach, superintendent of the Municipal Lodging House.

89. "No Place for Her to Rest Her Weary Head," *Chicago Tribune*, November 22, 1902, p. 37.

90. "How Women of Chicago Protect Girl Strangers," *Chicago Tribune*, October 14, 1906, p. F4.

91. "Plan New Home for Girls to Replace Old Building," *Chicago Tribune*, November 1, 1908, p. A3; "Ideal Hotel Home for Chicago Girl Workers," *Chicago Tribune*, October 24, 1909, p. 15.

92. "Plead in Vain for Increase in Pay," *Chicago Tribune*, December 29, 1909, p. 3. See also "Army of Women Seeks Lodgings," *Chicago Tribune*, November 9, 1909, p. 5. For a report of the League of Cook County Clubs support for this idea, see "Booms City Lodging House," *Chicago Tribune*, November 28,1909, p. A7. For the CWC's support, see Chicago Woman's Club, *Annals*, 263. See also Woman's City Club of Chicago, *Its Book* (Chicago: Woman's City Club of Chicago, 1915), 76, for the club's promotion of this issue in 1911–1912. For confirmation of this appropriation, see *Journal of the Proceedings of the City Council of Chicago*, February 19, 1908, p. 3960. The city council had appropriated relatively comparable amounts each previous year for the men's lodging house, as recorded in the annual *Journal*. See also "Lodging House Stays Open," *Chicago Tribune*, March 26, 1911, p. 3.

93. Quoted in "Army of Women Seeks Lodgings," 5.

94. "Lodging House for Women Crying Need of Chicago," *Chicago Tribune*, January 30, 1910, p. A5.

95. "Model Lodging House for the Needy Woman," *Chicago Tribune*, September 18, 1910, p. 13. See also "City to Give Women Lodgings," *Chicago Tribune*, April 25, 1910, p. 2.

96. See Anne Meis Knupfer, *Toward a Tenderer Humanity and a Nobler Womanhood: African American Women's Clubs in Turn-of-the-Century Chicago* (New York: New York University Press, 1996), 81–84.

97. "Other Cities' Idle Flock to Chicago," *Chicago Tribune*, January 10, 1914, p. 13; "Warning—Keep Out," *Chicago Tribune*, November 21, 1914, p. 5.

98. "Lodging Houses Report Habitués Eager for Work," *Chicago Tribune*, January 7, 1918, p. 3.

99. "The Friend of the People," *Chicago Tribune*, December 1, 1915, p. 8.

100. "Women Ask City Lodging House," *Chicago Tribune*, July 19, 1913, p. 3.

101. "News of the Women's Clubs," *Chicago Tribune*, October 25, 1914, p. F3.

102. "News of the Chicago Women's Clubs," *Chicago Tribune*, May 13, 1917; "News of the Chicago Women's Clubs," *Chicago Tribune*, November 16, 1919, p. D3; "Lodging House for Destitute Women Urged," *Chicago Tribune*, May 13, 1922, p. 15; "Stevenson Club to Hold Benefit," *Chicago Tribune*, February 19, 1933, p. E3; "Group to Meet in Memory of Dr. Stevenson," *Chicago Tribune*, January 7, 1934, p. E6.

103. Jeanne Catherine Lawrence, "Chicago's Eleanor Clubs: Housing Working Women in the Early Twentieth Century," in *People, Power, Places: Perspectives in Vernacular Architecture*, ed. Sally McMurry and Annemarie Adams (Knoxville: University of Tennessee Press, 2000), 220–222.

104. Mary Jo Deegan, *Jane Addams and the Men of the Chicago School, 1892-1918* (New Brunswick, NJ: Transactions, 1988), 49.

105. See various descriptions and coverage in "Dawes Hotel to Open," *Chicago Tribune*, January 1, 1914, p. 10; "Homeless Fill Rufus F. Dawes Memorial Hotel," *Chicago Tribune*, January 2, 1914, p. 13; "Dawes Hotel Fills Up Early," *Chicago Tribune*, January 3, 1914, p. 13; "Give 4,100 Beds to Jobless Men, *Chicago Tribune*, December 16, 1914, p. 3; "Down and Outs Eat Big Dinners," *Chicago Tribune*, December 26, 1914, p. 3; "Purposes of Hotel," *Chicago Tribune*, January 7, 1915, p. 8; "What the Rufus F. Dawes Hotel Did," *Chicago Tribune*, January 7, 1916, p. 17.

106. "Purposes of Hotel," *Chicago Tribune*, February 17, 1917, p. 8.

107. *Chicago Tribune*, January 7, 1915.

108. *Journal of the Proceedings of the City Council of Chicago*, June 3, 1918, pp. 330–331, and June 10, 1918, pp. 366–367.

109. "The Municipal Lodging House," *Chicago Tribune*, January 11, 1922, p. 8 (it is unclear from the paper's article whether these are Mulcahy's words or those of the *Tribune* reporter).

110. "Aldermen Order Inquiry on City Lodging House," *Chicago Tribune*, December 17, 1921, p. 10;"Complete Plans for Opening the Municipal Lodging House," *Chicago Tribune*, February 3, 1922, p. 11; "Council to Act on Sending Idle Workmen Home," *Chicago Tribune*, March 11, 1922, p. 5.

111. "City Club Asks Mayor to Form Jobs Bureau," *Chicago Tribune*, March 26, 1921, p. 2; City Club of Chicago, "Mayor Asked to Relieve Situation," *Bulletin*, April 11, 1921, p. 62.

112. "Lodging House for Destitute Women Urged," *Chicago Tribune*, May 13, 1922, p. 15.

CHAPTER 4

1. Richard Dennis, *Cities in Modernity: Representations and Productions of Metropolitan Space, 1840–1930* (Cambridge: Cambridge University Press, 2008), 35.

2. For an argument about the unity of the modern self (male) and the modern environment, see Marshall Berman, *All That Is Solid Melts into the Air: the Experience of Modernity* (London: Verso Books, 1983), esp. 74, 101, and 132.

3. Despina Stratigakos, *A Women's Berlin: Building the Modern City* (Minneapolis: University of Minnesota Press, 2008), 1.

4. David Harvey, *Paris, Capital of Modernity* (New York: Routledge, 2003), 183.

5. See Stratigakos, *A Women's Berlin*, 6. Emile Zola's 1883 novel *Au Bonheur des Dames* introduced this idea into popular consciousness.

6. Erika Rappaport, *Shopping for Pleasure: Women in the Making of London's West End* (Princeton, NJ: Princeton University Press, 2000), 52.

7. Elizabeth Wilson, *The Sphinx in the City: Urban Life, the Control of Disorder and Women* (Berkeley: University of California Press, 1992), 87, 157, 8. See also Janet Wolff, "The Invisible *Flâneuse*: Women and the Literature of Modernity," *Theory, Culture and Society* 2, no. 3 (1985): 37–48. See Berman, *All That Is Solid*, for his analysis of the new "Faustian" man bringing authority, adventure, and renewal to the city.

8. Robert E. Lee, "The 'Modern City'—Its Hopes and Aspirations and Claims for Support," *Modern City*, February 1917: 5.

9. Dennis, *Cities in Modernity*, 29.

10. For more on how male promoters of new urban environments consistently marginalized women's ideas about and participation in movements to reform the built environment while simultaneously praising women for their feminine qualities, see Meryl Aldridge, "Garden Cities: The Disappearing 'Woman Question,'" in *Urban Space and Identity in the European City, 1890s to 1930s*, ed. S. Zimmermann (Budapest: Central European University, 1995), 13–23; and Helen Meller, "Gender, Citizenship and the Making of the Modern Environment," in *Women and the Making of Built Space in England, 1870–1950*, ed. Elizabeth Darling and Lesley Whitworth (Aldershot, UK: Ashgate, 2007), 21–26. According to Meller, Geddes believed in the "Man/Woman dichotomy at the cutting edge of what was bringing about the future." Women's role in this dichotomy was to support the ideas and activities of men. Meller, "Gender, Citizenship," 24. See also Doreen Massey, *Space, Place, and Gender* (Minneapolis: University of Minnesota Press, 1994). I use *embound* in this book to mean to "encircle, enclose, or surround."

11. Theodore Dreiser, *Sister Carrie* (New York: Doubleday, Page, 1900), 557.

12. Wilson, *Sphinx in the City*, 157; see also chaps. 4 and 6 for further analysis of male fears of the city.

13. Stratigakos, *A Women's Berlin*, 6–7.

14. Seth Koven, *Slumming: Sexual and Social Politics in Victorian London* (Princeton, NJ: Princeton University Press, 2006), 229.

15. See Toynbee Hall, *Sixth Annual Report of the Universities' Settlement in East London* (London: Toynbee Hall, 1890); and Toynbee Hall, *Twenty-Third Annual Report of the Universities' Settlement in East London* (London: Toynbee Hall, 1907).

16. Werner Picht, *Toynbee Hall and the English Settlement Movement* (London: G. Bell, 1914), 72.

17. Ibid., 237.

18. See ibid., 31-32, for a brief list of positions held by some of these men demonstrating the relationship between Toynbee Hall and government positions. See also Philip Lyttleton Gell, "The Work of Toynbee Hall," in *Johns Hopkins University Studies in Historical and Political Science*, ed. Herbert B. Adams, vol. 7, *Social Science, Municipal and Federal Government* (Baltimore: Johns Hopkins University Press, 1889), 57-64.

19. Will Reason, ed., *University and Social Settlements* (London: Methuen, 1898), 25.

20. Ibid., 183.

21. Ibid., 92.

22. Ibid., 95, 96.

23. Sara Z. Burke, *Seeking the Highest Good: Social Service and Gender at the University of Toronto, 1888-1937* (Toronto: University of Toronto Press, 1996), 45-47, 76.

24. For an overview of the settlement houses in the city and religious affiliations, see Cathy James, "Reforming Reform: Toronto's Settlement House Movement, 1900-1920," *Canadian Historical Review* 82, no. 1 (2001): 55-90.

25. "Headworkers' Report," December 17, 1911-January 18, 1912, in *Minutes*, April 1911-September 1913, File 1, Box 2-149133, Central Neighbourhood House Fonds 1005, Toronto City Archives.

26. "Minutes of the Organizing Committee," August 31, 1911, in *Record Book #2*, 1911-September 1912, File 59, Box 4-149150, Central Neighbourhood House Fonds 1005, Toronto City Archives. Toronto Local Council of Women, *Monthly Meeting Minutes*, March 8, 1911, and May 10, 1911, Box 805-MU6362, Toronto Local Council of Women Fonds, Archives of Ontario.

27. Cudmore subsequently headed the Dominion Bureau of Statistics. See Burke, *Seeking the Highest Good*, 45-47, 50-51, 59-60.

28. See Ellen Fitzpatrick, *Endless Crusade: Women Social Scientists and Progressive Reform* (New York: Oxford University Press, 1990), 196-200; and Robin F. Bachin, *Building the South Side: Urban Space and Civic Culture in Chicago, 1890-1919* (Chicago: University of Chicago Press, 2004), 108-109, 123-124. See also Helen Jarvis with Paula Kantor and Jonathan Cloke, *Cities and Gender: Critical Introductions to Urbanism and the City* (London: Routledge, 2009), 56-57.

29. Jane Addams, "The Objective Value of a Social Settlement," in *Philanthropy and Social Progress: Seven Essays* (New York: Crowell, 1893), 49-52.

30. Jane Addams, "The Subjective Necessity for Social Settlements," in *Philanthropy and Social Progress*, 1.

31. Jane Addams, *Democracy and Social Ethics*, ed. Charlene Haddock Seigfried (Urbana: University of Illinois Press, 2002), 98-99.

32. C. M. Lloyd, "Labour Politics: A Socialist Outlook," in Toynbee Hall, *Annual Report* (1906-1907), 30-31.

33. Mary McDowell, "The University of Chicago Settlement," 1901, pp. 12-13, 19-20, Mary McDowell Collection, Chicago History Museum.

34. Graham Taylor, "A Social Center for Civic Co-operation: Chicago Commons," *The Commons*, December 1904, p. 4; see also pp. 38-40. Taylor was a minister who had also founded the School of Civics and Philanthropy but later broke with the women of the school over its direction.

35. Jane Addams, "Preferatory Note," in *Hull-House Maps and Papers*, by Residents of Hull-House (New York: Crowell, 1895), vii-viii.

36. Rima Lunin Schultz, "Introduction," in *Hull-House Maps and Papers* (Urbana: University of Illinois Press, 2007), 13.

37. Joseph Schumpeter, *Capitalism, Socialism, and Democracy* (New York: Harper, 1942), 83.

38. Max Page, *The Creative Destruction of Manhattan, 1900-1940* (Chicago: University of Chicago Press, 1990), 3.

39. Dennis, *Cities in Modernity*, 113.

40. Richard Dennis, "Modern London," in *The Cambridge Urban History of Britain*, ed. Martin Daunton (Cambridge: Cambridge University Press, 2000), 3:112-113 (emphasis in original).

41. Page, *Creative Destruction*, 3.

42. Ruth Livesey, "Women Rent Collectors and the Rewriting of Space, Class and Gender in East London, 1870-1900," in Darling and Whitworth, *Women and the Making of Built Space in England*, 93.

43. Page, *Creative Destruction*, 3.

44. For representative examples from each city, see Robin L. Einhorn, *Property Rules: Political Economy in Chicago, 1833-1872* (Chicago: University of Chicago Press, 1991); Ruth McManus, *Dublin, 1910-1940: Shaping the City and Suburbs* (Dublin: Four Courts Press, 2002); John Davis, *Reforming London: The London Government Problem, 1855-1900* (London: Oxford University Press, 1988); and Peter Goheen, *Victorian Toronto, 1850-1900: Pattern and Process of Growth* (Chicago: University of Chicago Geography Department, 1970).

45. For representative examples from each city, see Georg Leidenberger, *Chicago's Progressive Alliance: Labor and the Bid for Public Streetcars* (DeKalb: Northern Illinois University Press, 2006); Ruth McManus, "Blue Collars, 'Red Forts,' and Green Fields: Working-Class Housing in Ireland in the Twentieth Century," *International Labor and Working-Class History* 64, no. 1 (2003): 38-54; Martin Daunton, *House and Home in the Victorian City: Working-Class Housing, 1850-1914* (London: Edward Arnold, 1983); and Raphaël Fischler, "Development Controls in Toronto in the Nineteenth Century," *Urban History Review* 36, no. 1 (2007): 16-31. See also Maureen A. Flanagan, *Charter Reform in Chicago* (Carbondale: Southern Illinois University Press, 1987), which uses sources from women to see how they engaged with municipal charter reform.

46. Martin J. Daunton, "American Cities," in *Housing the Workers, 1850-1914*, 2nd ed., ed. Martin J. Daunton (Leicester, UK: University of Leicester Press, 1990), 275.

47. Thomas Blashill, "Report on Housing in the Suburbs," May 1898, LCC/HSG/GEN/02, London County Council Collection, London Metropolitan Archives (LMA). See also Thomas Blashill, "Unhealthy Areas and Municipal Rehousing," 1899, pamphlet HD7/349, London School of Economics (LSE).

48. Peabody Trustees, "Minutes," March 18, 1882, p. 202, Sutton Trust Collection, LMA; Blashill, "Report on Housing in the Suburbs."

49. For examples, see Jon Teaford, *The Unheralded Triumph: City Government in America, 1780-1900* (Baltimore: Johns Hopkins University Press, 1984); Martin Melosi, *The Sanitary City: Urban Infrastructure in America from Colonial Times to the Present* (Baltimore: Johns Hopkins University Press, 2000); James Winter, *London's Teeming Streets, 1830-1914* (Abington, UK: Routledge, 1993); David Dickson, *Dublin: The Making of a Capital City* (Cambridge, MA: Harvard University Press, 2014); and Lawrence Solomon, *Toronto Sprawls: A History* (Toronto: University of Toronto Press, 2007).

50. Anthony Wohl, *The Eternal Slum: Housing and Social Policy in Victorian London*, 2nd ed. (London: Transaction, 2002), 194-195.

51. Winter, *London's Teeming Streets*, 160-161.

52. Toronto City Council, *Minutes* (Toronto: Toronto City Council, 1908), vol. 2, app. C, p. 12, Toronto City Archives.

53. Unidentified newspaper clippings, December 20, 1907, and December [?], 1907, Box F805-MU6362, Toronto Local Council of Women Fonds, Archives of Ontario.

54. "Unsafe Buildings," *Chicago Daily Inter-Ocean*, February 19, 1888, p. 5.

55. "Building and Loan," *Chicago Daily Inter-Ocean*, April 16, 1893, p. 21.

56. Margaret Garb, *City of American Dreams: A History of Home Ownership and Housing Reform in Chicago, 1871-1919* (Chicago: University of Chicago Press, 2005), chap. 2, esp. 50-59.

57. Quoted in Perry Duis, *Chicago: Coping with Everyday Life, 1837-1920* (Urbana: University of Illinois Press, 1998), 84-85.

58. For an example, see Toronto Harbour Commissioners, "Toronto: A City of Opportunities," June 1912, Digital Collection, Fisher Library, University of Toronto.

59. Solomon, *Toronto Sprawls*, 28. See also Richard Harris, *Unplanned Suburbs: Toronto's American Tragedy, 1900-1950* (Baltimore: Johns Hopkins University Press, 1999), esp. chap. 4.

60. Toronto Civic Guild, *Monthly Bulletin*, January 1913, p. 9; Richard Dennis, "Interpreting the Apartment House: Modernity and Metropolitism in Toronto, 1900–1930," *Journal of Historical Geography* 20, no. 3 (1994): 306.

61. Henry R. Aldridge, "House Building and Management," August 1907, pamphlet HD7/283, LSE.

62. P. C. Cowan, "The Difficulties of the Housing Problem and Some Attempts to Solve It," presidential address to the Engineering and Scientific Association of Ireland, January 31, 1916, pp. 15–16, National Library of Ireland, Dublin, Ireland.

63. Ebenezer Howard, "Garden Cities: Manufactures and Labour," paper presented at Garden City Conference, Bourneville, France, September 20–21, 1901, p. 54, LSE.

64. Anna E. Nicholes, "How Women Can Help in the Administration of a City," in *The Woman's Citizen Library* (Chicago: Civics Society, 1913), 9:2150–2151. See also Sandra Haar, "The Hull House Settlement and the Study of the City," in *Embodied Utopias: Gender, Social Change, and the Modern Metropolis*, ed. Amy Bingaman, Lise Sanders, and Rebecca Zorach (New York: Routledge, 2002), 111.

65. Toronto Local Council of Women, "Historical Sketch," p. 1, Toronto Local Council of Women Fonds, Archives of Ontario.

66. See *Sláinte*, March 1909, p. 42, National Library of Ireland; and Women's National Health Association, "Report, Balance Sheet, Donations, and Subscriptions of the WHNA of Ireland," 1909, pp. 2–6, Pamphlets-Medicine Collection, National Library of Ireland. For brief mentions of nurses, playgrounds, and a restaurant, see "Women's National Health Association: Infant Mortality and Babies' Clubs," *Irish Times*, February 10, 1910, p. 10; "Women's National Health Association: Babies Clubs," *Irish Times*, June 10, 1911, p. 4; and "Women's National Health Association," *Irish Times*, April 16, 1913, p. 7.

67. Haar, "Hull House Settlement," 113–114.

68. Massey, *Space, Place, and Gender*, 2.

69. Anonymous, "The Glorified Spinster," *Macmillan's Magazine* 58 (1888): 372.

70. The 1878 Public Health (Ireland) Act gave the corporation power to acquire government loans at 3½ percent to "supply homes for the working classes." Jacinta Prunty, *Dublin Slums, 1800–1925: A Study in Urban Geography* (Dublin: Irish Academic Press, 1998), 143.

71. Elizabeth Wilson, "Culture and Gender Concerns in Spatial Development," in *Women in the City* (Paris: Organisation for Economic Co-operation and Development, 1994), 41; Clara H. Greed, *Women and Planning: Creating Gendered Realities* (London: Routledge, 1994), 89. See also Helen Meller, "Women and Citizenship: Gender and the Built Environment in British Cities, 1870–1939," in *Cities of Ideas: Civil Society and Urban Governance in Britain, 1800–2000*, ed. Robert Colls and Richard Rodger (Aldershot, UK: Ashgate, 2004), esp. 232–234; Meller, "Gender, Citizenship," esp. 16–17, 20; and Kristine B. Miranne and Alma H. Young, eds., *Gendering the City: Women, Boundaries, and Visions of Urban Life* (Lanham, MD: Rowman and Littlefield, 2000).

72. See descriptions in Sarah Wise, *The Blackest Streets: The Life and Death of a Victorian Slum* (London: Random House, 2008); and R. Vladimir Steffel, "The Boundary Street Estate: An Example of Urban Redevelopment by the London County Council, 1889–1914," *Town Planning Review* 47, no. 2 (1976): 161–173.

73. Steffel, "Boundary Street Estate," 165. See also Owen Fleming, "Working Class Dwellings—the Rebuilding of the Boundary Street Estate," April 2, 1900, LCC/HSG/GEN/02/016, London County Council Collection, LMA.

74. The Peabody Trust still exists and recently constructed a new building in the Darbishire Buildings (Whitechapel, 1870) on the site of a building in the complex destroyed during World War II.

75. Wise, *Blackest Streets*, 255–256.

76. Ibid., 259.

77. Steffel, "Boundary Street Estate," 168, table I; "The Housing Question in London," 1891, LCC/HSG/GEN/02, London County Council Collection, LMA; "Housing of the Working Classes: Report of the Manager," 1903, Housing Manager's Annual Reports, 1902–1909, LCC/HSG/GEN/02, London County Council Collection, LMA. Charles Booth's map of poverty drawn in 1898–1899

showed the new layout and categorized the new residents as "fairly comfortable." Charles Booth, *Life and Labour of the People of London* (London: Macmillan, 1892).

78. "Statistical Returns," 1899, LCC/SG/GEN/02, Section XI, London County Council Collection, LMA.

79. Andrew Young and Edgar Harper, "Displacements by Private Enterprise," March 15, 1905, LCC/HSG/GEN/02, London County Council Collection, LMA.

80. London County Council, "Insanitary Areas before and after Clearance," March 1905, London County Council Collection, LMA.

81. Murray Fraser, *John Bull's Other Homes: State Housing and British Policy in Ireland, 1883–1922* (Liverpool: Liverpool University Press, 1996), 76.

82. Mary E. Daly, "Housing Conditions and the Genesis of Housing Reform in Dublin, 1880–1920," in *The Emergence of Irish Planning, 1880–1920*, ed. Michael Bannon (Dublin: Turoe Press, 1985), 96.

83. "Report of Artisans' Dwellings Committee," *Reports and Printed Documents of the Corporation of Dublin* 1, no. 56 (1897): 572–574; "Report of the Artisans' Dwellings Committee," *Reports and Printed Documents of the Corporation of Dublin* 2, no. 103 (1897): 941–942.

84. Jacinta Prunty, "Improving the Urban Environment: Public Health and Housing in Nineteenth-Century Dublin," in *Dublin through Space and Time*, ed. Joseph Brady and Anngret Simms (Dublin: Four Courts Press, 2001), 197. See the same conclusion in Daly, "Housing Conditions."

85. *Minutes of the Municipal Council of the City of Dublin*, no. 426 (1898): 368–369.

86. "Report of Special Committee," *Reports and Printed Documents of the Corporation of Dublin* 3, no. 148 (1900): 301–302.

87. For an account of a meeting adjudicating property claims, see "Bull Alley Improvement Scheme," *Freeman's Journal and Daily Commercial Advertiser*, June 19, 1900, p. 3.

88. F.H.A. Aalen, *The Iveagh Trust: The First Hundred Years, 1890–1990* (Dublin: Iveagh Trust, 1990), 16.

89. Ibid., 68.

90. Kevin C. Kearns, *Dublin Tenement Life: An Oral History* (Dublin: M. H. Gill, 2006), 34. See also Victoria Kelley, "The Streets for the People: London's Street Markets, 1850–1939," *Urban History* 43, no. 3 (2016): 410.

91. Aalen, *Iveagh Trust*, 55.

92. Ibid., 69.

93. See Daunton, *House and Home in the Victorian City*, 12–13, 15; and Prunty, *Dublin Slums*, 142.

94. "Report of Special Committee," *Reports and Printed Documents of the Corporation of Dublin* 3, no. 148 (1900): 301–302.

95. For a letter of complaint to the corporation about empty stalls because of high rents, see *Reports and Printed Documents of the Corporation of Dublin* 3, no. 147 (1909): 1–4.

96. *Minutes of the Municipal Council of the City of Dublin*, no. 398 (1900): 300–301; *Minutes of the Municipal Council of the City of Dublin*, no. 589 (1900): 492–494; *Minutes of the Municipal Council of the City of Dublin*, no. 590 (1900): 492–494; "Report of Artisans' Dwellings Committee," *Reports and Printed Documents of the Corporation of Dublin* 3, no. 129 (1898): 388–389.

97. Citizens' Association of Chicago, "Report of the Committee on Tenement Houses," 1884, pp. 18–19, Citizens' Association of Chicago Manuscript Collection, Chicago History Museum.

98. Ibid., 19–20; Garb, *City of American Dreams*, 139.

99. William T. Stead, *If Christ Came to Chicago* (Chicago: Laird and Lee, 1894).

100. Letter from T. W. Harvey to William Stead, quoted in Thekla Ellen Joiner, *Sin in the City: Chicago and Revivalism, 1880–1920* (Columbia: University of Missouri Press, 2007), 114. Harvey had been a leading figure in the Chicago Relief and Aid Society's control of rebuilding following the 1871 fire.

101. A copy of the handbill was printed in William T. Stead, *If Christ*, 453. Charitable institutions distributed tickets that were necessary for admission into their facilities.

102. For discussions of influential property owners resisting housing inspection, see Maureen A. Flanagan, *Seeing with Their Hearts: Chicago Women and the Vision of the Good City, 1871–1933*

(Princeton, NJ: Princeton University Press, 2002), 91–92; and Harold L. Platt, "Jane Addams and the Ward Boss Revisited: Class, Politics, and Public Health in Chicago, 1890–1930," *Environmental History* 5, no. 2 (2000): 194–222, 209.

103. Robert Hunter, *Tenement Conditions in Chicago* (Chicago: City Homes Association, 1901), 177–178.

104. Solomon, *Toronto Sprawls*, 19.

105. Toronto City Council, *Minutes* (Toronto: Toronto City Council, 1905), vol. 2, app. C, p. 2, Toronto City Archives.

106. Sean Purdy, "'This Is Not a Company; It Is a Cause': Class, Gender, and the Toronto Housing Company, 1912–1920," *Urban History Review* 21, no. 2 (1993): 77. See also Sean Purdy, "Industrial Efficiency, Social Order, and Moral Purity: Housing Reform Thought in English Canada, 1900–1950," *Urban History Review* 25, no. 2 (1997): 30–40.

107. For a brief discussion of Howard's early experiences, see Robert Kargon and Arthur Molella, *Invented Edens: Techno-Cities of the Twentieth Century* (Cambridge, MA: MIT Press, 2008), 7–11.

108. Ebenezer Howard, *Garden Cities of To-Morrow* (London: Sonnenschein, 1902), 11–12. See also David Pinder, *Visions of the City: Utopianism, Power and Politics in Twentieth-Century Urbanism* (New York: Routledge, 2005), 32–35. Howard's book was originally titled *Tomorrow: A Peaceful Path to Reform*.

109. Howard, *Garden Cities of To-Morrow*.

110. Ibid., 22–23. See also Robert Fishman, *Urban Utopias in the Twentieth Century: Ebenezer Howard, Frank Lloyd Wright, and Le Corbusier* (Cambridge, MA: MIT Press, 1991), 45–47.

111. Howard, *Garden Cities of To-Morrow*, 138–139.

112. Simon Parker, *Urban Theory and the Urban Experience: Encountering the City* (London: Routledge, 2004), 6.

113. Ibid., 53.

114. Howard, *Garden Cities of To-Morrow*, 134, 136, 20.

115. Parker, *Urban Theory*, 52–53; Patrick Geddes, *John Ruskin, Economist* (Edinburgh: William Brown, 1884), 43.

116. Octavia Hill, *Homes of the London Poor* (London: Macmillan, 1875), 200. For an observation that the break came after an exchange of letters that Hill finally answered by telling Ruskin that he was incapable of managing practical work, see Jane E. Lewis, *Women and Social Action in Victorian and Edwardian London* (Stanford, CA: Stanford University Press, 1991), 27.

117. Aldridge, "Garden Cities," 15, 16. See also Howard, *Garden Cities of To-Morrow*, following the postscript, for the list of Garden Cities Association council members and vice presidents, who were overwhelmingly men.

118. Fishman, *Urban Utopias*, 43.

119. Howard, *Garden Cities of To-Morrow*, contains his famous sketches of how the city was to be laid out in this fashion. See pp. 22–23 for these and his description of the Central Park, Crystal Palace, and circular streets. Howard's sketches have been reprinted in every work about him and about the garden city idea.

120. Fishman, *Urban Utopias*, 44.

121. Nicholes, "How Women Can Help in the Administration of a City," 9:2184.

122. Helen Meller, "Urban Renewal and Citizenship: The Quality of Life in British Cities, 1890–1990," *Urban History* 22, no. 1 (1995): 65.

123. Breckinridge quoted in Flanagan, *Seeing with Their Hearts*, 93.

124. Chicago Woman's Club Civics Committee, "The Tenement Housing Conditions in the Twentieth Ward, Chicago," 1912, p. 16, available at https://archive.org/details/tenementhousing c00chic.

125. For examples, see Daphne Spain, *How Women Saved the City* (Minneapolis: University of Minnesota Press, 2001); Darling and Whitworth, *Women and the Making of Built Space in England*; Massey, *Space, Place, and Gender*; Wilson, *Sphinx in the City*; and Stratigakos, *A Women's Berlin*.

126. David Pinder, *Visions of the City*, 51–52. For a discussion of controlling urban space through the control of the public visibility of disorderly human bodies, see Margaret E. Farrar,

"Making the City Beautiful: Aesthetic Reform and the (Dis)Placement of Bodies," in Bingaman, Sanders, and Zorach, *Embodied Utopias*, 37–53.

127. C. M. Knowles, "The Housing Problem in London," 1899, p. 18, pamphlet HD7/D101, LSE.

128. Howard, "Garden Cities: Manufactures and Labour," 54.

129. "Proceedings of the Conference with the Metropolitan Borough Councils," June 28, 1901, London County Council Collection, LMA.

130. T. C. Horsfall, "The Relation of Town-Planning to the National Life," paper presented at the Conference for Town-Planning and Co-partnership in Housing, 1908, pp. 13–14, LSE.

131. P. C. Cowan, "Address to the Section of Town Planning and the Housing of the Working-Classes of the Dublin Congress," 1911, pp. 7, 9, pamphlet HD7/287, LSE. For the co-partnership movement and its links to the garden city movement, see Denis Hardy, *From Garden Cities to New Towns: Campaigning for Town and Country Planning, 1899–1946* (London: Taylor and Francis, 1991), 89–91.

132. "Report of the Conference between the Parliamentary Representatives of the County and City of Dublin, the Corporation of Dublin, and the Dublin Trades Council, on the Subject of the Housing of the Working Classes," *Reports and Printed Documents of the Corporation of Dublin* 3, no. 176 (1903): 395. See also Prunty, *Dublin Slums*, 169–170.

133. *Minutes of the Municipal Council of the City of Dublin*, no. 500 (1905): 485, no. 501 (1905), and no. 779 (1910): 515.

134. *Minutes of the Municipal Council of the City of Dublin*, no. 396 (1911): 292.

135. Cowan, "Address to the Section of Town Planning," 7.

136. W. Thompson, "The Powers of Local Authorities," in *The House Famine and How to Relieve It*, Fabian Tract 101 (London: Fabian Society, 1900), 24–25, LSE.

137. Raymond Unwin, *Cottage Plans and Common Sense*, Fabian Tract 109 (London: Fabian Society, 1902), 11, LSE.

138. Helen Meller, "Planning Theory and Women's Role in the City," *Urban History* 17, no. 1 (1990), 85.

139. See Lord Shaftesbury, "The Housing of the Poor," *The Times*, June 27, 1885, p. 10.

140. Daunton, *House and Home in the Victorian City*, 272.

141. Helen Meller, *Patrick Geddes: Social Evolutionist and City Planner* (London: Routledge, 1994), 56–57. See also Helen Meller, *Towns, Plans and Society in Modern Britain* (Cambridge: Cambridge University Press, 1997).

142. Burke, *Seeking the Highest Good*, 48–60. See also James Mavor, *My Windows on the Street of the World* (Toronto: Dent, 1923), especially the chapter "London Circles in the Eighties" and his conclusion that shelters such as those of the Salvation Army "tended to perpetuate the need for their subsidised provision," 270, which he regarded anathema to a successful political economy. In addition, see James Mavor, "The Relation of Economic Study to Public and Private Charity," *Annals of the American Academy of Political and Social Science*, July 1, 1893, pp. 34–60.

143. Patrick Geddes, "Civics as Concrete and Applied Sociology," paper presented at the Sociological Society meeting, University of London, January 23, 1905, p. 58, available at https://www.gutenberg.org/files/13205/13205-h/13205-h.htm.

144. Howard, *Garden Cities of To-Morrow*, 17.

145. See ibid., 22. For a good sketch of the master key, see Kargon and Molella, *Invented Edens*, 10.

146. Anne Anderson and Elizabeth Darling, "The Hill Sisters: Cultural Philanthropy and the Embellishment of Lives in Late-Nineteenth Century England," in Darling and Whitworth, *Women and the Making of Built Space in England*, 45. See also Octavia Hill, "The Kyrle Society," *Charity Organization Review* 18, no. 108 (1905): 314–319. For a small sample of women's focus on depicting interiors, see Rappaport, *Shopping for Pleasure*; Stratigakos, *A Women's Berlin*; Spain, *How Women Saved the City*; and Flanagan, *Seeing with Their Hearts*.

147. Chapter 5 develops this issue more fully as it shows the intersection of city planning with housing.

148. J. S. Nettlefold, *Practical Town Planning: A Land and Housing Policy* (London: St. Catherine Press, 1914), 251.

149. Henrietta Barnett, "Proposed Garden Suburb at Hampstead Heath near London," paper presented at Congrès International des Habitations à Bon Marché, Liege, Belgium, 1905, pp. 47–48.

150. Lynn F. Pearson, *The Architectural and Social History of Cooperative Living* (London: Macmillan, 1988), 102–104. Barnett was subsequently a member of the women's subcommittee of the postwar Housing Advisory Committee (HAC) that produced a report singling out the continuing lack of accommodations for single working women that the male-dominated HAC ignored; see pp. 153–155.

151. Barnett, "Proposed Garden Suburb," 49.

152. Henrietta Barnett, *The Making of the Home* (London: Cassell, 1905), 1, 4.

153. Unwin, "Cottage Plans and Common Sense," 2, 3–4.

154. Raymond Unwin, *Town Planning in Practice: An Introduction to the Art of Designing Cities and Suburbs*, 2nd ed. (London: Unwin, 1911). See drawing 7805, "Hampstead Garden Suburb London NW," April 1911, at the end of the book. For a description of current Hampstead, see Gordon Cherry, *Cities and Plans: The Shaping of Urban Britain in the Nineteenth and Twentieth Centuries* (London: Edward Arnold, 1988), 63–64; and Nikolaus Pevsner and Bridget Cherry, *Buildings of England, London* (London: Penguin, 1983), 4:139–144.

155. Raymond Unwin, *Nothing Gained by Overcrowding! How the Garden City Type of Development May Benefit Both Owner and Occupier* (London: Garden Cities and Town Planning Association, 1912), 3–5.

156. *Canadian Architect and Builder*, August 1905, p. 115.

157. "Statistical Returns," 1899–1902, Section XI, London County Council Collection, LMA. In 1902, 27,486 residents had been or were going to be displaced with the ability to rehouse 22,746. See also Young and Harper, "Displacements by Private Enterprise." Other purposes included factories and workshops, business premises, shops and offices, railways, non-working-class housing, and government buildings. Land that had contained 1,278 rooms now stood vacant.

158. Arthur Crow, "Town Planning in Relation to Old and Congested Areas with Special Reference to London," paper presented at the Royal Institute of British Architects Town Planning Conference, London, October 1910, pp. 8, 5, LMA.

159. Ibid., 6.

160. Ibid., 14, 19. See also other papers presented at the conference, published in *Transactions* (London: Royal Institute of British Architects, 1911).

161. Raymond Unwin, "The City Development Plan," in *Transactions*, 247.

162. "Report of the Committee of the Whole House," *Reports and Printed Documents of the Corporation of Dublin* 1, no. 27 (1896): 308. For the response from the Dublin United Tramways, see *Reports and Printed Documents of the Corporation of Dublin*, no. 40 (1896): 593.

163. "Report of the Conference between the Parliamentary Representatives of the County and City of Dublin," 395.

164. "Cook Street Area Improvement Scheme," *Irish Times*, June 16, 1910, p. 9.

PART II

1. Michael Batty and Stephen Marshall, "The Evolution of Cities: Geddes, Abercrombie and the New Physicalism," *Town Planning Review* 80, no. 6 (2009): 551.

2. Richard Dennis, *Cities in Modernity: Representations and Productions of Metropolitan Space, 1840–1930* (Cambridge: University of Cambridge Press, 2008), 113.

3. Max Page, *The Creative Destruction of Manhattan, 1900–1940* (Chicago: University of Chicago Press, 1999), 2.

4. Michael Batty, "The Creative Destruction of Cities," *Environment and Planning B: Planning and Design* 34, no. 1 (2007): 3.

5. Henri Lefebvre, *The Production of Space*, trans. Donald Nicholson-Smith (Oxford: Oxford University Press, 1991).

6. Page, *Creative Destruction*, 3. See also Ruth Livesey, "Women Rent Collectors and the Rewriting of Space, Class and Gender in East London, 1870–1900," in *Women and the Making of*

Built Space in England, 1870-1950, ed. Elizabeth Darling and Lesley Whitworth (Aldershot, UK: Ashgate, 2007), 93.

7. Dolores Hayden, *The Power of Place: Urban Landscapes as Public History* (Cambridge, MA: MIT Press, 1996), 15-18; Doreen Massey, *Space, Place, and Gender* (Minneapolis: University of Minnesota Press, 1994), 2; Elizabeth Wilson, *The Sphinx in the City: Urban Life, the Control of Disorder, and Women* (Berkeley: University of California Press, 1992). One can find similar arguments in the various essays in Jane Rendell, Barbara Penner, and Iain Borden, eds., *Gender Space Architecture* (New York: Routledge, 2000); Kristine B. Miranne and Alma H. Young, eds., *Gendering the City: Women, Boundaries and Visions of Urban Life* (Lanham, MD: Rowman and Littlefield, 2000); Amy Bingaman, Lise Sanders, and Rebecca Zorach, eds., *Embodied Utopias: Gender, Social Change and the Modern Metropolis* (New York: Routledge, 2002); Helen Jarvis with Paula Kantor and Jonathan Cloke, *Cities and Gender* (London: Routledge, 2009); and Despina Stratigakos, *A Women's Berlin: Building the Modern City* (Minneapolis: University of Minnesota Press, 2008).

8. Elizabeth Darling, "The All-Europe House and Four Women's Spatial Practices," in Darling and Whitworth, *Women and the Making of Built Space in England*, 123-140.

9. Livesey, "Women Rent Collectors," 89.

10. See William Whyte, "The 1910 Royal Institute of British Architects' Conference: A Focus for International Town Planning?" *Urban History* 39, no. 1 (2012): 149-165, for his analysis that despite the celebration of this gathering as internationally significant, legal, professional, training, and other differences across national contexts meant that the import of the conference was mainly for "Anglophone connections" (156).

11. Barbara Hooper, "The Poem of Male Desires: Female Bodies, Modernity, and 'Paris, Capital of the Nineteenth Century,'" in *Making the Invisible Visible: A Multicultural History of Planning*, ed. Leonie Sandercock (Berkeley: University of California Press, 1998), 229.

12. Allan G. Johnson, *The Gender Knot: Unraveling Our Patriarchal Legacy*, 3rd ed. (Philadelphia: Temple University Press, 2014), 37.

13. Helen Meller, "Planning Theory and Women's Role in the City," *Urban History* 17, no. 1 (1990): 85-86. See also Helen Meller, "Women and Citizenship: Gender and the Built Environment in British Cities, 1870-1939," in *Cities of Ideas: Civil Society and Urban Governance in Britain, 1800-2000*, ed. Robert Colls and Richard Rodger (Aldershot, UK: Ashgate, 2004), 231-257.

CHAPTER 5

1. Helen Meller, "Women and Citizenship: Gender and the Built Environment in British Cities, 1870-1939," in *Cities of Ideas: Civil Society and Urban Governance in Britain, 1800-2000*, ed. Robert Colls and Richard Rodger (Aldershot, UK: Ashgate, 2004), 247-248. English planner Thomas Sharp wrote of woman, "Aesthetically she has few or none of the makings of a citizen." Quoted in Elizabeth Wilson, *The Sphinx in the City: Urban Life, the Control of Disorder, and Women* (Berkeley: University of California Press, 1992), 106.

2. Patrick Geddes, *Cities in Evolution: An Introduction to the Town Planning Movement and to the Study of Civics* (London: Williams and Norgate, 1915), 129.

3. The commission produced an eight-volume work, held in the Guildhall Library in London. *Report of the Royal Commission on the Means of Locomotion and Transport in London* (*RRCMLTL*) (London: Wyman, 1905), vol. 1, includes the summary of the commission's work and its recommendations.

4. Ibid., 1:17, 34-39, 88-92.

5. Ibid., 1:16.

6. "Minutes of Evidence," in ibid., 2:829, para. 22506.

7. Ibid., 2:266, para. 7119, 7120, 7122; "Appendices to the Evidence," in ibid., 3:272.

8. Ibid., 2:691, para. 18999, 19000, 19001, 19103. See also Charles Booth, "Improved Means of Locomotion as a Cure for the Housing Difficulties of London," 1901, p. 7, pamphlet HD7/377, London School of Economics (LSE). Booth also wanted to bar local authorities from building any new housing, leaving the task to private enterprise.

9. *RRCMLTL*, 2:791, para. 21397.

10. This board's complete recommendations are contained in ibid., vol. 7. A brief summary is in vol. 1, pp. 34–39.

11. Ibid., 2:466–467, para. 13640, 13641; "Memorandum," in ibid., 3:464.

12. David Rooney, "Visualization, Decentralization and Metropolitan Improvements: 'Light-and-Air' and London County Council Photographs, 1899–1908," *Urban History* 40, no. 3 (2013), 465–466.

13. Ibid., 466. Time-space compression is also referred to as time-geography in other publications.

14. See Booth, "Improved Means of Locomotion"; C. M. Knowles, "The Housing Problem in London," 1899, pamphlet HD7/D101, LSE; William Thompson, *The Housing Famine and How to Relieve It*, Fabian Tract 101 (London: Fabian Society, 1900), LSE; and Raymond Unwin, *Cottage Plans and Common Sense*, Fabian Tract 109 (London: Fabian Society, 1902), LSE.

15. "Minutes of Evidence," in *RRCMLTL*, 2:152, para. 4117, 4118; *RRCMLTL*, 1:103, para. 216.

16. Russell Haywood, "Railways, Urban Form and Town Planning in London: 1900–1947," *Planning Perspectives* 12, no. 1 (1997), 39.

17. "The L.C.C. and London Traffic," *The Times*, July 2, 1907, p. 11.

18. *Report of the London Traffic Branch of the Board of Trade* (London: Darling, 1908).

19. "The Traffic of London," *London Municipal Notes: A Monthly Review of Municipal Work and Progress* 10 (February 1910): 101.

20. Arthur Crow, "Housing and Town Re-planning," *Architects' Law Reports and Review* 4 (1909): 13; see pp. 2–3 for the scheme for the ten-mile double avenue with a double tramway system on 225-foot-wide arteries.

21. Arthur Crow, "Town Planning in Relation to Old and Congested Areas with Special Reference to London," in *Transactions* (London: Royal Institute of British Architects, 1911), 434.

22. "London Traffic," *The Times*, February 10, 1911, p. 7.

23. W. W. Thompson, *Handbook of Housing and Town Planning Act, 1909* (London: King, 1910), 24–25.

24. Ibid., 27.

25. See E. G. Bentley and S. Pointon Taylor, *A Practical Guide in the Preparation of Town Planning Schemes* (London: George Philip, 1911). Raymond Unwin and Henry Aldridge were advisors, and Unwin wrote the foreword to this publication.

26. Crow, "Town Planning in Relation to Old and Congested Areas."

27. Town Planning Committee of the Royal Institute of British Architects, "Suggestions to Promoters of Town Planning Schemes," *Royal Institute of British Architects Journal*, August 26, 1911, pp. 666, 663.

28. Daniel Burnham, "A City of the Future under Democratic Government," in *Transactions*, 370.

29. Crow, "Town Planning in Relation to Old and Congested Areas," 426.

30. Thomas Adams, "Town Planning in Greater London," *Town Planning Review* 5, no. 2 (1914): 96–97.

31. Helena Beaufoy, "'Order Out of Chaos': The London Society and the Planning of London, 1912–1920," *Planning Perspectives* 12, no. 2 (1997): 155, 136, 140. See also Philip Booth and Margo Huxley, "1909 and All That: Reflections on the Housing, Town Planning, Etc. Act 1909," *Planning Perspectives* 27, no. 2 (2012): 267–283. For more on the London Society, see Lucy Hewitt, "Toward a Greater Urban Geography: Regional Planning and Associational Networks in London during the Early Twentieth Century," *Planning Perspectives* 26, no. 4 (2011): 551–568.

32. See London Society, "The Development Plan of Greater London," 1914–1918, LCC/AR/TP/01/076, Town Planning File, 1918–1935, Miscellaneous Printed Reports, London County Council Collection, London Metropolitan Archives (LMA).

33. Booth and Huxley, "1909 and All That," 561–562. For an analysis of these men and their overlapping networks and memberships, see Hewitt, "Toward a Greater Urban Geography."

34. National Housing and Town Planning Council, "Memorandum," 1917, p. 2, LCC/HSG/GEN/01/011, London County Council Collection, LMA.

35. Adams, "Town Planning in Greater London," 92.

36. "National Congress to Consider Home Problems after the War," *Town Planning Review* 6, no. 4 (1916): 217.

37. "Waste of Road Space," *The Times*, June 4, 1927, p. 11; "Central London Traffic," *The Times*, April 28, 1932, p. 9.

38. "Waste of Road Space," 11.

39. Abigail Beach and Nick Tiratsoo, "The Planners and the Publics," in *Cambridge Urban History of Britain, 1840–1950*, ed. Martin Daunton (Cambridge: Cambridge University Press, 2000), 528.

40. Raymond Unwin, *Town Planning in Practice: An Introduction to the Art of Designing Cities and Suburbs*, 2nd ed. (London: Unwin, 1911), 12.

41. Raymond Unwin, "The City Development Plan," in *Transactions*, 252.

42. "Design in House Building," *The Times*, June 10, 1933, p. 9.

43. Helen Meller, "Gender, Citizenship and the Making of the Modern Environment," in *Women and the Making of Built Space in England, 1870–1950*, ed. Elizabeth Darling and Lesley Whitworth (Aldershot, UK: Ashgate, 2007), 16–17.

44. Crow, "Housing and Town Re-planning," 1–3.

45. Annie Hankinson, "Appendix XIII," in *Practical Town Planning: A Land and Housing Policy*, by J. S. Nettlefold (London: St. Catherine Press, 1914), 464.

46. Ibid., 465.

47. Ibid., 464.

48. Richard Dennis, *Cities in Modernity: Representations and Productions of Metropolitan Space, 1840–1930* (Cambridge: Cambridge University Press, 2008), 56.

49. Ibid., 70–72. See also "Planning by Diagram," *The Times*, October 25, 1920, p. 7, for an RIBA-held exhibition titled "Civic Survey Diagrams" that presented "in diagramatic form, the basis or ground-work for development in town planning."

50. See Geddes, *Cities in Evolution*, 356–357.

51. Town Planning Committee of the Royal Institute of British Architects, "Suggestions to Promoters of Town Planning Schemes," 662–663.

52. Meller, "Gender, Citizenship and the Making of the Modern Environment," 24.

53. London's Public Health Act (1891) gave local authorities power to build underground toilets.

54. *Surveyor and Municipal and County Engineer* 3 (1883): 280; "Building Notes," *British Architect* 23, no. 5 (1885): 60.

55. Vestry minutes and the local newspaper indicate that St. Pancras, for example, provided public toilets for men on High Street, Tottenham Court, Kentish Town Roads, and other streets. The vestry spent £2,000 alone on the Fortress Road toilets. Ordnance Survey maps show urinals at busy intersections, on major streets, by bridges, and along tram routes across the city. Court cases over land taxes indicate that there was a woman's toilet on Broad-street and one at Piccadilly Circus. See "King's Bench Division," *The Times*, November 11, 1903, p. 10; and "Supreme Court of Judicature," *The Times*, July 23, 1904, p. 10. See also Lynne Walker, "Vistas of Pleasure: Women Consumers of Urban Space in the West End of London, 1850–1900," in *Women in the Victorian Art World*, ed. Caroline Campbell (Manchester, UK: University of Manchester Press, 1995), 70–88.

56. George Bernard Shaw, *Women as Councillors*, Fabian Tract 93 (London: Fabian Society, 1900), 2, LSE.

57. See Barbara Penner, "A World of Unmentionable Suffering: Women's Public Conveniences in Victorian London," *Journal of Design History* 14, no. 1 (2001): 35–51. For an extended discussion of the issue of women's public toilets in the four cities being considered here, see Maureen Flanagan, "Private Needs, Public Space: Public Toilets Provision in the Anglo-Atlantic Patriarchal City: London, Dublin, Toronto, and Chicago," *Urban History* 41, no. 2 (2014): 265–290. See also Walker, "Vistas of Pleasure."

58. Quoted in Penner, "A World of Unmentionable Suffering," 35, 36. See also George Bernard Shaw, "The Unmentionable Case for Women's Suffrage," *Review of Reviews* 39, no. 232 (1909): 342. Shaw was a vestryman and then borough councillor of St. Pancras.

59. Penner, "A World of Unmentionable Suffering," 35.

60. Ibid., 41.

61. Ibid., 40, 41.

62. For a discussion of women's toilets in department stores, see Erica Rappaport, *Shopping for Pleasure: Women in the Making of London's West End* (Princeton, NJ: Princeton University Press, 2000).

63. Clara Greed, *Women and Planning: Creating Gendered Realities* (London: Routledge, 1994), 103.

64. Clara Greed, *Inclusive Urban Design: Public Toilets* (Oxford, UK: Architectural Press, 2003), 47.

65. Penner, "A World of Unmentionable Suffering," 39.

66. Women's Municipal Party, *Third Annual Report* (1916), 9, Woman's Municipal Party Collection, Women at Work Collection, Imperial War Museum, London. The WMP also distributed a leaflet demanding public baths and washhouses, women police, and women's lodging houses. See also Walker, "Vistas of Pleasure."

67. London County Council, "Public Conveniences in London," in *Report, Medical Officer of Health* (pamphlet), December 13, 1928, p. 8, table 1, Women's Library, LSE.

68. Ibid., 3, 5. See Greed, *Inclusive Urban Design*, for her analysis of contemporary conditions in the United Kingdom.

69. Alison Ravetz, *Council Housing and Culture: The History of a Social Experiment* (London: Routledge, 2001), 75.

70. See Mark Swenarton, *Homes Fit for Heroes: The Politics and Architecture of Early State Housing in Britain* (London: Heinemann, 1981).

71. T. P. Ritzema, "The Housing of the Working-Classes: Grave Outlook; A Suggested Solution to the Problem," 1919, p. 5, pamphlet HD7/103, LSE.

72. National Housing and Town Planning Council, "Programme of Greater London Regional Housing and Town Planning Conference," 1920, pp. 2–3, LMA.

73. Karen Hunt, "Gendering the Politics of the Working Woman's Home," in Darling and Whitworth, *Women and the Making of Built Space in England*, 111.

74. Mabel Lawrence, "Labour Woman" (August 1913), quoted in Caroline Rowan, "Women in the Labour Party, 1906–1920," *Feminist Review* 12 (October 1982), 87.

75. A. D. Sanderson Furniss and Marion Phillips, *The Working Woman's House* (London: Swarthmore Press, 1919), 10 (emphasis in original).

76. Ibid., 72–73. See p. 13 for list of organizations consulted. For more detailed explanation of the act, see *Housing and Town Planning, &C., Acts, 1919* (London: Local Government Journal, 1919).

77. Ministry of Reconstruction, *Women's Housing Sub-committee: First Interim Report* (London: His Majesty's Stationery Office, 1918), 4, 5. See also Rowan, "Women in the Labour Party, 1906–1920," 74–81.

78. Alison Ravetz, *The Place of Home: English Domestic Environments, 1914–2000* (Abingdon, UK: Taylor and Francis, 1995), 150. See also Swenarton, *Homes Fit for Heroes*, 91–92, and the 1919 Housing and Town Planning Act for the directive that local authorities were responsible for providing housing for the working classes in their district and prepare town plans. In London, the authority was the LCC, which worked through the LGB.

79. L.P.A., "Women's Housing Report to the Ministry of Reconstruction," *Town Planning Review* 8, no. 1 (1919): 47, 48.

80. Rowan, "Women in the Labour Party, 1906–1920," 89.

81. "The Ideal Cottage," *The Times*, January 28, 1919, p. 5.

82. Ibid.

83. Greed, *Women and Planning*, 118–119.

84. C. M. Lloyd, *Housing*, Fabian Tract 193 (London: Fabian Society, 1920), 21, LSE.

85. Ibid., 16.

86. Raymond Unwin, "Some Thoughts on the Development of London," in *London of the Future*, ed. Sir Aston Webb (New York: Dutton, 1921), 181, 183–184.

87. S. D. Adshead, "Central London," in Webb, *London of the Future*, 148, 150. The bulk of his essay dealt with planning roads and transportation systems.

88. W. R. Davidge, "The Housing of London," in Webb, *London of the Future*, 195, 204, 205. See also the account of the book in "London of the Future," *The Times*, October 5, 1921, p. 11.

89. "Building Policy," *The Times*, May 21, 1925, p. 5.

90. Mei-Po Kwan, "Gender Differences in Space-Time Constraints," *Area* 32, no. 2 (2000): 146. See also Helen Jarvis with Paula Kantor and Jonathan Cloke, *Cities and Gender: Critical Introductions to Urbanism and the City* (New York: Routledge, 2009), 144–147, which uses the term *time-geography*.

91. Davidge, "The Housing of London," diagrams facing 196, 198, and 200; photo facing 202.

92. Marion Roberts, "Gender and Housing: The Impact of Design," *Built Environment* 16, no. 4 (1990), 258.

93. Furniss and Phillips, *The Working Woman's House*, 58, 61.

94. "A Social Reform Programme for Women," *Daily Sketch*, [month obscured] 22, 1919, Women, War and Society Collection, Imperial War Museum.

95. "Views on Housing Bill," *The Times*, April 14, 1923, p. 7.

96. Hunt, "Gendering the Politics of the Working Woman's Home," 121.

97. Women's Municipal Party, "Objects and Programmes of the Women's Municipal Party," in *First Annual Report* (1914–1915), 5, Women, War and Society Collection, Imperial War Museum. Women's Municipal Party, *Third Annual Report*, lists a total of 1,360 members in the party.

98. Women's Municipal Party, "Women and Municipal Work: Their Claims to Share in Local Government," July 1916, in *Third Annual Report*, 3–4.

99. Women's Municipal Party, *Third Annual Report*, 17.

100. "Overcrowding in Somers Town," *The Times*, December 20, 1926, p. 18.

101. See Peter Malpass, "The Discontinuous History of Housing Associations in England," *Housing Studies* 15, no. 2 (2000): 204–205.

102. Elizabeth Darling, "'The Star in the Profession She Invented for Herself': A Brief Biography of Elizabeth Denby, Housing Consultant," *Planning Perspectives* 20, no. 3 (2005): 276. See this essay for an extensive treatment of Denby and information on the housing that she ultimately helped to design including these amenities.

103. Ibid., 282.

104. Irene T. Barclay and Evelyn E. Perry, "Report on Housing Conditions in the Metropolitan Borough of Southwark," 1929, pamphlet HD144, LSE. See also Mrs. Ant. Hare, survey, 1934, LSE.

105. Swenarton, *Homes Fit for Heroes*, 174.

106. Dennis, *Cities in Modernity*, 201, fig. 7.6, is a map showing the location of both the prewar and interwar LCC housing estates. They were either on the periphery of the county boundary or outside it. See also Meller, "Women and Citizenship," 250.

107. London County Council, *Annual Report of the Council, 1922* (London: London County Council, 1923), 3:117. More detailed information on the building of the estate can be found in the "Norbury Estate—Development—Committee Reports, etc." file, LCC/HSG/GEN/01/024, and "Norbury Estate—Development—Correspondence" file, LCC/HSG/GEN/01/025, London County Council Collection, LMA.

108. "New L.C.C. Housing Estate," *The Times*, October 21, 1927, p. 13.

109. Greed, *Women and Planning*, 42.

110. Gilda O'Neill, *My East End: Memories of Life in Cockney London* (London: Penguin, 1999), 82, 84.

111. Ibid., 85.

112. Ibid., 284.

113. Ibid., 285.

114. "Housing in London," *The Times*, June 6, 1928, p. 11.

115. Elizabeth Darling, "'The House That Is a Woman's Book Come True': The All-Europe House and Four Women's Spatial Practices in Inter-war England," in Darling and Whitworth, *Women and the Making of Built Space in England*, 131–132.

116. Quoted in Michael P. Collins, "The Development of Town Planning Education at University College London, 1914–1969: The Contributions of Professors S. D. Adshead, L. P. Abercrombie, and W. G. Holford," *Planning Perspectives* 31, no. 2 (2016), 285.

117. "Town Planning," *The Times*, April 1, 1924, p. 11.

118. "Thames Bridges," *The Times*, June 12, 1926, p. 10. Abercrombie was responding specifically to discussion about plans for the Charing Cross bridge, but his statements capture the fact that housing was just a minor aspect of the grand plan perspective for constructing a new London.

119. Quoted in Darling, "'The Star in the Profession She Invented for Herself,'" 287.

120. "Slums," *The Times*, October 26, 1927, p. 15.

121. "London Slum Centres," *The Times*, April 7, 1925, p. 12.

122. The 1933 Housing (Financial Provisions) Act, for instance, was to encourage building housing affordable to lower-paid workers, as the building of such accommodations was clearly lagging behind need.

123. Elizabeth Darling, *Re-forming Britain: Narratives of Modernity before Reconstruction* (London: Routledge, 2007).

124. See Greed, *Women and Planning*, 41.

125. "'Satellite' Towns," *The Times*, January 12, 1924, p. 5.

126. "The Next Step 'Ordered Plan' of Housing Needs," *The Times*, July 19, 1934, p. 7.

127. "A New Covent Garden," *The Times*, March 12, 1926, p. 11.

128. "The London Society and Traffic," *The Times*, March 24, 1926, p. 13.

129. "A New Covent Garden," 11.

130. "The Re-Planning of Bloomsbury," *The Times*, April 30, 1927, p. 9.

131. "Town-Planning in Central London," *The Times*, February 2, 1928, p. 9. For the entire scheme for the area, see "Town Planning Scheme #5 and #6," 1926–1927, LCC/AR/TP/01/012, 013, and 014, London County Council Collection, LMA. These schemes were generally referred to as the Holburn–St. Pancras schemes.

132. For a group of documents titled "Objections and Representations," see "Town Planning Scheme #5 and #6," 1926–1927, LCC/AR/TP/01/013 and 014. See also "L.C.C. Foundling Estate Scheme," *The Times*, February 14, 1928, p. 16, for news of a public gathering in which the residents of Holborn and St. Pancras drafted a petition against building on the Foundling Estate site and in favor of saving it for "public ends."

133. "Town-Planning in Holburn," *The Times*, January 14, 1928, p. 7.

134. "The Foundling Estate," *The Times*, December 10, 1926, p. 10.

135. Letter from St. Peter's Men's Club to London County Council, March 20, 1934, LCC/AR/TP/01/024, LMA. The previous year the Finsbury borough council had reported that property owners were keeping land vacant hoping to attract new business rather than use the land for housing. See "Slum Clearance in Finsbury," *The Times*, July 11, 1933, p. 11.

136. "Slum Clearance at Popular," *The Times*, August 30, 1934, p. 6.

137. Dennis, *Cities in Modernity*, 115.

138. See Ruth Durant, *Watling: A Survey of Social Life on a New Housing Estate* (London: King, 1939). The "Watling" Estate is really the Edgware Estate to the northwest outside the County boundary.

139. Ruth Durant, "Community and Association in a London Housing Estate," in *Readings in Urban Sociology*, ed. R. E. Pahl (Oxford, UK: Pergamon Press, 1968), 165.

140. Wilson, *Sphinx in the City*, 8.

141. Greed, *Women and Planning*, 52.

142. Dennis, *Cities in Modernity*, 118; see 119 for maps.

143. Ibid., 120–123.

144. Ibid., 124. See also the photo of Victoria Street taken in 1899, reproduced on p. 125. The Kingsway-Aldwych scheme that connected High Holburn Street on the north to the Strand on the south, cutting a swath through old neighborhoods obliterating small, narrow streets as well as the old Clare Market and clearing a wide path to the Waterloo Bridge are other examples. See Dirk Schubert and Anthony Sutcliffe, "The 'Haussmannization' of London? The Planning and Construction of the Kingsway-Aldwych, 1889–1935," *Planning Perspectives* 11, no. 2 (1996): 115–144.

145. David Harvey, *Paris, Capital of Modernity* (New York: Routledge, 2006), 112–113.

146. Barbara Hooper, "The Poem of Male Desires: Female Bodies, Modernity, and 'Paris, Capital of the Nineteenth Century,'" in *Making the Invisible Visible: A Multicultural Planning Reader*, ed. Leonie Sandercock (Berkeley: University of California Press, 1998), 243–244.

147. Greed, *Women and Planning*, 116.

148. Wilson, *Sphinx in the City*, 8.

149. Barbara Hooper, "Urban Space, Modernity, and Masculinist Desire: The Utopian Longings of Le Corbusier," in *Embodied Utopias: Gender, Social Change, and the Modern Metropolis*, ed. Amy Bingaman, Lise Sanders, and Rebecca Zorach (London: Routledge, 2002), 60.

150. Wilson, *Sphinx in the City*, 91, 92.

151. Robert Fishman, *Urban Utopias in the Twentieth Century: Ebenezer Howard, Frank Lloyd Wright, and Le Corbusier* (New York: Basic Books, 1977), 177; Le Corbusier, *Urbanisme* (Paris: G. Crès et Cie, 1925), 22–23, 37.

152. Le Corbusier, *The City of To-morrow and Its Planning*, trans. Frederick Etchells (New York: Dover, 1987), 5, 10. See also Hooper, "Urban Space," 60, 66, 71.

153. Abraham Akkerman, "Femininity and Masculinity in City-Form: Philosophical Urbanism as a History of Consciousness," *Human Studies* 29, no. 2 (2006): 242.

154. Quoted in Hooper, "Urban Space," 65.

155. Darling, *Re-forming Britain*, 6.

156. Abercrombie insisted that a complete survey "in which traffic, population, vital statistics, occupation, ownership, public services, [and] land values" be taken on the national, regional, and local levels as "the essential basis of all planning," and at a meeting of the London Society he called for a "proper plan for the whole of the metropolitan area." See "Need of a National Survey," *The Times*, January 5, 1938, p. 5; and "Blemishes on London," *The Times*, March 23, 1939, p. 18, respectively.

157. Matthew Hollow, "Utopian Urges: Visions for Reconstruction in Britain 1940–50," *Planning Perspectives* 27, no. 4 (2012): 571–572.

158. "Greater London of the Future," *The Times*, April 9, 1941, p. 2. See also "Planning the New London," *The Times*, April 5, 1941, p. 2.

159. "A Plan for London," *The Times*, July 10, 1943, p. 5; "London Replanned," *The Times*, July 13, 1943, p. 5. See also "County of London Plan, 1943," 1944–1945, LCC/AR/TP/01/096, London County Council Collection, LMA.

160. "A Plan for Greater London," *The Times*, December 14, 1944, p. 5.

161. "Rebuilding East London," *The Times*, February 2, 1946, p. 4. See also "London Replanned"; and "Labour's Plans for London," *The Times*, February 6, 1946, p. 2. The Town and Country Planning Association (the renamed Garden Cities Association) complained that the plan would not sufficiently reduce the density of the areas. "Replanning of London," *The Times*, March 8, 1946, p. 2. For one critique of aspects of the 1944 GLP, see Hugh Stowell Phillips, "The Abercrombie Greater London Plan," *Public Administration* 23, no. 1 (1945): 38–40.

162. Susan Cowan, "The People's Peace: The Myth of Wartime Unity and Public Consent for Town Planning," in *The Blitz and Its Legacy: Wartime Destruction to Post-war Reconstruction*, ed. Mark Clapson and Peter J. Larkham (Farnham, UK: Ashgate, 2013), 73–86.

163. Marco Amati and Robert Freestone, "All of London's a Stage: The 1943 County Plan of London Exhibition," *Urban History* 43, no. 4 (2016): 540.

164. Ibid., 552, 553, 555.

165. Patrick Abercrombie, "The Policy Aimed at the Detailed Movement of Population and Work," in *Greater London Plan, 1944* (London: His Majesty's Stationery Store, 1945), 56–57.

166. Darling, "'House That Is a Women's Book,'" 123–142. For a discussion of the career of one woman involved in new town planning, see Mark Clapson, "The Rise and Fall of Monica Felton, British Town Planner and Peace Activist, 1930s to 1950s," *Planning Perspectives* 30, no. 2 (2015): 211–229.

167. Stephen V. Ward, *Planning and Urban Change*, 2nd ed. (London: Sage, 2004), 101.

168. Greed, *Women and Planning*, 125.

169. Christine Booth and Rose Gilroy, "Dreaming the Possibility of Change," *Built Environment* 22, no. 1 (1996): 72.

170. Lewis Mumford, "On the Future of London," *Architectural Review* 97, no. 577 (1945): 8.

171. See J. H. Forshaw and Patrick Abercrombie, *County of London Plan* (London: Macmillan, 1943), color plate 1, for Abercrombie's mapping of the city as composed of isolated neighborhoods spinning out from the center.

172. W. Russell Tylor, "The Neighbourhood Unit Principle in Town Planning," *Town Planning Review* 18, no. 3 (1939): 176.

173. See National Council for Social Service, *Social Factors Influencing the Composition and Size of an Urban Unit* (London: Allen and Unwin, 1942); National Council for Social Service, "The Size and Social Structure of a Town" (London: Allen and Unwin, 1943).

174. Nicholas Bullock, *Building the Post-war World: Modern Architecture and Reconstruction in Britain* (London: Routledge, 2002), 161–163.

175. Greed, *Women and Planning*, 142.

176. Wilson, *Sphinx in the City*, 113.

177. Linda McDowell, "Towards an Understanding of the Gender Division of Urban Space," *Environment and Planning D: Society and Space* 1, no. 1 (1983): 59–72. See also Greed, *Women and Planning*, 141–143, for a discussion of how ideas of urban sociologists regarding the "traditional family" were incorporated into planning.

178. Logan Nash, "Middle-Class Castle: Constructing Gentrification at London's Barbican Estate," *Journal of Urban History* 39, no. 5 (2013): 909, 910, 912. For a map of the area showing the Barbican development superimposed over the prewar neighborhood, see http://assets.londonist .com/uploads/2015/01/barb1.jpg. For another map of the site before building, see Tatsuya Tsubaki, "'Model for a Short-Lived Future'? Early Tribulations of the Barbican Redevelopment in the City of London, 1940–1982," *Planning Perspectives* 27, no. 4 (2012): 531.

179. Nash, "Middle-Class Castle," 915.

CHAPTER 6

1. "Report of the Public Health Committee: In re Infantile Mortality," *Reports and Printed Documents of the Corporation of Dublin* 2, no. 156 (1906): 610. These figures were part of the report of Charles Cameron, medical officer of health. For the connections between health and housing, see Jacinta Prunty, *Dublin Slums, 1800–1925: A Study in Urban Geography* (Dublin: Irish Academic Press, 1998), chap. 5. For statistics on overall mortality rates, see pp. 153–157, table 5.1. For a comparison chart of world cities and death rates, see p. 154. For a graph of recorded death registrations from 1896–1911, see p. 160, table 5.2; in some years the annual deaths from tuberculosis rose as high as 1,800 and those from diarrheal diseases exceeded 600. The 1891 census showed Dublin proper's population slightly under 250,000, with approximately an additional 100,000 in the suburban districts. For an original report, see "Report of the Committee Appointed by the Local Government Board for Ireland to Inquire into the Public Health of the City of Dublin, 1900," *Public Health* 13 (October 1900–September 1901): 24–26. Charles Cameron headed the committee.

2. See Ruth McManus, *Dublin, 1910–1940: Shaping the City and Suburbs* (Dublin: Four Courts Press, 2002), 41–42.

3. Local Government Board for Ireland, *Report on the Housing Conditions of the Working Classes* (London: His Majesty's Stationery Office, 1914), para. 30, 33.

4. Quoted in Mary E. Daly, *Dublin, the Deposed Capital: A Social and Economic History, 1860–1914* (Cork, UK: Cork University Press, 1984), 293.

5. Prunty, *Dublin Slums*, 151–152. Cameron asserted that such housing would give "these people a chance of being useful to the community." "Housing of the Very Poor," *Irish Times*, July 3, 1897, p. 9A. See also "Housing of the Very Poor," *Irish Times*, June 10, 1897, p. 5. In 1893, the Guinness [Iveagh] Trust reported that the average weekly earnings of families in its buildings was 14s/2d per week. That figure had risen five years later to 18s/1¼d per week, with weekly rents in the building going for 1s/10¼d per room. See "The Guinness Trust," *The Times*, March 22, 1894, p. 11; and "The Guinness Trust," *The Times*, March 11, 1899, p. 6.

6. "Housing the Dublin Poor," *Freeman's Journal and Daily Commercial Advertiser*, September 3, 1897, p. 4.

7. Local Government Board for Ireland, *Report on the Housing Conditions of the Working Classes*, para. 42, reports that the Housing of the Very Poor Committee built 157 single-room dwellings.

8. See Daly, *Dublin, the Deposed Capital*, 285, for an example.

9. "Report of the Conference between the Parliamentary Representatives of the County and City of Dublin, the Corporation of Dublin, and the Dublin Trades Council, on the Subject of the Housing of the Working Classes," *Reports and Printed Documents of the Corporation of Dublin* 3, no. 176 (1903): 395.

10. Prunty, *Dublin Slums*, 3. See also "Arran Quay Ward Ratepayers' Association," *Freeman's Journal and Daily Commercial Advertiser*, October 7, 1898, p. 6.

11. *Minutes of the Municipal Council of the City of Dublin*, no. 501 (1905): 485.

12. "Report of the Public Health Committee," *Reports and Printed Documents of the Corporation of Dublin* 2, no. 144 (1905): 506.

13. For an explanation of the Clancy Act, see Daly, *Dublin, the Deposed Capital*, 310.

14. "Cook Street Area Improvement Scheme," *Irish Times*, June 16, 1910, p. 9. See also "Dublin Corporation Housing Schemes," *Irish Times*, June 15, 1910, p. 11.

15. Daly, *Dublin, the Deposed Capital*, 78.

16. Maria Luddy, *Prostitution in Irish Society, 1800–1940* (Cambridge: Cambridge University Press, 2007), 17–21, 27, 50, apps. 2, 3. See also Maria Luddy, "'Abandoned Women and Bad Characters': Prostitution in Nineteenth-Century Ireland," *Women's History Review* 6, no. 4 (1997): 485–504; and Daly, *Dublin, the Deposed Capital*, 78–79.

17. Quoted in "Minutes of a Special Meeting . . . the 19th. Day of October, 1910," *Minutes of the Municipal Council of the City of Dublin*, no. 758 (1910): 483.

18. Ibid., 483–484.

19. *Minutes of the Municipal Council of the City of Dublin*, no. 421 (1897): 375. See also "The Corporation," *Freeman's Journal and Daily Commercial Advertiser*, August 22, 1899, p. 2.

20. See, for example, *Minutes of the Municipal Council of the City of Dublin*, no. 46 (1898): 29; no. 111 (1898): 84; no. 326 (1899): 221; no. 332 (1899): 222–223; no. 339 (1899): 225; no. 521 (1900): 452; and "Report of the Public Health Committee," *Reports and Printed Documents of the Corporation of Dublin* 1, no. 9 (1898): 69; 2, no. 65 (1899): 373–375; 2, no. 72 (1899): 415–417; 2, no. 68 (1900): 445; 3, no. 3 (1900): 143, 828–830; 1, no. 53 (1901): 347–348.

21. "Report of the Improvements Committee," *Reports and Printed Documents of the Corporation of Dublin* 1, no. 12 (1902): 81–82. See also *Minutes of the Municipal Council of the City of Dublin*, no. 339 (1899): 225, and no. 365 (1901): 543.

22. "Report of Public Health Committee," *Reports and Printed Documents of the Corporation of Dublin* 1, no. 161 (1906): 649–650. For Cameron's continuing stress on private facilities for women, see "Report of Public Health Committee," *Reports and Printed Documents of the Corporation of Dublin* 2, no. 120 (1911): 451–452.

23. For the council's proposal, see *Minutes of the Municipal Council of the City of Dublin*, no. 591 (1907): 426–427.

24. *Minutes of the Municipal Council of the City of Dublin*, no. 177 (1907): 85.

25. "Alleged Obstruction by the Corporation," *Irish Times*, September 5, 1907, p. 3. The paper identified the plaintiffs as a watchmaker, chemist, tobacconist, and boot merchant.

26. Ibid. For the council's decision, see *Minutes of the Municipal Council of the City of Dublin*, no. 5 (1908): 7–8, and no. 740 (1908): 543–544.

27. "Report of the Public Health Committee," *Reports and Printed Documents of the Corporation of Dublin* 1, no. 2 (1911): 19–23; 1, no. 42 (1911): 19–23, 405; 2, no. 107 (1911): 375; 2, no. 120 (1911): 451–452. See also *Minutes of the Municipal Council of the City of Dublin*, no. 371 (1911): 269–270.

28. *Minutes of the Municipal Council of the City of Dublin*, no. 577 (1911): 394.

29. See "Report of the Public Health Committee," *Reports and Printed Documents of the Corporation of Dublin* 1, no. 42 (1911): 405–408. Urinals were free, while water closets cost 1d.

30. *Minutes of the Municipal Council of the City of Dublin*, no. 146 (1912): 110; see also no. 994 (1912): 691.

31. "Report of the Improvements, Public Health, and Cleansing Committees," *Reports and Printed Documents of the Corporation of Dublin* 1 (1915): 97.

32. Letter from Hodges and Sons, Aston Quay, to council, *Minutes of the Municipal Council of the City of Dublin*, no. 247 (1915): 121.

33. Letter from ratepayers to council, *Minutes of the Municipal Council of the City of Dublin*, no. 247 (1915): 119. See also "Dublin Port and Docks Board," *Irish Times*, February 12, 1915, p. 3.

34. *Minutes of the Municipal Council of the City of Dublin*, no. 654 (1921): 460; "Report of the Improvements Committee," *Reports and Printed Documents of the Corporation of Dublin* 2, no. 230 (1921): 575-579.

35. For an overview of this struggle, see Joseph V. O'Brien, *Dear, Dirty Dublin: A City in Distress, 1899-1916* (Berkeley: University of California Press, 1982), part II.

36. Frances Carruthers, "The Organisational Work of Lady Ishbel Aberdeen, Marchioness of Aberdeen and Temair (1857-1939)," Ph.D. diss., National University of Ireland Maynooth, 2001, p. 168.

37. See Women's National Health Association, "Reports, Balance Sheet, Donations, and Subscriptions of the WNHA of Ireland," 1909, Pamphlets-Medicine Collection, National Library of Ireland; *Sláinte*, March 1909, National Library of Ireland; and *Irish Independent*, November 10, 1911, August 30, 1912, and April 18, 1913. See also Carruthers, "The Organisational Work of Lady Ishbel Aberdeen," 161, 163.

38. "Report of the Housing Committee," *Reports and Printed Documents of the Corporation of Dublin* 2, no. 127 (1913): 255.

39. "Report of the Housing Committee," *Reports and Printed Documents of the Corporation of Dublin* 1, no. 248 (1917): 5-10. See also "Report of the Housing Committee," *Reports and Printed Documents of the Corporation of Dublin* 2, no. 23 (1914): 161; and "Women's National Health Association," *Irish Times*, December 2, 1914, p. 6.

40. "Notification of Births (Extension) Act, 1915," *Reports and Printed Documents of the Corporation of Dublin* 2, no. 163 (1916): 473. See also "Report of the Public Health Committee," *Reports and Printed Documents of the Corporation of Dublin* 3, no. 178 (1916): 10-11; and *Minutes of the Municipal Council of the City of Dublin*, no. 694 (1916): 434, 475.

41. See Carruthers, "The Organisational Work of Lady Ishbel Aberdeen," 168-171.

42. Ibid., 172.

43. P. C. Cowan, "Address to the Section of Town Planning and the Housing of the Working-Classes of the Dublin Congress," 1911, p. 7, pamphlet HD7/287, London School of Economics.

44. See Patrick Geddes, *Cities in Evolution: An Introduction to the Town Planning Movement and to the Study of Civics* (London: Williams and Norgate, 1915), 258-259; flyer announcing the Cities and Town Planning Exhibition, 1911, Miscellaneous Pamphlet Collection, Dublin City Archives, Pearse Street Library, Dublin; and Helen Meller, *Patrick Geddes: Social Evolutionist and City Planner* (London: Routledge, 1990), 182-183.

45. "A Secret Housing Inquiry," *Irish Times*, October 21, 1913, p. 6; "Dublin Corporation (2): Housing Problem," *Irish Times*, October 21, 1913, p. 5; "The Housing Inquiry," *Irish Times*, November 6, 1913, p. 4; and "Housing the Workers: Deputations to the Castle Demand for Viceregal Commission," *Irish Times*, November 8, 1913, p. 13; "The Dublin Slums," *Irish Times*, November 8, 1913, p. 10.

46. "Dublin Corporation: Housing Problem Committee of Inquiry Critised," *Irish Times*, November 11, 1913, p. 7.

47. "The Dublin Slums," *Irish Times*, November 25, 1913, p. 7.

48. "Housing in Dublin," *Irish Times*, November 14, 1913, p. 5. The article also noted that there were a large number of "ladies" in attendance.

49. "Housing in Dublin," *Irish Times*, March 14, 1914, p. 9.

50. Daly, *Dublin, the Deposed Capital*, 315. See also Local Government Board for Ireland, *Report on the Housing Conditions of the Working Classes*, para. 30, 33.

51. "Report of the Housing Committee," *Reports and Printed Documents of the Corporation of Dublin* 2, no. 120 (1914): 156, 162.

52. Local Government Board for Ireland, *Report on the Housing Conditions of the Working Classes*, para. 28.

53. "Report of the Housing Committee," *Reports and Printed Documents of the Corporation of Dublin* 2, no. 120 (1914): 167.

54. "Dublin Housing Inquiry," *The Times*, November 19, 1913, p. 10; November 20, 1913, p. 5; November 21, 1913, p. 5; November 25, 1913, p. 10; December 20, 1913, p. 4; and December 22, 1913, p. 5.

55. "Scandal of the Dublin Slums," *The Times*, February 19, 1914, p. 8.

56. Ibid.; McManus, *Dublin, 1910–1940*, 35–36.

57. Daly, *Dublin, the Deposed Capital*, 315–317. For parliamentary discussion comparing housing and sanitation in Dublin and Belfast, in which the superiority of unionist government over nationalist government was contended, see "Parliament," *The Times*, April 17, 1914, p. 12.

58. "Dublin Housing Inquiry," *The Times*, November 25, 1913, p. 10.

59. Ruth McManus, *Such Happy Harmony: Early Twentieth Century Co-operation to Solve Dublin's Housing Problems* (Dublin: Dublin City Libraries, 2005), 13.

60. Letter from Presbytery of Dublin to city council, October 9, 1913, *Minutes of the Municipal Council of the City of Dublin*, no. 845 (1913): 533–534.

61. *Minutes of the Municipal Council of the City of Dublin*, no. 206 (1913): 150–151.

62. For more details and discussion of the competition's directives, see Michael J. Bannon, "Dublin Town Planning Competition: Ashbee and Chettle's New Dublin—a Study in Civics," *Planning Perspectives* 14, no. 2 (1999): 145–162; and Michael J. Bannon, "The Genesis of Modern Irish Planning," in *The Emergence of Irish Planning, 1880–1920*, ed. Michael J. Bannon (Dublin: Turoe Press, 1985), 189–260. Building a municipal art gallery had been a priority of a city council committee. See *Minutes of the Municipal Council of the City of Dublin*, no. 261 (1913): 184–189.

63. Patrick Abercrombie, Sydney Kelly, and Arthur Kelly, *Dublin of the Future: The New Town Plan* (Liverpool: University Press of Liverpool, 1922), 20–23.

64. "Report of the Housing Committee," *Reports and Printed Documents of the Corporation of Dublin* 1, no. 17 (1914): 85.

65. Raymond Unwin and Patrick Geddes, "Report to the Town Clerk," *Reports and Printed Documents of the Corporation of Dublin* 1, no. 17 (1915): 710.

66. For an example of the council's plans for the area, see "Report of the Improvements Committee," *Reports and Printed Documents of the Corporation of Dublin* 3, no. 145 (1903): 147–155. For more on the playground, see "Report of the Housing Committee," *Reports and Printed Documents of the Corporation of Dublin* 2, no. 23 (1914): 161.

67. Unwin and Geddes, "Report to the Town Clerk, 712–713. See also Andrew Kincaid, *Postcolonial Dublin: Imperial Legacies and the Built Environment* (Minneapolis: University of Minnesota Press, 2006), 2–3.

68. Unwin and Geddes, "Report to the Town Clerk," 718–721.

69. "Report of the Sub-committee Appointed to Consider the Foregoing Reports," *Reports and Printed Documents of the Corporation of Dublin* 1 (1915): 752. See also Unwin and Geddes, "Report to the Town Clerk," 715–716.

70. "Report of the Sub-committee," 753.

71. Kincaid, *Postcolonial Dublin*, 2–3.

72. Raymond Unwin and Patrick Geddes, "Memorandum no. 3," *Reports and Printed Documents of the Corporation of Dublin* 1, no. 17 (1915): 729.

73. The subtitle to Geddes's *Cities in Evolution* was *An Introduction to the Town Planning Movement and the Study of Civics*. See also Bannon, "Dublin Town Planning Competition," 148–149.

74. Quoted in Bannon, "The Genesis of Modern Irish Planning," 205.

75. "Architects and City Improvements," *Irish Times*, April 30, 1913, p. 9.

76. For letters exchanged between the housing committee and the LGB, see "Report of the Housing Committee," *Reports and Printed Documents of the Corporation of Dublin* 1, no. 240 (1915): 11–12, 105–122.

77. R. M. Butler, "The Reconstruction of O'Connell Street, Dublin," *Studies: An Irish Quarterly Review* 5, no. 20 (1916): 570.

78. McManus, *Dublin, 1910–1940*, 69.

79. "Royal Institute of Architects of Ireland; The Town Planning Competition," *Irish Times*, December 20, 1915, p. 3; "An Ideal City of Dublin: Aberdeen's Prize Winners Plans," *Irish Times*, September 23, 1916, p. 7. See also "Dublin Replanned," *The Times*, August 28, 1916, p. 3.

80. Abercrombie, Kelly, and Kelly, *Dublin of the Future*, 5.

81. For details of this traffic center, see ibid., plate 27.

82. Ibid., 36–37. References to monumental edifices of continental cities were abundant in the plan.

83. Ibid., 38–39.

84. Ibid., 31, 30.

85. Ibid., 44.

86. "Report of the Work and Conclusions of the Expert Committee," *Reports and Printed Documents of the Corporation of Dublin* 3, no. 226 (1916): 617–640, contains Unwin's report.

87. "Report of the Housing Committee," *Reports and Printed Documents of the Corporation of Dublin* 1, no. 13 (1918): 113.

88. Ibid., 81–145.

89. P. C. Cowan, "Report on Dublin Housing," 1918, p. 19, Dublin City Archives. See also *Minutes of the Municipal Council of the City of Dublin*, no. 214 (1917): 130, for letter from Dublin Industrial Development Corporation urging the corporation to appoint a committee of experts to draw up a plan for the city "to which all future developments and improvements should conform."

90. Prunty, *Dublin Slums*, 330.

91. McManus, *Dublin, 1910–1940*, provides the most detailed overview of planning in these years.

92. *Irish Independent*, July 4, 1922. Since O'Rourke did not retire until 1945, his tenure coincided with planning and reconstruction activity of Dublin up to that date.

93. Abercrombie, Kelly, and Kelly, *Dublin of the Future*, vi.

94. Bannon, "Dublin Town Planning Competition," 151.

95. Ibid., 153.

96. Ibid., 160–161.

97. "A Civic Survey," *Irish Times*, March 1, 1924, p. 9.

98. David Dickson, *Dublin: The Making of a Capital City* (Cambridge, MA: Cambridge University Press, 2014), 474–475.

99. See Patrick Abercrombie, "A Civic Society: An Outline of Its Scope, Formation and Functions," *Town Planning Review* 8, no. 2 (1920): 79–92.

100. Horace O'Rourke, *The Dublin Civic Survey Report* (Dublin: Civics Institute, 1925), xv, available at https://digital.ucd.ie/get/ucdlib:33060/content. The two women among the twenty-one members of the survey committee represented the Irish Women Citizen's and Local Government Association and the Dublin Citizen's Housing Association. But their voices are not found in the report, so it is impossible to know what they might have contributed or how they may have felt about such a conclusion. The men were politicians and representatives of professional and civic organizations.

101. Ibid., 58–59.

102. Ibid., 59.

103. Ibid., 69.

104. Ruth McManus, "Public Utility Societies, the Dublin Corporation and the Development of Dublin, 1920–1940," *Irish Geography* 29, no. 1 (1996): 27–37. For the terms set by the corporation, see also "Report of the Housing, Workshops, and Supplies Section," *Reports and Printed Documents of the Corporation of Dublin* 2, no. 177 (1925): 252–254. For a revision of these terms to include those enterprises building houses for sale so that private enterprise would not be retarded, see "Report of the Housing, Workshops, and Supplies Section," *Reports and Printed Documents of the Corporation of Dublin* 2, no. 262 (1925): 525–528.

105. McManus, *Dublin, 1910–1940*, 94. From the end of 1918, the city architect had argued that new housing schemes in Dublin accept the standards of larger housing schemes containing larger

dwellings that were being promoted in the English Tudor Walters report. See "Report of the Housing Committee," *Reports and Printed Documents of the Corporation of Dublin* 3, no. 210 (1919): 51.

106. See, for example, Ruth McManus, "Blue Collars, 'Red Forts,' and Green Fields: Working-Class Housing in Ireland in the Twentieth Century," *International Labor and Working-Class History* 64, no. 1 (2003): 38-54.

107. Other developments that were under way at the same time exhibited many of the same elements, but Marino is the exemplar most cited. See the detailed analysis of various housing schemes of this type in McManus, *Dublin, 1910-1940*.

108. See James Killen, "Transport in Dublin: Past, Present and Future," in *Dublin City and County: From Prehistory to Present*, ed. F.H.A. Aalen and Kevin Whelan (Dublin: Geography, 1992), 310.

109. O'Rourke, *Dublin Civic Survey Report*, 69.

110. McManus, *Dublin, 1910-1940*, 93, 202-205. See also Mervyn Miller, "Raymond Unwin and the Planning of Dublin," in Bannon, *The Emergence of Irish Planning, 1880-1920*, 263-305.

111. For examples, see "Report of the Public Health Committee," *Reports and Printed Documents of the Corporation of Dublin* 1, no. 203 (1923): 183.

112. "Public Health Section Report," *Reports and Printed Documents of the Corporation of Dublin* 2, no. 153 (1926): 426; *Minutes of the Municipal Council of the City of Dublin*, no. 119 (1928): 60.

113. Prunty, *Dublin Slums*, 98, 159.

114. Under the 1924 and 1925 Housing Acts the city turned the housing issue over to "assisted private enterprise," largely public utility societies.

115. "Report of the Reconstruction Committee," *Reports and Printed Documents of the Corporation of Dublin* 2, no. 154 (1923): 751.

116. "Report of the Reconstruction Committee," *Reports and Printed Documents of the Corporation of Dublin* 1, no. 13 (1925): 45-46.

117. McManus, *Dublin, 1910-1940*, 72-74; "The Street Architecture of Dublin," *Irish Builder and Engineer*, January 28, 1922, p. 50.

118. McManus, *Dublin, 1910-1940*, 76-77.

119. "Report of the Town Planning Committee," *Reports and Printed Documents of the Corporation of Dublin*, no. 30 (1933): 162-166; no. 31 (1933): 167-171. Patrick Abercrombie had previously proposed a scheme of low-density flats and cottage housing for this area. His sketches can be found at http://archiseek.com/2011/1922-urban-flats-and-cottages-townsend-st/#.U0hevVcqQlQ.

120. "Report of the Housing Committee," *Reports and Printed Documents of the Corporation of Dublin*, no. 28 (1934): 173. See also "Report on Housing by City Manager," *Reports and Printed Documents of the Corporation of Dublin*, no. 16 (1934): 121-134, for the report of the city manager to the council about the housing situation.

121. Fergal McGrath, "Homes for the People," *Studies: An Irish Quarterly Review* 21, no. 82 (1932): 271, 272. This journal was published by the Jesuits. For more on such arguments, accompanied by a focus on property ownership for men, see McManus, "Blue Collars."

122. Quoted in McManus, "Blue Collars," 49.

123. Mary E. Daly, "Oh, Kathleen Ni Houlihan, Your Way's a Thorny Way," in *Gender and Sexuality in Modern Ireland*, ed. Maryann Gialanella Valiulis and Anthony Bradley (Amherst: University of Massachusetts Press, 1997), 112-113.

124. Helen Jarvis with Paula Kantor and Jonathan Cloke, *Cities and Gender: Critical Introductions to Urbanism and the City* (London: Routledge, 2009), 47.

125. Ibid., 220.

126. Lynne Walker, "Women and Architecture," in *Gender Space Architecture: An Interdisciplinary Introduction*, ed. Jane Rendell, Barbara Penner, and Iain Borden (London: Routledge, 2000), 254.

127. Elizabeth Darling and Lesley Whitworth, "Introduction: Making Space and Re-making History," in *Women and the Making of Built Space in England, 1870-1950*, ed. Elizabeth Darling and Lesley Whitworth (Aldershot, UK: Ashgate, 2007), 5.

128. Daly, "Oh, Kathleen Ni Houlihan," 113.

129. See, for example, Maryann Gialanella Valiulis, "The Politics of Gender in the Irish Free State, 1922–1937," *Women's History Review* 20, no. 4 (2011): 569–578, esp. 575, 576.

130. I distinguish here between Dublin-focused women's organizations and Irish women's organizations such as the Irish Women Worker's Union and the Irish Women's Citizens' Association, which were more broadly focused on securing women's rights.

131. *Irish Independent*, June 17, 1925.

132. In particular, see Ruth Livesey, "Women Rent Collectors and the Rewriting of Space, Class and Gender in East London, 1870–1900," in Darling and Whitworth, *Women and the Making of Built Space in England*, 87–105.

133. See Darling and Whitworth, *Women and the Making of Built Space in England*. For more on Denby, see Elizabeth Darling, "'The Star in the Profession She Invented for Herself': A Brief Biography of Elizabeth Denby, Housing Consultant," *Planning Perspectives* 20, no. 3 (2005): 271–300.

134. Máirín Johnston, *Around the Banks of Pimlico* (Dublin: Attic Press, 1985), 94.

135. Quoted in Kevin C. Kearns, *Dublin Tenement Life: An Oral History* (Dublin: Gill and Macmillan, 1994), 92 (emphasis in original).

136. Ibid., 166.

137. Ibid., 170–171, 34.

138. See the photo in Prunty, *Dublin Slums*, 324.

139. Kearns, *Dublin Tenement Life*, 159.

140. Town and Regional Planning Act (1934), part 1.3.

141. "Report of the Town Planning Committee," *Reports and Printed Documents of the Corporation of Dublin*, no. 12 (1937): 107, 111. See also "Report of the Town Planning Committee," *Reports and Printed Documents of the Corporation of Dublin*, no. 416 (1938): 206.

142. "Corporation's Consultants Plans and Suggestions," *Irish Times*, November 4, 1939, p. 7.

143. Patrick Abercrombie, Sydney Kelly, and Manning Robertson, *Town Planning Report: Sketch Development Plan* (Dublin: Corporation of Dublin, 1941), 34. See also Patrick Abercrombie, Sydney A. Kelly, and Manning Robertson, *County Borough of Dublin and Neighbourhood Town Planning Report: Sketch Development Plan* (Dublin: Corporation of Dublin, 1939); and Patrick Abercrombie, "The Dublin Town Plan," *Studies: An Irish Quarterly Review* 31, no. 122 (1942): 155–170.

144. "Town-Planning Report Adopted," *Irish Times*, December 11, 1940, p. 6; "Town-Planning Report Adopted," *Irish Times*, December 14, 1940, p. 9. The appendix to Abercrombie, Kelly, and Robertson, *County Borough of Dublin*, contains the report of the 1939 Town and Planning Committee with a notation that the council's General Purposes Committee adopted this report and the SDP with amendments. For more information on the development plan, see Dickson, *Dublin*; and Seán O'Leary, *Sense of Place: A History of Irish Planning* (Dublin: History Press of Ireland, 2014).

145. Abercrombie, Kelly, and Robertson, *County Borough of Dublin*. For more on *Abercrombie* and regional planning, see Patrick Abercrombie, "Regional Planning," *Town Planning Review* 10, no. 2 (1923): 109–118.

146. Joseph Brady, *Dublin, 1930–1950: The Emergence of the Modern City* (Dublin: Four Courts Press, 2014), 94. See also T.W.T. Dillon, "Slum Clearance: Past and Present," *Studies: An Irish Quarterly Review* 34, no. 133 (1945): 13–20.

147. *Minutes of the Municipal Council of the City of Dublin*, no. 13 (1939): 6–7; see also no. 71 (1939): 78.

148. Maryann Gialanella Valiulis, "Power, Gender, and Identity in the Irish Free State," *Journal of Women's History* 6, no. 4 (1995): 126, 128. The Civil Service Bill (1925) restricted women from the upper levels of the Civil Service; the Juries Bill (1927) removed women from the jury service rolls; the Conditions of Employment Bill (1935) gave the government power to limit the number of women employed in individual industries; and a ban on married women as teachers was enacted (1932). Article 41 of the 1937 constitution defined women's citizenship in relation to their role in the family and home. For women's organized campaigns against such legislation and the 1937 constitution, see Catriona Beaumont, "Women, Citizenship, and Catholicism in the Irish Free State, 1922–1948," *Women's History Review* 6, no. 4 (1997): 563–585.

149. Erika Hanna, *Modern Dublin: Urban Change and the Irish Past, 1957–1973* (Oxford: Oxford University Press, 2013), 34–35, 41–42.

150. Dickson, *Dublin: The Making of a Capital City*, 482.

151. Alison Ravetz, *Council Housing and Culture: The History of a Social Experiment* (London: Routledge, 2001), 9.

152. Brady, *Dublin, 1930–1950*, 59. By 1938, 1,120 cottage-type houses were being built in Crumlin to the southwest, with an additional 2,100 planned for the area and 3,000 planned for Cabra West (northwest) and Donnycarney (northeast). Brady, *Dublin, 1930–1950*, 220–223, 228.

153. McManus, *Dublin, 1910–1940*, 123–139; McManus, "Blue Collars," 38–54.

154. For a list of all corporation schemes between 1917 and 1939, which totaled 2,249 flats, see Brady, *Dublin, 1930–1950*, 205; see p. 202 for the overall total of corporation schemes completed between 1933 and 1938 that focused on suburban development.

155. McManus, "Blue Collars," 49. For further discussion of the Alexandra Guild houses, see McManus, *Dublin, 1910–1940*, 446, 150–151. See also Brady, *Dublin, 1930–1950*, 67–68.

156. Mary P. Corcoran, "Re-imagining the Built Environment: Place, Community, and Neighborhood in the City of Dublin," in *Re-Imagining Ireland*, ed. Andrew Higgins Wyndham (Charlottesville: University of Virginia Press, 2006), 176.

157. For examples, see Kearns, *Dublin Tenement Life*.

CHAPTER 7

1. Quoted in untitled newspaper clippings, December [n.d.] and December 20, 1907, Box 805-MU 6362, Toronto Local Council of Women Fonds, Archives of Ontario (AO).

2. Toronto Local Council of Women, *14th Annual Report*, 1908, Gerritsen Collection of Aletta Jacobs (GCAJ), available at http://www.proquest.com/products-services/gerritsen.html. The city finally began to build this filtration plant, as reported in Toronto City Council, "Mayor's Inaugural Address," in *Minutes* (Toronto: Toronto City Council, 1908), app. C, p. 6, Toronto City Archives (TCA).

3. See, for example, *Annual Report of the City Engineer of Toronto for 1901* (Toronto: Carswell, 1902).

4. Lawrence Solomon, *Toronto Sprawls: A History* (Toronto: University of Toronto Press, 2007), 20.

5. Ibid., 3–5.

6. Ibid., 3.

7. Ian MacLachlan, *Kill and Chill: Restructuring Canada's Beef Commodity Chain* (Toronto: University of Toronto Press, 2001), 110–111.

8. Albert E. Kelsey, "Modern City Making," *Canadian Architect and Builder* 14, no. 160 (1901): 80, available at https://archive.org/stream/canadianarchitec05onta#page/n69/mode/2up.

9. Ontario Association of Architects, "Proceedings of the Annual Convention," *Canadian Architect and Builder* 15, no. 169 (1902): 9, available at https://archive.org/stream/canadianarchitec05onta#page/n195/mode/2up; Ontario Association of Architects, "Editorial," *Canadian Architect and Builder* 15, no. 172 (1902): 45, available at https://archive.org/stream/canadianarchitec05onta#page/n219/mode/2up.

10. W. A. Langton, "City Planning," *Canadian Architect and Builder* 15, no. 172 (1902): 49, available at https://archive.org/stream/canadianarchitec05onta#page/n221/mode/2up.

11. "The Toronto Fire," *Canadian Architect and Builder* 17, no. 4 (1904): 66. There are two different online versions of this journal, and the content of some issues varies between versions. For this and subsequent citations, I consulted the digitized version on the McGill University Library website, at http://digital.library.mcgill.ca/cab/search/browse_frameset.htm. The quotation represents exactly the type of rhetoric used by Chicago businessmen following the 1871 fire.

12. Toronto City Council "Mayor's Address," in *Minutes* (Toronto: Toronto City Council, 1908), vol. 2, app. C, p. 1, TCA.

13. Byron E. Walker, "The Plan of Improvements to Toronto," *Canadian Architect and Builder* 19, no. 2 (1906): 20.

14. "Report on a Comprehensive Plan for Systematic Improvements in Toronto by Toronto Guild of Civic Art," 1909, pp. 10–13, Urban Affairs Library, University of Toronto. The plan called for the diagonals to be 100–125 feet wide.

15. Toronto City Council, *Minutes* (Toronto: Toronto City Council, 1910), p. 12, TCA.

16. Ibid., 217–218, app. A, 1483. The council did constitute a Civic Improvement Committee, composed of politicians, professional men, and businessmen with Langton and other guild members. See James Lemon, "Plans for Early 20th-Century Toronto: Lost in Management," *Urban History Review* 18, no. 1 (1989): 11.

17. Alexander Fraser, *Official Guide and Souvenir of Toronto, the Queen City of Canada* (Toronto: Toronto City Council, 1901), 18.

18. William T. James, *Toronto as It Was and Is: a Graphic Historical Sketch of the City of Toronto* (Toronto: James and Williams, 1903), 26.

19. W. A. Langton, "Apartment Life," *Canadian Architect and Builder* 16, no. 5 (1903): 71. Langton was future editor of the publication and chair of the Plan Committee of the Guild of Civic Art.

20. Ibid., 71–72.

21. Quoted in Richard Dennis, *Cities in Modernity: Representations and Productions of Metropolitan Space, 1840–1930* (Cambridge: Cambridge University Press, 2008), 132.

22. Bureau of Municipal Research, "What Is 'the Ward' Going to Do with Toronto?" *Bulletin* 71 (1918): 67–68.

23. Ibid., 13. No women were listed as guarantors or members of the bureau.

24. See "Toronto Health Matters," *Canada Lancet* 37, no. 9 (1904): 851. *Annual Report of the City Engineer of Toronto for 1904* (Toronto: Carswell, 1905) also records public conveniences in the St. Lawrence and St. Andrews markets.

25. *Annual Report of the City Engineer of Toronto for 1906* (Toronto: Carswell, 1907), 163. In 1907, the three facilities were averaging a daily use by 2,293 people with heaviest usage at the Queen and Spadina location. See *Annual Report of the City Engineer of Toronto for 1907* (Toronto: Carswell, 1908), 22.

26. Richard Harris and A. Victoria Bloomfield, "The Impact of Industrial Decentralization on the Gendered Journey to Work, 1900–1940," *Economic Geography* 73, no. 1 (1997): 109, 111.

27. Toronto Local Council of Women, *16th Annual Report*, 1910, GCAJ; Toronto Local Council of Women, *19th Annual Report*, 1912, GCAJ.

28. Sites proposed for public lavatories were at College and Spadina, St. Clair and Dufferin, Queen Street east and Kingston Road, Gerrard and Greenwood, King and Queen Streets at Roncesvalles, and Broadview and Danforth.

29. "A West End Controller Has His Eye on the East End," *Toronto Star*, January 8, 1910, p. 1; "Shop over Lavatory," *Toronto Star*, May 30, 1911, p. 1; "Board of Works Votes," *Toronto Star*, February 1, 1913, p. 2.

30. "Board of Works Votes," 2.

31. "Restaurant's Wash-Basins," *Toronto Star*, February 16, 1915, p. 6.

32. Richard Dennis, "Interpreting the Apartment House: Modernity and Metropolitism in Toronto, 1900–1930," *Journal of Historical Geography* 20, no. 3 (1994): 313.

33. Solomon, *Toronto Sprawls*, 24.

34. Toronto City Council, "Report of the Local Board of Health," in *Minutes* (Toronto: Toronto City Council, 1911), vol. 2, app. A, p. 1822, TCA.

35. Toronto City Council, "Report of the Local Board of Health," in *Minutes* (Toronto: Toronto City Council, 1912), vol. 2, app. A, pp. 1292–1293, TCA. For record of the council again approving a motion to consider forming a special committee to investigate the housing problem, see Toronto City Council, "Meeting of 13 January 1913," in *Minutes* (Toronto: Toronto City Council, 1913), vol. 1, app. A, p. 154, TCA.

36. "Address of Mr. R. S. Gourlay, President of the Board of Trade of the City of Toronto," January 1912, p. 37.

37. Toronto City Council, "Mayor's Inaugural Address," in *Minutes* (Toronto: Toronto City Council, 1913), vol. 2, app. C, pp. 12–13, 16–17, TCA.

38. Letter from Vincent Basevi to G. Frank Beer, April 9, 1912, Folder 1905–13, "General Correspondence, 1905–29" series, Box F177-MU59, G. Frank Beer Fonds, AO.

39. See a description of this act in "Report of the Ontario Housing Committee," *Sessional Papers* 51, part 10 (1919): 41.

40. Sean Purdy, "'This Is Not a Company: It Is a Cause': Class, Gender, and the Toronto Housing Company, 1912–1920," *Urban History Review* 21, no. 2 (1993): 78.

41. Toronto Housing Company, "Better Housing in Ontario: The Ontario Plan," in *First Annual Report of the Toronto Housing Company, Ltd, 1913* (Toronto: Toronto Housing Company), 19, Urban Affairs Library, Toronto.

42. Untitled clipping, *Toronto Daily News*, November 10, 1914, "Clippings" folder, Series II, Box F177-MU61, Beer Fonds, AO. The company was originally called the Toronto Co-partnership Garden Suburbs, Ltd.

43. Letter from G. Frank Beer to John McDougald (chair of the provincial Board of Inquiry), January 15, 1914, Folder 1914, Box F177-MU59, Beer Fonds, AO. See also letter from McDougald to Beer, January 13, 1914, Folder 1914, Box F177-MU59, Beer Fonds, AO.

44. *Toronto Globe and Mail*, June 25, 1940, "Clippings" folder, Beer Fonds, AO.

45. Wilfrid S. Dinnick, Lawrence Park scheme, "Lawrence Park Plans" folder, Box 175-MU919, Dinnick Family Fonds, AO. Dinnick was also vice president of the Standard Loan Company and director of Canadian Casualty. His other housing schemes were Dawes Park Estates, Waverley Subdivision, and Glebe Manor Estates.

46. Untitled, undated typescripts, "Toronto Real Estate" folder, Dinnick Family Fonds, AO.

47. Wilfrid Dinnick, "Tremendous Toronto," 1914, p. 13, available at https://archive.org/details/cihm_87456.

48. Toronto Local Council of Women, *19th Annual Report*. Calling for this housing committee was one of fifteen measures that the women wanted the city council to adopt and which they labeled their Municipal Platform. They were still agitating for public toilets for women.

49. Toronto Local Council of Women, *14th Annual Report*, 1908, GCAJ.

50. Toronto Local Council of Women, "Report of Sub-committee on Working Mothers' Homes," in *19th Annual Report*.

51. Unidentified clipping, September 29, 1912, File 1: 1911–1930, Box 11, Central Neighbourhood House Fonds 1005, TCA. See also "Minutes of the Organizing Committee," August 31, 1911, File 59: 1911–Sept. 1912, Box 4, TCA. This file includes a letter from the TLCW about how it was soliciting funds for this effort.

52. Toronto Local Council of Women, *21st Annual Report*, 1914, GCAJ.

53. Purdy, "'This Is Not a Company; It Is a Cause,'" 87.

54. Suzanne Mackenzie, "Building Women, Building Cities: Toward Gender Sensitive Theory in the Environmental Disciplines," in *Life Spaces: Gender, Household, Employment*, ed. Caroline Andrew and Beth Moore Milroy (Vancouver: University of British Columbia Press, 1988), 20–21.

55. Purdy, "'This Is Not a Company; It Is a Cause,'" 83.

56. G. Frank Beer, *A Plea for City Planning Organization* (Toronto: Bryant Press, 1914), 9.

57. Quoted in Purdy, "'This Is Not a Company; It Is a Cause,'" 77.

58. Quoted in Sean Purdy, "Industrial Efficiency, Social Order, and Moral Purity: Housing Thought in English Canada, 1900–1950," *Urban History Review* 25, no. 2 (1997): 35.

59. Toronto Local Council of Women, "Regular Meetings," March 15 and April 19, 1921, in *Monthly Meeting Minutes*, Box F805-MU6362, Toronto Local Council of Women Fonds, AO.

60. Toronto Local Council of Women, "Regular Meetings," October 16 and December 13, 1921, and March 21, 1922, in *Monthly Meeting Minutes*, Box F805-MU6362, Toronto Local Council of Women Fonds, AO. The 1919 Ontario Housing Act and the $25 million are discussed later in the chapter.

61. Quoted in Purdy, "Industrial Efficiency, Social Order, and Moral Purity," 35.

62. Quoted in Richard Harris, *Unplanned Suburbs: Toronto's American Tragedy, 1900–1950* (Baltimore: Johns Hopkins University Press, 1994), 93, 99.

63. "Danforth, N. Toronto New House Districts," *Toronto Star*, December 3, 1918, p. 18.

64. "Labor and House Building after the War," *Toronto Star*, December 3, 1918, p. 6.

65. "Danforth."

66. "Report to the Chairman and Members of the Board of Control," March 1, 1920, p. 5, Series 60, Fonds 2, City of Toronto Reports Collection, TCA. See also File 5, Box 2, Bureau of Municipal Research Fonds 1003, TCA; Bureau of Municipal Research, "The Toronto Housing

Commission," *White Papers*, no. 27, May 14, 1919, Series 973, Subseries 2, Bureau of Municipal Research Fonds 1003, TCA.

67. "Social Service Board Attacks Housing Here," *Toronto Star*, October 8, 1920, p. 3.

68. Toronto City Council, *Minutes* (Toronto: Toronto City Council, 1921), vol. 1, pp. 20, 23, 101–102, TCA.

69. *The Globe*, October 12, 1907, quoted in Gene Desfor, Lucian Vesalon, and Jennefer Laidley, "Establishing the Toronto Harbour Commission and Its 1912 Waterfront Development Plan," in *Reshaping Toronto's Waterfront*, ed. Gene Desfor and Jennefer Laidley (Toronto: University of Toronto Press, 2011), 65.

70. Desfor, Vesalon, and Laidley, "Establishing the Toronto Harbour Commission," 68–69.

71. Ibid., 59–60. See also Board of Trade of the City of Toronto, *Year Book*, 1914, Fonds 1030, Board of Trade of the City of Toronto Collection, TCA, for its assessment of the role the board played in securing the Harbour Commission.

72. Paul S. B. Jackson, "From Liability to Profitability: How Disease, Fear, and Medical Science Cleaned up the Marshes of Ashbridge's Bay," in Desfor and Laidley, *Reshaping Toronto's Waterfront*, 95.

73. Toronto Harbour Commissioners, "Toronto: A City of Opportunities," June 1912, Digital Collection, Fisher Library, University of Toronto.

74. "Improvements Commission Suggested for Toronto," *Toronto Star*, November 27, 1912.

75. Robert S. Gourlay, "Basic Principles of Water-Front Development as Illustrated by the Plans of the Toronto Harbor Commissioners," in *Proceedings of the 6th National Conference on City Planning, Toronto, May 25–27, 1914* (Boston: University Press, 1914), 17, 20–21, 33.

76. Toronto Civic Guild, "Report of the Civic Improvement Committee for the City of Toronto," 1911, p. 7, Urban Affairs Library.

77. Civic Guild, "Reports on Second Toronto Improvements Conference," *Bulletin*, October 1912, p. 1. For confirmation that ratepayers' committees were male organizations, see Toronto Local Council of Women, "Citizenship Committee," in *21st Annual Report*, 41–42.

78. C. H. Mitchell, "Town Planning and Civic Improvement," address to the first meeting of the Ontario Town Planning Congress, December 11, 1912, in *Bulletin*, January 1913, p. 3.

79. Ibid., 9.

80. "Wider Streets to Cost Million," *Toronto Star*, April 4, 1911, p. 9. See also "Money Well Spent," *Toronto Star*, June 25, 1912, p. 6; "Works Committee Says 66 Feet for Terauley Street," *Toronto Star*, September 21, 1912, p. 6; and "Board of Works Votes 86-Foot for Terauley Street," *Toronto Star*, February 1, 1913, p. 2.

81. "Start Terauley Street Widening at Once," *Toronto Star*, January 27, 1914, p. 2.

82. Terauley Street originally ran between Queen Street and College Street (north of Bay Street).

83. "Danforth Lands Assessed," *Toronto Star*, May 22, 1914, p. 1. For information on the widening of Bloor Street, see "City Hall News Notes and Other Activities," *Toronto Star*, September 8, 1914, p. 14.

84. "Yonge Street Widening," *Toronto Star*, November 14 1914, p. 16; "Yonge St. Widening, By-law Rescinded," *Toronto Star*, November 18, 1914, p. 13.

85. Dinnick, "Tremendous Toronto," 12.

86. See Dennis, *Cities in Modernity*, 14–20.

87. "Bloor Street Viaduct Months ahead of Schedule," *Toronto Star*, December 5, 1915, p. 7.

88. "To Finish Viaduct before the Time Limit," *Toronto Star*, January 20, 1916, p. 1.

89. Dennis, *Cities in Modernity*, 14.

90. Ibid., 18.

91. "Viaduct Will Bring Don Seven Minutes from Yonge Street," *Toronto Star*, October 2, 1915, p. 4.

92. See Bureau of Municipal Research, memorandum marked "Not for Publication," April 9, 1914, in *Minute Books* (April 1914), p. 52, Series 969, Subseries 1, Bureau of Municipal Research Fonds 1003, TCA; Bureau of Municipal Research, "Meeting of January 17, 1917," in *Minute Books* (January 1917), File 2, Box 2, Bureau of Municipal Research Fonds 1003, TCA; "Treasurer's Report," in *Minute Books* (April 1925–March 1926), File 4, Box 3, Bureau of Municipal Research

Fonds 1003, TCA; and Bureau of Municipal Research, "17th Annual Report," 1931, Series 973, Subseries 9, Bureau of Municipal Research Fonds 1003, TCA.

93. Bureau of Municipal Research, meetings of February 9 and 19, 1914, in *Minute Books*, Series 969, Subseries 1, Bureau of Municipal Research Fonds 1003, TCA.

94. Bureau of Municipal Research, "First Annual Report," 1915, p. 4, Series 973, Subseries 9, Bureau of Municipal Research Fonds 1003, TCA.

95. Bureau of Municipal Research, meeting of September 15, 1915, in *Minute Books*, Series 969, Subseries 1, Bureau of Municipal Research Fonds 1003, TCA.

96. Toronto City Council, *Minutes* (Toronto: Toronto City Council, 1914), vol. 1, app. A, p. 262, TCA.

97. See Thomas Adams, "Town Planning in Canada and the United States," *Town Planning Review* 5, no. 2 (1914): 157, 158. See also Commission of Conservation of Canada, "Draft of Town Planning Act," in *Sixth Annual Meeting* (Toronto: Bryant Press, 1919), 247–258.

98. Commission of Conservation of Canada, *Civic Improvement League for Canada: Report of the Preliminary Conference* (Ottawa: Commission of Conservation of Canada, 1916), 26, available at https://archive.org/stream/civicimprovement00canaiala.

99. Ibid., 31.

100. Ibid., 32.

101. Ibid., 34–35.

102. I believe this is Elizabeth Shortt, who was also a doctor.

103. Commission of Conservation of Canada, *Report of the Preliminary Conference*, 38.

104. Ibid., 39.

105. Ibid., 38.

106. Commission of Conservation of Canada, *Civic Improvement: Report of the Conference of the Civic Improvement League of Canada* (Ottawa: Commission of Conservation of Canada, 1916), 16–17, available at https://babel.hathitrust.org/cgi/pt?id=uc2.ark:/13960/t6930qk9x.

107. Ibid., 28, 30.

108. Ibid., 32.

109. Bureau of Municipal Research, "What Is 'the Ward' Going to Do with Toronto?" 9, 11, 32; see also 37, 57, 58, 66–67.

110. Ibid., 57, 58.

111. Ibid., 66–67.

112. Ibid., 31.

113. Bureau of Municipal Research, "A Home Owning Citizenship," *White Papers*, no. 236, December 20, 1938, Series 2, Subseries 2, Bureau of Municipal Research Fonds 1003, TCA.

114. Jill Delaney, "The Garden Suburb of Lindenlea, Ottawa: A Model Project for the First Federal Housing Policy, 1918–24," *Urban History Review* 19, no. 3 (1991): 154, 156. See also MacKenzie, "Building Women, Building Cities."

115. Bureau of Municipal Research, meeting of December 8, 1915, in *Minute Books*, Series 969, Subseries 1, Bureau of Municipal Research Fonds 1003, TCA.

116. Bureau of Municipal Research, "Third Annual Report," 1917, pp. 22–23, Series 973, Subseries 9, Bureau of Municipal Research Fonds 1003, TCA.

117. Bureau of Municipal Research, "Toronto Gives: A Description of Haphazard vs. Planned Philanthropy," June 1917, File 3, Series 973, Subseries 2, Bureau of Municipal Research Fonds 1003, TCA.

118. Bureau of Municipal Research, "How Are the Bureau's Activities Estimated by Some Citizens Who Have Been in Touch with Its Work?" June 4, 1918, behind p. 275, in *Minute Books*, File 4, Box 2, Bureau of Municipal Research Fonds 1003, TCA.

119. Bureau of Municipal Research, "Planning versus Confusion," *White Papers*, no. 98, April 12, 1926, File 2, Box 149216, Bureau of Municipal Research Fonds 1003, TCA; Bureau of Municipal Research, "City Planning," *White Papers*, no. 126, March 16, 1928, File 3, Bureau of Municipal Research Fonds 1003, TCA.

120. Bureau of Municipal Research, "Second Annual Report," 1915–1916, p. 19, Bureau of Municipal Research Fonds 1003, TCA.

121. "City Planning Commission Accepted after Long Debate," *Toronto Star*, May 15, 1928, p. 8.

122. Ibid.
123. Ibid.
124. "City Planners' 15-Year Program $13,000,000," *Toronto Star*, March 11, 1929, p. 1.
125. Ibid.
126. "Report of the Civic Department Heads re: the Advisory City Planning Commission Report for the Improvement of the City of Toronto," 1929, pp. 3, 14, Urban Affairs Library. See also the brief narrative on the commission's plan in Mark Osbaldeston, *Unbuilt Toronto: A History of the City that Might Have Been* (Toronto: Dundurn Press, 2008), 26.
127. "Report of the Civic Department Heads," 10.
128. "Straight Extension of University Avenue Undesirable—Harris," *Toronto Star*, November, 1929, pp. 1–2; "Ratepayers to Vote on Civic Improvement Bylaw on New Years'," *Toronto Star*, November 27, 1929, p. 8. For more discussion of support and opposition, see "Let's Have a Better Toronto," *Toronto Star*, December 14, 1929, p. 6; "Citizens' Commission for a Greater Toronto Announces Its Organization," *Toronto Star*, December 14, 1929, p. 11; various articles supporting the vote, *Toronto Star*, December 26, 1929; and "Workers Are Solid for Planning Project, Union Leaders Reply," *Toronto Star*, December 28, 1929, pp. 1–2.
129. "Civic Improvement Plan Still Vital Need," *Toronto Star*, January 2, 1930, p. 3.
130. "University Avenue Extension Urged by Commissioners," *Toronto Star*, March 28, 1930, p. 1.
131. "Hint Master Plan for City Is only Skeleton," *Toronto Star*, May 13, 1929, pp. 1–2; "Complete Master Plan for City Released," *Toronto Star*, May 14, 1930, p. 1; "Anxious Council Jumps at Wemp's City Plan," *Toronto Star*, May 15, 1930, p. 3; *Toronto Star*, June 19, 1931. Tracy leMay's name is variously spelled LeMay and leMay. I use the latter spelling, which seems more common.
132. "Richmond Widening Blocked by Council," *Toronto Star*, May 19, 1931, p. 33; "Working Without a Plan," *Toronto Star*, May 23, 1931, p. 6.
133. Solomon, *Toronto Sprawls*, 30. The figures had kept increasing with every decade rather than decreasing: 9.2 percent in1911, 10.2 percent in 1912, and 23.2 percent in 1931. See Demographia, "Canada City Population History: Montreal, Ottawa, Toronto and Vancouver," 2003, available at http://demographia.com/db-cancityhist.htm.
134. Dennis, *Cities in Modernity*, 254–255.
135. Herbert A. Bruce, "Report of the Lieutenant-Governor's Committee on Housing Conditions in Toronto, 1934," Canadian Urban Policy Archive, available at http://www.urbancentre.uto ronto.ca/policyarchive/11policyarchivehousing.html. See also "Downtown Slums Found Breeding Place of Disease, Delinquency," *Toronto Star*, November 5, 1934, pp. 1–2, for coverage of the council's review of the report.
136. "Downtown Slums." See also John Sewell, *The Shape of the City: Toronto Struggles with Modern Planning* (Toronto: University of Toronto Press, 1993).
137. "Mayor Tells Bruce Council behind Plan," *Toronto Star*, January 21, 1935, p. 3.
138. See, for example, a report of meeting of the council's special housing committee eighteen months after the report was issued in "Slum Clearance Benefit to Toronto," *Toronto Star*, May 12, 1936, 3; and "Would Ensure $2,000,000 Used for Slum Clearance," *Toronto Star*, November 2, 1937, p. 2.
139. Bruce, "Report of the Lieutenant-Governor's Committee," 6.
140. Helen Jarvis with Paula Kantor and Jonathan Cloke, *Cities and Gender* (London: Routledge, 2009), 220.
141. John Sewell, *The Shape of the Suburbs: Understanding Toronto's Sprawl* (Toronto: University of Toronto Press, 2009), 30.
142. "Controllers Recommend City Planning Commission," *Toronto Star*, December 1, 1941, p. 2.
143. "City Lags Behind in Motor Mishaps," *Toronto Star*, January 4, 1939, p. 2.
144. Sewell, *Shape of the Suburbs*, 31, 53. The plan was published as a pamphlet that can be found in the Urban Affairs Library at the Toronto Public Library. The city's current density was double the 10,000 figure.

145. "Include All Suburbs in 'Master Projects,'" *Toronto Star*, September 22, 1943, p. 3; Sewell, *Shape of the Suburbs*, 34. See also "Declares City Doing Nothing on Housing," *Toronto Star*, September 22, 1943, p. 3, for presentations to a meeting called by the TLCW housing and planning committee.

146. "Know Your City," *Toronto Star*, March 24, 1945, p. 4.

147. "1,690 Housing Units Seen Possible in Conboy Plan," *Toronto Star*, October 22, 1942, p. 8.

148. "Homes for 1,100 Families Held City's Immediate Need," *Toronto Star*, September 10, 1943, p. 2.

149. "Get Houses by Mail Forecast after War," *Toronto Star*, March 4, 1942.

150. Sylvia Novac, "Not Seen, Not Heard: Women in Housing Policy," in *Canadian Woman Studies: An Introductory Reader*, ed. Nuzhat Amin, Frances Beer, Kathryn McPherson, Andrea Medovarski, Angela Miles, and Goli Rezar-Roshti (Toronto: Inn, 1999), 173.

CHAPTER 8

1. J. Paul Goode, *The Geographic Background of Chicago* (Chicago: University of Chicago Press, 1926), 66, 70.

2. For the best overview of the Haymarket affair, see Paul Avrich, *Haymarket* (Princeton, NJ: Princeton University Press, 1984).

3. "Real Estate Dinner," *Chicago Daily Inter-Ocean*, February 28, 1893, p. 6.

4. See "League Under Way: Organization for Municipal Improvement Launched," *Chicago Tribune*, October 27, 1894, p. 14; "Lake Front Plans," *Chicago Tribune*, August 10, 1895, p. 9; "For a Public Park," *Chicago Daily Inter-Ocean*, December 16, 1894, p. 5; "Will Discuss Lake Front," *Chicago Daily Inter-Ocean*, June 2, 1895, p. 2; "Concerning Parks," *Chicago Daily Inter-Ocean*, June 4, 1895, p. 6; "New Plan Favored," *Chicago Daily Inter-Ocean*, October 3, 1895, p. 5; and "Plans for Lake Front and South Shore Drive," *Chicago Daily Inter-Ocean*, October 11, 1896, p. 25.

5. "Plans for Lake Front and South Shore Drive," 25; "Burnham on His Lakeside Paris," *Chicago Tribune*, February 12, 1897, p. 4.

6. "Make a Fine Park," *Chicago Tribune*, December 30, 1894, p. 1. The Commercial Club was organized in 1877 with a small membership limited to men of "conspicuous success." John J. Glessner, *The Commercial Club of Chicago: Its Beginnings and Something of Its Work* (Chicago: private printing, 1910), 21.

7. "Favor Grent [*sic*] Park," *Chicago Tribune*, March 29, 1897, p. 5.

8. Daniel Bluestone, *Constructing Chicago* (New Haven, CT: Yale University Press, 1991), 187.

9. Carl Smith, *The Plan of Chicago: Daniel Burnham and the Making of the American City* (Chicago: University of Chicago Press, 2006), 32.

10. "Board for Lake Park," *Chicago Tribune*, March 30, 1897, p. 7.

11. Smith, *Plan of Chicago*, chap. 2, discusses Burnham's involvement in lakefront planning.

12. "Plans for Lake Front Park and South Shore Drive," 25.

13. "Plan for New Park," *Chicago Daily Inter-Ocean*, August 10, 1895. See also "Lake-Front Plans," *Chicago Tribune*, August 10, 1895, p. 9, for a description of the proposed plan.

14. "The Lake Front Wins," *Chicago Daily Inter-Ocean*, October 16, 1895, p. 6.

15. "Prominent Citizens Endorse Burnham's New Scheme," *Chicago Tribune*, March 30, 1897, p. 5. See also "Chicago to Be a Mecca," *Chicago Tribune*, April 4, 1897, p. 3; and "Decide for Lake Park," *Chicago Tribune*, April 17, 1897, p. 5.

16. Private money built the Art Institute of Chicago on the western edge of the area in 1893; dry-goods merchant Marshall Field heavily funded the Field Museum of Natural History that would ultimately be relocated from Jackson Park on the city's south side to the south end of Grant Park; and the John A. Shedd Aquarium and the Max Adler Planetarium (both named for prominent businessmen) opened in 1929 and 1930 respectively on the lake toward the south end of the park. Monumental sculptures of Christopher Columbus and Abraham Lincoln and an equestrian statue of Illinois native and Civil War hero Major General John Logan were erected in the park, as was the massive Buckingham fountain, a gateway into the park on its east side, donated by the

sister of businessman Clarence Buckingham. The area was renamed Grant Park in 1901 after the late Republican president Ulysses S. Grant. The north end of the park was redesigned and renamed Millennium Park to mark the 2000 millennium year. The one prominent businessman who opposed Burnham's plan was dry-goods merchant Aaron Montgomery, who feared that it would devalue property on Michigan Avenue.

17. Maureen A. Flanagan, *Seeing with Their Hearts: Chicago Women and the Vision of the Good City, 1871-1933* (Princeton, NJ: Princeton University Press, 2002).

18. "For Clean Streets," *Chicago Tribune*, March 19, 1892, p. 9; "To Make Chicago a Clean City," *Chicago Tribune*, March 26, 1892, p. 6; "Now Ready for Work: Municipal Order League Organization Completed," *Chicago Tribune*, March 29, 1892, p. 6; "For a Clean City," *Chicago Tribune*, June 28, 1892; "It Should Be Burned," *Chicago Tribune*, June 29, 1892, p. 3; "Conditions According to Wealth: Florence Kelley Gives Some Facts about West Side Streets and Alleys," *Chicago Tribune*, July 3, 1892, p. 19.

19. "Baths and Lavatories Needed," *Chicago Tribune*, March 28, 1892, p. 1.

20. "Free Lake Baths for the Poor," *Chicago Tribune*, July 26, 1892, p. 3.

21. "Reform the City," *Chicago Daily Inter-Ocean*, November 29, 1892.

22. "Baths and Lavatories Needed," 1.

23. "Free Public Baths on the West Side," *Chicago Tribune*, June 7, 1893, p. 10.

24. For the best discussion of the public bath issue in Chicago and other U.S. cities, see Daphne Spain, *How Women Saved the City* (Minneapolis: University of Minnesota Press, 2001). For more on Ada Sweet, see Suellen Hoy, "Ada C. Sweet," in *Women Building Chicago, 1790-1990: A Biographical Dictionary* (Bloomington: Indiana University Press, 2001), 862-864.

25. For more on the MOL and public baths, see Lucy Cleveland, "The Public Baths of Chicago," *Modern Sanitation* 5 (October 1908): 5-17.

26. "End of Municipal Order League," *Chicago Tribune*, April 30, 1895, p. 12; "Baths Cause a Row," *Chicago Tribune*, June 9, 1895, p. 6. Both men and women belonged to the Civic Federation, but it was a male-dominated and -led organization. For a report of the MOL's earlier attempt to recruit the support of men's organizations, see "To Enlist the Clubs and Clergymen," *Chicago Tribune*, November 8, 1892, p. 9.

27. See Lucy Cleveland, "The Public Baths of Chicago," in *Souvenir of Dedication of the "South Side Bath"* (Chicago: Free Bath and Sanitary League, 1897), Newberry Library, Chicago.

28. "Baths and Lavatories Needed," 1.

29. "Underground Lavatories," *Chicago Tribune*, February 3, 1901, p. 38.

30. *Journal of the Proceedings of the City Council of Chicago*, July 1, 1907, p. 925. Public toilets in Chicago, especially when referring to women's facilities, were usually called "comfort stations."

31. "Comfort Stations Favored by Hamilton Club Committee," *Chicago Tribune*, October 3, 1907, p. 5; "Plans for Comfort Stations," *Chicago Tribune*, October 19, 1907, p. 5; "Loud Demand for Public Comfort Booths," *Chicago Tribune*, October 25, 1907, p. 4; "Public Comfort Stations Will Dot Loop District," *Chicago Tribune*, November 10, 1907, p. 3. See also City Club of Chicago, "Public Comfort Stations," *Bulletin*, November 20, 1907, pp. 247-253; and the agenda for a 1907 meeting organized by the Rotary Club of Chicago to discuss public toilets in "Rotary Scrap Book," *The Rotarian*, February 1940, available at https://www.rghfhome.org/first100/library/rotarian/1940 scrapbook/1940scrapbook1.htm#.WgSFEIhrw2w. Despite the optimistic reports in the *Chicago Tribune*, public toilets were not built at this time.

32. See *Journal of the Proceedings of the City Council of Chicago*, January 6, 1908, p. 3647; February 19, 1908, p. 3970; December 21, 1908, p. 2216. See also "Part of the Worker in Building New City Hall," *Chicago Tribune*, January 1, 1911, p. E1; "City's First Comfort Room Will Be Opened Next Week," *Chicago Tribune*, September 30, 1911, p. 3; and "Civics and Philanthropy Department of Chicago Women's Aid," *Chicago Tribune*, December 10, 1911, p. 13.

33. "Public Comfort Stations Planned for Small Parks," *Chicago Tribune*, May 6, 1908, p. 10; *Chicago City Manual* (Chicago: Bureau of Statistics and Municipal Library, 1912), 8.

34. "Saloons Provide Facilities for Public Comfort," *Chicago Tribune*, June 10, 1913, p. 1. This article also notes the existence of two public toilets outside City Hall, one for each sex.

35. See Woman's City Club of Chicago, *Bulletin*, December 1914; November 1915; and March 1923, p. 303.

36. *Chicago City Manual* (Chicago: Bureau of Statistics, 1916), 175.

37. "Public Comfort Stations," *Bulletin of the Department of Public Welfare, City of Chicago*, no. 3 (October 1916). See also Woman's City Club of Chicago, *Bulletin*, September 1916; and "Plan 38 Public Comfort Stations," *Chicago Tribune*, December 16, 1916, p. 5.

38. Woman's City Club of Chicago, *Bulletin*, August, p. 3; September, p. 2; October, pp. 3–4; and December 1917, p. 7.

39. Woman's City Club of Chicago, *Bulletin*, July 1918, pp. 5–6; and August 1918, pp. 4–5.

40. *Journal of the Proceedings of the City Council of Chicago*, August 5, 1918, pp. 839–840.

41. Woman's City Club of Chicago, *Bulletin*, September 1917, p. 2; June 1920, p. 10; April 1921, p. 23; January 1923, p. 233; and May 1925, p. 26.

42. "Approve Plans for 17 Comfort Stations in W. Park System," *Chicago Tribune*, January 16, 1926, p. 2.

43. Early members of the Commercial Club were dry-goods merchant Marshall Field, industrialist Cyrus McCormick, car works owner George Pullman, and meatpacker George Armour. For some earlier examples of the club members' attitudes, see Commercial Club of Chicago, meetings of February 22, 1897, and March 27 and April 24, 1886, in *General Club Minutes, December 27, 1877–December 28, 1889*, Folder 4, Box 1, Commercial Club Collection, Chicago History Museum (CHM).

44. Committee on Plan of Chicago, "Committee Minutes, 1907," in *Encyclopedia of Chicago* (Chicago: Chicago Historical Society, 2005), available at http://www.encyclopedia.chicagohistory.org/pages/10853.html.

45. Commercial Club of Chicago, "Meeting of December 13, 1908," 1908, Folder 7, Box 26, Commercial Club Collection, CHM. See also Folder 6 (August–December 1907), Box 26, Commercial Club Collection, CHM, for the club's discussion of widening Michigan Avenue as "one of the greatest and most immediate needs of the City of Chicago."

46. "Plan Underway for City Beauty," *Chicago Tribune*, December 13, 1906, p. 8.

47. "Ready to Begin on 'Chicago Plan,'" *Chicago Tribune*, November 2, 1909, p. 2; Chicago Plan Commission, "Meeting of November 4, 1909," pp. 1–2, 5, Folder 1909–1912, Chicago Plan Commission Collection, CHM. A complete list of the members of the commission can be found in Chicago Plan Commission, *Ten Years Work of the Chicago Plan Commission, 1909–1919: A Resume of the Work on the Plan of Chicago* (Chicago: Burmeister, 1920).

48. "Unionist Scores the Chicago Plan," *Chicago Tribune*, November 4, 1909, p. 7.

49. Robert Jackson was elected alderman of the city's second ward in 1918, so he was a later member of the Chicago Plan Commission (CPC).

50. The 1908 photo is in the Chicago History Museum and published as the frontispiece to Chicago Plan Commission, *Ten Years Work*. The two sketches were published in E. J. Goodspeed, *History of the Great Fires of Chicago and the West* (New York: Goodspeed, 1871).

51. Smith, *Plan of Chicago*, 78.

52. Chicago Plan Commission, *The Plan of Chicago in 1925: Fifteen Years' Work of the Chicago Plan Commission* (Chicago: Chicago Plan Commission, 1925), 1.

53. "European Cities Spur to Chicago," *Chicago Tribune*, November 23, 1910, p. 14.

54. Quoted in *Proceedings of the Fifth National Conference on City Planning, Chicago, Illinois, May 5–7, 1913* (Boston: National Conference on City Planning, 1913), 230.

55. "'City Practical' Is Chicago Slogan," *Chicago Tribune*, March 6, 1911, p. 9.

56. For lists of the various projects completed or begun by 1919, including estimated costs and bond proposals for Twelfth Street and Michigan Avenue, see Chicago Plan Commission, *Ten Years Work*, 4–5, 31–38. For additional details on completed projects, see Smith, *Plan of Chicago*, 134–140.

57. Chicago Plan Commission, "Proceedings of the Twenty-Second Meeting of the Executive Committee of the Chicago Plan Commission, Held in the Main Dining Room, Hotel La Salle, Chicago, January 24, 1913," p. 36, Folder 1913–1914, Chicago Plan Commission Collection, CHM.

58. Smith, *Plan of Chicago*, 135.

59. Walter Moody, speech, in Chicago Plan Commission, "Proceedings of the Twenty-Second Meeting of the Executive Committee," 27, 28, 19.

60. Chicago Plan Commission, *Ten Years Work*, 32; Chicago Plan Commission, *Plan of Chicago in 1925*, 13–22.

61. Chicago Plan Commission, *Ten Years Work*, 43–45.

62. Chicago Plan Commission, "Proceedings of the Twenty-Second Meeting of the Executive Committee," 37–38.

63. Thomas Hines, *Burnham of Chicago: Architect and Planner* (Chicago: University of Chicago Press, 1979), 327, 332.

64. "Among the Women's Clubs: Club Women Eager for Loop Playground," *Chicago Tribune*, February 1, 1913, p. 10.

65. Robin F. Bachin, *Building the South Side: Urban Space and Civic Culture in Chicago, 1890–1919* (Chicago: University of Chicago Press, 2004), 143–146.

66. Commercial Club of Chicago, *Year-Book, 1919–20* (Chicago: Executive Committee, 1920), 325. See also Smith, *Plan of Chicago*, 145–147. For more on the humanitarian and commercial worth of the forest preserves, see Chicago Plan Commission, *Ten Years Work*, 59; and Chicago Plan Commission, *Plan of Chicago in 1925*, 7–9.

67. For an extensive discussion of the Small Parks Commission, see Bachin, *Building the South Side*, 140–159.

68. Patrick Abercrombie, "Town Planning Schemes in America: Chicago," *Town Planning Review* 1, no. 1 (1910): 56.

69. Smith, *Plan of Chicago*, xv.

70. Chicago Plan Commission, *Ten Years Work*, 25.

71. "Citizen Members of the Mayor's Harbor Commission," *Chicago Tribune*, January 14, 1908, p. 3; "The Harbor Commission," *Chicago Tribune*, January 15, 1908, p. 8. The members were Charles Wacker, real estate; F. A. Delano, railroads; G. H. Conover, mercantile; Randolph Isham, engineer; and John M. Ewan, building interests. See also "Summary of Harbor Commission' Recommendations," *Chicago Tribune*, February 28, 1909, p. 6.

72. "Report of the City Council Subcommittee on Harbor Development, October 1911," *Journal of the Proceedings of the City Council of Chicago*, 1911, pp. 17–18. The journal also contains a sketch of the proposed harbor facilities. For additional coverage of the subcommittee's proposal, see "Outlines Plans of Chicago Harbor," *Chicago Tribune*, October 28, 1911, p. 11; "Aldermen Adopt City Harbor Plan," *Chicago Tribune*, January 18, 1912, p. 3; and "OK Harbor Plan," *Chicago Tribune*, February 10, 1912, p. 2.

73. City Club of Chicago, "Harbor Development and the Proposed Bond Issue," *Bulletin*, March 29, 1912, p. 82.

74. "Mayor for Speed on Chicago Harbor," *Chicago Tribune*, July 16, 1913, p. 3; "Refuse to Delay Harbor," *Chicago Tribune*, July 26, 1913, p. 12; "Aldermen Vote $300,000 to Pay for Harbor Site," *Chicago Tribune*, July 29, 1913, p. 3.

75. "Realty Men Jab Harbor Bill," *Chicago Tribune*, June 5, 1913, p. 8.

76. "Agree on Plan for Lakefront," *Chicago Tribune*, December 24, 1914, p. 4; Chicago Plan Commission, "Sixth Annual Report, Meeting of March 16, 1916," Folder 1915–1919, Chicago Plan Commission Collection, CHM.

77. Chicago Plan Commission, *Ten Years Work*, 45–50.

78. "Chicago Harbor," *Chicago Tribune*, January 23, 1928, p. 10. See also "Putnam Lists Five Sites for Chicago Harbor," *Chicago Tribune*, November 5, 1926, p. 15; and "Aldermen Are Urged to Keep Word, Adopt Chicago Harbor Plan," *Chicago Tribune*, October 30, 1929, p. 13.

79. As early as 1924, Mayor Dever and the council had begun to pursue federal help for the Calumet Harbor. See "Chicago Council Events," *Illinois Municipal Review* 2, no. 6 (1924): 153.

80. "Women Work on Child Problem," *Chicago Tribune*, March 7, 1896, p. 13; "Plead for Little Tots," *Chicago Tribune*, May 10, 1896, p. 4. The circulated letter of invitation was signed by Jane Addams, Dr. Sarah Hackett Stevenson, Florence Kelley, Ellen Henrotin, Corinne Brown, Dr. Julia Holmes Smith, Julia Lathrop, and Lucy Flower, among others.

81. Woman's City Club of Chicago, *Bulletin*, August 1916.

82. For evidence of such bids, see "Municipal Pier Rents May Pay Upkeep Expense," *Chicago Tribune*, February 9, 1916, p. 15.

83. Charles Wacker, "Gaining Public Support for a City Planning Movement," in *Proceedings of the Fifth National Conference*, 232.

84. Quoted in City Club of Chicago, "The Housing Problem in Chicago," *Bulletin*, January 12, 1910, p. 112.

85. "Houses for Poor a Huge Problem," *Chicago Tribune*, October 8, 1910, p. 3.

86. City Club of Chicago, "Civic Associations' Night," *Bulletin*, May 27, 1912, p. 209.

87. Wacker, "Gaining Public Support," 232; Chicago Plan Commission, *Ten Years Work*, 20.

88. "Houses for Poor a Huge Problem," 3.

89. Chicago Woman's Club Civics Committee, "Tenement Housing Conditions in the Twentieth Ward, Chicago," 1912, p. 16, available at https://archive.org/details/tenementhousing c00chic.

90. Wacker, "Gaining Public Support," 236, 239–240.

91. "News of Chicago Women's Clubs: Housing Council Formed to Work for Better Homes," *Chicago Tribune*, June 18, 1916, p. G3. These groups included the CWC, WCC, CWA, PEL, and Jewish Chicago Woman's Aid, among others. See also Woman's City Club of Chicago, *Bulletin*, July 1916.

92. Thomas Lee Philpott, *The Slum and the Ghetto: Neighborhood Deterioration and Middle-Class Reform, Chicago, 1880–1930* (New York: Oxford University Press, 1989), 205. For her tentative plans, see Folder 14, Box 2, Mary McDowell Collection, CHM.

93. City Club of Chicago, "Chicago's Housing Crisis," *Bulletin*, January 17, 1921.

94. For a brief overview of housing conditions during the first years of the migration, see James R. Grossman, *Land of Hope: Chicago, Black Southerners, and the Great Migration* (Chicago: University of Chicago Press, 1989), 132–139; and Philpott, *Slum and the Ghetto*, 189–198.

95. T. Arnold Hill, "Housing for the Negro Wage Earner," in *Proceedings of the Sixth National Conference on Housing, Chicago, October 15, 16, and 17, 1917* (New York: National Housing Association, 1917), 309–313; "Civic League Meets," *Chicago Defender*, May 24, 1919, p. 16.

96. For MacChesney's role in the restrictive covenants, see Philpott, *Slum and the Ghetto*, 189–190.

97. Letter from Sophonisba Breckinridge to Julia Lathrop, December 23, 1909, Microfilm Reel 2, Container 740–41, Breckinridge Family Collection, Library of Congress, Washington, DC.

98. Alzina P. Comstock, "Chicago Housing Conditions, VI: The Problem of the Negro," *American Journal of Sociology* 18, no. 2 (1912): 241.

99. Ibid., 254–257.

100. Sophonisba Breckinridge, "The Color Line in the Housing Problem," *The Survey* 29 (February 1913): 575–576.

101. Philpott, *Slum and the Ghetto*, 207.

102. "Discuss Housing Problem," *Chicago Defender*, June 28, 1919, p. 16.

103. Carl Sandburg, *The Chicago Race Riots, July 1919* (New York: Harcourt, Brace and Howe, 1919), 14.

104. The most complete analysis of the 1919 events is William M. Tuttle, *Race Riot: Chicago in the Red Summer of 1919* (Urbana: University of Illinois Press, 1970). For more on the Hyde Park–Kenwood Association, see pp. 174–183.

105. Chicago Plan Commission, *Ten Years Work*, 3.

106. Chicago Commission on Race Relations, *The Negro in Chicago: A Study of Race Relations and a Race Riot* (Chicago: University of Chicago Press, 1922), 644–646. See also "Commission on Race Relations," *Chicago Defender*, October 7, 1922, p. 12. The *Chicago Tribune* gave almost no coverage to the commission and its report.

107. "Armour Could Have Helped," *Chicago Defender*, January 29, 1921, p. 12.

108. "The Housing Problem," *Chicago Defender*, April 18, 1925, p. A12.

109. Mary McDowell, "Report on Race Relations and Civic Betterment," WCC *Bulletin*, January 20, 1920, pp. 2–4.

110. Woman's City Club of Chicago, *Bulletin*, December 1920, pp. 10–11.

111. "Better Housing Plan Launched for Black Belt," *Chicago Tribune*, August 8, 1919, p. 2. See Philpott, *Slum and the Ghetto*, 215–219, for an overview of housing plans on the part of private organizations before and after, including the Real Estate Board and the Chamber of Commerce.

112. "The Housing Problem," *Chicago Defender*, April 18, 1925, p. A12.

113. Patrick Abercrombie, Sydney Kelly, and Arthur Kelly, *Dublin of the Future: The New Town Plan* (Liverpool: University Press of Liverpool, 1922), 35.

114. Robert Park, "The City: Suggestions for the Investigation of Human Behavior in the City Environment," *American Journal of Sociology* 20, no. 5 (1915): 577–578.

115. Ibid., 612.

116. Ellen Fitzpatrick, *Endless Crusade: Women Social Scientists and Progressive Reform* (New York: Oxford University Press, 1990), 41. For additional information on the steady erosion of the university's social science department focus on practicality, see pp. 40–44.

117. Helen Jarvis with Paula Kantor and Jonathan Cloke, *Cities and Gender* (London: Routledge, 2009), 12. See pp. 56–57 for more on the Chicago school of sociology.

118. Ernest W. Burgess, "The Interdependence of Sociology and Social Work," *Journal of Social Forces* 1, no. 4 (1923): 369.

119. J. Laurence Laughlin (one of the founders of the *American Journal of Sociology*), quoted in Fitzpatrick, *Endless Crusade*, 43.

120. Quoted in Fitzpatrick, *Endless Crusade*, 200.

121. John Nolen, *New Ideals in the Planning of Towns and Cities* (New York: American City Bureau, 1919), 96.

122. City Club of Chicago, *Bulletin*, January 20, 1919, p. 18; City Club of Chicago, "The City Club and Zoning," *Bulletin*, December 22, 1919, pp. 1–2. For an analysis of Chicago zoning as industrial policy, see Robert Lewis, "Industrial Policy and Zoning: Chicago, 1910-1930," *Urban History* 40, no. 1 (2013): 92–113.

123. "Citizens' Zone Plan Conference to Be Held This Week," *Chicago Tribune*, December 14, 1919, p. 12.

124. A. C. Holliday, "Zoning for Use," *Town Planning Review* 9, no. 4 (1922): 218–219.

125. Joseph Heathcote, "'The Whole City Is Our Laboratory': Harland Bartholomew and the Production of Urban Knowledge," *Journal of Planning History* 4, no. 9 (2005): 322–355.

126. "Zoning Board to Study Plans of Other Cities," *Chicago Tribune*, July 29, 1921, p. 8. See also Philpott, *Slum and the Ghetto*, 246.

127. "Zone Plan Ready in 1922," *Chicago Tribune*, November 17, 1921, p. 11.

128. City Club of Chicago, "Zoning Apothegms," *Bulletin*, January 23, 1922, p. 16. Two years earlier Ball gave a talk stressing that the two great results of zoning would be to eliminate fear of property devaluation and eliminate the need for annual tax ratings. See City Club of Chicago, *Bulletin*, July 26, 1920, p. 156.

129. "Sees Zone Plan as Specific for Business Slump," *Chicago Tribune*, November 14, 1921, p. 21.

130. Chicago Zoning Commission, "Zoning Chicago," April 1922, pp. 10–11, available at https://babel.hathitrust.org/cgi/pt?id=chi.46984694.

131. Philpott, *Slum and the Ghetto*, 247, 249.

132. "Sees Zoning System as Aid to Home Owning," *Chicago Tribune*, August 5, 1921, p. 2.

133. Woman's City Club of Chicago, "Zoning Is No Longer a Reformer's Dream," *Bulletin*, July–August 1921, pp. 2–3.

134. Woman's City Club of Chicago, "The Question of Zoning for Chicago," *Bulletin*, December 1919, pp. 1–2.

135. Chicago Zoning Commission, "Zoning Chicago," front cover.

136. "The Value of Zoning," *Chicago Tribune*, May 1, 1922, p. 8. The paper would continue to reiterate this stance as the plan was being released. See, for example, "To Guard Chicago's Prosperity," *Chicago Tribune*, January 12, 1923, p. 8.

137. Chicago Zoning Commission, "Zoning Chicago," 3.

138. "Black Belt Zone Puzzle Baffles City Commission," *Chicago Tribune*, October 20, 1922, p. 17.

139. "Property Owners Assn. in Sunday Afternoon Meeting," *Chicago Defender*, July 22, 1922, p. 2; "Zoning of Chicago," *Chicago Defender*, August 12, 1922, p. 3; "City Planning," *Chicago Defender*, September 29, 1923, p. 4; "City Planning," *Chicago Defender*, October 13, 1923, p. 10.

140. Letter from women's clubs to the zoning commission (February 10, 1923), WCC *Bulletin*, March 1923, pp. 288–289.

141. The present zones by comparison were single-family homes to Bridgeport, Connecticut; manufacturing to Mitchell, South Dakota; commercial to St. Louis, Missouri; two-family apartments to Chattanooga, Tennessee; and multiple-family apartments to Marshalltown, Iowa.

142. Chicago Zoning Commission, "Zoning Chicago," 9. See also "Zoning Board Asks Creation of Five Districts," *Chicago Tribune*, April 19, 1922, p. 21.

143. "Council Votes Zoning Law at Final Session," *Chicago Tribune*, April 6, 1923, p. 1.

144. "City Club Backs Comprehensive Plan for Zoning," *Chicago Tribune*, March 4, 1923, p. 6; Woman's City Club of Chicago, *Bulletin*, April 1923, p. 332.

145. Philpott, *Slum and the Ghetto*, 245–246.

146. Ibid., 228–239, gives the best overview of the association's membership, purposes, and work, including McDowell's reluctant support.

147. City Club of Chicago, "Helping to Solve the Housing Problem," *Bulletin*, July 26, 1920, p. 157.

148. "An Investment in Citizenship," *Chicago Tribune*, July 26, 1920, p. 6.

149. Woman's City Club of Chicago, *Bulletin*, February 1919, March and June 1920, April and July–August 1921; "Fight Housing Bill as Peril to Building Boom," *Chicago Tribune*, March 18, 1919, p. 16. For other examples of opposition to new housing legislation, see "Wiping Out the Slums," *Chicago Tribune*, April 19, 1919, p. 8; "Bill Would Add $120,000,000 to Chicago Burden," *Chicago Tribune*, May 12, 1919, p. 22; and "In the Housing Problem," *Chicago Tribune*, February 19, 1921, p. 6.

150. Woman's City Club of Chicago, *Bulletin*, May 1921.

151. Department of Public Welfare, "Annual Report," WCC *Bulletin*, February 1925, pp. 176–177.

152. Woman's City Club of Chicago, *Bulletin*, February 1925, pp. 184, 186.

153. Mary McDowell, "Living Conditions of Migrant Negroes and Mexicans in Chicago," WCC *Bulletin*, January 1926, pp. 178–179. See also "Housing Relief for Small Wage-Earners Planned: Survey Reveals Crowding of Laborers' Families," *Chicago Tribune*, April 7, 1926, p. 29, for preliminary reports and intent to arrange another housing conference.

154. Woman's City Club of Chicago, *Bulletin*, May 1926, pp. 119–120.

155. "All Day Housing Conference" (flyer), Folder 17, Box 2, Mayor William Dever Collection, CHM. See also "Foster on Mayor's Housing Commission," *Chicago Defender*, July 24, 1926, p. 3.

156. "Housing Commission Is Named by Dever," *Chicago Tribune*, July 7, 1926, p. 29. A list with a few additional members is found in Folder 14, Box 2, Mary McDowell Collection, CHM.

157. "Mayor's Commission Meets to Organize Fight against Slums," *Chicago Tribune*, August 4, 1926, p. 31. After the conference, Walling had asked Dever to appoint "a commission of men well informed in the basic needs of the population to give continuing attention to the problems of housing." Letter from Willoughby Walling to William Dever, May 11, 1926, Folder 17, Box 2, Mayor William Dever Collection, CHM.

158. "City Club to Hold Housing Conference: Women's Club Page," *Chicago Tribune*, October 30, 1927, p. D3.

159. "Woman Quotes King George V on Poor's Needs," *Chicago Tribune*, November 4, 1927, p. 16.

160. "Parks Should Replace Slums, Say Planners," *Chicago Tribune*, November 26, 1931, p. 42.

161. "City Beautiful Planners Were Busy Every Day," *Chicago Tribune*, January 1, 1923, p. A1.

162. For examples of these arguments and proposals, see "'Widen, Repair,' 1924's Sign for Road Builders," *Chicago Tribune*, January 1, 1924, p. A8; "Open Up the City," *Chicago Tribune*, April 26, 1924, p. 8; "Opposition from Evanston May Halt New Road," *Chicago Tribune*, July 12, 1927, p. 8; and "City Streets Weakest Link in Road Plan: Superhighways Needed to Relieve Congestion," *Chicago Tribune*, July 27, 1930, p. A7.

163. "Complete Plan for $6,000,000 Airport in Lake," *Chicago Tribune*, July 1, 1933, p. 4; "Sprague Tells First Aims of City Planners: Superhighway, Downtown Airport, Link Bridge," *Chicago Tribune*, February 13, 1935, p. 6.

164. "Chicago Plan Group Studies Blighted Areas," *Chicago Tribune*, September 2, 1934, p. A10.

165. "Kelly Begins Slum Clearing Work Today: Starts to Raze 25 Buildings," *Chicago Tribune*, June 1, 1934, p. 35.

166. See Devereaux Bowly Jr., *The Poorhouse: Subsidized Housing in Chicago, 1895–1976* (Carbondale: Southern Illinois University Press, 1978), 61.

167. Letter from Elizabeth Wood to Lea Taylor (chair of the WCC Housing Committee), June 28, 1934, "Housing, 1927–1940" folder, Box 17, Lea Taylor Collection, CHM. Wood was MHC executive director, but professional men led the council.

168. Arnold R. Hirsch, *Making the Second Ghetto: Race and Housing in Chicago, 1940–1960* (New York: Cambridge University Press, 1983), 18; "More Dwellings Torn Down than Erected in City," *Chicago Tribune*, December 26, 1939, p. 8.

169. See "Report of the Housing Committee of the Woman's City Club, April 28, 1931," "Housing, 1927–1940" folder, Box 17, Lea Taylor Collection, CHM; "Name Groups to Develop State Housing Plans," *Chicago Tribune*, February 3, 1932, p. 28; "Women to Hold Housing Rally on South Shore," *Chicago Tribune*, August 25, 1935, p. S2; "Housing Parlay, Exhibit Will Be Held March 19," *Chicago Tribune*, March 13, 1936, p. 37; "Conference on Housing to Be Event of the Week: Program All Day Thursday under Auspices of Women's Council," *Chicago Tribune*, March 15, 1936, p. C4; and "Housing Conference Will Be Held at Woman's Club," *Chicago Tribune*, March 19, 1936, p. 21.

170. "Kelly Appoints Five to Form Housing Authority for City," *Chicago Tribune*, January 6, 1937, p. 18. The men were T. J. Carney, vice president of Sears; Coleman Woodbury, director of the National Association of Housing Officials; Victor Olander, secretary-treasurer of the Illinois Federation of Labor; John R. Fugard, architect and president of the MHC; and W. J. Lynch, building contractor.

171. "Mayor to Press Move to Legalize Planning Board," *Chicago Tribune*, April 10, 1939, p. 3. The council approved the ordinance in July 1939.

172. "180 Appointed as New Chicago Plan Advisors," *Chicago Tribune*, November 5, 1939, p. SW2; "Mayor Appoints 11 Members of Planning Group," *Chicago Tribune*, January 12, 1940, p. 6; "City Planning Personnel to Be Unchanged," *Chicago Tribune*, December 15, 1940, p. 27; "Stewart Put on City Plan Commission," *Chicago Defender*, July 6, 1940, p. 8. Exact numbers fluctuated, but the 1939 and 1940 appointees were an accurate representation of the membership across the following years.

173. David Pinder, *Visions of the City: Utopianism, Power and Politics in Twentieth-Century Urbanism* (New York: Routledge, 2005), 107–109.

174. Chicago Plan Commission, *Report of the Chicago Land Use Survey*, vol. 1, *Residential Chicago* (Chicago: City of Chicago, 1942), xxi.

175. Chicago Plan Commission, *Report of the Chicago Land Use Survey*, vol. 2, *Land Use in Chicago* (Chicago: City of Chicago, 1942), vii.

176. Chicago Plan Commission, *Residential Chicago*, xxxvi.

177. D. Bradford Hunt, *Blueprint for Disaster: The Unraveling of Chicago Public Housing* (Chicago: University of Chicago Press, 2009), 69. For the complete report, see Chicago Plan Commission, *Master Plan of Residential Land Use* (Chicago: Chicago Plan Commission, 1943). For definitions of "blighted" and "near-blighted," see pp. 74, 87, 72, table 17.

178. "Post-war Plans Envision New 'Old Chicago,'" *Chicago Tribune*, April 7, 1944, p. 2.

179. "Slum Cleanup Held City's Big Post-war Job," *Chicago Tribune*, December 17, 1944, p. C10.

180. Chicago Plan Commission, *Building New Neighborhoods: Subdivision Design and Standards* (Chicago: Chicago Plan Commission, 1943), 3, 6, 18–23. For proposed reconstruction of this "blighted" area on the near north side, first of 109 acres and then expanded to 200 acres that could become a garden spot, see, for example, "Slum Areas Viewed as Garden Spots," *Chicago Tribune*, February 8, 1945, p. 25; "Map Slum Clearance," *Chicago Tribune*, June 8, 1945, p. 11.

181. Chicago Plan Commission, *Building New Neighborhoods*, 34–35, 37, 39. Getting children in and out of cars and then keeping hold of their hands while shopping is not as easy as putting

them into strollers (prams) and wheeling them to the shop on the street. See, for example, Clara Greed, *Women and Planning: Creating Gendered Realities* (London: Routledge, 1994), 132. For a discussion on planners' emphasis on these "externalities" (quantifiable elements) versus shoppers' (overwhelmingly women) focus on "internalities" (qualitative elements), such as how the shopping area can be used, see p. 45. See p. 46 for her critique.

182. Chicago Plan Commission, *Housing Goals for Chicago* (Chicago: Chicago Plan Commission, 1946), 62.

183. Ibid., 197.

184. The earlier survey had included data on birth rates, percent of male juvenile delinquency, and rates of communicable diseases by neighborhood, among other social factors. For examples, see "Slum Removal Urged to Curb Population Dip," *Chicago Tribune*, February 14, 1942, p. 25.

185. Chicago Plan Commission, *Housing Goals for Chicago*, 197, 198.

186. See Gwendolyn Wright, *Building the Dream: A Social History of Housing in America* (Cambridge, MA: MIT Press, 1983), 220–239.

187. See Hunt, *Blueprint for Disaster*, 58, 76–78, 94–95; and Bowly, *The Poorhouse*, 59–60.

188. D. Bradford Hunt and Jon V. DeVries, *Planning Chicago* (Chicago: Chicago Planning Commission, 2013), 98.

189. Chicago Plan Commission, *Housing Goals for Chicago*, 115.

CONCLUSION

1. Obituary for Lady Unwin, *The Planner* 35, no. 4 (1949): 129.

2. "Planner of the New London," *The Times*, June 9, 1943, p. 2.

3. John Sewell, *The Shape of the City: Toronto Struggles with Modern Planning* (Toronto: University of Toronto Press, 1993), 4.

4. David Pinder, *Visions of the City: Utopianism, Power and Politics in Twentieth-Century Urbanism* (New York: Routledge, 2005), 107, 108.

5. For an examination of the career and scholarly treatment of another female English architect, see Jill Seddon, "'Part-Time Practice as Before': The Career of Sadie Speight, Architect," in *Women and the Making of Built Space in England, 1870–1950*, ed. Elizabeth Darling and Lesley Whitworth (Aldershot, UK: Ashgate, 2007), 143–160. For a discussion of the women involved in the 1930s "New Housing for Old" campaign, the first exhibition of which was all curated or designed by women, see also Helen Meller, "Women and Citizenship: Gender and the Built Environment in British Cities, 1870–1939," in *Cities of Ideas: Civil Society and Urban Governance in Britain, 1800–2000*, ed. Robert Colls and Richard Rodger (Aldershot, UK: Ashgate, 2004), 252–253.

6. Elizabeth Darling, "'The Star in the Profession She Invented for Herself': A Brief Biography of Elizabeth Denby, Housing Consultant," *Planning Perspectives* 20, no. 3 (2005): 282–283.

7. Clara Greed, *Women and Planning: Creating Gendered Realities* (London: Routledge, 1994), 86–87.

8. Helen Jarvis with Paula Kantor and Jonathan Cloke, *Cities and Gender* (London: Routledge, 2009), 236.

9. Clara Greed, "Promise or Progress: Women and Planning," *Built Environment* 22, no. 1 (1996): 12.

10. Elizabeth Darling, *Re-forming Britain: Narratives of Modernity before Reconstruction* (London: Routledge, 2007), 116–120.

11. Greed, *Women and Planning*, 86–87.

12. Jarvis, *Cities and Gender*, 131.

13. Helen Meller, "Gender, Citizenship and the Making of the Modern Environment," in *Women and the Making of Built Space in England, 1870–1950*, ed. Elizabeth Darling and Lesley Whitworth (Aldershot, UK: Ashgate, 2007), 16.

14. Jarvis, *Cities and Gender*, 131.

15. Jody Beck, *John Nolen and the Metropolitan Landscape* (New York: Routledge, 2013), 32.

16. Carolyn Whitzman, "Feminist Activism for Safer Social Space in High Park Toronto: How Women Got Lost in the Woods," *Canadian Journal of Urban Research* 11, no. 2 (2002): 304, 308–309.

17. Ibid., 311, 313, 314, 315.

18. Gerda Wekerle, "Gender Planning in Public Transit: Institutionalizing Feminist Policies, Discourse, and Practices," in *Gender and Planning: A Reader*, ed. Susan S. Fainstein and Lisa J. Servon (New Brunswick, NJ: Rutgers University Press, 2005), 291–292.

19. Eeva Berglund with Barbra Wallace, "Women's Design Service as Counter-expertise," in *Fair Shared Cities: The Impact of Gender Planning in Europe*, ed. Inés Sánchez de Madariaga and Marion Roberts (Farnham, UK: Ashgate, 2013), 250.

20. Ibid., 256.

21. Elmer Johnson, *Chicago Metropolis 2020: A Plan for the Twenty-First Century* (Chicago: University of Chicago Press, 2001).

22. Rob Imrie and Loretta Lees, eds., *Sustainable London? The Future of a Global City* (Bristol, UK: Policy Press, 2014), 3.

23. Sylvia Bashevkin, *Tales of Two Cities: Women and Municipal Restructuring in London and Toronto* (Vancouver: University of British Columbia Press, 2006), 75–76.

24. Jarvis, *Cities and Gender*, 10.

25. Greed, *Women and Planning*, 53.

26. Johnson, *Chicago Metropolis 2020*.

INDEX

Maureen A. Flanagan is Emerita Professor of History at the Illinois Institute of Technology and Michigan State University. She is the author of *America Reformed: Progressives and Progressivisms, 1890s–1920s*, *Seeing with Their Hearts: Chicago Women and the Vision of the Good City, 1871–1933*, and *Charter Reform in Chicago*.

Also in the series *Urban Life, Landscape, and Policy*:

Jerome Hodos, *Second Cities: Globalization and Local Politics in Manchester and Philadelphia*

Julia L. Foulkes, *To the City: Urban Photographs of the New Deal*

William Issel, *For Both Cross and Flag: Catholic Action, Anti-Catholicism, and National Security Politics in World War II San Francisco*

Lisa Hoffman, *Patriotic Professionalism in Urban China: Fostering Talent*

John D. Fairfield, *The Public and Its Possibilities: Triumphs and Tragedies in the American City*

Andrew Hurley, *Beyond Preservation: Using Public History to Revitalize Inner Cities*

www.ingramcontent.com/pod-product-compliance
Lightning Source LLC
Chambersburg PA
CBHW040146270326
41929CB00025B/3395